MASTERING
NEW TESTAMENT
GREEK

MASTERING
NEW TESTAMENT
GREEK

Essential Tools for Students

THOMAS A. ROBINSON

 HENDRICKSON PUBLISHERS

Mastering New Testament Greek: Essential Tools for Students
© 2007 by Hendrickson Publishers, Inc.
P. O. Box 3473
Peabody, Massachusetts 01961-3473

ISBN 978-1-56563-576-0

Mastering New Testament Greek: Essential Tools for Students is revised from *Mastering Greek Vocabulary,* second revised edition, copyright ©1990, 1991.

Printed in the United States of America

Second Printing, Third Edition — December 2008

Cover Art: The cover artwork is taken from the purple Codex Rossanensis, a sixth-century manuscript famous for being one of the oldest illustrated manuscripts in the world and for its unique purple parchment. In addition to the Gospel of Matthew and almost the entire Gospel of Mark, the manuscript contains inscriptions and forty verses from the Psalms and Prophets. The writing is silver with extra large, square letters called "biblical capital." Location: Biblioteca Arcivescovile, Rossano, Italy. Photo Credit: Erich Lessing / Art Resource, N.Y. Used with permission.

Library of Congress Cataloging-in-Publication Data

Robinson, Thomas A. (Thomas Arthur), 1951–
    Mastering New Testament Greek : essential tools for students / Tom Robinson.
        p. cm.
    Includes indexes.
    ISBN-13: 978–1–56563–576–0 (alk. paper)
    1. Greek language, Biblical—Vocabulary. 2. Greek language, Biblical—Grammar. 3. Bible. N.T.—Language, style. I. Title.
    PA817.R59 2006
    487'.4—dc22
                            2006021313

For Bethany

Lover of Language
Lover of Life

CONTENTS

ABBREVIATIONS

acc	accusative case
act	active voice
adj	adjective
adv	adverb
aor	aorist tense
cj	conjunction
dat	dative case
fem	feminine gender
fut	future tense
gen	genitive case
impf	imperfect tense
impv	imperative mood
ind	indicative mood
interj	interjection
masc	masculine gender
mid	middle voice
neut	neuter gender
nom	nominative case
opt	optative mood
pass	passive voice
perf	perfect tense
pl	plural
plup	pluperfect tense
prep	preposition
pres	present tense
pron	pronoun
pt	particle
sg	singular
subj	subjunctive mood
vb	verb
voc	vocative case

INTRODUCTION

Even for the student of New Testament Greek who has little desire to read extensively in Greek literature outside of the New Testament, the New Testament vocabulary is itself quite large and difficult enough to master. Various attempts have been made to give students a "working" vocabulary of the New Testament. Rather than learning the entire vocabulary from Ἀαρών to ὠφέλιμος, students often learn words in order of their frequency of occurrence within the New Testament. Thus, instead of learning over five thousand words (the total vocabulary of the New Testament), the student would be presented with a much shorter list of words from which the less frequent words have been omitted.

This learning approach is sound. Why require of a student the effort to learn words that will be encountered only rarely in the entire New Testament? Over one third of the words in the New Testament vocabulary occur only once—obviously not the most pressing working vocabulary for a reader of the New Testament. If one were to learn the more frequently occurring words in the New Testament, however, one could make quick gains. For example, the thirty most frequent words in the New Testament represent fully one half of all word occurrences. Of course, many of these words are common prepositions, particles, the definite article, etc., which may not in themselves significantly enhance the understanding of the passage being translated. Nevertheless, this example illustrates a solid pedagogical principle: one can most quickly gain a working vocabulary by learning the most frequently occurring words first. Expending a minimal effort with the words most commonly used in the New Testament most readily exposes the student to a fairly substantial working vocabulary.

In the vocabulary lists that follow I have modified this approach slightly, while honoring this central insight. I have based the order in which words are listed on the frequency of the occurrence of the *cognate root* rather than on the frequency of the individual word. The reason for this approach is that most often in New Testament vocabulary one root is reflected in several related words. Thus by learning the most frequent roots, one can gain a solid working vocabulary even more quickly than by memorizing only the most frequent individual words. In the lists that follow, all cognate groups with twenty or more occurrences in the New Testament are given.

Two other features help make these vocabulary lists an effective way to learn Greek vocabulary. First, for the majority of roots, an easy memory aid is provided. For example, for the Greek root ἀκου, which means "to hear," the memory aid provided is the English word "acoustic." The English derivative, thus, illustrates the meaning of the Greek word. In this way, the student learns Greek by finding common ground between Greek and English. In addition, since words have been grouped in terms of their common root, by learning, for example, that the root ἀκου means "to hear," the student has the basic meaning not just of one word but of all eleven Greek words that are based on that root.

The final feature of these lists is a breakdown of all the Greek words into their roots, prefixes and suffixes. By learning how a particular prefix or suffix can affect the basic sense of a word's root, the student will be able to gain clues as to the meaning of a complex word. This arrangement will not only give the student ready access to a solid working vocabulary, but will, as well, provide help in determining the meanings of words that are encountered for the first time. Since in the final analysis the meaning of any word needs to be determined by its usage in the context in which it originally appeared, the clues provided by a word's components do not in themselves determine its definition. For this the standard Greek lexical tools should be consulted. However, an understanding of basic root meanings, coupled with a measure of insight into how these meanings are impacted by various prefixes and suffixes, can take the student a long way in the direction of comprehending a complex word's resultant meaning and can provide significant help in fixing new vocabulary in the memory.

This third revised edition of *Mastering New Testament Greek* broadens the scope of the original work significantly by providing several additional resources. The first of these, the Index of Greek Word Endings, offers the student help in one of the most difficult areas of the acquisition of New Testament Greek—the parsing of the myriad of inflectional forms one encounters in translation. Prior to the creation of this tool, students without a complete analytical guide at hand have often felt at a loss to decipher the various inflectional endings they encounter in doing their translation work. One reason for this is that traditional Greek tools are designed to enable only the analysis of complete words by looking them up one by one, in alphabetical order. This new resource enables the student to look up word endings in *reverse alphabetical order,* beginning with the last letter of the word and working backward until the puzzling form has been identified. Because this new resource provides an easy method for finding the forms of difficult Greek words, it is likely to get the most sustained use both from students and from those using the language later in their career.

Another new resource, the section dealing with Prepositions and Cases, provides an intuitive visual model that illustrates the correlation between the various Greek prepositions and the cases these prepositions employ in establishing relationships between nouns or pronouns. Because prepositions, in their most basic sense, deal with the basic spatial positions or relationships between objects (under, inside, with, through, etc.), their meanings may be illustrated using pictures or diagrams. This new section contains a series of small diagrams that go beyond the common prepositional charts to show not only the basic directional or locational sense of each preposition, but also the case (genitive, dative, or accusative) the prepositional object normally takes to complete its meaning. The basic, spatial sense of a preposition, once mastered, can be used as a link to the many other shades of meaning (temporal, logical, etc.) that the preposition may communicate in various contexts. Thus the preposition "under," beside having the basic, spatial sense of being literally underneath something, can also refer to being under the power or sway of a force or concept.

A third new resource, the Mini Greek-English Cognate Dictionary, builds on the Derived English Words section of the previous editions. The Derived English Words list served to create a link between known English words that had their origins in Greek and the Greek vocabulary words from which those English words have been derived. The Mini Greek-English Cognate Dictionary serves a similar purpose, but in reverse order. It provides a list of Greek roots that have made their way into a host of English words. Greek roots can be looked up in Greek alphabetical order to gain deeper insight into the meaning of a particular Greek root, to see its host of connections with English cognate words, and to discover useful aids for riveting the root in the memory.

The revised and expanded vocabulary-building resources from the previous edition, coupled with new material providing a unique new parsing aid, make this third edition of *Mastering New Testament Greek* an even more valuable resource for students of New Testament Greek.

INSTRUCTIONS

The purpose of this revised edition of *Mastering New Testament Greek* goes a step beyond that of the earlier editions. Its original intent was to assist the beginning student of New Testament Greek in quickly gaining a working vocabulary. This edition expands that original thrust and includes various added innovative features, such as the Index of Greek Word Endings, which provides a helpful aid in parsing Greek words, and the Prepositions and Cases charts, which provide visual help in associating the proper cases of nouns with their accompanying preposition. The various features of this collection will appeal to each user differently. A simple, primary word of advice is therefore in order: use those sections that you find helpful and ignore the ones that are less helpful.

Some guidance in using this volume may help. I suggest the following approach:

I. Become aware of the Greek words you have already acquired by learning English. By reviewing Section 1 (*Identical Greek/English Words*) you can gain—without the need to memorize new words—a vocabulary of about 250 words (and an even larger vocabulary, if all the cognates of these words are considered). All the English words listed in this section are *transliterations* of Greek words. In other words, they are simply Greek words spelled using the English alphabet (with only minor variations). But not only do these words have similar spellings, their meanings are quite similar as well. By using this list you can begin to build a working Greek vocabulary by tapping your existing knowledge of Greek embedded in your English vocabulary.

II. Use Cognate Groups to expand your working Greek vocabulary.

a. Familiarize yourself with the Cognate Groups.

(1)				(2)
ἀγ ἀγωγ				449
bring / lead (3)				
Memory Aid: synagogue, demagogue, agent (4)				
≥25 ἄγω	lead	vb	ω	
ἀγωγή ῆς	manner of life	fem	η	
ἀνάγαιον ου	upstairs room	neut	ἀνα-[√]-ον	
≥10 ἀνάγω	lead up, bring up	vb	ἀνα-[√]-ω	
(5) (6)	(7)	(8)	(9)	

Each Cognate Group has nine main parts:

    (1) The Greek root (variant forms are often included)
    (2) The frequency of that root in the New Testament
    (3) The general meaning of that root (in English)
    (4) English words derived from (or suggestive of) the Greek root. These are to serve as Memory Aids.

Following this general information, contained on the first three lines of the cognate entry, is a list of Greek words sharing the same root along with some aids for prioritizing, defining, and identifying the terms:

    (5) Symbol column:
        ≥25 indicates that the word occurs 25 times or more in the New Testament.
        ≥10 indicates that the word occurs 10–24 times.
            A blank space indicates that the word occurs fewer than ten times.
    (6) Greek word column
    (7) English translation column
    (8) Part of speech column (see Abbreviations for details)
    (9) Prefix, Root, and Suffix

Roots listed elsewhere in the Cognate Lists are enclosed in brackets [v], while roots not listed in the Cognate Lists are enclosed in parentheses (v).

    b. Study each Cognate Group as a whole in order to get a sense of the various relationships of words in this group. Pay particularly attention to the Memory Aids (on line three). If the meaning of a derived English word in the Memory Aid section is unfamiliar, look up the word in Section 5 (*Derived English Words*). You can also consult section 6 (the *Mini Greek-English Cognate Dictionary*), which enables you to look up the various Greek roots to discover their basic meaning, English cognates, and useful memory aids. If no common English derivative could be found as a memory aid, suggestive words (not cognates) or sentences sometimes have been provided. If you find them helpful, use them. Where I have been unable to provide a useful memory aid, I have left a blank space where you can fill in your own memory device.

    c. Beginning with the most frequent Cognate Groups and choosing from the most frequent words in each group, memorize a basic set of vocabulary words. The most frequent words are marked by the symbol ≥25 or ≥10, as explained above. (Note: words are listed in each Cognate Group in alphabetical order of the Greek words.)

    d. Note any prefixes and suffixes attached to the Greek root. Individual prefixes and suffixes generally alter the meaning of the root in regular ways. Refer to Section 3 (*Explanation of Greek Prefixes and Suffixes*) for a detailed description of how the various prefixes and suffixes affect the root. In some cases, Greek and English share the same prefixes and suffixes. See Section 4 (*Identical Greek /English Prefixes and Suffixes*) for a list of these shared prefixes and suffixes.

III. Master frequent non-cognate Greek words. Nearly ninety words occur in the New Testament between 10 and 19 times that are not part of any Cognate Group. These are listed in *Index 1: Words Occurring 10–19 Times*. Some of these terms will be easy to learn by association (e.g., δράκων = dragon, or ῥαββί = rabbi), while others will require memorization (e.g., ἐξουθενέω = despise). For many of these words an English cognate or memory aid is provided. For others you may wish to develop your own memory aid.

IV. Use visual memory aids to become familiar with common Greek prepositions. Prepositions are among the most commonly used words in any language, and Greek is no exception. A firm grasp of the basic sense of each of the Greek prepositions can carry you a long way toward a mastery of Greek vocabulary. Review Section 7 (*Prepositions & Cases*) to become familiar with the basic, spatial or directional sense of each of the prepositions listed. As you encounter prepositions in the process of building your working Greek vocabulary, refer to the series of illustrations in that section to become more thoroughly familiar both with the basic meaning of the preposition you are learning and the case it normally requires to complete its meaning. As your working vocabulary grows, refer to the entire section again and again to get a better feel for the complete range of Greek prepositions.

V. Get a better grasp of the ways in which Greek words inflect. Use *Index 2: Greek Word Endings* to assist you in distinguishing between the parts of a Greek word that change (inflect) to fit various contexts and those which remain constant (the root or stem and its prefix[es]). With this index you look up words in *reverse order*, taking the last letter of the word first. To look up the ending of the word λύομαι, for example, you must first find the section where word endings are listed under the last letter, iota, then take the next to last letter, alpha, and so on, until the ending in question (ομαι) is found along with its parsing: *pres ind mid/pass 1 sg.* (Note that the index lists *complete* endings rather than partial ones. Thus the perfect active indicative ending μαι is distinguished from the present active indicative ending ομαι and the first aorist ending σομαι. Normally the *longest* ending on the list that fits the word in question is the one that best describes how the word should be parsed.)

Mastering New Testament Greek comes with a CD that includes classroom-tested programs designed to help you learn how to form and pronounce letters of the Greek alphabet, master and review vocabulary and verbs forms, determine word endings, and hear the pronunciation of Greek words. The CD also provides a link to *GIG* (Greek Internet Grammar), an introductory illustrated grammar for beginning students.

1

Identical Greek/English Words

A number of Greek words have been merely transliterated to create words in the English language. The student should review these words first, since this will give the student some confidence that Greek is not entirely foreign. Words are listed below even if the root occurs fewer than twenty times (a requirement of all roots that occur in the main Cognate Groups list), since no real effort is required to learn these words (other than for some attention to endings). Proper names are not included. These are capitalized in any New Testament Greek text, and straight transliteration will usually give the rough English equivalent. Names of plants, minerals, and coins are not included either. There should be no trouble with such words when they are met in a text. Prepositional prefixes are included even if they do not occur as separate words.

One main point to remember is that consonants are considerably more stable than vowels.

ἀββά – abba
ἄβυσσος – abyss
ἄγγελος – angel, messenger
ἄγκυρα – anchor
ἄγνωστος – agnostic, unknown
ἀγωνία – agony
ἀγωνίζομαι – agonize, struggle
ᾅδης – Hades
ἀήρ – air
ἄθλησις – athletics, struggle
αἴνιγμα – enigma, obscurity
αἵρεσις – heresy, faction
αἱρετικός – heretic, division-causing
αἴσθησις – aesthetics, insight
αἰών – eon, age
ἀλάβαστρον – alabaster jar
ἀλληγορέω – allegorize
ἀλληλουϊά – hallelujah
ἄλφα – alpha
ἀμήν – amen

ἀνάθεμα – anathema
ἀναθεματίζω – anathematize
ἀντί – prefix "anti-"
ἀντίτυπος – antitype, copy
ἀντίχριστος – antichrist
ἀποκάλυψις – apocalypse
ἀπόκρυφος – apocryphal, secret
ἀπολογία – apology, defense
ἀποστασία – apostasy
ἀπόστολος – apostle
ἀρχάγγελος – archangel
ἀρχαῖος – archaic, old
ἀρχιτέκτων – architect, master builder
ἄρωμα – aroma
ἀστήρ – star
αὐστηρός – austere, severe
αὐτόματος – automatic

βαπτίζω – baptize
βάπτισμα – baptism

βαπτιστής — baptist
βάρβαρος — barbarian
βιβλίον — book (Bible)
βίβλος — book (Bible)
βίος — prefix "bio-," life
βλασφημέω — blaspheme
βλασφημία — blasphemy
βλάσφημος — blasphemous

γάγγραινα — gangrene
γέεννα — gehenna, hell
γενεαλογία — genealogy
γνῶσις — gnosis, knowledge

δαίμων — demon
δέρμα — epidermis, skin
δεσπότης — despot, lord
διάγνωσις — diagnosis, discernment
διάδημα — diadem, crown
διάκονος — deacon, servant
διαλέγομαι — dialogue, discuss
διάλεκτος — dialect, language
διασπορά — diaspora
διδακτικός — didactic
δόγμα — dogma, rule
δράκων — dragon
δυσεντέριον — dysentery
δῶμα — dome, roof

ἐγώ — ego
ἐθνάρχης — ethnarch, governor
εἴδωλον — idol
εἰκών — icon, likeness
εἰρηνικός — irenic, peaceful
ἑκατόν — hecto (metric measure prefix,
    meaning 100)
ἐκκλησία — ecclesia, church
ἔκστασις — ecstasy
ἐμέω — emit
ἐμπόριον — emporium, market
ἐν — in
ἐνδύω — endue, clothe
ἐνέργεια — energy, working
ἔξοδος — exodus
ἐξορκίζω — exorcize
ἐξορκιστής — exorcist
ἐπιγραφή — epigraph, inscription
ἐπισκοπή — episcopacy
ἐπιστολή — epistle, letter

ἐπιφάνεια — epiphany, appearing
ἔσχατον — eschaton, end
εὐαγγελίζω — evangelize
εὐαγγελιστής — evangelist
εὐγενής — eugenic
εὐλογέω — eulogize
εὐλογία — eulogy
εὐνοῦχος — eunuch
εὐφημία — euphemism, good reputation
εὐχαριστία — eucharist, thanksgiving

ζηλεύω — be zealous
ζῆλος — zeal
ζηλόω — be zealous

ἡγεμονία — hegemony, rule
ἡμι — prefix, like the English prefix
    "hemi," half

θέατρον — theatre
θεραπεία — therapy
θρόνος — throne
θώραξ — thorax, chest

ἰουδαΐζω — judaize

καθαρισμός — catharsis, cleansing
Καῖσαρ — Kaiser, Caesar
καλέω — call
κάμηλος — camel
κανών — canon, rule
κατακλυσμός — cataclysm
καταλέγω — catalogue, enroll
καταστροφή — catastrophe
καῦσις — caustic, burning
κεντυρίων — centurion
κεραμικός — ceramic, clay
κήρυγμα — kerygma
κίνησις — English suffix "kinesis,"
    meaning "motion"
κοινωνία — koinonia, fellowship
κολωνία — colony
κόσμος — cosmos, world
κρανίον — cranium, skull
κύμβαλον — cymbal

λαμπάς — lamp
λάρυγξ — larynx, throat
λεγιών — legion
λέπρα — leprosy

λεπρός – leper
λέων – lion
λίνον – linen
λογικός – logical, rational

μαγεία – magic
μαγεύω – do magic
μάγος – magi, wise man
μάμμη – mamma, grandmother
μαμωνᾶς – mammon, money
μανία – mania, madness
μάννα – manna
μάρτυς – martyr, witness
μεταμορφόομαι – metamorphose, change
μέτρον – meter, measure
μίλιον – mile
μιμέομαι – mimic
μόρφωσις – English suffix "morph," meaning "form"
μουσικός – musician
μῦθος – myth
μύλος – mill
μυριάς – myriad
μυστήριον – mystery, secret
μωρός – moron, fool

ὀρφανός – orphan

παραβολή – parable
παράδεισος – paradise
παράδοξος – paradoxical, incredible
παράκλητος – Paraclete, comforter
παραλύομαι – be paralyzed
παραλυτικός – paralytic
παρουσία – parousia, coming
πατριάρχης – patriarch
πεντηκοστή – Pentecost
πέτρα – Peter, rock
πλάξ – plaque, tablet
πλαστός – plastic, made-up
πληγή – plague
πλήρωμα – pleroma, fullness
πόλεμος – polemic, war
πόλις – polis, city
πρεσβύτης – presbyter, elderly man
πρόγνωσις – prognosis, foreknowledge
προσήλυτος – proselyte
προφητεία – prophecy
προφητεύω – prophesy

προφήτης – prophet
προφητικός – prophetic
προφῆτις – prophetess
πυλών – pylon, gateway

ῥαββι – rabbi
ῥαίνω – rain, sprinkle

σάββατον – Sabbath
σανδάλιον – sandal
Σατανᾶς – Satan
σκανδαλίζω – scandalize
σκάνδαλον – scandal
σκορπίος – scorpion
σοφία – Sophia, wisdom
σπένδομαι – spend, give one's life
σπέρμα – sperm, seed
σπίλος – spill, spot, stain
σπόγγος – sponge
σπορά – spore, seed
σπόρος – spore, seed
στεῖρα – sterile woman
στίγμα – stigma, mark
στοά – stoa, porch
στόμαχος – stomach
στῦλος – stele, pillar
συκομορέα – sycamore tree
συμπαθής – sympathy
συμπαθέω – sympathize
συμπόσιον – symposium
συμφωνία – symphony, music
συνέδριον – Sanhedrin
συνοδία – synod
σχῆμα – scheme, form
σχίσμα – schism
σχολή – school, lecture hall
σωματικός – somatic, bodily

ταβέρνη – tavern, inn
ταῦρος – Taurus, bull
τέχνη – technique, craft
τεχνίτης – technician
τίτλος – title, notice
τραῦμα – trauma, wound
τραυματίζω – traumatize, wound
τρέμω – tremble
τύπος – type, pattern

ὕβρις – hubris
ὑγιής – hygienic, sound

ὕμνος – hymn
ὑπερβολή – hyperbole, excess
ὑπόκρισις – hypocrisy
ὑποκριτής – hypocrite
ὕσσωπος – hyssop
φαντασία – fantasy, imagination
φάντασμα – phantom
φαρμακεία – pharmacy, sorcery
φάρμακος – pharmacist, sorcerer (from use of drugs)
φιλανθρωπία – philanthropy
φιλοσοφία – philosophy
φιλόσοφος – philosopher
φυλακτήριον – phylactery
φυλή – phylum, tribe
φυσικός – English prefix "physico-," having to do with "nature"

χαρακτήρ – character, likeness
χάρισμα – charism, gift
χάρτης – chart, paper
χάσμα – chasm
χορός – chorus, dancing
χρῖσμα – chrism, anointing
Χριστιανός – Christian
Χριστός – Christ

ψαλμός – psalm
ψευδής – English prefix "pseudo-," false

ὦ – O!
ᾠδή – ode, song
ὥρα – hour, time
ὡσαννά – hosanna

2

Cognate Groups

ὁ ἡ το				21,117
the / who / which				
Memory Aid: See Appendix 2, Chart B.				
≥25 ὁ ἡ τό	the	adj		
≥10 ὅδε ἥδε τόδε	this	adj		
≥25 ὅς ἥ ὅ	who, which, what	pron	ος	
ὅσπερ ἥπερ ὅπερ	who, which	pron	[√]-περ	

καὶ				9,039
and				
Memory Aid:				
≥25 κἀγώ	and I, I also	cj/pt	[ἐγω]	
≥25 καί	and, also, but	cj/pt		
καίπερ	though	cj/pt	[√]-περ	
καίτοι	yet, though	cj/pt		
καίτοιγε	yet, though	cj/pt		

αὐτυ				5,943
self				
Memory Aid: autobiography, autograph, automatic, autistic, prefix auto-				
αὐτόματος η ον	automatic	adj	[√]-τος	
≥25 αὐτός ἡ ό	self, same, he, she, it	pron	[√]-ος	
≥25 ἑαυτοῦ ἧς οῦ	himself, herself, itself	pron		
≥25 ἐμαυτοῦ ἧς	myself, my own	pron		
ἐξαυτῆς	at once	adv	ἐκ-[√]	
≥25 σεαυτοῦ ἧς	yourself	pron	[σ]-[√]	
φίλαυτος ον	selfish (>self-loving)	adj	[φιλ]-[√]-ος	

δε[1]				2,771
but				
Memory Aid:				
≥25 δέ	but, rather	cj/pt		

ἐν				2,725
in				
Memory Aid: in, endemic, include, instill, inside, intake, insert, inscribe				

≥25	ἐν (*dat*)	in	prep	
	ἐνθάδε	here, in this place	adv	
	ἔνθεν	from here	adv	[√]-θεν
	ἐντός (*gen*)	within	prep	

εἰμι εἰ¹ ἐσ οὐσ ὀντ
be / exist   2,554

Memory Aid: parousia, ontological, essence

	ἄπειμι	be away	vb	ἀπο-[√]-μι
	ἀπουσία ας	absence	fem	ἀπο-[√]-ια
≥25	εἰμί	be, exist	vb	[√]-μι
	ἔνειμι	be in(side)	vb	ἐν-[√]-μι
≥25	ἔξεστι	it is proper / possible	vb	ἐκ-[√]-μι
≥10	ὄντως	really	adv	[√]-ως
	οὐσία ας	property	fem	[√]-ια
	πάρειμι	be present	vb	[√]-μι
≥10	παρουσία ας	coming, parousia	fem	παρα-[√]-ια
	περιούσιος ον	special	adj	περι-[√]-ιος
	συμπάρειμι	be present with	vb	συν-παρα-[√]-μι
	σύνειμι	be with, come together	vb	συν-[√]-μι

οὐ οὐκ οὐχ
no   1,920

Memory Aid:

≥10	οὔ	no	cj/pt	
≥25	οὐ	not	cj/pt	
	οὐδαμῶς	by no means	adv	[√]-ως
≥25	οὐδέ	neither, nor	cj/pt	
≥25	οὔτε	not, nor	cj/pt	
≥25	οὐχί	not, no (emphatic)	cj/pt	

εἰς ἐσω
into   1,776

Memory Aid: eisegesis, esophagus

≥25	εἰς (*acc*)	into, to	prep	
	ἔσω	inside	adv	[√]-ω
≥10	ἔσωθεν	from within	adv	[√]-ω-θεν
	ἐσώτερος α ον	inner (adj), behind / in (prep)	adj/prep	[√]-τερος

ἐγω
I   1,713

Memory Aid: ego, egocentric

| ≥25 | ἐγώ | I (first person pronoun) | pron | |

οὑτ αὑτ τουτ
this   1,652

Memory Aid:

≥25	οὗτος αὕτη τοῦτο	this, this one	adj	[√]-ος
≥25	οὕτως [οὕτω]	thus (>in this way)	adv	[√]-ως
≥25	τοιοῦτος αὕτη οὗτον	such, similar	adj	[√]-ος

ἐρχ
come
Memory Aid:

	ἀνέρχομαι	go (come) up	vb	ἀνα-[√]-ω
	ἀντιπαρέρχομαι	pass by the other side	vb	ἀντι-παρα-[√]-ω
≥25	ἀπέρχομαι	go (away)	vb	ἀπο-[√]-ω
≥25	διέρχομαι	go / come through	vb	δια-[√]-ω
≥25	εἰσέρχομαι	come, enter, share in	vb	εἰς-[√]-ω
≥25	ἐξέρχομαι	come / go out, escape	vb	ἐκ-[√]-ω
	ἐπανέρχομαι	return	vb	ἐπι-ἀνα-[√]-ω
	ἐπεισέρχομαι	come upon	vb	ἐπι-εἰς-[√]-ω
≥25	ἐπέρχομαι	come, come upon	vb	ἐπι-[√]-ω
≥10	κατέρχομαι	come / go down	vb	κατα-[√]-ω
	παρεισέρχομαι	come in	vb	παρα-εἰς-[√]-ω
≥25	παρέρχομαι	pass (by, away)	vb	παρα-[√]-ω
	περιέρχομαι	travel (go) about	vb	περι-[√]-ω
	προέρχομαι	go ahead	vb	προ-[√]-ω
≥25	προσέρχομαι	come to, agree with	vb	προς-[√]-ω
	συνεισέρχομαι	enter in	vb	συν-εἰς-[√]-ω
≥25	συνέρχομαι	come together	vb	συν-[√]-ω

1,392

θε¹ θεο θει
god
Memory Aid: theology, atheist, pantheon, polytheism

	ἄθεος ον	without God (>atheist)	adj	ἀ-[√]-ος
	θεά ᾶς	goddess	fem	[√]-α
	θεῖος α ον	divine	adj	[√]-ιος
	θειότης ητος	deity	fem	[√]-οτης
	θεομάχος ον	God-opposing	adj	[√]-[μαχ]-ος
	θεόπνευστος ον	God-inspired	adj	[√]-[πνευ]-τος
≥25	θεός οῦ	God	masc	[√]-ος
	θεοσέβεια ας	religion	fem	[√]-[σεβ]-ειᾳ
	θεοσεβής ές	religious	adj	[√]-[σεβ]-ης
	θεοστυγής ές	God-hating	adj	[√]-(στύγος)-ης
	θεότης ητος	deity	fem	[√]-οτης
	κατάθεμα ματος	God-cursed thing	neut	κατα-[√]-μα
	φιλόθεος ον	God-loving	adj	[√]-[φιλ]-ος

1,328

ὅτι
that / because
Memory Aid: [Similar to Greek: τι *Why?*– ὅτι *Because.*]

≥25	ὅτι	that, because	cj/pt

1,285

παν πασ παντ
all
Memory Aid: Pan America, panorama, panacea, pantheon, pandemic

≥25	ἅπας ἅπασα ἅπαν	each, all	adj	
	πανταχῇ	everywhere	adv	[√]-η
	πανταχοῦ	everywhere	adv	[√]-ου

1,278

πάντη	in every way	adv	
πάντοθεν	from all directions	adv	[√]-θεν
πάντως	by all means	adv	[√]-ως
≥25 πᾶς πᾶσα πᾶν	each, all	adj	

τι τις τιν²   *1,224*
who / what / any

Memory Aid: See Appendix 2, Chart B.

≥25 ὅστις ἥτις ὅ τι	whoever, whichever	adj/pron	[ὁ]
≥25 τὶς τὶ	anyone, anything	adj/pron	
≥25 τίς τί	who? what? (τι why?)	adj/pron	

μη   *1,164*
not

Memory Aid:

≥25 μή	not	cj/pt	
μήγε	otherwise	cj/pt	
μηδαμῶς	no, by no means	adv	[√]-ως
≥25 μηδέ	nor	cj/pt	
≥25 μήτε	and not	cj/pt	
≥10 μήτι	(negative answer)	cj/pt	

ἀρ γαρ   *1,085*
then / therefore

Memory Aid:

≥25 ἄρα	then, therefore, thus	cj/pt	
≥25 γάρ	for, since, then	cj/pt	

σ   *1,084*
you

Memory Aid: [S is the sign of the Second person.]

≥25 σός σή σόν	your, yours	adj	[√]-ος
≥25 σύ	you	pron	

ἐκ ἐξ   *1,006*
out / from

Memory Aid: exit, exodus, exorcise, excommunicate, exegesis, exile

≥25 ἐκ (*gen*)	from, out from	prep	
ἐκτός (*gen*)	outside, except	prep	[√]
≥25 ἔξω (*gen*)	out, outside	adv/prep	[√]-ω
≥10 ἔξωθεν (*gen*)	from outside	adv/prep	[√]-θεν
ἐξωθέω	drive out, run aground	vb	[√]-εω (ὠθέω)
ἐξώτερος α ον	outer	adj	[√]-τερος
παρεκτός (*gen*)	except	prep	παρα-[√]

γεν γιν γον   *949*
family / birth

Memory Aid: genetic, generation, genesis, genealogy, genre, genocide

ἀγενεαλόγητος ον	without genealogy	adj	ἀ-[√]-[λεγ]-τος
ἀγενής ές	insignificant, inferior	adj	ἀ-[√]-ης

ἀναγεννάω	give new birth to	vb	ἀνα-[√]-αω
ἀπογίνομαι	have no part in	vb	ἀπο-[√]-ω
ἀρτιγέννητος ον	newborn	adj	[ἀρτι]-[√]-τος
≥25 γενεά ᾶς	generation, age, family	fem	[√]-α
γενεαλογέομαι	descend from	vb	[√]-[λεγ]-εω
γενεαλογία ας	genealogy	fem	[√]-[λεγ]-ια
γενέσια ων (*pl*)	birthday party	neut	[√]-ιον
γένεσις εως	birth, lineage	fem	[√]-σις
γενετή ῆς	birth	fem	[√]-η
γένημα ματος	harvest, product	neut	[√]-μα
≥25 γεννάω	be father of, bear	vb	[√]-αω
γέννημα ματος	offspring	neut	[√]-μα
γέννησις εως	birth	fem	[√]-σις
γεννητός ά όν	born	adj	[√]-τος
≥10 γένος ους	family, race	neut	[√]-ς
≥25 γίνομαι	become, be, happen	vb	[√]-ω
≥10 γονεύς έως	parent	masc	[√]-ευς
διαγίνομαι	pass (of time)	vb	δια-[√]-ω
ἔκγονον ου	grandchild	neut	ἐκ-[√]-ον
ἐπιγίνομαι	spring up, come on	vb	ἐπι-[√]-ω
εὐγενής ές	high born (>eugenics)	adj	εὐ-[√]-ης
μονογενής ές	only, unique born	adj	[μονο]-[√]-ης
παλιγγενεσία ας	rebirth	fem	παλιν-[√]-ια
≥25 παραγίνομαι	come, appear, stand by	vb	παρα-[√]-ω
προγίνομαι	happen previously	vb	προ-[√]-ω
πρόγονος ου	parent (>progenitor)	masc/fem	προ-[√]-ος
συγγένεια ας	relatives	fem	συν-[√]-εια
συγγενής οῦς	relative	masc	συν-[√]-ς
συγγενίς ίδος	female relative	fem	συν-[√]-ς
συμπαραγίνομαι	assemble	vb	συν-παρα-[√]-ω

εἰ²   *942*
if

Memory Aid:

≥25 ἐάν	if, even if, though	cj/pt	[√]-[ἀν¹]
ἐάνπερ	if only	cj/pt	[√]-[ἀν¹]-περ
≥25 εἰ	if	cj/pt	
εἴπερ	since, if it is true that	cj/pt	[√]-περ
≥10 εἶτα	then, moreover	adv	
≥25 εἴτε	if, whether	cj/pt	

ἀλλ   *937*
other / change

Memory Aid: allegory, alias, allotrope, parallel, alien

≥25 ἀλλά	but	cj/pt	
ἀλλάσσω	change	vb	[√]-σσω
ἀλλαχόθεν	at another place	adv	[√]-θεν
ἀλλαχοῦ	elsewhere	adv	[√]-ου

≥25	ἀλλήλων οις ους	one another	pron	[√]-ος
	ἀλλογενής ους	foreigner	masc	[√]-[γεν]-ς
≥25	ἄλλος η ο	another, other	adj	[√]-ος
≥10	ἀλλότριος α ον	of another, foreign	adj	[√]-ιος
	ἄλλως	otherwise	adv	[√]-ως
	ἀντάλλαγμα ματος	thing in exchange	neut	ἀντι-[√]-μα
	ἀπαλλάσσω	set free	vb	ἀπο-[√]-σσω
	ἀποκαταλλάσσω	reconcile	vb	ἀπο-κατα-[√]-σσω
	διαλλάσσομαι	be reconciled	vb	δια-[√]-σσω
	καταλλαγή ῆς	reconciliation	fem	κατα-[√]-η
	καταλάσσω	reconcile	vb	κατα-[√]-σσω
	μεταλάσσω	exchange	vb	μετα-[√]-σσω
	παραλλαγή ῆς	variation, change	fem	παρα-[√]-η
	συναλλάσσω	reconcile	vb	συν-[√]-σσω

ὡς   914
as / how (manner)
Memory Aid: See Appendix 2, Chart A.

≥25	καθώς	as, just as	adv	κατα-[√]
	καθώσπερ	as, just as	adv	κατα-[√]-περ
≥25	ὅπως	that, in order that	cj/pt	[√]-ως
≥25	πῶς	how? in what way?	cj/pt	
≥10	πώς	somehow, in some way	cj/pt	
≥25	ὡς	as, like	cj/pt	
≥10	ὡσαύτως	likewise	adv	[√]-[αὐτ]-ως
≥10	ὡσεί	like, as	cj/pt	
≥25	ὥσπερ	as, just as	cj/pt	[√]-περ
	ὡσπερεί	as (though)	prep	[√]-περ
≥25	ὥστε	that, so that, thus	prep	

ἐπι   896
on
Memory Aid: epidermis, epicenter, epidemic, epitaph

| ≥10 | ἐπάνω (*gen*) | on, above, over | adv/prep | [√]-ἀνα-ω |
| ≥25 | ἐπί (*gen, dat, acc*) | upon, on, over | prep | |

ἐχ οχ   852
have / hold
Memory Aid:

≥10	ἀνέχομαι	tolerate (>hold up under)	vb	ἀνα-[√]-ω
	ἀνοχή ῆς	tolerance	fem	ἀνα-[√]-η
	ἀντέχομαι	be loyal to, hold firmly	vb	ἀντι-[√]-ω
≥10	ἀπέχω	receive in full	vb	ἀπο-[√]-ω
	ἐνέχω	have grudge	vb	ἐν-[√]-ω
	ἔνοχος ον	liable	adj	ἐν-[√]-ος
	ἐπέχω	notice	vb	ἐπι-[√]-ω
≥25	ἔχω	have	vb	[√]-ω
≥10	κατέχω	hold fast, keep	vb	κατα-[√]-ω
	μετέχω	share in, eat, have	vb	μετα-[√]-ω

	μετοχή ῆς	partnership	fem	μετα-[√]-η
	μέτοχος ου	partner	masc	μετα-[√]-ος
≥10	παρέχω	cause	vb	παρα-[√]-ω
	περιέχω	seize, overcome	vb	περι-[√]-ω
	προέχομαι	be better off	vb	προ-[√]-ω
	προκατέχω	have previously	vb	προ-κατα-[√]-ω
	προσανέχω	approach	vb	προς-ἀνα-[√]-ω
≥10	προσέχω	pay close attention to	vb	προς-[√]-ω
	συμμέτοχος ου	sharer	masc	συν-μετα-[√]-ος
≥10	συνέχω	surround, control	vb	συν-[√]-ω
	ὑπερέχω	surpass, govern	vb	ὑπερ-[√]-ω
	ὑπεροχή ῆς	position of authority	fem	ὑπερ-[√]-η
	ὑπέχω	undergo, suffer	vb	ὑπο-[√]-ω

προσ   744
to / toward
Memory Aid: prosthesis

≥25	ἔμπροσθεν (*gen*)	before	prep	ἐν-[√]-θεν
≥25	πρός (*acc*)	to, toward	prep	

κυρι   737
lord / power
Memory Aid: kyrios [*czar, kaiser, caesar*]

	κατακυριεύω	have power over	vb	κατα-[√]-ευω
	κυρία ας	lady	fem	[√]-ια
	κυριακός ή όν	belonging to the Lord	adj	[√]-ακος
	κυριεύω	rule, have power	vb	[√]-ευω
≥25	κύριος ου	lord, master	masc	[√]-ιος
	κυριότης ητος	power, authority	fem	[√]-οτης

ἵνα   679
in order that
Memory Aid:

≥25	ἵνα	in order that	cj/pt	
	ἵνατί	why?	cj/pt	[√]-[τι]

λεγ λογ λεκτ   673
say / word
Memory Aid: dialogue, eulogy, prologue, lexicon, dialect, elect

	ἄλογος ον	unreasoning, wild	adj	ἀ-[√]-ος
	ἀναλογία ας	proportion	fem	ἀνα-[√]-ια
	ἀναλογίζομαι	consider closely	vb	ἀνα-[√]-ιζω
	ἀναπολόγητος ον	without excuse	adj	ἀ-ἀπο-[√]-τος
	ἀνθομολογέομαι	give thanks	vb	ἀντι-[ὁμο]-[√]-εω
	ἀντιλέγω	object to	vb	ἀντι-[√]-ω
	ἀντιλογία ας	argument, hatred	fem	ἀντι-[√]-ια
≥10	ἀπολογέομαι	speak in one's defense	vb	ἀπο-[√]-εω
	ἀπολογία ας	defense (>apology)	fem	ἀπο-[√]-ια
	βατταλογέω	babble	vb	(βάττος)-[√]-εω

≥10 διαλέγομαι	discuss	vb	δια-[√]-ω
διάλεκτος ου	language (>dialect)	fem	[√]-τος
διαλογίζομαι	discuss	vb	[√]-ιζω
διαλογισμός οῦ	opinion, thought	masc	[√]-ισμος
δίλογος ον	two-faced	adj	[δευ]-[√]-ος
≥10 ἐκλέγομαι	choose, select (>elect)	vb	ἐκ-[√]-ω
≥10 ἐκλεκτός ή όν	chosen (>elected)	adj	ἐκ-[√]-τος
ἐκλογή ῆς	election, choosing	fem	ἐκ-[√]-η
ἐλλογέω	record	vb	ἐν-[√]-εω
ἐνευλογέω	bless	vb	ἐν-[√]-εὐ-[√]-εω
≥10 ἐξομολογέω	agree, consent, admit	vb	ἐκ-[ὁμο]-[√]-εω
ἐπιλέγω	call, name	vb	ἐπι-[√]-ω
≥25 εὐλογέω	bless (>eulogize)	vb	εὐ-[√]-εω
εὐλογητός ή όν	blessed, praised	adj	εὐ-[√]-τος
≥10 εὐλογία ας	blessing (>eulogy)	fem	εὐ-[√]-ια
καταλέγω	enroll (>catalogue)	vb	κατα-[√]-ω
κατευλογέω	bless	vb	κατα-εὐ-[√]-εω
≥25 λέγω	say	vb	[√]-ω
λόγια ων	oracles, words	neut	[√]-ια
≥25 λογίζομαι	count, consider	vb	[√]-ιζω
λογικός ή όν	rational, spiritual	adj	[√]-ικος
λόγιος α ον	eloquent, learned	adj	[√]-ιος
λογισμός οῦ	thought, reasoning	masc	[√]-ισμος
λογομαχέω	fight about words	vb	[√]-[μαχ]-εω
λογομαχία ας	quarrel about words	fem	[√]-[μαχ]-ια
≥25 λόγος ου	word, message	masc	[√]-ος
≥25 ὁμολογέω	confess, declare	vb	[ὁμο]-[√]-εω
ὁμολογία ας	confession	fem	[ὁμο]-[√]-ια
ὁμολογουμένως	undeniably	adv	[ὁμο]-[√]-ως
παραλογίζομαι	deceive	vb	παρα-[√]-ιζω
προλέγω	say (>prologue)	vb	προ-[√]-ω
προσλέγω	answer, reply	vb	προς-[√]-ω
συλλογίζομαι	discuss	vb	συν-[√]-ιζω

δια
through
Memory Aid: diameter, diarrhea

≥25 διά (*gen, acc*)	through, on account of	prep	

666

ἀπο ἀπ ἀφ
from
Memory Aid: apostasy, apostle

≥25 ἀπό (*gen*)	from	prep	

645

διδ δο δω
give
Memory Aid: antidote, dose [*donor, donate, dole*]

ἀναδίδωμι	deliver (>give up)	vb	ἀνα-[√]-μι
ἀνταποδίδωμι	repay, return	vb	ἀντι-ἀπο-[√]-μι

644

ἀνταπόδομα ματος	repayment	neut	ἀντι-ἀπο-[√]-μα
ἀνταπόδοσις εως	repayment	fem	ἀντι-ἀπο-[√]-σις
≥25 ἀποδίδωμι	give, pay	vb	ἀπο-[√]-μι
διαδίδωμι	distribute	vb	δια-[√]-μι
≥25 δίδωμι	give	vb	[√]-μι
δόμα ματος	gift	neut	[√]-μα
δόσις εως	gift	fem	[√]-σις
δότης ου	giver	masc	[√]-της
ἐκδίδομαι	let out, lease	vb	ἐκ-[√]-μι
ἔκδοτος ον	given over	adj	ἐκ-[√]-τος
≥10 ἐπιδίδωμι	deliver, give way	vb	ἐπι-[√]-μι
εὐμετάδοτος ον	liberal, generous	adj	εὐ-μετα-[√]-τος
μεταδίδωμι	give, share	vb	μετα-[√]-μι
≥25 παραδίδωμι	hand over, deliver	vb	παρα-[√]-μι
≥10 παράδοσις εως	tradition	fem	παρα-[√]-σις
πατροπαράδοτος ον	handed from ancestors	adj	[πατρ]-παρα-[√]-τος
προδίδωμι	give first	vb	προ-[√]-μι
προδότης ου	traitor	masc	προ-[√]-της

πιστ   602
belief / faith

Memory Aid: epistemology, epistemic

ἀπιστέω	fail to believe	vb	ἀ-[√]-εω
≥10 ἀπιστία ας	unbelief	fem	ἀ-[√]-ια
≥10 ἄπιστος ον	unfaithful, unbelieving	adj	ἀ-[√]-ος
ὀλιγοπιστία ας	little faith	fem	[ὀλιγ]-[√]-ια
ὀλιγόπιστος ον	of little faith	adj	[ὀλιγ]-[√]-ος
≥25 πιστεύω	believe	vb	[√]-ευω
πιστικός ή όν	genuine	adj	[√]-ικος
≥25 πίστις εως	faith, trust, belief	fem	[√]-ς
πιστόομαι	firmly believe, entrust	vb	[√]-οω
≥25 πιστός ή όν	faithful, believing	adj	[√]-τος

ποι   595
make / do

Memory Aid: poem

ἀχειροποίητος ον	not made by hands	adj	ἀ-[χειρ]-[√]-τος
εὐποιΐα ας	doing of good	fem	εὐ-[√]-ια
περιποιέομαι	obtain, preserve	vb	[περι]-[√]-εω
περιποίησις εως	obtaining, possession	fem	[περι]-[√]-σις
≥25 ποιέω	make, do	vb	[√]-εω
ποίημα ματος	something made	neut	[√]-μα
ποίησις εως	undertaking	fem	[√]-σις
ποιητής οῦ	one who does, doer	masc	[√]-της
προσποιέομαι	pretend	vb	προσ-[√]-εω
συζωοποιέω	make alive together	vb	συν-[ζω]-[√]-εω
χειροποίητος ον	hand / man-made	adj	[χειρ]-[√]-τος

ἱστη στα στη
stand

Memory Aid: static, status, system, ecstasy, stamina

	ἀκαταστασία ας	disorder	fem	ἀ-κατα-[√]-ια
	ἀκατάστατος ον	unstable	adj	ἀ-κατα-[√]-τος
≥25	ἀνάστασις εως	resurrection	masc/fem	ἀνα-[√]-σις
	ἀναστατόω	agitate, incite a revolt	vb	ἀνα-[√]-οω
≥10	ἀνθίστημι	resist	vb	ἀντι-[√]-μι
≥25	ἀνίστημι	raise up, appoint	vb	ἀνα-[√]-μι
	ἀντικαθίστημι	resist	vb	ἀντι-κατα-[√]-μι
	ἀποκαθίστημι	reestablish, cure	vb	ἀπο-κατα-[√]-μι
	ἀποκατάστασις εως	restoration	fem	ἀπο-κατα-[√]-σις
	ἀποστασία ας	apostasy	fem	ἀπο-[√]-ια
	ἀποστάσιον ου	notice of divorce	neut	ἀπο-[√]-ιον
	ἀστατέω	be homeless, wander	vb	ἀ-[√]-εω
≥10	ἀφίσταμαι	leave	vb	ἀπο-[√]-μι
	διάστημα ματος	interval	neut	δια-[√]-μα
	διΐστημι	part, pass time	vb	δια-[√]-μι
	διχοστασία ας	division	fem	[δευ]-[√]-ια
	ἔκστασις εως	amazement (>ecstasy)	fem	ἐκ-[√]-σις
	ἐνίστημι	be present	vb	ἐν-[√]-μι
	ἐξανάστασις εως	resurrection	fem	ἐκ-ἀνα-[√]-σις
	ἐξανίστημι	have, stand up	vb	ἐκ-ἀνα-[√]-μι
≥10	ἐξίστημι	be amazed, amaze	vb	ἐκ-[√]-μι
	ἐπανίσταμαι	turn against, rebel	vb	ἐπι-ἀνα-[√]-μι
≥10	ἐπίσταμαι	know, understand	vb	ἐπι-[√]-μι
	ἐπίστασις εως	pressure, stirring up	fem	ἐπι-[√]-σις
	ἐπιστάτης ου	Master	masc	ἐπι-[√]-της
	ἐπισήμων ον	understanding	adj	ἐπι-[√]-μων
	εὐπερίστατος ον	holding on tightly	adj	εὐ-περι-[√]-τος
≥10	ἐφίστημι	come to, approach	vb	ἐπι-[√]-μι
≥25	ἵστημι	set, stand	vb	[√]-μι
≥10	καθίστημι	put in charge	vb	κατα-[√]-μι
	κατάστημα ματος	behavior	neut	κατα-[√]-μα
	κατεφίστημι	attack, set upon	vb	κατα-ἐπι-[√]-μι
	μεθίστημι	remove, mislead	vb	μετα-[√]-μι
≥25	παρίστημι	present	vb	παρα-[√]-μι
	περιΐστημι	stand around	vb	περι-[√]-μι
	προΐστημι	be a leader, manage	vb	προ-[√]-μι
	προστάτις ιδος	helper (>stand before)	fem	προ-[√]-ς
	στασιαστής οῦ	rebel	masc	[√]-της
	στάσις εως	dispute, revolt	fem	[√]-σις
≥10	στήκω	stand	vb	[√]-ω
	συνεφίστημι	join in an attack	vb	συν-ἐπι-[√]-μι
≥10	συνίστημι	recommend, show	vb	συν-[√]-μι
	ὑπόστασις εως	conviction, confidence	fem	ὑπο-[√]-σις

ἀνθρωπ 561
man
Memory Aid: anthropology, anthropomorphic

	ἀνθρώπινος η ον	human	adj	[√]-ινος
	ἀνθρωποκτόνος ου	murderer	masc	[√]-[κτειν]-ος
≥25	ἄνθρωπος ου	man, person	masc	[√]-ος
	φιλανθρωπία ας	kindness	fem	[φιλ]-[√]-ια
	φιλανθρώπως	considerately	adv	[φιλ]-[√]-ως

κρι 553
judge
Memory Aid: critical, critic, crisis, critique, crime

	ἀδιάκριτος ον	without favoritism	adj	ἀ-δια-[√]-τος
	ἀκατάκριτος ον	uncondemned	adj	ἀ-κατα-[√]-τος
≥10	ἀνακρίνω	question, examine	vb	ἀνα-[√]-ω
	ἀνάκρισις εως	investigation	fem	ἀνα-[√]-σις
	ἀνταποκρίνομαι	reply	vb	ἀντι-ἀπο-[√]-ω
	ἀνυπόκριτος ον	sincere, genuine	adj	ἀ-ὑπο-[√]-τος
	ἀπόκριμα ματος	sentence	neut	ἀπο-[√]-μα
≥25	ἀποκρίνομαι	answer, reply	vb	ἀπο-[√]-νω
	ἀπόκρισις εως	answer, reply	fem	ἀπο-[√]-σις
	αὐτοκατάκριτος ον	self-condemned	adj	[αὐτο]-κατα-[√]-τος
≥10	διακρίνω	evaluate (mid doubt)	vb	δια-[√]-ω
	διάκρισις εως	ability to discriminate	fem	δια-[√]-σις
	ἐγκρίνω	class with	vb	ἐν-[√]-ω
	εἰλικρίνεια α	sincerity	fem	(ἔλη)-[√]-εια
	εἰλικρινής ές	sincere, pure	adj	(ἔλη)-[√]-ης
	ἐπικρίνω	decide	vb	ἐπι-[√]-ω
	κατάκριμα ματος	condemnation	neut	κατα-[√]-μα
≥10	κατακρίνω	condemn, judge	vb	κατα-[√]-ω
	κατάκρισις εως	condemnation	fem	κατα-[√]-σις
≥25	κρίμα τος	judgment, decision	neut	[√]-μα
≥25	κρίνω	judge, consider	vb	[√]-ω
≥25	κρίσις εως	judgment	fem	[√]-σις
	κριτήριον ου	court (judgment hall)	neut	[√]-τηριον
≥10	κριτής οῦ	judge	masc	[√]-της
	κριτικός ή όν	able to judge	adj	[√]-τικος
	πρόκριμα ματος	prejudice (>pre-judging)	neut	προ-[√]-μα
	συγκρίνω	compare, interpret	vb	συν-[√]-ω
	συνυποκρίνομαι	act insincerely with	vb	συν-ὑπο-[√]-ω
	ὑποκρίνομαι	pretend, be a hypocrite	vb	ὑπο-[√]-ω
	ὑπόκρισις εως	hypocrisy	fem	ὑπο-[√]-σις
≥10	ὑποκριτής οῦ	hypocrite	masc	ὑπο-[√]-της

χρι χρις 549
anoint
Memory Aid: Christ, christen, chrism

	ἀντίχριστος ου	Antichrist	masc	ἀντι-[√]-τος

ἐγχρίω	rub on	vb	ἐν-[√]-ω
ἐπιχρίω	smear	vb	ἐπι-[√]-ω
χρῖσμα ματος	anointing	neut	[√]-μα
Χριστιανός οῦ	Christian	masc	[√]-ος
≥25 Χριστός οῦ	Christ	masc	[√]-τος
χρίω	anoint	vb	[√]-ω
ψευδόχριστος ου	false Christ	masc	[ψευδ]-[√]-τος

κατ καθ¹
down / according to   523

Memory Aid: catacomb, catapult, cataract, cataclysm

καθά	as, just as	cj/pt/adv	
≥10 καθάπερ	as, just as	cj/pt/adv	[√]-περ
καθό	as, according as	adv	
≥25 κατά (*gen, acc*)	down, according to	prep	
κάτω	down, below	adv	[√]-ω
κατώτερος α ον	lower	adj	[√]-τερος
κατωτέρω	under	adv	[√]-ω
≥10 ὑποκάτω (*gen*)	under	prep	ὑπο-[√]-ω

οτε
when   523

Memory Aid: See Appendix 2, Chart A.

δήποτε	whatever	adv	
μηδέποτε	never	adv	[μη]-[√]
≥25 μήποτε	lest, whether, never	cj/pt	[μη]-[√]
ὁπότε	when	adv	[ὁπ]-[√]
≥25 ὅταν	when, whenever	adv	[√]-[ἀν]
≥25 ὅτε	when, while	cj/pt	
≥10 οὐδέποτε	never	adv	[οὐ]-[√]
≥25 πάντοτε	always, at all times	adv	[παν]-[√]
≥25 ποτέ	once, ever	cj/pt	
≥10 πότε	when?	adv	
πώποτε	ever, at any time	adv	
≥25 τότε	then	adv	

καλ² κλη
call   515

Memory Aid: call, paraclete, ecclesiastical

ἀνέγκλητος ον	beyond reproach	adj	ἀ-ἐν-[√]-τος
ἀντικαλέω	invite in return	vb	ἀντι-[√]-εω
ἐγκαλέω	accuse	vb	ἐν-[√]-εω
ἔγκλημα ματος	accusation	neut	ἐν-[√]-μα
εἰσκαλέομαι	invite in	vb	εἰς-[√]-εω
≥25 ἐκκλησία ας	church, assembly	fem	ἐκ-[√]-ια
≥25 ἐπικαλέω	call, name	vb	ἐπι-[√]-εω
≥25 καλέω	call, name	vb	[√]-εω
≥10 κλῆσις εως	call, calling	fem	[√]-σις
≥10 κλητός ή όν	called, invited	adj	[√]-τος

μετακαλέομαι	send for, invite	vb	μετα-[√]-εω
≥25 παρακαλέω	beg, encourage	vb	παρα-[√]-εω
≥25 παράκλησις εως	encouragement, help	fem	παρα-[√]-σις
παράκλητος ου	helper (the Paraclete)	masc	παρα-[√]-τος
προκαλέομαι	irritate	vb	προ-[√]-εω
≥25 προσκαλέομαι	summon, invite	vb	προς-[√]-εω
συγκαλέω	call together, summon	vb	συν-[√]-εω
συμπαρακαλέομαι	be encouraged together	vb	συν-παρα-[√]-εω

ἀγγελ   *505*
message
Memory Aid: angel, evangelist

ἀγγελία ας	message, news	fem	[√]-ια
ἀγγέλλω	tell	vb	[√]-ω
≥25 ἄγγελος ου	angel, messenger	masc	[√]-ος
≥10 ἀναγγέλλω	tell, proclaim	vb	ἀνα-[√]-ω
≥25 ἀπαγγέλλω	tell, proclaim	vb	ἀπο-[√]-ω
ἀρχάγγελος ου	archangel	masc	[ἀρχ]-[√]-ος
διαγγέλλω	preach, proclaim	vb	δια-[√]-ω
ἐξαγγέλλω	tell, proclaim	vb	ἐκ-[√]-ω
≥25 ἐπαγγελία ας	promise, decision	fem	ἐπι-[√]-ια
≥10 ἐπαγγέλλομαι	promise, confess	vb	ἐπι-[√]-ω
ἐπάγγελμα ματος	promise	neut	ἐπι-[√]-μα
≥25 εὐαγγελίζω	evangelize	vb	εὐ-[√]-ιζω
≥25 εὐαγγέλιον ου	good news, gospel	neut	εὐ-[√]-ιον
εὐαγγελιστής οῦ	evangelist	masc	εὐ-[√]-ιστης
ἰσάγγελος ον	angel-like	adj	[ἰσ]-[√]-ος
καταγγελεύς έως	proclaimer	masc	κατα-[√]-ευς
≥10 καταγγέλλω	proclaim	vb	κατα-[√]-ω
παραγγελία ας	order, instruction	fem	παρα-[√]-ια
≥25 παραγγέλλω	command, order	vb	παρα-[√]-ω
προεπαγγέλλομαι	promise before	vb	προ-ἐπι-[√]-ω
προευαγγελίζομαι	evangelize before	vb	προ-εὐ-[√]-ιζω
προκαταγγέλλω	announce before	vb	προ-κατα-[√]-ω

ἀκο ἀκου   *504*
hear
Memory Aid: acoustic

≥10 ἀκοή ῆς	hearing, report, news	fem	[√]-η
≥25 ἀκούω	hear, understand	vb	[√]-ω
διακούω	hear (legal cases)	vb	δια-[√]-ω
εἰσακούω	hear, obey (>listen to)	vb	εἰς-[√]-ω
ἐπακούω	hear, listen to	vb	ἐπι-[√]-ω
παρακοή ῆς	disobedience, disloyalty	fem	παρα-[√]-η
παρακούω	refuse to listen, disobey	vb	παρα-[√]-ω
προακούω	hear before	vb	προ-[√]-ω
≥10 ὑπακοή ῆς	obedience	fem	ὑπο-[√]-η
≥10 ὑπακούω	obey	vb	ὑπο-[√]-ω
ὑπήκοος ον	obedient	adj	ὑπο-[√]-ος

οὖν
therefore
Memory Aid:

	οὐκοῦν	so, then	adv	[οὐ]-[√]
≥25	οὖν	therefore	cj/pt	
	τοιγαροῦν	therefore, then	cj/pt	[ἀρ]-[√]

497

μετα
with / after
Memory Aid: metaphysics, metamorphosis, metabolism

| ≥25 | μετά (*gen, acc*) | with, after | prep | |
| | μεταξύ (*gen*) | between, among | prep | |

476

ἀγ ἀγωγ
lead / bring
Memory Aid: synagogue, demagogue, agent

≥25	ἄγω	lead	vb	[√]-ω
	ἀγωγή ῆς	manner of life	fem	[√]-η
	ἀνάγαιον ου	upstairs room	neut	ἀνα-[√]-ον
≥10	ἀνάγω	lead up, bring up	vb	ἀνα-[√]-ω
	ἀνεκδιήγητος ον	indescribable	adj	ἀ-ἐκ-δια-[√]-τος
≥10	ἀπάγω	lead away, bring before	vb	ἀπο-[√]-ω
	ἀποσυνάγωγος ον	excommunicated	adj	ἀπο-συν-[√]-ος
	ἀρχισυνάγωγος ου	chief of a synagogue	masc	[ἀρχ]-συν-[√]-ος
	διάγω	lead, spend (a life)	vb	δια-[√]-ω
	διηγέομαι	tell fully	vb	δια-[√]-εω
	διήγησις εως	account	fem	δια-[√]-σις
≥10	εἰσάγω	lead / bring in	vb	εἰς-[√]-ω
	ἐκδιηγέομαι	tell fully	vb	ἐκ-δια-[√]-εω
≥10	ἐξάγω	lead / bring out	vb	ἐκ-[√]-ω
	ἐξηγέομαι	tell, explain	vb	ἐκ-[√]-εω
	ἐπάγω	bring upon	vb	ἐπι-[√]-ω
	ἐπανάγω	return, put out	vb	ἐπι-ἀνα-[√]-ω
	ἐπεισαγωγή ῆς	bringing in	fem	ἐπι-εἰς-[√]-η
	ἐπισυνάγω	gather	vb	ἐπι-συν-[√]-ω
	ἐπισυναγωγή ῆς	assembly	fem	ἐπι-συν-[√]-η
	καθηγητής οῦ	teacher	masc	κατα-[√]-της
	κατάγω	bring (down)	vb	κατα-[√]-ω
≥10	κατηγορέω	accuse (bring against)	vb	κατα-[√]-εω
	κατηγορία	accusation	fem	κατα-[√]-ια
	κατήγορος ου	accuser	masc	κατα-[√]-ος
	κατήγωρ ορος	accuser	masc	κατα-[√]-ρ
	μετάγω	guide, direct	vb	μετα-[√]-ω
≥10	παράγω	pass by (away)	vb	παρα-[√]-ω
	παρεισάγω	bring in	vb	παρα-εἰς-[√]-ω
	περιάγω	go around	vb	περι-[√]-ω
≥10	προάγω	go before	vb	προ-[√]-ω
	προηγέομαι	outdo, lead the way	vb	προ-[√]-εω

455

προσάγω	bring to or before	vb	προς-[√]-ω
προσαγωγή ῆς	access	fem	προς-[√]-η
συλαγωγέω	make captive	vb	(συλάω)-[√]-εω
≥25 συνάγω	gather	vb	συν-[√]-ω
≥25 συναγωγή ῆς	synagogue	fem	συν-[√]-η
συναπάγομαι	be carried away	vb	συν-ἀπο-[√]-ω
≥25 ὑπάγω	go (away)	vb	ὑπο-[√]-ω
χειραγωγέω	lead by the hand	vb	[χειρ]-[√]-εω
χειραγωγός οῦ	one who leads	masc	[χειρ]-[√]-ος

γνο γνω γινω   445
know

Memory Aid: agnostic, gnosis, gnosticism, diagnosis [knowledge: *see Grimm's Law*]

≥10 ἀγνοέω	be ignorant, disregard	vb	ἀ-[√]-εω
ἀγνόημα ματος	sin done in ignorance	neut	ἀ-[√]-μα
ἄγνοια ας	ignorance	fem	ἀ-[√]-ια
ἀγνωσία ας	lack of spiritual insight	fem	ἀ-[√]-ια
ἄγνωστος ον	unknown	adj	ἀ-[√]-τος
ἀκατάγνωστος ον	above criticism	adj	ἀ-κατα-[√]-τος
≥25 ἀναγινώσκω	read	vb	ἀνα-[√]-σκω
ἀναγνωρίζομαι	make known again	vb	ἀνα-[√]-ιζω
ἀνάγνωσις εως	reading	fem	ἀνα-[√]-σις
≥25 γινώσκω	know, learn	vb	[√]-σκω
γνώμη ης	purpose, will, opinion	fem	[√]-η
≥25 γνωρίζω	make known, know	vb	[√]-ιζω
≥25 γνῶσις εως	knowledge	fem	[√]-σις
γνώστης ου	one familiar with	masc	[√]-της
≥10 γνωστός ή όν	known (acquaintance)	adj	[√]-τος
διαγινώσκω	investigate, decide	vb	δια-[√]-σκω
διάγνωσις εως	decision (>diagnosis)	fem	δια-[√]-σις
≥25 ἐπιγινώσκω	know, perceive	vb	ἐπι-[√]-σκω
≥10 ἐπίγνωσις εως	knowledge	fem	ἐπι-[√]-σις
καταγινώσκω	condemn	vb	κατα-[√]-σκω
προγινώσκω	know already	vb	προ-[√]-σκω
πρόγνωσις εως	foreknowledge, purpose	fem	προ-[√]-σις
συγγνώμη ης	permission	fem	συν-[√]-η

πατρ πατηρ   436
father

Memory Aid: paternity, patriarch [father: *see Grimm's Law*]

ἀπάτωρ ορος	the fatherless	masc	ἀ-[√]-ρ
≥25 πατήρ πατρός	father	masc	[√]-ρ
πατριά ᾶς	family, nation	fem	[√]-ια
πατριάρχης ου	patriarch	masc	[√]-[ἀρχ]-ης
πατρικός ή όν	paternal	adj	[√]-ικος
πατρίς ίδος	homeland	fem	[√]-ς
πατρῷος α ον	belonging to ancestors	adj	[√]-ιος
προπάτωρ ορος	forefather	masc	προ-[√]-ρ

ἀρχ   435
begin / old / rule / chief
Memory Aid: monarch, archangel, archbishop, archetype, archaeology

ἀπαρχή ῆς	first-fruits	fem	ἀπο-[√]-η
≥10 ἀρχαῖος α ον	old, ancient, former	adj	[√]-ιος
≥25 ἀρχή ῆς	beginning, rule	fem	[√]-η
ἀρχηγός οῦ	leader, founder	masc	[√]-[ἀγ]-ος
ἀρχιερατικός όν	highpriestly	adj	[√]-τικος
≥25 ἀρχιερεύς έως	high priest	masc	[√]-ευς
ἀρχιποίμην ενος	chief shepherd	masc	[√]-[ποιμ]-ην
≥25 ἄρχω	govern (mid begin)	vb	[√]-ω
≥25 ἄρχων οντος	ruler	masc	[√]-ων
≥10 ἑκατοντάρχης ου	centurion	masc	(ἑκατ)-[√]-ης
ἐνάρχομαι	begin	vb	ἐν-[√]-ω
ἐπαρχεία ας	province (>thing ruled)	fem	ἐπι-[√]-εια
προενάρχομαι	begin, begin before	vb	προ-ἐν-[√]-ω
προϋπάρχω	exist previously	vb	προ-ὑπο-[√]-ω
ὕπαρξις εως	possession	fem	ὑπο-[√]-σις
≥25 ὑπάρχω	be under one's rule	vb	ὑπο-[√]-ω
≥10 χιλίαρχος ου	tribune, officer	masc	[χιλι]-[√]-ος

ἡμερ   435
day
Memory Aid: ephemeral

ἀνήμερος ον	fierce	adj	ἀ-[√]-ος
ἐφημερία ας	division	fem	ἐπι-[√]-ια
ἐφήμερος ον	daily	adj	ἐπι-[√]-ος
≥25 ἡμέρα ας	day	fem	[√]-α
καθημερινός ή όν	daily	adj	κατα-[√]-ινος
ὀκταήμερος ον	on the eighth day	adj	(ὀκτώ)-[√]-ος
≥25 σήμερον	today	adv	[√]-ον

πν πνευ   429
spirit / wind / breath
Memory Aid: pneumonia, pneumatic

ἀποπνίγω	choke, drown	vb	ἀπο-[√]-ω
ἐκπνέω	die	vb	ἐκ-[√]-ω
ἐμπνέω	breathe	vb	ἐν-[√]-ω
≥25 πνεῦμα ματος	spirit, self, wind	neut	[√]-μα
≥25 πνευματικός ή όν	spiritual	adj	[√]-τικος
πνευματικῶς	spiritually, symbolically	adv	[√]-τικος-ως
πνέω	blow	vb	[√]-ω
πνίγω	choke, drown	vb	[√]-ω
πνικτός ή όν	strangled	adj	[√]-τος
πνοή ῆς	wind, breath	fem	[√]-η
ὑποπνέω	blow gently	vb	ὑπο-[√]-ω

εἷς μια ἑν   424
one
Memory Aid: henotheism

≥25 εἷς μία ἕν	one, only	adj	
ἑνότης ητος	unity	fem	[√]-οτης
≥25 μηδείς μηδεμία μηδέν	no one	adj	[μη]-[√]

λαμβ λημ λαβ   424
take / receive
Memory Aid: syllable, dilemma

≥10 ἀναλαμβάνω	take (up)	vb	ἀνα-[√]-ανω
ἀνάλημψις εως	ascension (>taking up)	fem	ἀνα-[√]-σις
ἀνεπίλημπτος ον	above reproach	adj	ἀ-ἐπι-[√]-τος
ἀντιλαμβάνομαι	help	vb	ἀντι-[√]-ανω
ἀντίλημψις εως	ability to help, helper	fem	ἀντι-[√]-σις
ἀπολαμβάνω	receive, get back	vb	ἀπο-[√]-ανω
ἀπροσωπολήμπτως	impartially	adv	ἀ-[προσωπ]-[√]-ως
≥10 ἐπιλαμβάνομαι	take, seize, help	vb	ἐπι-[√]-ανω
εὐλάβεια ας	godly fear, reverence	fem	εὐ-[√]-εια
εὐλαβέομαι	act in reverence	vb	εὐ-[√]-εω
εὐλαβής ές	reverent	adj	εὐ-[√]-ης
≥10 καταλαμβάνω	obtain, attain, overtake	vb	κατα-[√]-ανω
≥25 λαμβάνω	take, receive	vb	[√]-ανω
λῆμψις εως	receiving	fem	[√]-σις
μεταλαμβάνω	receive, share in	vb	μετα-[√]-ανω
μετάλημψις εως	receiving, accepting	fem	μετα-[√]-σις
≥25 παραλαμβάνω	take (along), receive	vb	παρα-[√]-ανω
προλαμβάνω	do (take) ahead of time	vb	προ-[√]-ανω
≥10 προσλαμβάνομαι	welcome, accept	vb	προς-[√]-ανω
πρόσλημψις εως	acceptance	fem	προς-[√]-σις
≥10 συλλαμβάνω	seize, arrest	vb	συν-[√]-ανω
συμπαραλαμβάνω	take / bring along with	vb	συν-παρα-[√]-ανω
συμπεριλαμβάνω	embrace, hug	vb	συν-περι-[√]-ανω
συναντιλαμβάνομαι	(come to) help	vb	συν-ἀντι-[√]-ανω
ὑπολαμβάνω	suppose, take away	vb	ὑπο-[√]-ανω

οἰκ   418
house
Memory Aid: economy, ecology, ecosystem, ecumenical, diocese

ἀνοικοδομέω	rebuild	vb	[ἀνα]-[√]-[δημ]-εω
ἐγκατοικέω	live among	vb	ἐν-κατα-[√]-εω
ἐνοικέω	live in	vb	ἐν-[√]-εω
ἐποικοδομέω	build on / build up	vb	ἐπι-[√]-(δέμω)-εω
≥25 κατοικέω	live, inhabit	vb	κατα-[√]-εω
κατοίκησις εως	home	fem	κατα-[√]-σις
κατοικητήριον ου	house, home	neut	κατα-[√]-τηριον
κατοικία ας	place where one lives	fem	κατα-[√]-ια
κατοικίζω	place, put	vb	κατα-[√]-ιζω
μετοικεσία ας	carrying off	fem	μετα-[√]-ια
μετοικίζω	deport / send off	vb	μετα-[√]-ιζω
οἰκεῖος ου	family member	masc	[√]-ιος

οἰκετεία ας	household	fem	[√]-εια
οἰκέτης ου	house servant	masc	[√]-της
οἰκέω	live, dwell	vb	[√]-εω
οἴκημα ματος	prison cell	neut	[√]-μα
οἰκητήριον ου	home, dwelling	neut	[√]-τηριον
≥25 οἰκία ας	home, family	fem	[√]-ια
οἰκιακός οῦ	member of household	masc	[√]-ακος
οἰκοδεσποτέω	run a household	vb	[√]-(δεσπότης)-εω
≥10 οἰκοδεσπότης ου	master, householder	masc	[√]-(δεσπότης)-της
≥25 οἰκοδομέω	build, encourage	vb	[√]-(δέμω)-εω
≥10 οἰκοδομή ῆς	structure	fem	[√]-(δέμω)-η
οἰκοδόμος ου	builder	masc	[√]-(δέμω)-ος
οἰκονομέω	be a manager, steward	vb	[√]-[νομ]-εω
οἰκονομία ας	task, responsibility	fem	[√]-[νομ]-ια
≥10 οἰκονόμος ου	manager, steward	masc	[√]-[νομ]-ος
≥25 οἶκος ου	house	masc	[√]-ος
≥10 οἰκουμένη ης	world (>oikomenia)	fem	[√]-η
οἰκουργός όν	domestic	adj	[√]-[ἐργ]-ος
πανοικεί	with one's household	adv	[παν]-[√]
παροικέω	live in, live as a stranger	vb	παρα-[√]-εω
παροικία ας	stay, visit	fem	παρα-[√]-ια
πάροικος ου	alien, stranger	masc	παρα-[√]-ος
περιοικέω	live in a neighborhood	vb	περι-[√]-εω
περίοικος ου	neighbor	masc	περι-[√]-ος
συνοικέω	live with	vb	συν-[√]-εω

ἐκει ἐκειν   411
there / that
Memory Aid:

≥25 ἐκεῖ	there	adv	
≥25 ἐκεῖθεν	from there	adv	[√]-θεν
ἐκείνης	there	adv	
≥25 ἐκεῖνος η ο	that	adj/pron	[√]-ος
ἐκεῖσε	there	adv	
ἐπέκεινα (*gen*)	beyond	prep	ἐπι-[√]-α
≥10 κἀκεῖ	and there	adv	[και]
≥10 κἀκεῖθεν	from there	adv	[και]-[√]-θεν
≥10 κἀκεῖνος η ο	and that one	pron	[και]-[√]-ος
ὑπερέκεινα (*gen*)	beyond	prep	ὑπερ-[√]-α

βαλ βολ βλη   394
throw
Memory Aid: ball, ballistic, diabolical, problem

ἀμφιβάλλω	cast a net	vb	ἀμφι-[√]-ω
ἀμφίβληστρον ου	casting net	neut	ἀμφι-[√]-τρον
ἀναβάλλομαι	postpone	vb	ἀνα-[√]-ω
ἀναβολή ῆς	delay	fem	ἀνα-[√]-η
ἀντιβάλλω	exchange	vb	ἀντι-[√]-ω

ἀποβάλλω	throw off	vb	ἀπο-[√]-ω
ἀπόβλητος ον	rejected	adj	ἀπο-[√]-τος
ἀποβολή ῆς	loss, rejection	fem	ἀπο-[√]-η
≥25 βάλλω	throw	vb	[√]-ω
βλητέος α ον	must be put, poured	adj	[√]-ος
βολή ῆς	throw	fem	[√]-η
βολίζω	measure depth	vb	[√]-ιζω
διαβάλλω	accuse (>throw against)	vb	δια-[√]-ω
διάβολος ον	accusing (falsely)	adj	δια-[√]-ος
≥25 διάβολος ου	devil (the accuser)	masc	δια-[√]-ος
≥25 ἐκβάλλω	force out, exclude	vb	ἐκ-[√]-ω
ἐκβολή ῆς	throwing overboard	fem	ἐκ-[√]-η
ἐμβάλλω	throw	vb	ἐν-[√]-ω
≥10 ἐπιβάλλω	lay (hands) on	vb	ἐπι-[√]-ω
καταβάλλω	knock down	vb	κατα-[√]-ω
≥10 καταβολή ῆς	beginning, foundation	fem	κατα-[√]-η
μεταβάλλομαι	change one's mind	vb	μετα-[√]-ω
παραβάλλω	arrive	vb	παρα-[√]-ω
παραβολεύομαι	risk	vb	παρα-[√]-ευω
≥25 παραβολή ῆς	parable, symbol	fem	παρα-[√]-η
παρεμβάλλω	set up	vb	παρα-ἐν-[√]-ω
≥10 παρεμβολή ῆς	barracks, camp	fem	παρα-ἐν-[√]-η
≥10 περιβάλλω	put on, clothe	vb	περι-[√]-ω
περιβόλαιον ου	cloak, covering	neut	περι-[√]-ιον
προβάλλω	put forward	vb	προ-[√]-ω
συμβάλλω	meet, discuss	vb	συν-[√]-ω
ὑπερβαλλόντως	much more	adv	ὑπερ-[√]-ως
ὑπερβάλλω	surpass (>overthrow)	vb	ὑπερ-[√]-ω
ὑπερβολή ῆς	the extreme (>hyperbole)	fem	ὑπερ-[√]-η
ὑποβάλλω	bribe	vb	ὑπο-[√]-ω

δυνα δυναμ
power / ability

388

Memory Aid: dynamic, dynamite, dynasty, dynamo

ἀδυνατεῖ	it is impossible	vb	ἀ-[√]-εω
≥10 ἀδύνατος ον	impossible, unable	adj	ἀ-[√]-τος
≥25 δύναμαι	be able	vb	[√]-μι
≥25 δύναμις εως	power, strength	fem	[√]-ς
δυναμόω	make strong	vb	[√]-οω
δυνάστης ου	ruler	masc	[√]-της
δυνατέω	be able, be strong	vb	[√]-εω
≥25 δυνατός ή όν	able, possible, strong	adj	[√]-τος
ἐνδυναμόω	strengthen	vb	ἐν-[√]-οω
καταδυναστεύω	oppress	vb	κατα-[√]-ευω

ἀδελφ
brother / sister

380

Memory Aid: Philadelphia

≥25	ἀδελφή ῆς	sister	fem	[√]-η
≥25	ἀδελφός οῦ	brother, countryman	masc	[√]-ος
	ἀδελφότης ητος	brotherhood	fem	[√]-οτης
	φιλαδελφία ας	brotherly love	fem	[φιλ]-[√]-ια
	φιλάδελφος ον	brother-loving	adj	[φιλ]-[√]-ος
	ψευδάδελφος ου	false brother	masc	[ψευδ]-[√]-ος

υἱ
son
380

Memory Aid:

| | υἱοθεσία ας | adoption | fem | [√]-[τιθ]-ια |
| ≥25 | υἱός οῦ | son, descendant | masc | [√]-ος |

ἐργ οὐργ
work
375

Memory Aid: liturgy, energy, ergonomic, suffix -urgy

	ἀργέω	be idle (>not working)	vb	ἀ-[√]-εω
	ἀργός ἡ όν	idle, unemployed	adj	ἀ-[√]-ος
	δημιουργός οῦ	builder	masc	[δημ]-[√]-ος
	ἐνέργεια ας	work (>energy)	fem	ἐν-[√]-εια
≥10	ἐνεργέω	work	vb	ἐν-[√]-εω
	ἐνέργημα ματος	working, activity	neut	ἐν-[√]-μα
	ἐνεργής ές	active, effective	adj	ἐν-[√]-ης
≥25	ἐργάζομαι	work, do	vb	[√]-αζω
	ἐργασία ας	gain, doing	fem	[√]-σια
≥10	ἐργάτης ου	worker	masc	[√]-της
≥25	ἔργον ου	work, action	neut	[√]-ον
	εὐεργεσία ας	service, kind act	fem	εὐ-[√]-ια
	εὐρεργετέω	do good	vb	εὐ-[√]-εω
	εὐεργέτης ου	benefactor	masc	εὐ-[√]-της
≥25	καταργέω	destroy	vb	κατα-[√]-εω
≥10	κατεργάζομαι	do, accomplish	vb	κατα-[√]-αζω
	λειτουργέω	serve, worship	vb	[λα]-[√]-εω
	λειτουργία ας	service, worship	fem	[λα]-[√]-ια
	λειτουργικός ἡ όν	serving, ministering	adj	[λα]-[√]-ικος
	λειτουργός οῦ	servant, minister	masc	[λα]-[√]-ος
	πανουργία ας	trickery	fem	[παν]-[√]-ια
	πανοῦργος ον	tricky	adj	[παν]-[√]-ος
	περιεργάζομαι	be a busybody	vb	περι-[√]-αζω
	περίεργος ου	busybody	masc	περι-[√]-ος
	προσεργάζομαι	make more	vb	προς-[√]-αζω
	ῥαδιούργημα ματος	wrongdoing	neut	[ῥά]-[√]-μα
	ῥαδιουργία ας	wrongdoing	fem	[ῥά]-[√]-ια
	συνεργέω	work with	vb	συν-[√]-εω
≥10	συνεργός οῦ	fellow-worker	masc	συν-[√]-ος
	συνυπουργέω	join in, help	vb	συν-ὑπο-[√]-εω

πολλ πολυ
much / many
367

Memory Aid: polytheistic, polygamy

πολλάκις	often	adv	[√]-κις
πολλαπλασίων ον	more	adj	[√]-(πλασίων)-ων
πολυλογία ας	many words	fem	[√]-[λεγ]-ια
πολυμερῶς	many times, bit by bit	adv	[√]-[μερ]-ως
πολυποίκιλος ον	in varied forms	adj	[√]-(ποικίλος)-ος
≥25 πολύς πολλή πολύ	much, many	adj	[√]-υς
πολύσπλαγχνος ον	very compassionate	adj	[√]-(σπλάγχνον)-ος
πολυτελής ές	expensive	adj	[√]-[τελ]-ης
πολύτιμος ον	expensive	adj	[√]-[τιμ]-ος
πολυτρόπως	in many ways, variously	adv	[√]-[τρεπ]-ως

γραφ γραπ γραμ
write
345

Memory Aid: geography, calligraphy, graphite, grammar

ἀγράμματος ον	uneducated	adj	ἀ-[√]-τος
ἀπογραφή ῆς	registration, census	fem	ἀπο-[√]-η
ἀπογράφω	register	vb	ἀπο-[√]-ω
≥10 γράμμα ματος	letter, Scripture, account	neut	[√]-μα
≥25 γραμματεύς έως	scribe	masc	[√]-ευς
γραπτός ή όν	written	adj	[√]-τος
≥25 γραφή ῆς	Scripture	fem	[√]-η
≥25 γράφω	write	vb	[√]-ω
ἐγγράφω	write, record	vb	ἐν-[√]-ω
ἐπιγραφή ῆς	inscription (>epigraph)	fem	ἐπι-[√]-η
ἐπιγράφω	write on	vb	ἐπι-[√]-ω
καταγράφω	write	vb	κατα-[√]-ω
προγράφω	write beforehand	vb	προ-[√]-ω
ὑπογραμμός οὗ	example	masc	ὑπο-[√]-ος
χειρόγραφον ου	record of debt	neut	[χειρ]-[√]-ον

ἤ
or / than
344

Memory Aid:

≥25 ἤ	or, than	cj/pt	
ἤπερ	than	cj/pt	[√]-περ
ἤτοι	or	cj/pt	

τιθ θε² θη
put / place
336

Memory Aid: synthesis, epithet, bibliotheca, thesis, antithesis

ἄθεσμος ον	lawless	adj	ἀ-[√]-μος
≥10 ἀθετέω	reject, ignore (>not put)	vb	ἀ-[√]-εω
ἀθέτησις εως	nullification (>not put)	fem	ἀ-[√]-σις
ἀμετάθετος ον	unchangeable	adj	ἀ-μετα-[√]-τος
ἀνάθεμα ματος	cursed, anathematized	neut	ἀνα-[√]-μα
ἀναθεματίζω	curse, anathematize	vb	ἀνα-[√]-ιζω
ἀνάθημα ματος	offering, gift	neut	ἀνα-[√]-μα
ἀνατίθεμαι	present	vb	ἀνα-[√]-μι
ἀνεύθετος ον	unsuitable (>not well put)	adj	ἀ-εὐ-[√]-τος

ἀντιδιατίθεμαι	oppose	vb	ἀντι-δια-[√]-μι
ἀντίθεσις εως	antithesis, contradiction	fem	ἀντι-[√]-σις
ἀπόθεσις εως	removal	fem	ἀπο-[√]-σις
ἀποθήκη ης	barn	fem	ἀπο-[√]-η
ἀποτίθημι	throw (take) off	vb	ἀπο-[√]-μι
ἀσύνθετος ον	faithless, disloyal	adj	ἀ-συν-[√]-τος
≥25 διαθήκη ης	covenant	fem	δια-[√]-η
διατίθεμαι	make (a covenant)	vb	δια-[√]-μι
ἔκθετος ον	abandoned	adj	ἐκ-[√]-τος
ἐκτίθεμαι	explain, expound	vb	ἐκ-[√]-μι
ἐπίθεσις εως	laying on (of hands)	fem	ἐπι-[√]-σις
≥25 ἐπιτίθημι	put on, place	vb	ἐπι-[√]-μι
εὔθετος ον	suitable (>well placed)	adj	εὐ-[√]-τος
θήκη ης	sheath	fem	[√]-η
καταθεματίζω	curse	vb	κατα-[√]-ιζω
κατατίθημι	lay, place	vb	κατα-[√]-μι
μετάθεσις εως	removal, change	fem	μετα-[√]-σις
μετατίθημι	remove, change	vb	μετα-[√]-μι
παραθήκη ης	something entrusted	fem	παρα-[√]-η
≥10 παρατίθημι	place before, give	vb	παρα-[√]-μι
περίθεσις εως	wearing (of jewelry)	fem	περι-[√]-σις
περιτίθημι	put around	vb	περι-[√]-μι
≥10 πρόθεσις εως	purpose, plan	fem	προ-[√]-σις
προσανατίθεμαι	go for advice, add to	vb	προς-ἀνα-[√]-μι
≥10 προστίθημι	add, increase, continue	vb	προς-[√]-μι
προτίθεμαι	plan, intend	vb	προ-[√]-μι
συγκατάθεσις εως	joint agreement	fem	συν-κατα-[√]-σις
συγκατατίθεμαι	agree with	vb	συν-κατα-[√]-μι
συνεπιτίθεμαι	join in the attack	vb	συν-ἐπι-[√]-μι
συντίθεμαι	agree, arrange	vb	συν-[√]-μι
≥25 τίθημι	put, place, lay	vb	[√]-μι
ὑποτίθημι	risk (>place under)	vb	ὑπο-[√]-μι

περι   332
around / concerning
Memory Aid: perimeter, peripheral, periscope

≥25 περί (*gen, acc*)	about, concerning	prep	
πέριξ	around	adv	

λαλ   328
speak
Memory Aid: glossolalia

ἀλαλάζω	wail (>not speaking)	vb	ἀ-[√]-αζω
ἀλάλητος ον	inexpressible	adj	ἀ-[√]-τος
ἄλαλος ον	unable to speak, dumb	adj	ἀ-[√]-ος
ἀνεκλάλητος ον	inexpressible in words	adj	ἀ-ἐκ-[√]-τος
διαλαλέω	discuss	vb	δια-[√]-εω
ἐκλαλέω	tell (>speak out)	vb	ἐκ-[√]-εω

καταλαλέω	slander (>speak against)	vb	κατα-[√]-εω
καταλαλιά ᾶς	slander	fem	κατα-[√]-ια
κατάλαλος ου	slanderer	masc	κατα-[√]-ος
≥25 λαλέω	speak	vb	[√]-εω
λαλιά ᾶς	what is said, accent	fem	[√]-ια
μογιλάλος ον	mute, dumb	adj	(μόγος)-[√]-ος
προσλαλέω	speak to	vb	προς-[√]-εω
συλλαλέω	talk with	vb	συν-[√]-εω

οἰδ
know
322

Memory Aid:

≥25 οἶδα	know	vb	[√]-ω
σύνοιδα	share knowledge with	vb	συν-[√]-ω

ἀγαπ
love
318

Memory Aid: agape

≥25 ἀγαπάω	love	vb	[√]-αω
≥25 ἀγάπη ης	love	fem	[√]-η
≥25 ἀγαπητός ή όν	beloved	adj	[√]-τος

ζω ζα
life
317

Memory Aid: zoology, zoo, protozoa, zodiac

ἀναζάω	revive	vb	ἀνα-[√]-ω
≥25 ζάω	live	vb	[√]-ω
≥25 ζωή ῆς	life	fem	[√]-η
ζωογονέω	save life	vb	[√]-[γεν]-εω
≥10 ζῷον ου	animal (>living thing)	neut	[√]-ον
≥10 ζωοποιέω	make alive	vb	[√]-[ποι]-εω
συζάω	live with	vb	συν-[√]-ω

βασιλ
royal
311

Memory Aid: basilica

≥25 βασιλεία ας	reign, kingdom	fem	[√]-εια
βασίλειος ον	royal	adj	[√]-ιος
≥25 βασιλεύς έως	king	masc	[√]-ευς
≥10 βασιλεύω	rule, reign	vb	[√]-ευω
βασιλικός ή όν	royal	adj	[√]-ικος
βασίλισσα ης	queen	fem	[√]-ισσα
συμβασιλεύω	live together as kings	vb	συν-[√]-ευω

δικ
just / judgment
309

Memory Aid: syndicate

≥25 ἀδικέω	wrong	vb	ἀ-[√]-εω
ἀδίκημα ματος	crime, sin, wrong	neut	ἀ-[√]-μα
ἀδικία ας	wrongdoing, evil	fem	ἀ-[√]-ια

≥10 ἄδικος ον	evil, sinful	adj	ἀ-[√]-ος
ἀδίκως	unjustly	adv	ἀ-[√]-ως
ἀντίδικος ου	opponent at law, enemy	masc	ἀντι-[√]-ος
δικαιοκρισία ας	just judgment	fem	[√]-[κρι]-ια
≥25 δίκαιος α ον	just, right	adj	[√]-ιος
≥25 δικαιοσύνη ης	righteousness, justice	fem	[√]-συνη
≥25 δικαιόω	acquit, make righteous	vb	[√]-οω
≥10 δικαίωμα ματος	judgment, acquittal	neut	[√]-μα
δικαίως	justly	adv	[√]-ως
δικαίωσις εως	acquittal	fem	[√]-σις
δικαστής οῦ	judge	masc	[√]-της
δίκη ης	justice, punishment	fem	[√]-η
ἐκδικέω	avenge, punish	vb	ἐκ-[√]-εω
ἐκδίκησις εως	punishment	fem	ἐκ-[√]-σις
ἔκδικος ου	one who punishes	masc	ἐκ-[√]-ος
ἔνδικος ον	just, deserved	adj	ἐν-[√]-ος
καταδικάζω	condemn	vb	κατα-[√]-αζω
καταδίκη ης	sentence, condemnation	fem	κατα-[√]-η
ὑπόδικος ον	answerable to	adj	ὑπο-[√]-ος

οὐραν
heaven
301

Memory Aid: Uranus

≥10 ἐπουράνιος ον	heavenly	adj	ἐπι-[√]-ιος
οὐράνιος ον	heavenly	adj	[√]-ιος
οὐρανόθεν	from heaven	adv	[√]-θεν
≥25 οὐρανός οῦ	heaven	masc	[√]-ος

ἁγι ἁγν
holy / sacred
296

Memory Aid: hagiology, Hagia Sophia

≥25 ἁγιάζω	make holy, purify	vb	[√]-αζω
≥10 ἁγιασμός οῦ	consecration	masc	[√]-σμος
≥25 ἅγιος α ον	holy, consecrated	adj	[√]-ιος
ἁγιότης ητος	holiness	fem	[√]-οτης
ἁγιωσύνη ης	holiness, consecration	fem	[√]-συνη
ἁγνεία ας	moral purity	fem	[√]-εια
ἁγνίζω	purify (>holy + ize)	vb	[√]-ιζω
ἁγνισμός οῦ	purification	masc	[√]-ισμος
ἁγνός ή όν	holy, pure	adj	[√]-ος
ἁγνότης ητος	purity, sincerity	fem	[√]-οτης
ἁγνῶς	purely	adv	[√]-ως

μαθ μανθ
learn
295

Memory Aid: math

ἀμαθής ές	ignorant	adj	ἀ-[√]-ης
καταμανθάνω	consider, observe	vb	κατα-[√]-ανω
μαθητεύω	make a disciple	vb	[√]-ευω

≥25	μαθητής οῦ	disciple, pupil	masc	[√]-της
	μαθήτρια ας	woman disciple	fem	[√]-τρια
≥25	μανθάνω	learn, discover	vb	[√]-ανω
	συμμαθητής οῦ	fellow disciple	masc	συν-[√]-της

πατ
walk
Memory Aid: peripatetic

	ἐμπεριπατέω	live among	vb	ἐν-περι-[√]-εω
≥25	καταπατέω	trample on, despise	vb	κατα-[√]-εω
	πατέω	walk, trample	vb	[√]-εω
≥25	περιπατέω	walk, move about, live	vb	περι-[√]-εω

290

φα φη φημ
say / report
Memory Aid: prophet, euphemistic, blaspheme, fame

	διαφημίζω	spread around	vb	δια-[√]-ιζω
	δυσφημέω	slander	vb	δυσ-[√]-εω
	δυσφημία ας	slander	fem	δυσ-[√]-ια
	εὐφημία ας	good reputation	fem	εὐ-[√]-ια
	εὔφημος ον	worthy of praise	adj	εὐ-[√]-ος
≥10	προφητεία ας	prophesying	fem	προ-[√]-εια
≥25	προφητεύω	prophesy, preach	vb	προ-[√]-ευω
≥25	προφήτης ου	prophet	masc	προ-[√]-της
	προφητικός ή όν	prophetic	adj	προ-[√]-τικος
	προφῆτις ιδος	prophetess	fem	προ-[√]-ς
	σύμφημι	agree with	vb	συν-[√]-μι
	φάσις εως	news, report	fem	[√]-σις
	φάσκω	claim, assert	vb	[√]-σκω
	φήμη ης	report, news	fem	[√]-η
≥25	φημί	say	vb	[√]-μι
≥10	ψευδοπροφήτης ου	false prophet	masc	[ψευδ]-προ-[√]-της

286

γη γε[1]
earth
Memory Aid: geography, George

	γεωργέω	cultivate (>work earth)	vb	[√]-[ἐργ]-εω
	γεώργιον ου	field (>worked earth)	neut	[√]-[ἐργ]-ιον
≥10	γεωργός οῦ	farmer (>earth-worker)	masc	[√]-[ἐργ]-ος
≥25	γῆ γῆς	earth, land, region	fem	[√]-η
	ἐπίγειος ον	earthly	adj	ἐπι-[√]-ιος

276

στελ στολ
send / equip
Memory Aid: apostle

≥25	ἀποστέλλω	send	vb	ἀπο-[√]-ω
	ἀποστολή ῆς	apostleship	fem	ἀπο-[√]-η
≥25	ἀπόστολος ου	apostle, messenger	masc	ἀπο-[√]-ος
	διαστέλλομαι	order	vb	δια-[√]-ω

275

διαστολή ῆς	distinction	fem	δια-[√]-η
≥10 ἐξαποστέλλω	send off	vb	ἐκ-ἀπο-[√]-ω
ἐπιστέλλω	write	vb	ἐπι-[√]-ω
≥10 ἐπιστολή ῆς	letter	fem	ἐπι-[√]-η
καταστέλλω	quiet	vb	κατα-[√]-ω
στέλλομαι	avoid	vb	[√]-ω
συναποστέλλω	send along with	vb	συν-ἀπο-[√]-ω
συστέλλω	carry out	vb	συν-[√]-ω
ὑποστέλλω	draw back, hold back	vb	ὑπο-[√]-ω
ὑποστολή ῆς	shrinking / turning back	fem	ὑπο-[√]-η

ἁμαρτ
sin
Memory Aid: hamartiology

≥25 ἁμαρτάνω	sin	vb	[√]-ανω
ἁμάρτημα ματος	sin	neut	[√]-μα
≥25 ἁμαρτία ας	sin	fem	[√]-ια
≥25 ἁμαρτωλός όν	sinful	adj	[√]-λος
ἀναμάρτητος ον	sinless	adj	ἀ-[√]-τος
προαμαρτάνω	sin previously	vb	προ-[√]-ανω

270

θελ
will
Memory Aid: monothelite

≥25 θέλημα ματος	will, desire	neut	[√]-μα
θέλησις εως	will	fem	[√]-σις
≥25 θέλω	wish, want	vb	[√]-ω

270

θαν θνη
death
Memory Aid: euthanasia

ἀθανασία ας	immortality	fem	ἀ-[√]-ια
≥25 ἀποθνήσκω	die, face death	vb	ἀπο-[√]-σκω
ἐπιθανάτιος ον	sentenced to death	adj	ἐπι-[√]-ιος
ἡμιθανής ές	half dead	adj	[ἡμι]-[√]-ης
θανάσιμον ου	deadly poison	neut	[√]-ιμος
θανατηφόρος ον	deadly	adj	[√]-[φερ]-ος
≥25 θάνατος ου	death	masc	[√]-ος
≥10 θανατόω	kill (>make dead)	vb	[√]-οω
θνῄσκω	die	vb	[√]-σκω
θνητός ή όν	mortal	adj	[√]-τος
συναποθνῄσκω	die with	vb	συν-ἀπο-[√]-σκω

269

χαρι χαριστ
gift
Memory Aid: charismatic, charity, Eucharist

ἀχάριστος ον	ungrateful	adj	ἀ-[√]-τος
≥25 εὐχαριστέω	thank, be thankful	vb	εὐ-[√]-εω
≥10 εὐχαριστία ας	thanksgiving (eucharist)	fem	εὐ-[√]-ια

262

	εὐχάριστος ον	thankful	adj	εὐ-[√]-τος
≥10	χαρίζομαι	give, forgive	vb	[√]-ιζω
	χάριν	for the sake of, because of	prep	
≥25	χάρις ιτος	grace, favor, kindness	fem	[√]-ς
≥10	χάρισμα ματος	gift	neut	[√]-μα
	χαριτόω	give freely (>make a gift)	vb	[√]-οω

βαιν βα βη βασ
go / foot
261

Memory Aid: Anabasis, acrobat, base

≥25	ἀναβαίνω	go up, ascend, grow	vb	ἀνα-[√]-ω
	ἀναβιβάζω	make to go, draw, drag	vb	ἀνα-[√]-αζω
	ἀπαράβατος ον	permanent	adj	ἀ-παρα-[√]-τος
	ἀποβαίνω	get out, go from	vb	ἀπο-[√]-ω
	βαθμός οῦ	standing, position	masc	[√]-μος
	βάσις εως	foot (>base)	fem	[√]-ς
≥10	βῆμα ματος	judgment bench	neut	[√]-μα
	διαβαίνω	cross, cross over	vb	δια-[√]-ω
	ἐκβαίνω	leave, go out	vb	ἐκ-[√]-ω
≥10	ἐμβαίνω	get in, embark	vb	ἐν-[√]-ω
	ἐπιβαίνω	embark, arrive	vb	ἐπι-[√]-ω
≥25	καταβαίνω	descend, fall	vb	κατα-[√]-ω
	κατάβασις εως	descent, slope	fem	[√]-ς
≥10	μεταβαίνω	leave, move	vb	μετα-[√]-ω
	παραβαίνω	break, disobey	vb	παρα-[√]-ω
	παράβασις εως	disobedience	fem	παρα-[√]-ς
	παραβάτης ου	one who disobeys	masc	παρα-[√]-της
	προβαίνω	go on	vb	προ-[√]-ω
	προσαναβαίνω	move up	vb	προς-ἀνα-[√]-ω
	συγκαταβαίνω	come down with	vb	συν-κατα-[√]-ω
	συμβαίνω	happen, come about	vb	συν-[√]-ω
	συμβιβάζω	bring together	vb	συν-[√]-αζω
	συναναβαίνω	come up together	vb	συν-ἀνα-[√]-ω
	ὑπερβαίνω	do wrong to	vb	ὑπερ-[√]-ω

προ πρω πρωτ
before / first
254

Memory Aid: prologue, prophesy, prototype, prognosis

≥10	πρίν	before	cj/pt	
≥25	πρό (*gen*)	before	prep	
≥10	πρότερος α ον	former, earlier	adj	[√]-τερος
≥10	πρωΐ	morning	adv	
	πρωΐα ας	morning	fem	[√]-ια
	πρωϊνός ή όν	morning	adj	[√]-ινος
	πρῴρα ης	prow, bow	fem	[√]-α
	πρωτεύω	have first place	vb	[√]-ευω
≥25	πρῶτον	in the first place, earlier	adv	[√]-ον
≥25	πρῶτος η ον	first, earlier, leading	adj	[√]-τος

πρωτοστάτης ου	ring-leader	masc	[√]-[ἰστη]-της
πρωτοτόκια ων	birthright	neut	[√]-[τεκν]-ια
πρωτότοκος ον	first-born	adj	[√]-[τεκν]-ος
πρώτως	for the first time, firstly	adv	[√]-ως
φιλοπρωτεύω	desire to be first	vb	[√]-[φιλ]-ευω

νομ   253
law
Memory Aid: nomos, antinomian, astronomy, Deuteronomy, anomoly

≥10	ἀνομία ας	lawlessness, wickedness	fem	ἀ-[√]-ια
	ἄνομος ον	lawless	adj	ἀ-[√]-ος
	ἀνόμως	lawlessly, without law	adv	ἀ-[√]-ως
	ἔννομος ον	legal, subject to law	adj	ἐν-[√]-ος
≥10	νομίζω	suppose	vb	[√]-ιζω
	νομικός ή όν	legal	adj	[√]-ικος
	νομίμως	lawfully	adv	[√]-ως
	νόμισμα ματος	coin (>legal tender)	neut	[√]-μα
	νομοδιδάσκαλος ου	teacher of law	masc	[√]-[διδασκ]-ος
	νομοθεσία ας	giving of the law	fem	[√]-[τιθ]-ια
	νομοθετέομαι	be given the law	vb	[√]-[τιθ]-εω
	νομοθέτης ου	lawgiver	masc	[√]-[τιθ]-της
≥25	νόμος ου	law	masc	[√]-ος
	παρανομέω	act contrary to the law	vb	παρα-[√]-εω
	παρανομία ας	offense	fem	παρα-[√]-ια

πορ   240
journey
Memory Aid: emporium, pore [fare, far: *see Grimm's Law*]

	διαπορεύομαι	go through	vb	δια-[√]-ευω
≥10	εἰσπορεύομαι	go / come in, enter	vb	εἰς-[√]-ευω
≥25	ἐκπορεύομαι	go / come out	vb	ἐκ-[√]-ευω
	ἐμπορεύομαι	be in business, exploit	vb	ἐν-[√]-ευω
	ἐμπορία ας	business	fem	ἐν-[√]-ια
	ἐμπόριον ου	market (>emporium)	neut	ἐν-[√]-ιον
	ἔμπορος ου	merchant	masc	ἐν-[√]-ος
	ἐπιπορεύομαι	come to	vb	ἐπι-[√]-ευω
	εὐπορέομαι	have financial means	vb	εὐ-[√]-εω
	εὐπορία ας	wealth	fem	εὐ-[√]-ια
	παραπορεύομαι	pass by, go	vb	παρα-[√]-ευω
	πορεία ας	journey	fem	[√]-εια
≥25	πορεύομαι	journey, go, live	vb	[√]-ευω
	πόρρω	far away	adv	[√]-ω
	πόρρωθεν	from a distance	adv	[√]-θεν
	πορρώτερον	farther	adv	[√]-τερος
	προπορεύομαι	go before	vb	προ-[√]-ευω
	προσπορεύομαι	come to	vb	προς-[√]-ευω
	συμπορεύομαι	go along with	vb	συν-[√]-ευω

ὀνομ
name
Memory Aid: onomatopoeia, synonym, pseudonym, anonymous

	ἐπονομάζομαι	call oneself	vb	ἐπι-[√]-αζω
≥25	ὄνομα ματος	name	neut	[√]-μα
	ὀνομάζω	name, call	vb	[√]-αζω
	ψευδώνυμος ον	so-called	adj	[ψευδ]-[√]-ος

δοξ
glory
Memory Aid: doxology

≥25	δόξα ης	glory, power	fem	[√]-α
≥25	δοξάζω	praise, honor	vb	[√]-αζω
	ἐνδοξάζομαι	receive glory	vb	ἐν-[√]-αζω
	ἔνδοξος ον	glorious, fine	adj	ἐν-[√]-ος
	κενοδοξία ας	conceit (>empty glory)	fem	[κενο]-[√]-ια
	κενόδοξος ον	conceited	adj	[κενο]-[√]-ος
	συνδοξάζομαι	share in glory	vb	συν-[√]-αζω

πλη πληθ πληρ
full
Memory Aid: plethora, pleroma, plenary, plenty

	ἀναπληρόω	meet requirements	vb	ἀνα-[√]-οω
	ἀνταναπληρόω	complete (>make full)	vb	ἀντι-ἀνα-[√]-οω
	ἀποπληρόω	meet requirements	vb	ἀπο-[√]-οω
	ἐκπληρόω	fulfill (>make happen)	vb	ἐκ-[√]-οω
≥10	ἐκπλήρωσις εως	completion, end	fem	ἐκ-[√]-σις
	ἐμπίμπλημι	fill, satisfy, enjoy	vb	ἐν-[√]-μι
	παμπληθεί	together	adv	[παν]-[√]
≥10	πίμπλημι	fill, end	vb	[√]-μι
≥25	πλῆθος ους	crowd	neut	[√]-ς
≥10	πληθύνω	increase	vb	[√]-υνω
	πλήμμυρα ης	flood	fem	[√]-α
≥10	πλήρης ες	full	adj	[√]-ης
	πληροφορέω	accomplish	vb	[√]-[φερ]-εω
	πληροφορία ας	certainty	fem	[√]-[φερ]-ια
≥25	πληρόω	fulfill (>make happen)	vb	[√]-οω
≥10	πλήρωμα ματος	fullness	neut	[√]-μα
	πλησμονή ῆς	satisfaction	fem	[√]-η
	προσαναπληρόω	supply, provide	vb	προς-ἀνα-[√]-οω
	συμπληρόω	draw near, end	vb	συν-[√]-οω

φερ φορ
bring / bear / carry
Memory Aid: transfer, ferry, euphoria, paraphernalia [bear: *see Grimm's Law*]

	ἀναφέρω	offer (>bring up)	vb	ἀνα-[√]-ω
	ἀποφέρω	take, carry away	vb	ἀπο-[√]-ω
	ἀποφορτίζομαι	unload	vb	ἀπο-[√]-ιζω

239

235

232

231

≥10 διαφέρω	be superior, carry through	vb	δια-[√]-ω
δωροφορία ας	a bearing of gifts	fem	[δωρ]-[√]-ια
εἰσφέρω	bring in	vb	εἰς-[√]-ω
ἐκφέρω	carry out, yield	vb	ἐκ-[√]-ω
ἐπιφέρω	bring upon, inflict	vb	ἐπι-[√]-ω
εὐφορέω	produce good crops	vb	εὐ-[√]-εω
καταφέρω	bring against	vb	κατα-[√]-ω
παραφέρω	remove, carry away	vb	παρα-[√]-ω
παρεισφέρω	exert	vb	παρα-εἰς-[√]-ω
περιφέρω	carry about, bring	vb	περι-[√]-ω
≥25 προσφέρω	offer, do	vb	προς-[√]-ω
προσφορά ᾶς	offering, sacrifice	fem	προς-[√]-α
προφέρω	progress, produce	vb	προ-[√]-ω
≥10 συμφέρω	be helpful / useful	vb	συν-[√]-ω
σύμφορον ου	advantage, benefit	neut	συν-[√]-ον
τροφοφορέω	care for	vb	[τρεφ]-[√]-εω
ὑποφέρω	endure, bear up under	vb	ὑπο-[√]-ω
≥25 φέρω	bring, carry	vb	[√]-ω
φορέω	wear	vb	[√]-εω
φόρος ου	tax (>burden)	masc	[√]-ος
φορτίζω	burden, load	vb	[√]-ιζω
φορτίον ου	burden, cargo	neut	[√]-ιον

ἰδ   229
see
Memory Aid: idea, idol

εἰδέα ας	appearance, form	fem	[√]-α
εἶδος ους	visible form, sight	neut	[√]-ς
≥25 ἴδε	Behold! here is	interj	
≥25 ἰδού	Behold! here is	interj	

ἀνηρ ἀνδρ   221
man
Memory Aid: android, androgynous

ἀνδραποδιστής οῦ	kidnapper, slave dealer	masc	[√]-[πο²]-ιστης
ἀνδρίζομαι	act like a man	vb	[√]-ιζω
ἀνδροφόνος ου	murderer	masc	[√]-(φενω)-ος
≥25 ἀνήρ ἀνδρός	man, husband	masc	[√]-ρ
ὕπανδρος ον	married (>under + man)	adj	ὑπο-[√]-ος
φίλανδρος ον	husband-loving	adj	[φιλ]-[√]-ος

ὑπο   217
under / by means of
Memory Aid: hypodermic, hypothermia

≥10 ὑπό (*gen, acc*)	under, by means of	prep	

μεγ μεγαλ   215
great
Memory Aid: megaphone, megaton, megalomania, megalith

	μεγαλεῖον ου	great / mighty act	neut	[√]-ιον
	μεγαλειότης ητος	greatness, majesty	fem	[√]-οτης
	μεγαλύνω	enlarge	vb	[√]-υνω
	μεγαλωσύνη ης	greatness, majesty	fem	[√]-συνη
	μεγάλως	greatly	adv	[√]-ως
≥25	μέγας μεγάλη μέγα	great, large	adj	
	μέγεθος ους	greatness	neut	[√]-ς
	μεγιστάν ᾶνος	person of high position	masc	[√]-ς
	μέγιστος η ον	very great, greatest	adj	[√]-ιστος

διδασκ διδακ διδαχ
teach
214

Memory Aid: didactic, Didache

	διδακτικός ή όν	able to teach	adj	[√]-τικος
	διδακτός ή όν	taught	adj	[√]-τος
≥10	διδασκαλία ας	teaching, instruction	fem	[√]-ια
≥25	διδάσκαλος ου	teacher	masc	[√]-ος
≥25	διδάσκω	teach	vb	[√]-ω
≥25	διδαχή ῆς	instruction	fem	[√]-η
	ἑτεροδιδασκαλέω	teach different doctrine	vb	[ἑτερ]-[√]-εω
	θεοδίδακτος ον	taught by God	adj	[θε]-[√]-τος
	καλοδιδάσκαλος ον	teaching what is good	adj	[καλ¹]-[√]-ος

γυνη γυναικ
woman
211

Memory Aid: gynecology, polygyny, androgynous

	γυναικάριον ου	foolish woman	neut	[√]-αριον
	γυναικεῖος α ον	female	adj	[√]-ιος
≥25	γυνή αικός	woman, wife	fem	[√]-ς

μεν² μον
wait / remain
207

Memory Aid: remain

	ἀναμένω	wait expectantly	vb	ἀνα-[√]-ω
	διαμένω	remain, stay	vb	δια-[√]-ω
	ἐμμένω	remain faithful	vb	ἐν-[√]-ω
≥10	ἐπιμένω	remain, continue	vb	ἐπι-[√]-ω
	καταμένω	remain, stay, live	vb	κατα-[√]-ω
≥25	μένω	remain	vb	[√]-ω
	μονή ῆς	room	fem	[√]-η
	παραμένω	remain, stay	vb	παρα-[√]-ω
	περιμένω	wait for	vb	περι-[√]-ω
	προσμένω	remain (with)	vb	προς-[√]-ω
≥10	ὑπομένω	endure (>stay under)	vb	ὑπο-[√]-ω
≥25	ὑπομονή ῆς	endurance (>stay under)	fem	ὑπο-[√]-η

φων
voice
207

Memory Aid: symphony, telephone, phonetics, euphony, phoneme

	ἀναφωνέω	call out	vb	ἀνα-[√]-εω

ἀσύμφωνος ον	in disagreement	adj	ἀ-συν-[√]-ος
ἄφωνος ον	dumb, silent	adj	ἀ-[√]-ος
ἐπιφωνέω	shout	vb	ἐπι-[√]-εω
κενοφωνία ας	foolish (empty) talk	fem	[κενο]-[√]-ια
προσφωνέω	call to, address	vb	προς-[√]-εω
συμφωνέω	agree with	vb	συν-[√]-εω
συμφώνησις εως	agreement	fem	συν-[√]-σις
συμφωνία ας	music (>symphony)	fem	συν-[√]-ια
σύμφωνον ου	mutual consent	neut	συν-[√]-ον
≥25 φωνέω	call	vb	[√]-εω
≥25 φωνή ῆς	voice, sound	fem	[√]-η

κοσμ   200
world / order
Memory Aid: cosmos, cosmetics, cosmopolitan

≥10 κοσμέω	adorn, put in order	vb	[√]-εω
κοσμικός ή όν	worldly, man-made	adj	[√]-ικος
κόσμιος ον	ordered, well-behaved	adj	[√]-ιος
κοσμοκράτωρ ορος	world-ruler	masc	[√]-[κρατ]-τωρ
≥25 κόσμος ου	world, universe	masc	[√]-ος

μαρτυρ   198
witness
Memory Aid: martyr

ἀμάρτυρος ον	without witness	adj	ἀ-[√]-ος
≥10 διαμαρτύρομαι	declare solemnly	vb	δια-[√]-ω
ἐπιμαρτυρέω	witness, declare	vb	ἐπι-[√]-εω
καταμαρτυρέω	witness against	vb	κατα-[√]-εω
≥25 μαρτυρέω	testify, affirm	vb	[√]-εω
≥25 μαρτυρία ας	witness, testimony	fem	[√]-ια
≥10 μαρτύριον ου	witness, testimony	neut	[√]-ιον
μαρτύρομαι	witness, testify, urge	vb	[√]-ω
≥25 μάρτυς μάρτυρος	witness, martyr	masc	[√]-ς
προμαρτύρομαι	predict	vb	προ-[√]-ω
συμμαρτυρέω	testify in support of	vb	συν-[√]-εω
συνεπιμαρτυρέω	add further witness	vb	συν-ἐπι-[√]-εω

αἰων   193
age
Memory Aid: aeon

| ≥25 αἰών ῶνος | age, eternity | masc | [√]-ων |
| ≥25 αἰώνιος ον | eternal | adj | [√]-ιος |

μεν¹   193
particle of contrast
Memory Aid:

≥25 μέν	(used to show contrast)	cj/pt	
μενοῦν	rather	cj/pt	[√]-[ουν]
μέντοι	but	cj/pt	

παρα
by
Memory Aid: parallel, paramedic, paragraph, parasite

≥25	παρά (*gen, dat, acc*) by, with	prep	

ἀν¹
particle indicating contingency
Memory Aid:

≥25	ἄν	(signals contingency)	cj/pt	
	ἐπάν	when	cj/pt	ἐπι-[√]
≥10	κἄν (καὶ ἐάν)	even if	cj/pt	[και]-[√]-[εἰ]

ου
where
Memory Aid: [Sounds like French *où: where.*] See Appendix 2, Chart A.

	δήπου	of course	adv	
≥25	ὅπου	where	adv	
≥10	οὗ	where	adv	
≥25	πόθεν	from where, where	adv	[√]-θεν
	πού	somewhere	adv	
≥25	ποῦ	where?	adv	

χειρ
hand
Memory Aid: chiropractic, enchiridion

	αὐτόχειρ ος	doer	masc/fem	[αὐτ]-[√]-ρ
	διαχειρίζομαι	seize and kill	vb	δια-[√]-ιζω
	ἐπιχειρέω	undertake	vb	ἐπι-[√]-εω
	προχειρίζομαι	choose in advance	vb	προ-[√]-ιζω
	προχειροτονέω	choose in advance	vb	προ-[√]-[τεν]-εω
≥25	χείρ χειρός	hand	fem	[√]-ρ

βλεπ βλεψ βλεμ
see
Memory Aid: [A *blemish* is a *visible* flaw.]

≥25	ἀναβλέπω	look up, regain sight	vb	ἀνα-[√]-ω
	ἀνάβλεψις εως	restoration of sight	fem	ἀνα-[√]-σις
	ἀποβλέπω	keep one's eyes on	vb	ἀπο-[√]-ω
	βλέμμα ματος	what is seen, sight	neut	[√]-μα
≥25	βλέπω	see, look	vb	[√]-ω
	διαβλέπω	see clearly	vb	δια-[√]-ω
≥10	ἐμβλέπω	look at, consider	vb	ἐν-[√]-ω
	ἐπιβλέπω	look upon (with care)	vb	ἐπι-[√]-ω
	περιβλέπομαι	look around	vb	περι-[√]-ω
	προβλέπομαι	provide	vb	προ-[√]-ω

ἀληθ
true
Memory Aid:

≥25	ἀλήθεια ας	truth, truthfulness	fem	[√]-εια

	ἀληθεύω	be truthful, honest	vb	[√]-ευω
≥25	ἀληθής ές	true, truthful, genuine	adj	[√]-ης
≥25	ἀληθινός ή όν	real, true, genuine	adj	[√]-ινος
≥10	ἀληθῶς	truly, actually	adv	[√]-ως

δευτερ δυο   182
two
Memory Aid: duo, duet, Deuteronomy

	δευτεραῖος α ον	in two days	adj	[√]-ιος
	δευτερόπρωτος ον	the next	adj	[√]-[προ]-ος
≥25	δεύτερος α ον	second	adj	[√]-ος
≥25	δύο	two	adj	

δουλ   180
slave
Memory Aid: [*Slaves do lots.*]

	δουλαγωγέω	bring under control	vb	[√]-[ἀγ]-εω
	δουλεία ας	slavery	fem	[√]-εια
≥25	δουλεύω	serve, be enslaved	vb	[√]-ευω
	δούλη ης	female servant	fem	[√]-η
	δοῦλος η ον	slave-like	adj	[√]-ος
≥25	δοῦλος ου	servant, slave	masc	[√]-ος
	δουλόω	enslave (>make a slave)	vb	[√]-οω
	καταδουλόω	make a slave of	vb	κατα-[√]-οω
≥10	σύνδουλος ου	fellow-slave (servant)	masc	συν-[√]-ος

ἐγειρ ἐγερ γρηγορ   180
raise / rouse
Memory Aid: [*Gregory* the Great *raised* the papal office.]

≥10	γρηγορέω	be awake, watch	vb	[√]-εω
	διαγρηγορέω	become fully awake	vb	δια-[√]-εω
	διεγείρω	awake	vb	δια-[√]-ω
≥25	ἐγείρω	raise	vb	[√]-ω
	ἔγερσις εως	resurrection	fem	[√]-σις
	ἐξεγείρω	raise	vb	ἐκ-[√]-ω
	ἐπεγείρω	stir up	vb	ἐπι-[√]-ω
	συνεγείρω	raise together	vb	συν-[√]-ω

ἱη ε   180
let / send
MemoryAid:

	ἄνεσις εως	relief (>let up)	fem	ἀνα-[√]-σις
	ἀνίημι	loosen, stop, desert	vb	ἀνα-[√]-μι
	ἀσύνετος ον	without understanding	adj	ἀ-συν-[√]-τος
≥10	ἄφεσις εως	forgiveness	fem	ἀπο-[√]-σις
≥25	ἀφίημι	forgive, cancel	vb	ἀπο-[√]-μι
	ἐγκάθετος ου	spy, lie in wait	masc	ἐν-κατα-[√]-τος
	καθίημι	let down	vb	κατα-[√]-μι
	παρίημι	neglect (>let [go] by)	vb	παρα-[√]-μι

τελ

180

end / far

Memory Aid: telescope, telephone, television, teleology, Anatolia

	ἀνατέλλω	rise	vb	ἀνα-[√]-ω
≥10	ἀνατολή ῆς	rising, dawn, east	fem	ἀνα-[√]-η
	ἀποτελέω	accomplish	vb	ἀπο-[√]-εω
	διατελέω	continue	vb	δια-[√]-εω
	ἐκτελέω	finish, complete	vb	ἐκ-[√]-εω
	ἐξανατέλλω	sprout, spring up	vb	ἐκ-ἀνα-[√]-ω
≥10	ἐπιτελέω	complete	vb	ἐπι-[√]-εω
	παντελής ές	complete	adj	[παν]-[√]-ης
	συντέλεια ας	end, completion	fem	συν-[√]-εια
	συντελέω	end, complete	vb	συν-[√]-εω
≥10	τέλειος α ον	complete	adj	[√]-ιος
	τελειότης ητος	completeness	fem	[√]-οτης
≥10	τελειόω	make perfect	vb	[√]-οω
	τελείως	fully	adv	[√]-ως
	τελείωσις εως	fulfillment	fem	[√]-σις
	τελειωτής οῦ	perfecter	masc	[√]-της
	τελεσφορέω	produce mature fruit	vb	[√]-[φερ]-εω
≥10	τελευτάω	die	vb	[√]-αω
	τελευτή ῆς	death	fem	[√]-η
≥25	τελέω	finish (make an end)	vb	[√]-εω
≥25	τέλος ους	end	neut	[√]-ς

εὑρ

179

find

Memory Aid: heuristic, Eureka!

	ἀνευρίσκω	find	vb	ἀνα-[√]-σκω
≥25	εὑρίσκω	find	vb	[√]-σκω
	ἐφευρετής οῦ	inventor	masc	ἐπι-[√]-της

ὀχλ

179

crowd / mob

Memory Aid: ochlocracy

	ἐνοχλέω	trouble (>crowd in)	vb	ἐν-[√]-εω
	ὀχλέομαι	crowd, trouble, harass	vb	[√]-εω
	ὀχλοποιέω	gather a crowd	vb	[√]-[ποι]-εω
≥25	ὄχλος ου	crowd, mob	masc	[√]-ος
	παρενοχλέω	add extra difficulties	vb	παρα-ἐν-[√]-εω

πιπτ πτω

176

fall

Memory Aid: symptom [Sounds something like pit, as in *pit-fall*.]

≥10	ἀναπίπτω	sit, lean	vb	ἀνα-[√]-ω
	ἀντιπίπτω	resist, fight against	vb	ἀντι-[√]-ω
	ἀποπίπτω	fall from	vb	ἀπο-[√]-ω
≥10	ἐκπίπτω	fall off, lose	vb	ἐκ-[√]-ω

ἐμπίπτω	fall into or among	vb	ἐν-[√]-ω
≥10 ἐπιπίπτω	fall upon, close in on	vb	ἐπι-[√]-ω
καταπίπτω	fall (down)	vb	κατα-[√]-ω
παραπίπτω	apostatize (>fall away)	vb	παρα-[√]-ω
≥10 παράπτωμα ματος	sin	neut	παρα-[√]-μα
περιπίπτω	encounter	vb	περι-[√]-ω
≥25 πίπτω	fall	vb	[√]-ω
προσπίπτω	fall at someone's feet	vb	προς-[√]-ω
πτῶμα ματος	body, corpse (>the fallen)	neut	[√]-μα
πτῶσις εως	fall	fem	[√]-σις
συμπίπτω	collapse	vb	συν-[√]-ω

λυ λυτρ   175
loose / redeem

Memory Aid: analysis, paralysis [*loose*]

ἀκατάλυτος ον	indestructible	adj	ἀ-κατα-[√]-τος
ἀλυσιτελής ές	of no advantage / help	adj	ἀ-[√]-[τελ]-ης
ἀνάλυσις εως	death (>releasing)	fem	ἀνα-[√]-σις
ἀναλύω	come back	vb	ἀνα-[√]-ω
ἀντίλυτρον ου	ransom	neut	ἀντι-[√]-τρον
≥10 ἀπολύτρωσις εως	deliverance	fem	ἀπο-[√]-σις
≥25 ἀπολύω	release, send away	vb	ἀπο-[√]-ω
διαλύω	scatter	vb	δια-[√]-ω
ἐκλύομαι	give up, faint	vb	ἐκ-[√]-ω
ἐπίλυσις εως	interpretation	fem	ἐπι-[√]-σις
ἐπιλύω	explain, settle	vb	ἐπι-[√]-ω
κατάλυμα ματος	room, guest room	neut	κατα-[√]-μα
≥10 καταλύω	destroy, stop	vb	κατα-[√]-ω
λύσις εως	separation (loosed from)	fem	[√]-σις
λύτρον ου	means of release	neut	[√]-τρον
λυτρόομαι	redeem, set free	vb	[√]-οω
λύτρωσις εως	redemption	fem	[√]-σις
λυτρωτής οῦ	liberator	masc	[√]-της
≥25 λύω	loose, free	vb	[√]-ω
παραλύομαι	be paralyzed	vb	παρα-[√]-ω
≥10 παραλυτικός οῦ	paralytic	masc	παρα-[√]-τικος

νυν   174
now

Memory Aid: *now*

≥25 νῦν	now	adv	
≥10 νυνί	now	adv	
τοίνυν	therefore, then	prep	

πολι   173
city

Memory Aid: metropolis, political, polis, police

≥25 πόλις εως	city, town	fem	[√]-ς
πολιτάρχης ου	city official	masc	[√]-[ἀρχ]-ης

πολιτεία ας	citizenship, state	fem	[√]-εια
πολίτευμα ματος	place of citizenship	neut	[√]-μα
πολιτεύομαι	live, be a citizen	vb	[√]-ευω
πολίτης ου	citizen	masc	[√]-της
συμπολίτης ου	fellow citizen	masc	συν-[√]-της

πορν πονηρ   173
evil
Memory Aid: pornographic [fornication: *see Grimm's Law*]

≥25	ἐκπορνεύω	live immorally	vb	ἐκ-[√]-ευω
	πονηρία ας	wickedness	fem	[√]-ια
≥25	πονηρός ά όν	evil	adj	[√]-ρος
≥25	πορνεία ας	fornication	fem	[√]-εια
	πορνεύω	commit fornication	vb	[√]-ευω
≥10	πόρνη ης	prostitute	fem	[√]-η
≥10	πόρνος ου	immoral person	masc	[√]-ος

ἐθν   168
nation / Gentile
Memory Aid: ethnic, ethnology, ethnarch

	ἐθνάρχης ου	governor, ethnarch	masc	[√]-[ἀρχ]-ης
	ἐθνικός ή όν	pagan, Gentile	adj	[√]-ικος
	ἐθνικῶς	like a Gentile	adv	[√]-ικως
≥25	ἔθνος ους	nation, Gentiles	neut	[√]-ς

ζητ   165
seek / discuss
Memory Aid:

	ἀναζητέω	seek after	vb	ἀνα-[√]-εω
	ἐκζητέω	seek diligently	vb	ἐκ-[√]-εω
	ἐκζήτησις εως	speculation	fem	ἐκ-[√]-σις
≥10	ἐπιζητέω	seek, desire	vb	ἐπι-[√]-εω
≥25	ζητέω	seek, try	vb	[√]-εω
	ζήτημα ματος	question	neut	[√]-μα
	ζήτησις εως	discussion	fem	[√]-σις
≥10	συζητέω	discuss, argue	vb	συν-[√]-εω
	συζήτησις εως	discussion, argument	fem	συν-[√]-σις
	συζητητής οῦ	skillful debater	masc	συν-[√]-της

ἐτι   161
still / yet
Memory Aid:

≥25	ἔτι	still, yet	adv	
≥10	μηκέτι	no longer	adv	[μη]
≥25	οὐκέτι	no longer	adv	[οὐ]

καρδ   161
heart
Memory Aid: cardiac

≥25	καρδία ας	heart	fem	[√]-ια

καρδιογνώστης ου	knower of hearts	masc	[√]-[γνο]-της
σκληροκαρδία ας	hard-heartedness	fem	(σκληρός-[√]-ια

καθ² καθεδρ   *158*
sit (compare with κατ)
Memory Aid: cathedral

ἀνακαθίζω	sit up	vb	ἀνα-[√]-ιζω
ἐπικαθίζω	sit, sit on	vb	ἐπι-[√]-ιζω
καθέδρα ας	chair	fem	[√]-α
καθέζομαι	sit	vb	[√]-ω
≥25 κάθημαι	sit, live	vb	[√]-μι
≥25 καθίζω	sit	vb	[√]-ιζω
παρακαθέζομαι	sit	vb	παρα-[√]-ω
πρωτοκαθεδρία ας	place of honor	fem	[προ]-[√]-ια
συγκάθημαι	sit with	vb	συν-[√]-μι
συγκαθίζω	sit together with	vb	συν-[√]-ιζω

σαρξ σαρκ   *158*
flesh
Memory Aid: sarcophagus, sarcastic

σαρκικός ή όν	belonging to the world	adj	[√]-ικος
σάρκινος η ον	belonging to the world	adj	[√]-ινος
≥25 σάρξ σαρκός	flesh, physical body	fem	[√]-ξ

φοβ   *158*
fear
Memory Aid: all the "phobias"

ἀφόβως	without fear	adv	ἀ-[√]-ως
ἐκφοβέω	frighten, terrify	vb	ἐκ-[√]-εω
ἔκφοβος ον	frightened	adj	ἐκ-[√]-ος
ἔμφοβος ον	full of fear	adj	ἐν-[√]-ος
≥25 φοβέομαι	fear, be afraid, respect	vb	[√]-εω
φοβερός ά όν	fearful	adj	[√]-ρος
φόβητρον ου	fearful thing	neut	[√]-τρον
≥25 φόβος ου	fear	masc	[√]-ος

ὑπερ   *157*
over
Memory Aid: hypersensitive, hyperactive, hyperbole

≥25 ὑπέρ (*gen, acc*)	over	prep/adv	
ὑπεράνω (*gen*)	far above, above	prep	[√]-ἀνα
ὑπερέκεινα (*gen*)	beyond	prep	[√]-[ἐκει]-α
ὑπερῷον ου	upstairs room	neut	[√]-ιον

τιμ   *155*
honor / price
Memory Aid: [Paul asked the Corinthians *to honor Timothy*.]

ἀτιμάζω	dishonor	vb	ἀ-[√]-αζω
ἀτιμία ας	dishonor, shame	fem	ἀ-[√]-ια
ἄτιμος ον	dishonored, despised	adj	ἀ-[√]-ος

βαρύτιμος ον	very expensive	adj	[βαρ]-[√]-ος
ἔντιμος ον	valuable, esteemed	adj	ἐν-[√]-ος
≥25 ἐπιτιμάω	order, rebuke	vb	ἐπι-[√]-αω
ἐπιτιμία ας	punishment	fem	ἐπι-[√]-ια
ἰσότιμος ον	equally valuable	adj	[ἰσο]-[√]-ος
≥10 τιμάω	honor	vb	[√]-αω
≥25 τιμή ῆς	honor, price	fem	[√]-η
≥10 τίμιος α ον	precious, respected	adj	[√]-ιος
τιμιότης ητος	wealth, abundance	fem	[√]-οτης
≥10 Τιμόθεος ου	Timothy	masc	[√]-[θε]-ος

τρι
three

Memory Aid: triangle, trilogy, trinity, trio, triplet

154

≥25 τρεῖς τρία	three	adj	
≥10 τριάκοντα	thirty	adj	[√]-κοντα
τριακόσιοι αι α	three hundred	adj	[√]-κοσιοι
τριετία ας	period of three years	fem	[√]-ια
τρίμηνον ου	three months	neut	[√]-[μην]-ον
≥10 τρίς	three times, a third time	adv	
τρίστεγον ου	third floor	neut	[√]-(στέγω)-ον
τρισχίλιοι αι α	three thousand	adj	[√]-χιλιοι
τρίτον	the third time	adv	[√]-τος
≥25 τρίτος η ον	third	adj	[√]-τος

δεχ δεκ δοχ δοκ[1]
receive

Memory Aid: *Dock:* place where ships *receive* goods onto their *deck.*

150

ἀναδέχομαι	receive, welcome	vb	ἀνα-[√]-ω
ἀνένδεκτος ον	impossible	adj	ἀ-ἐν-[√]-τος
ἀπεκδέχομαι	await	vb	ἀπο-ἐκ-[√]-ω
ἀπόδεκτος ον	pleasing	adj	ἀπο-[√]-τος
ἀποδέχομαι	welcome, receive	vb	ἀπο-[√]-ω
ἀποδοχή ῆς	acceptance	fem	ἀπο-[√]-η
δεκτός ή όν	acceptable	adj	[√]-τος
≥25 δέχομαι	receive, take	vb	[√]-ω
διαδέχομαι	receive possession of	vb	δια-[√]-ω
διάδοχος ου	successor	masc	δια-[√]-ος
δοχή ῆς	reception	fem	[√]-η
εἰσδέχομαι	welcome, receive	vb	εἰς-[√]-ω
ἐκδέχομαι	wait for, expect	vb	ἐκ-[√]-ω
ἐκδοχή ῆς	expectation	fem	ἐκ-[√]-η
ἐνδέχεται	it is possible	vb	ἐπι-[√]-ω
ἐπιδέχομαι	receive, welcome	vb	ἐπι-[√]-ω
εὐπρόσδεκτος ον	acceptable	adj	εὐ-[√]-τος
πανδοχεῖον ου	inn (>receive all)	neut	παν-[√]-ειον
πανδοχεύς έως	inn-keeper	masc	παν-[√]-ευς
παραδέχομαι	accept, receive, welcome	vb	παρα-[√]-ω

≥10	προσδέχομαι	wait for, expect, receive	vb	προς-[√]-ω
≥10	προσδοκάω	wait for, expect	vb	προς-[√]-αω
	προσδοκία ας	expectation	fem	προς-[√]-ια
	ὑποδέχομαι	receive as a guest	vb	ὑπο-[√]-ω

οσ   150
much / many
Memory Aid: See Appendix 2, Chart A.

≥25	ὅσος η ον	as much as, as great as	pron	[√]-ος
	ποσάκις	how often?	adv	[√]-κις
≥25	πόσος η ον	how much, how many	pron	[√]-ος
≥10	τοσοῦτος αὕτη οὗτον	so much, so great	adj	[√]-[οὗτ]

ὁρα   148
see
Memory Aid: panorama

	ἀόρατος ον	invisible, unseen	adj	ἀ-[√]-τος
	ἀφοράω	fix one's eyes on	vb	ἀπο-[√]-ω
	ἐφοράω	take notice of	vb	ἐπι-[√]-αω
	καθοράω	perceive clearly	vb	κατα-[√]-ω
≥10	ὅραμα ματος	vision, sight	neut	[√]-μα
	ὅρασις εως	vision, appearance	fem	[√]-σις
	ὁρατός ή όν	visible	adj	[√]-τος
≥25	ὁράω	see, perceive	vb	[√]-ω
	προοράω	see ahead of time	vb	προ-[√]-ω
	συνοράω	realize, learn	vb	συν-[√]-ω
	ὑπεροράω	overlook	vb	ὑπερ-[√]-ω
	φρουρέω	guard	vb	προ-[√]-εω

φαν φαιν φανερ   147
display / appear
Memory Aid: phenomenon, phantom, theophany, epiphany

	ἀναφαίνω	come into sight	vb	ἀνα-[√]-ω
	ἀφανής ές	hidden	adj	ἀ-[√]-ης
	ἀφανίζω	ruin	vb	ἀ-[√]-ιζω
	ἀφανισμός οῦ	disappearance	masc	ἀ-[√]-μος
	ἄφαντος ον	invisible	adj	ἀ-[√]-τος
	ἐμφανής ές	visible, revealed	adj	ἐν-[√]-ης
≥10	ἐμφανίζω	inform, reveal	vb	ἐν-[√]-ιζω
	ἐπιφαίνω	appear, give light	vb	ἐπι-[√]-ω
	ἐπιφάνεια ας	appearance, coming	fem	ἐπι-[√]-εια
	ἐπιφανής ές	glorious	adj	ἐπι-[√]-ης
	ὑπερηφανία ας	arrogance	fem	ὑπερ-[√]-ια
	ὑπερήφανος ον	arrogant	adj	ὑπερ-[√]-ος
≥25	φαίνω	shine, appear	vb	[√]-ω
≥10	φανερός ά όν	known, visible, plain	adj	[√]-ρος
≥25	φανερόω	make known, reveal	vb	[√]-οω
	φανερῶς	openly, clearly	adv	[√]-ως
	φανέρωσις εως	disclosure	fem	[√]-σις

φανός οὗ	lantern	masc	[√]-ος
φαντάζομαι	appear	vb	[√]-αζω
φαντασία ας	pomp	fem	[√]-σια
φάντασμα ματος	phantom, ghost	neut	[√]-μα

σῶμα 146
body / physical
Memory Aid: somatic, psychosomatic

	σύσσωμος ον	of same body	adj	συν-[√]-ος
≥25	σῶμα ματος	body, substance	neut	[√]-μα
	σωματικός ή όν	physical	adj	[√]-τικος
	σωματικῶς	in bodily (human) form	adv	[√]-τικως

ἕως 145
until
Memory Aid:

≥25	ἕως (*gen*)	until	conj/prep	

δε³ 144
lack
Memory Aid:

≥10	δέησις εως	prayer, request	fem	[√]-σις
≥25	δεῖ	it is necessary	vb	
≥10	δέομαι	ask, beg	vb	[√]-ω
	ἐνδεής ές	needy (>in need)	adj	ἐν-[√]-ης
	προσδέομαι	need	vb	προς-[√]-ω

χωρ 142
place
Memory Aid: anchorite

≥10	ἀναχωρέω	withdraw, return	vb	ἀνα-[√]-εω
	ἀποχωρέω	go away, leave	vb	ἀπο-[√]-εω
	ἀποχωρίζομαι	separate	vb	ἀπο-[√]-ιζω
	διαχωρίζομαι	leave	vb	δια-[√]-ιζω
	ἐκχωρέω	leave	vb	ἐκ-[√]-εω
	εὐρύχωρος ον	wide, spacious	adj	(εὐρύς)-[√]-ος
	περίχωρος ου	neighborhood	fem	περι-[√]-ος
	στενοχωρέομαι	be held in check	vb	(στένος)-[√]-εω
	στενοχωρία ας	distress	fem	(στένος)-[√]-ια
	ὑποχωρέω	withdraw, go away	vb	ὑπο-[√]-εω
≥25	χώρα ας	country, land	fem	[√]-α
≥10	χωρέω	make room for, accept	vb	[√]-εω
≥10	χωρίζω	separate, leave	vb	[√]-ιζω
≥10	χωρίον ου	field, piece of land	neut	[√]-ιον
≥25	χωρίς	without, separately (*dat*)	prep	

λα 141
people
Memory Aid: laity

≥25	λαός οῦ	people, nation	masc	[√]-ος

στρεφ στροφ   *140*
turn
Memory Aid: apostrophe, catastrophe

	ἀναστρέφω	return (pass live)	vb	ἀνα-[√]-ω
≥10	ἀναστροφή ῆς	manner of life	fem	ἀνα-[√]-η
	ἀποστρέφω	turn away, remove	vb	ἀπο-[√]-ω
	διαστρέφω	pervert, distort	vb	δια-[√]-ω
	ἐκστρέφομαι	be perverted	vb	ἐκ-[√]-ω
≥25	ἐπιστρέφω	turn back	vb	ἐπι-[√]-ω
	ἐπιστροφή ῆς	converstion	fem	ἐπι-[√]-η
	καταστρέφω	overturn	vb	κατα-[√]-ω
	καταστροφή ῆς	ruin (>catastrophe)	fem	κατα-[√]-η
	μεταστρέφω	change, alter	vb	μετα-[√]-ω
	στρεβλόω	distort, twist	vb	[√]-οω
≥10	στρέφω	turn	vb	[√]-ω
≥25	ὑποστρέφω	return	vb	ὑπο-[√]-ω

χαρ χαιρ   *140*
rejoice
Memory Aid:

	συγχαίρω	rejoice with	vb	συν-[√]-ω
≥25	χαίρω	rejoice	vb	[√]-ω
≥25	χαρά ᾶς	joy	fem	[√]-α

νο   *139*
mind
Memory Aid: nous, paranoia

	ἀμετανόητος ον	unrepentant	adj	ἀ-μετα-[√]-τος
	ἀνόητος ον	foolish, ignorant	adj	ἀ-[√]-τος
	ἄνοια ας	stupidity, foolishness	fem	ἀ-[√]-ια
	διανόημα ματος	thought	neut	δια-[√]-μα
≥10	διάνοια ας	mind, understanding	fem	δια-[√]-ια
	δυσνόητος ον	difficult to understand	adj	δυσ-[√]-τος
	ἔννοια ας	attitude, thought	fem	ἐν-[√]-ια
	ἐπίνοια ας	intent, purpose	fem	ἐπι-[√]-ια
	εὐνοέω	make friends	vb	εὐ-[√]-εω
	εὔνοια ας	good will, eagerness	fem	εὐ-[√]-ια
≥10	κατανοέω	consider	vb	κατα-[√]-εω
≥25	μετανοέω	repent	vb	μετα-[√]-εω
≥10	μετάνοια ας	repentance	fem	μετα-[√]-ια
≥10	νοέω	understand	vb	[√]-εω
	νόημα τος	mind, thought	neut	[√]-μα
	νουθεσία ας	instruction	fem	[√]-[τιθ]-σια
	νουθετέω	instruct (>place in mind)	vb	[√]-[τιθ]-εω
	νουνεχῶς	wisely	adv	[√]-[ἐχ]-ως
	νοῦς νοος	mind	masc	[√]-ς
	προνοέω	plan	vb	προ-[√]-εω
	πρόνοια ας	provision	fem	προ-[√]-ια

| ὑπονοέω | suppose, suspect | vb | ὑπο-[√]-εω |
| ὑπόνοια ας | suspicion | fem | ὑπο-[√]-ια |

παλ
again
139

Memory Aid: palindrome, palimpsest

| ≥25 | πάλιν | again, once | adv | |

καλ¹
good / proper
137

Memory Aid: calligraphy, calisthenics, kaleidoscope

	κάλλιον	very well	adv	[√]-ων
	καλοποιέω	do what is good	vb	[√]-[ποι]-εω
≥25	καλός ή όν	good, proper	adj	[√]-ος
≥25	καλῶς	well	adv	[√]-ως

ὁδ
way / travel
136

Memory Aid: exodus, odometer, synod

	ἄμφοδον ου	street	neut	ἀμφι-[√]-ον
	διέξοδος ου	outlet, passage	fem	δια-ἐκ-[√]-ος
	διοδεύω	go about	vb	δια-[√]-ευω
	εἴσοδος ου	coming, entrance	fem	εἰς-[√]-ος
	ἔξοδος ου	departure (>exodus)	fem	ἐκ-[√]-ος
	εὐοδόομαι	have things go well	vb	εὐ-[√]-οω
	μεθοδεία ας	trickery	fem	μετα-[√]-εια
	ὁδεύω	travel	vb	[√]-ευω
	ὁδηγέω	lead, guide	vb	[√]-[ἀγ-εω
	ὁδηγός οῦ	guide, leader	masc	[√]-[ἀγ]-ος
	ὁδοιπορέω	travel	vb	[√]-[πορ]-εω
	ὁδοιπορία ας	journey	fem	[√]-[πορ]-ια
≥25	ὁδός οῦ	way, journey	fem	[√]-ος
	πάροδος ου	passage	fem	παρα-[√]-ός
	συνοδεύω	travel with	vb	συν-[√]-ευω
	συνοδία ας	group (synod)	fem	συν-[√]-ια

αἰρ
take
135

Memory Aid:

≥25	αἴρω	take	vb	[√]-ω
	ἀπαίρω	take away	vb	ἀπο-[√]-ω
	ἐξαίρω	remove, drive out	vb	ἐκ-[√]-ω
≥10	ἐπαίρω	raise, lift up	vb	ἐπι-[√]-ω
	μεταίρω	leave	vb	μετα-[√]-ω
	συναίρω	settle with	vb	συν-[√]-ω
	ὑπεραίρομαι	be puffed up with pride	vb	ὑπερ-[√]-ω

παι παιδ
child
134

Memory Aid: encyclopaedia, pedagogue, pedantic, pediatrician

ἀπαίδευτος ον	ignorant (>not learned)	adj	ἀ-[√]-τος
ἐμπαιγμονή ῆς	mockery, ridicule	fem	ἐν-[√]-η
ἐμπαιγμός οῦ	public ridicule	masc	ἐν-[√]-μος
≥10 ἐμπαίζω	ridicule	vb	ἐν-[√]-ιζω
ἐμπαίκτης ου	mocker	masc	ἐν-[√]-της
παιδαγωγός οῦ	instructor (>pedagogue)	masc	[√]-[ἀγ]-ος
παιδάριον ου	boy	neut	[√]-αριον
παιδεία ας	discipline, instruction	fem	[√]-εια
παιδευτής οῦ	teacher	masc	[√]-της
≥10 παιδεύω	instruct, correct	vb	[√]-ευω
παιδιόθεν	from childhood	adv	[√]-θεν
≥25 παιδίον ου	child, infant	neut	[√]-ιον
≥10 παιδίσκη ης	maid, slave	fem	[√]-η
παίζω	play, dance	vb	[√]-ιζω
≥10 παῖς παιδός	child, servant	masc/fem	[√]-ς

νεκρ   133
death
Memory Aid: necropolis

≥25 νεκρός ά όν	dead	adj	[√]-ος
νεκρόω	put to death, make dead	vb	[√]-οω
νέκρωσις εως	death, barrenness	fem	[√]-σις

τεκν τικ τοκ   133
child
Memory Aid: [A *child* is a little *tike*.]

ἄτεκνος ον	childless	adj	ἀ-[√]-ος
τεκνίον ου	little child	neut	[√]-ιον
τεκνογονέω	have children	vb	[√]-[γεν]-εω
τεκνογονία ας	childbirth	fem	[√]-[γεν]-ια
≥25 τέκνον ου	child	neut	[√]-ον
τεκνοτροφέω	bring up children	vb	[√]-[τρεφ]-εω
≥10 τίκτω	give birth to, yield	vb	[√]-ω
τόκος ου	interest (>child of money)	masc	[√]-ος
φιλότεκνος ον	child-loving	adj	[φιλ]-[√]-ος

εὐχ   129
pray
Memory Aid:

εὐχή ῆς	prayer, vow	fem	[√]-η
εὔχομαι	pray	vb	[√]-ω
≥25 προσευχή ῆς	prayer	fem	προς-[√]-η
≥25 προσεύχομαι	pray	vb	προς-[√]-ω

δεκα   128
ten
Memory Aid: decade, decalogue, decimate

ἀποδεκατόω	tithe, make one tithe	vb	ἀπο-[√]-οω
≥25 δέκα	ten	adj	
δεκαοκτώ	eighteen	adj	(ὀκτώ)

δεκαπέντε	fifteen	adj	[√]-[πεντ]
Δεκάπολις εως	Decapolis (ten city area)	fem	[√]-[πολ]-ς
δεκάτη ης	tithe	fem	[√]-η
δέκατος η ον	tenth	adj	[√]-τος
δεκατόω	collect (pay) tithes	vb	[√]-οω
≥25 δώδεκα	twelve	adj	[δευ]-[√]
δωδέκατος η ον	twelfth	adj	[δευ]-[√]-τος
ἕνδεκα	eleven	adj	[ἑις]-[√]
ἑνδέκατος η ον	eleventh	adj	[ἑις]-[√]-τος

ψυχ   *128*
self / soul / cold (unspiritual)

Memory Aid: psyche, psychology, psychiatry

ἀνάψυξις εως	refreshment	fem	ἀνα-[√]-σις
ἀναψύχω	refresh (>cooled)	vb	ἀνα-[√]-ω
ἀποψύχω	faint	vb	ἀπο-[√]-ω
ἄψυχος ον	inanimate	adj	ἀ-[√]-ος
δίψυχος ον	undecided (>two minds)	adj	[δευ]-[√]-ος
ἐκψύχω	die	vb	ἐκ-[√]-ω
εὐψυχέω	be encouraged	vb	εὐ-[√]-εω
ἰσόψυχος ον	sharing same feelings	adj	[ἰσ]-[√]-ος
καταψύχω	cool, refresh	vb	κατα-[√]-ω
σύμψυχος ον	united	adj	συν-[√]-ος
≥25 ψυχή ῆς	self, person	fem	[√]-η
ψυχικός ή όν	unspiritual, material	adj	[√]-ικος
ψύχομαι	grow cold	vb	[√]-ω
ψῦχος ους	cold	neut	[√]-ς
ψυχρός ά όν	cold	adj	[√]-ρος

ἀμην   *126*
truly

Memory Aid: amen

| ≥25 ἀμήν | amen, truly | adv | |

μιμν μν μνη μνημ   *123*
remember

Memory Aid: mnemonic, amnesia, amnesty [*memory, memorial*]

ἀναμιμνήσκω	remind	vb	ἀνα-[√]-σκω
ἀνάμνησις εως	reminder, remembrance	fem	ἀνα-[√]-σις
ἐπαναμιμνήσκω	remind	vb	ἐπι-ἀνα-[√]-σκω
≥10 μιμνήσκομαι	remember	vb	[√]-σκω
μνεία ας	remembrance, mention	fem	[√]-εια
≥10 μνῆμα ματος	grave, tomb (>memorial)	neut	[√]-μα
≥25 μνημεῖον ου	grave, monument	neut	[√]-ειον
μνήμη ης	remembrance, memory	fem	[√]-η
≥10 μνημονεύω	remember	vb	[√]-ευω
μνημόσυνον ου	memorial	neut	[√]-συνη-ον
ὑπομιμνήσκω	remind	vb	ὑπο-[√]-σκω
ὑπόμνησις εως	remembrance	fem	ὑπο-[√]-σις

πο¹ ποδ πεδ πεζ   *123*
foot

Memory Aid: podiatry, podium, tripod, pedestrian, orthopedic

ὀρθοποδέω	be consistent	vb	(ὀρθός)-[√]-εω
πέδη ης	chain (for feet)	fem	[√]-η
πεδινός ή όν	level (ground)	adj	[√]-ινος
πεζεύω	travel by land	vb	[√]-ευω
πεζῇ	on foot, by land	adv	[√]-η
≥25 πούς ποδός	foot	masc	[√]-ς
≥10 τράπεζα ης	table (>four legs)	fem	[τεσσ]-[πεζ]-α
ὑποπόδιον ου	footstool	neut	ὑπο-[√]-ιον

ἀγαθ   *122*
good

Memory Aid: [*good Agatha* Christie mysteries]

ἀγαθοεργέω	do good, be generous	vb	[√]-[ἐγρ]-εω
ἀγαθοποιέω	do good, be helpful	vb	[√]-[ποι]-εω
ἀγαθοποιΐα ας	good-doing	fem	[√]-[ποι]-ια
ἀγαθοποιός οῦ	good doer	masc	[√]-[ποι]-ος
≥25 ἀγαθός ή όν	good, useful	adj	[√]-ος
ἀγαθουργέω	do good, be kind	vb	[√]-[ἐργ]-εω
ἀγαθωσύνη ης	goodness	fem	[√]-συνη
ἀφιλάγαθος ον	not good-loving	adj	ἀ-[φιλ]-[√]-ος
φιλάγαθος ον	good-loving	adj	[φιλ]-[√]-ος

αἰτ   *122*
ask / reason / cause / accusation

Memory Aid: etiology

≥25 αἰτέω	ask, require	vb	[√]-εω
αἴτημα ματος	request, demand	neut	[√]-μα
≥10 αἰτία ας	reason, cause, charge	fem	[√]-ια
αἴτιον ου	guilt, reason	neut	[√]-ιον
αἴτιος ου	cause, source	masc	[√]-ιος
αἰτίωμα ματος	charge, accusation	neut	[√]-μα
ἀναίτιος ον	not guilty (>no charge)	adj	ἀ-[√]-ιος
ἀπαιτέω	demand (in return)	vb	ἀπο-[√]-εω
ἐξαιτέομαι	ask, demand	vb	ἐκ-[√]-εω
ἐπαιτέω	beg	vb	ἐπι-[√]-εω
≥10 παραιτέομαι	ask for, excuse	vb	παρα-[√]-εω
προαιτιάομαι	accuse beforehand	vb	προ-[√]-αω
προσαιτέω	beg	vb	προς-[√]-εω
προσαίτης ου	beggar	masc	προς-[√]-της

μονο   *122*
only

Memory Aid: monopoly, monologue, monotone, monarch

μονογενής ές	only begotten, unique	adj	[√]-[γεν]-ης
≥25 μόνον	only, alone	adv	[√]-ον

| μονόομαι | be left alone | vb | [√]-οω |
| ≥25 μόνος η ον | only, alone | adj | [√]-ος |

ταγ τακ ταξ ταχ¹ τασσ
order

Memory Aid: tactic, syntax, paratactic, taxonomy, taxidermist

ἀνατάσσομαι	compile, draw up	vb	ἀνα-[√]-σσω
ἀντιτάσσομαι	resist, oppose	vb	ἀντι-[√]-σσω
ἀνυπότακτος	disorderly	adj	ἀ-ὑπο-[√]-τος
ἀτακτέω	be lazy (>not ordered)	vb	ἀ-[√]-εω
ἄτακτος ον	lazy (>not ordered)	adj	ἀ-[√]-τος
ἀτάκτως	lazily	adv	ἀ-[√]-τως
διαταγή ῆς	decree	fem	δια-[√]-η
διάταγμα ματος	order, decree	neut	δια-[√]-μα
≥10 διατάσσω	command	vb	δια-[√]-σσω
ἐπιδιατάσσομαι	add to (a will)	vb	ἐπι-δια-[√]-σσω
ἐπιταγή ῆς	command, authority	fem	ἐπι-[√]-η
≥10 ἐπιτάσσω	order	vb	ἐπι-[√]-σσω
προστάσσω	command	vb	προς-[√]-σσω
συντάσσω	direct, instruct	vb	συν-[√]-σσω
τάγμα ματος	proper order	neut	[√]-μα
τακτός ή όν	appointed, fixed	adj	[√]-τος
τάξις εως	order, division	fem	[√]-σις
τάσσω	appoint	vb	[√]-ω
ὑποταγή ῆς	obedience, submission	fem	ὑπο-[√]-η
≥25 ὑποτάσσω	subject	vb	ὑπο-[√]-σσω

122

λειπ λοιπ λειμ λιμ
leave / lack

Memory Aid: eclipse

ἀδιάλειπτος ον	endless, constant	adj	ἀ-δια-[√]-τος
ἀδιαλείπτως	constantly, always	adv	ἀ-δια-[√]-ως
ἀνέκλειπτος ον	never decreasing	adj	ἀ-ἐκ-[√]-τος
ἀπολείπω	leave behind	vb	ἀπο-[√]-ω
διαλείπω	cease, stop	vb	δια-[√]-ω
διαλιμπάνω	stop, quit	vb	δια-[√]-ανω
≥10 ἐγκαταλείπω	forsake, leave	vb	ἐν-κατα-[√]-ω
ἐκλείπω	fail, cease, leave	vb	ἐκ-[√]-ω
ἐπιλείπω	run short	vb	ἐπι-[√]-ω
ἐπίλοιπος ον	remaining	adj	ἐπι-[√]-ος
≥10 καταλείπω	leave, forsake	vb	κατα-[√]-ω
κατάλοιπος ον	rest, remaining	adj	κατα-[√]-ος
λεῖμμα ματος	remnant	neut	[√]-μα
λείπω	lack, leave	vb	[√]-ω
≥25 λοιπός ή όν	rest, remaining	adj	[√]-ος
περιλείπομαι	remain	vb	περι-[√]-ω
ὑπόλειμμα ματος	remnant	neut	ὑπο-[√]-μα
ὑπολείπω	leave	vb	ὑπο-[√]-ω
ὑπολιμπάνω	leave	vb	ὑπο-[√]-ανω

121

ἐρωτ				120
ask				
Memory Aid:				
διερωτάω	learn	vb	δια-[√]-αω	
≥25 ἐπερωτάω	ask, ask for	vb	ἐπι-[√]-αω	
ἐπερώτημα ματος	promise, answer	neut	ἐπι-[√]-μα	
≥25 ἐρωτάω	ask	vb	[√]-αω	

βαπτ				119
baptize / dip				
Memory Aid: baptize, baptism				
≥25 βαπτίζω	baptize	vb	[√]-ιζω	
≥10 βάπτισμα ματος	baptism	neut	[√]-μα	
βαπτισμός οῦ	washing, baptism	masc	[√]-ισμος	
≥10 βαπτιστής οῦ	Baptist (Baptizer)	masc	[√]-ιστης	
βάπτω	dip	vb	[√]-ω	
ἐμβάπτω	dip	vb	ἐν-[√]-ω	
καταβαπτίζομαι	wash oneself	vb	κατα-[√]-ιζω	

ἰδι				118
own				
Memory Aid: idiosyncratic, idiomatic				
≥25 ἴδιος α ον	one's own, personal	adj	[√]-ιος	
ἰδιώτης ου	untrained person	masc	[√]-της	

ἰερ ἰερατ				117
priest				
Memory Aid: hierarchy, hieroglyph				
ἰερατεία ας	priestly office	fem	[√]-εια	
ἰεράτευμα ματος	priesthood	neut	[√]-μα	
ἰερατεύω	serve as a priest	vb	[√]-ευω	
≥25 ἰερεύς έως	priest	masc	[√]-ευς	
ἰερόθυτος ον	sacrificial	adj	[√]-[θυ]-τος	
≥25 ἰερόν οῦ	temple	neut	[√]-ον	
ἰεροπρεπής ές	reverent	adj	[√]-(πρέπω)-ης	
ἰερός ά όν	sacred	adj	[√]-ος	
ἰεροσυλέω	commit sacrilege	vb	[√]-(συλάω)-εω	
ἰερόσυλος ου	sacrilegious person	masc	[√]-(συλάω)-ος	
ἰερουργέω	work as a priest	vb	[√]-[ἐργ]-εω	
ἰερωσύνη ης	priesthood	fem	[√]-συνη	

ὀπ ὀπτ ωπ				117
see				
Memory Aid: optical, autopsy				
≥25 ἐνώπιον (*gen*)	before (>in sight of)	prep	ἐν-[√]-ιον	
ἐποπτεύω	see, observe	vb	ἐπι-[√]-ευω	
ἐπότης ου	observer, eyewitness	masc	ἐπι-[√]-της	
ἔσοπτρον ου	mirror	neut	εἰς-[√]-τρον	
κατοπτρίζω	behold	vb	κατα-[√]-ιζω	

μέτωπον ου	forehead	neut	μετα-[√]-ον
μυωπάζω	be shortsighted	vb	(μύω)-[√]-αζω
ὀπτάνομαι	appear (>gain sight of)	vb	[√]-ανω
ὀπτασία ας	vision	fem	[√]-σια
πρόσωπον	face	neut	προσ-[√]-ον
σκυθρωπός ή όν	sad	adj	(σκυθρός)-[√]-ος
ὑπωπιάζω	control (>under the eye)	vb	ὑπο-[√]-αζω

κακ   *116*
bad
Memory Aid: cacography, cacophony, caca

ἄκακος ον	innocent	adj	ἀ-[√]-ος
ἀνεξίκακος ον	tolerant	adj	ἀνα-[ἐχ]-[√]-ος
ἐγκακέω	become discouraged	vb	ἐν-[√]-εω
κακία ας	evil, trouble	fem	[√]-ια
κακοήθεια ας	meanness	fem	[√]-(>ἔθος)-εια
κακολογέω	speak evil of, curse	vb	[√]-[λεγ]-εω
κακοπάθεια ας	suffering, endurance	fem	[√]-[παθ]-εια
κακοπαθέω	suffer, endure	vb	[√]-[παθ]-εω
κακοποιέω	do evil	vb	[√]-[ποι]-εω
κακοποιός οῦ	criminal, wrongdoer	masc	[√]-[ποι]-ος
κακός ή όν	evil, bad	adj	[√]-ος
κακοῦργος ου	criminal	masc	[√]-[ἐργ]-ος
κακουχέομαι	be treated badly	vb	[√]-[ἐχ]-εω
κακόω	treat badly, harm	vb	[√]-οω
κακῶς	badly	adv	[√]-ως
κάκωσις εως	oppression, suffering	fem	[√]-σις
συγκακουχέομαι	suffer with	vb	συν-[√]-[ἐχ]-εω

ὁμο ὁμοι   *115*
same / like
Memory Aid: homogeneous, homonym, homoousion, homoiousion

	ἀφομοιόω	be like	vb	ἀπο [√] οω
	ὁμοιάζω	resemble	vb	[√]-αζω
	ὁμοιοπαθής ές	similar (>same feelings)	adj	[√]-[παθ]-ης
≥25	ὅμοιος α ον	like	adj	[√]-ιος
	ὁμοιότης ητος	likeness	fem	[√]-οτης
≥10	ὁμοιόω	make like, compare	vb	[√]-οω
	ὁμοίωμα ματος	likeness	neut	[√]-μα
≥25	ὁμοίως	too, in the same way	adv	[√]-ως
	ὁμοίωσις εως	likeness	fem	[√]-σις
	ὁμοῦ	together	adv	[√]-ου
	ὅμως	even	adv	[√]-ως
	παρομοιάζω	be like	vb	παρα-[√]-αζω
	παρόμοιος ον	like, similar	adj	παρα-[√]-ος

σῳζ (≈ σωτηρ, p. 74)   *115*
save
Memory Aid: creosote

| διασῴζω | rescue | vb | δια-[√]-ω |

ἐκσῴζω	save, keep safe	vb	ἐκ-[√]-ω
≥25 σῴζω	save, rescue, preserve	vb	[√]-ω

θυμ
feelings (emotions)   114
Memory Aid:

ἀθυμέω	become discouraged	vb	ἀ-[√]-εω
διενθυμέομαι	think over	vb	δια-ἐν-[√]-εω
ἐνθυμέομαι	think about, think	vb	ἐν-[√]-εω
ἐνθύμησις εως	thought, idea	fem	ἐν-[√]-σις
≥10 ἐπιθυμέω	desire, covet, lust for	vb	ἐπι-[√]-εω
ἐπιθυμητής οῦ	one who desires	masc	ἐπι-[√]-της
≥25 ἐπιθυμία ας	desire, lust	fem	ἐπι-[√]-ια
εὐθυμέω	take courage, be happy	vb	εὐ-[√]-εω
εὔθυμος ον	encouraged	adj	εὐ-[√]-ος
εὐθύμως	cheerfully	adv	εὐ-[√]-ως
θυμομαχέω	be very angry	vb	[√]-[μαχ]-εω
θυμόομαι	be furious	vb	[√]-οω
≥10 θυμός οῦ	anger	masc	[√]-ος
≥10 ὁμοθυμαδόν	with one mind	adv	[ὁμο]-[√]-δον
παραμυθέομαι	console	vb	παρα-[√]-εω
παραμυθία ας	comfort	fem	παρα-[√]-ια
παραμύθιον ου	comfort	neut	παρα-[√]-ιον
προθυμία ας	willingness, zeal	fem	προ-[√]-ια
πρόθυμος ον	willing	adj	προ-[√]-ος
προθύμως	willingly, eagerly	adv	προ-[√]-ως

ὁλ
whole / all   114
Memory Aid: whole, holocaust, catholic, holistic

καθόλου	completely, altogether	adv	[√]-κατα
≥25 ὅλος η ον	whole, all	adj	[√]-ος
ὁλοτελής ές	wholly	adj	[√]-[τελ]-ης
ὅλως	at all, actually	adv	[√]-ως

ῥη ῥητ
word   113
Memory Aid: orator, rhetoric

ἀναντίρρητος ον	undeniable	adj	ἀ-ἀντι-[√]-τος
ἀναντιρρήτως	without objection	adv	ἀ-ἀντι-[√]-ως
ἄρρητος ον	unutterable (>unflowing)	adj	ἀ-[√]-τος
≥25 παρρησία ας	openness (>all flowing)	fem	[παρ]-[√]-ια
παρρησιάζομαι	speak boldly	vb	[παρ]-[√]-αζω
≥25 ῥῆμα ματος	word, thing, event	neut	[√]-μα
ῥήτωρ ορος	lawyer, spokesperson	masc	[√]-τωρ
ῥητῶς	expressly	adv	[√]-ως

σπερ σπειρ σπορ
scatter   113
Memory Aid: sperm, sporadic, diaspora

	διασπείρω	scatter	vb	δια-[√]-ω
	διασπορά ᾶς	dispersion (>diaspora)	fem	δια-[√]-α
	ἐπισπείρω	sow in addition	vb	ἐπι-[√]-ω
≥25	σπείρω	sow	vb	[√]-ω
≥25	σπέρμα ματος	seed, offspring	neut	[√]-μα
	σπερμολόγος ου	gossiper (>word scatterer)	masc	[√]-[λεγ]-ος
	σπορά ᾶς	seed, origin	fem	[√]-α
	σπόριμα ων (*pl*)	grainfields	neut	[√]-ον
	σπόρος ου	seed	masc	[√]-ος

φρ φρο φρον   *113*
think
Memory Aid: schizophrenia

	ἀφροσύνη ης	folly	fem	ἀ-[√]-συνη
≥10	ἄφρων ον	foolish	adj	[√]-ων
≥10	εὐφραίνω	make glad	vb	εὐ-[√]-αινω
	εὐφροσύνη ης	gladness	fem	εὐ-[√]-συνη
	καταφρονέω	despise	vb	κατα-[√]-εω
	καταφρονητής οῦ	scoffer	masc	κατα-[√]-της
	ὁμόφρων ον	of one mind	adj	[ὁμο]-[√]-ων
	παραφρονέω	be insane	vb	παρα-[√]-εω
	παραφρονία ας	insanity	fem	παρα-[√]-ια
	περιφρονέω	esteem lightly, disregard	vb	περι-[√]-εω
	σωφρονέω	be sane, sensible	vb	[σωζ]-[√]-εω
	σωφρονίζω	train, teach	vb	[σωζ]-[√]-ιζω
	σωφρονισμός οῦ	sound judgment	masc	[σωζ]-[√]-ισμος
	σωφρόνως	sensibly	adv	[σωζ]-[√]-ως
	σωφροσύνη ης	good sense	fem	[σωζ]-[√]-συνη
	σώφρων ον	sensible	adj	[σωζ]-[√]-ων
	ὑπερφρονέω	hold high opinion of	vb	ὑπερ-[√]-εω
	φιλοφρόνως	kindly	adv	[φιλ]-[√]-ως
	φρήν φρενός	thought, understanding	fem	[√]-ην
≥25	φρονέω	think	vb	[√]-εω
	φρόνημα ματος	way of thinking, mind	neut	[√]-μα
	φρόνησις εως	insight, wisdom	fem	[√]-σις
≥10	φρόνιμος ον	wise	adj	[√]-μος
	φρονίμως	wisely	adv	[√]-ως
	φροντίζω	concentrate on	vb	[√]-ιζω

καθαρ καθαιρ   *112*
clean
Memory Aid: catharsis, Cathar

≥10	ἀκαθαρσία ας	impurity	fem	ἀ-[√]-ια
≥25	ἀκάθαρτος ον	unclean	adj	ἀ-[√]-τος
	διακαθαίρω	clean out	vb	δια-[√]-ω
	διακαθαρίζω	clean out	vb	δια-[√]-ιζω
	ἐκκαθαίρω	clean out	vb	ἐκ-[√]-ω
	καθαίρω	clean, prune	vb	[√]-ω

≥25	καθαρίζω	cleanse	vb	[√]-ιζω
	καθαρισμός οῦ	cleansing	masc	[√]-ισμος
≥25	καθαρός ά όν	clean, pure	adj	[√]-ρος
	καθαρότης ητος	purification, purity	fem	[√]-οτης
	περικάθαρμα ματος	rubbish	neut	περι-[√]-μα

ὡρ   *112*
time / hour
Memory Aid: horoscope, hour

	ἡμίωρον ου	half an hour	neut	ἡμι-[√]-ον
≥25	ὥρα ας	moment, time	fem	[√]-α
	ὡραῖος α ον	timely, welcome	adj	[√]-ιος

χρη χρα χρει   *111*
need / use
Memory Aid:

	ἀπόχρησις εως	process of being used	fem	ἀπο-[√]-σις
	ἀχρειόομαι	be worthless	vb	ἀ-[√]-οω
	ἀχρεῖος ον	worthless, mere	adj	ἀ-[√]-ιος
	ἄχρηστος ον	of little use, useless	adj	ἀ-[√]-τος
	εὔχρηστος ον	useful	adj	εὐ-[√]-τος
	καταχράομαι	use, use fully	vb	κατα-[√]-ω
≥10	παραχρῆμα	immediately	adv	παρα-[√]-μα
	συγχράομαι	associate with	vb	συν-[√]-ω
	χράομαι	use	vb	[√]-αω
≥25	χρεία ας	need	fem	[√]-εια
	χρή	it ought	vb	
	χρῄζω	need	vb	[√]-ιζω
	χρῆμα ματος	possessions, wealth	neut	[√]-μα
	χρήσιμον ου	good, value	neut	[√]-ιμος
	χρῆσις εως	sexual intercourse	fem	[√]-σις
	χρηστός ή όν	useful	adj	[√]-τος
≥10	χρηστότης ητος	goodness	fem	[√]-οτης

μελλ   *110*
be about
Memory Aid:

| ≥25 | μέλλω | be going, be about | vb | [√]-ω |

ὀλλ   *109*
destroy
Memory Aid: Apollyon

≥25	ἀπόλλυμι	destroy	vb	ἀπο-[√]-μι
≥10	ἀπώλεια ας	destruction	fem	ἀπο-[√]-εια
	συναπόλλυμαι	perish with	vb	συν-ἀπο-[√]-μι

ἐξουσ   *108*
authority
Memory Aid:

| ≥25 | ἐξουσία ας | authority, official | fem | [√]-ια |

ἐξουσιάζω	have power over	vb	[√]-αζω
ἐξουσιαστικός ή όν	authoritative	adj	[√]-τικος
κατεξουσιάζω	rule over	vb	κατα-[√]-αζω

ἀκολουθ
follow
106

Memory Aid: acolyte

≥25	ἀκολουθέω	follow, be a disciple	vb	[√]-εω
	ἐξακολουθέω	follow, be obedient	vb	ἐκ-[√]-εω
	ἐπακολουθέω	follow	vb	ἐπι-[√]-εω
	κατακολουθέω	follow, accompany	vb	κατα-[√]-εω
	παρακολουθέω	follow closely	vb	παρα-[√]-εω
	συνακολουθέω	follow, accompany	vb	συν-[√]-εω

πεμπ
send
106

Memory Aid: pompous

	ἀναπέμπω	send, send back / up	vb	ἀνα-[√]-ω
	ἐκπέμπω	send out / away	vb	ἐκ-[√]-ω
	μεταπέμπομαι	send for	vb	μετα-[√]-ω
≥25	πέμπω	send	vb	[√]-ω
	προπέμπω	send on one's way, escort	vb	προ-[√]-ω
	συμπέμπω	send along with	vb	συν-[√]-ω

δοκ² δογ δοξ
think / seem
104

Memory Aid: Docetic, paradox

	δόγμα ατος	decree	neut	[√]-μα
≥25	δοκέω	think, seem	vb	[√]-εω
≥10	εὐδοκέω	be pleased, choose, will	vb	εὐ-[√]-εω
	εὐδοκία ας	good will, pleasure	fem	εὐ-[√]-ια
	παράδοξος ον	incredible (>paradox)	adj	παρα-[√]-ος
	συνευδοκέω	approve of	vb	συν-ευ-[√]-εω

τεσσαρ τεταρ τετρα
four
104

Memory Aid: tetrahedron, tetrarch, tetris

	δεκατέσσαρες	fourteen	adj	[δεκα]-[√]
≥10	τεσσαράκοντα	forty	adj	[√]-κοντα
≥25	τέσσαρες α	four	adj	[√]-ες
	τεσσαρεσκαιδέκατος	fourteenth	adj	[√]-και-[δεκα]-τος
	τεταρταῖος α ον	on the fourth day	adj	[√]-ιος
≥10	τέταρτος η ον	fourth	adj	[√]-τος
	τετααρχέω	be tetrarch, be ruler	vb	[√]-[ἀρχ]-εω
	τετραάρχης ου	tetrarch (ruler)	masc	[√]-[ἀρχ]-ης
	τετράγωνος ον	squared (>four-angled)	adj	[√]-(γωνία)-ος
	τετράδιον ου	squad (of four men)	neut	[√]-ιον
	τετρακισχίλιοι αι α	four thousand	adj	[√]-κις-χιλιοι
	τετρακόσιοι αι α	four hundred	adj	[√]-κοσιοι

τετράμηνος ου	period of four months	fem	[√]-[μην]-ος
τετραπλοῦς ἦ οὖν	four times as much	adj	[√]-[πλει]-ος
τετράπουν ποδος	animal (>four-footed)	neut	[πο(1)]

ὀφθαλμ   103
eye
Memory Aid: ophthalmology

	ἀντοφθαλμέω	head into, face	vb	ἀντι-[√]-εω
	ὀφθαλμοδουλία ας	eye-service	fem	[√]-[δουλ]-ια
≥25	ὀφθαλμός οῦ	eye	masc	[√]-ος

εὐθ   101
immediate / straight
Memory Aid:

≥25	εὐθέως	immediately, soon	adv	[√]-ως
	εὐθύνω	make straight	vb	[√]-υνω
≥25	εὐθύς	immediately	adv	
	εὐθύς εῖα ύ	straight, (up)right	adj	[√]-υς
	εὐθύτης ητος	uprightness, justice	fem	[√]-οτης
	κατευθύνω	direct, guide	vb	κατα-[√]-υνω

καιρ   100
time
Memory Aid:

	ἀκαιρέομαι	be without opportunity	vb	ἀ-[√]-εω
	ἀκαίρως	untimely	adv	ἀ-[√]-ως
	εὐκαιρέω	have time, spend time	vb	εὐ-[√]-εω
	εὐκαιρία ας	opportune moment	fem	εὐ-[√]-ια
	εὔκαιρος ον	suitable, timely	adj	εὐ-[√]-ος
	εὐκαίρως	when the time is right	adv	εὐ-[√]-ως
≥25	καιρός οῦ	time, age	masc	[√]-ος
	πρόσκαιρος ον	temporary	adj	προς-[√]-ος

τοπ   100
place
Memory Aid: topography, Utopia, isotope

	ἄτοπος ον	improper	adj	ἀ-[√]-ος
	ἐντόπιος α ον	local (*pl* residents)	adj	ἐν-[√]-ιος
≥25	τόπος ου	place	masc	[√]-ος

αἱμ   99
blood
Memory Aid: hemophilia, hemorrhage, anemia, hemoglobin

≥25	αἷμα τος	blood, death	neut	[√]-α
	αἱματεκχυσία ας	shedding of blood	fem	[√]-ἐκ-[χε]-ια
	αἱμορροέω	hemorrhage, bleed	vb	[√]-[ῥε]-εω

εἰρην   99
peace
Memory Aid: irenic, Irene

| | εἰρηνεύω | be at peace | vb | [√]-ευω |

≥25	εἰρήνη ης	peace	fem	[√]-η
	εἰρηνικός ή όν	peaceful, irenic	adj	[√]-ικος
	εἰρηνοποιέω	make peace	vb	[√]-[ποι]-εω
	εἰρηνοποιός οῦ	peace-maker	masc	[√]-[ποι]-ος

ἕτερ   99
other / different
Memory Aid: heterodox, heterosexual

≥10	ἕτερος α ον	other, different	adj	[√]-ος
	ἑτέρως	otherwise, differently	adv	[√]-ως

διακον   98
serve
Memory Aid: deacon

≥25	διακονέω	serve, care for	vb	[√]-εω
≥25	διακονία ας	service, help	fem	[√]-ια
≥25	διάκονος ου	servant, deacon	masc/fem	[√]-ος

ἀρτ[1]   97
bread
Memory Aid:

≥25	ἄρτος ου	bread, food	masc	[√]-ος

πυρ   96
fire
Memory Aid: pyre, Pyrex, pyromaniac [fire: *see Grimm's Law*]

	ἀναζωπυρέω	stir into flame	vb	ἀνα-[ζω]-[√]-εω
≥25	πῦρ ός	fire	neut	[√]-ρ
	πυρά ᾶς	fire	fem	[√]-α
	πυρέσσω	be sick with fever	vb	[√]-σσω
	πυρετός οῦ	fever	masc	[√]-ος
	πύρινος η ον	fiery red (color)	adj	[√]-ινος
	πυρόομαι	burn	vb	[√]-οω
	πυρράζω	be red (for sky)	vb	[√]-αζω
	πυρρός ά όν	red (color)	adj	[√]-ος
	πύρωσις εως	burning, ordeal	fem	[√]-σις

φωσ φωτ   96
light
Memory Aid: photograph, photosynthesis, phosphorus

	ἐπιφώσκω	dawn, draw near	vb	ἐπι-[√]-σκω
≥25	φῶς φωτός	light, fire	neut	[√]-ς
	φωστήρ ῆρος	light, star	masc	[√]-τηρ
	φωσφόρος ου	morning star	masc	[√]-[φερ]-ος
	φωτεινός ή όν	full of light	adj	[√]-ινος
≥10	φωτίζω	give light, shine on	vb	[√]-ιζω
	φωτισμός οῦ	light, revelation	masc	[√]-μος

ἀντι   95
oppose / replace
Memory Aid: Antichrist, anti-aircraft, antibiotic, Antarctic, antidote

≥10 ἀντί (*gen*)	in place of, against	prep	
ἄντικρυς (*gen*)	opposite, off	prep	
ἀντιπέρα (*gen*)	opposite	prep	
ἀπαντάω	meet	vb	ἀπο-[√]-αω
ἀπάντησις εως	meeting	fem	ἀπο-[√]-σις
ἀπέναντι (*gen*)	opposite, before	prep	ἀπο-ἐν-[√]
ἔναντι (*gen*)	before (in judgment of)	prep	ἐν-[√]
ἐναντίον (*gen*)	before (in judgment of)	prep	ἐν-[√]
ἐναντιόομαι	oppose, contradict	vb	ἐν-[√]-οω
ἐναντίος α ον	against, hostile	adj	ἐν-[√]-ιος
≥10 καταντάω	come, arrive	vb	κατα-[√]-αω
κατέναντι (*gen*)	opposite	prep/adv	κατα-ἐν-[√]
συναντάω	meet, happen	vb	συν-[√]-αω
τουναντίον	on the contrary	adv	(τὸ ἐναντίον)
≥10 ὑπαντάω	meet, fight, oppose	vb	ὑπο-[√]-αω
ὑπάντησις εως	meeting	fem	ὑπο-[√]-σις
ὑπεναντίος α ον	against	adj	ὑπο-ἐν-[√]-ιος

ὁρ   94
boundary
Memory Aid: aphorism, horizon

ἀποδιορίζω	cause divisons	vb	ἀπο-δια-[√]-ιζω
≥10 ἀφορίζω	separate, exclude	vb	ἀπο-[√]-ιζω
ὁρίζω	decide, determine	vb	[√]-ιζω
≥10 ὅριον ου	territory, vicinity	neut	[√]-ιον
ὁροθεσία ας	limit, boundary	fem	[√]-[τιθ]-ια
≥25 ὅρος ου	limit, boundary	masc	[√]-ος

ἑπτ   93
seven
Memory Aid: Heptateuch

≥25 ἑπτά	seven	adj	
ἑπτάκις	seven times	adv	[√]-κις
ἑπτακισχίλιοι αι α	seven thousand	adj	[√]-κις-χιλιοι
ἑπταπλασίων ον	seven times as much	adj	[√]-ων (πλασίων)

θαλλασ   93
sea
Memory Aid: thallassic

διθάλασσος ον	between the seas	adj	[δευ]-[√]-ος
≥25 θάλασσα ης	sea	fem	[√]-α
παραθαλάσσιος α ον	by the sea or lake	adj	παρα-[√]-ιος

πλε πλο   93
sail
Memory Aid: [A boat *plies* the sea.]

ἀποπλέω	set sail	vb	ἀπο-[√]-ω
διαπλέω	sail across	vb	δια-[√]-ω
ἐκπλέω	sail	vb	ἐκ-[√]-ω

καταπλέω	sail	vb	κατα-[√]-ω
παραπλέω	sail past	vb	παρα-[√]-ω
πλέω	sail	vb	[√]-ω
πλοιάριον ου	boat	neut	[√]-αριον
≥25 πλοῖον ου	boat	neut	[√]-ιον
πλοῦς πλοός	voyage	masc	[√]-ς
ὑποπλέω	sail under the shelter of	vb	ὑπο-[√]-ω

μαλ μαλλ
more
Memory Aid:

≥10 μάλιστα	most of all	adv	[√]-ιστος
≥25 μᾶλλον	more	adv	[√]-ον

92

περισσ
abundance
Memory Aid:

ἐκπερισσῶς	emphatically	adv	ἐκ-[√]-ως
περισσεία ας	abundance	fem	[√]-εια
περίσσευμα ματος	abundance	neut	[√]-μα
≥25 περισσεύω	be left over, abound	vb	[√]-ευω
περισσός ή όν	more	adj	[√]-ος
≥10 περισσότερος α ον	greater, more	adj	[√]-τερος
≥10 περισσοτέρως	all the more	adv	[√]-τερος-ως
περισσῶς	all the more	adv	[√]-ως
υπερεκπερισσοῦ	with all earnestness	adv	ὑπερ-ἐκ-[√]-ου
ὑπερπερισσεύω	increase abundantly	vb	ὑπερ-[√]-ευω
ὑπερπερισσῶς	completely	adv	ὑπερ-[√]-ως

91

σημ
sign / indication
Memory Aid: semantics, semaphore

ἄσημος ον	insignificant	adj	ἀ-[√]-ος
ἐπίσημος ον	well known	adj	ἐπι-[√]-ος
εὔσημος ον	intelligible	adj	εὐ-[√]-ος
παράσημος ον	marked by a figurehead	adj	παρα-[√]-ος
σημαίνω	indicate	vb	[√]-αινω
≥25 σημεῖον ου	sign, miracle	neut	[√]-ιον
σημειόομαι	take / make note of	vb	[√]-οω
σύσσημον ου	signal, sign	neut	συν-[√]-ον

90

κρατ
strong / power
Memory Aid: autocratic, democracy, democrat, -cracy

ἀκρασία ας	lack of self control	fem	ἀ-[√]-ια
ἀκρατής ές	uncontrolled, violent	adj	ἀ-[√]-ης
ἐγκράτεια ας	self-control	fem	ἐν-[√]-εια
ἐγκρατεύομαι	be self-controlled	vb	ἐν-[√]-ευω
ἐγκρατής ές	self-controlled	adj	ἐν-[√]-ης

89

κραταιόομαι	become strong	vb	[√]-οω
κραταιός ά όν	strong	adj	[√]-ιος
≥25 κρατέω	hold, seize	vb	[√]-εω
κράτιστος η ον	most excellent	adj	[√]-ιστος
≥10 κράτος ους	strength, power	neut	[√]-ς
≥10 παντοκράτωρ ορος	the All-Powerful	masc	[παν]-[√]-ρ
περικρατής ές	in control of	adj	περι-[√]-ης

θεα θεωρ   88
see
Memory Aid: theatre, theory

ἀναθεωρέω	observe closely	vb	ἀνα-[√]-εω
≥10 θεάομαι	see, observe	vb	[√]-ω
θεατρίζω	expose to public shame	vb	[√]-ιζω
θέατρον ου	theatre, spectacle	neut	[√]-τρον
≥25 θεωρέω	see, observe	vb	[√]-εω
θεωρία ας	sight	fem	[√]-ια
παραθεωρέω	overlook	vb	παρα-[√]-εω

κει   88
lie
Memory Aid: cemetery

≥10 ἀνάκειμαι	be seated (lie) at a table	vb	ἀνα-[√]-μι
ἀντίκειμαι	oppose	vb	ἀντι-[√]-μι
ἀπόκειμαι	be stored away	vb	ἀπο-[√]-μι
ἐπίκειμαι	lie on, crowd	vb	ἐπι-[√]-μι
≥10 κατάκειμαι	lie, be sick	vb	κατα-[√]-μι
≥10 κεῖμαι	lie, be laid, be	vb	[√]-μι
παράκειμαι	be present	vb	παρα-[√]-μι
περίκειμαι	be placed around	vb	περι-[√]-μι
πρόκειμαι	be set before, be present	vb	προ-[√]-μι
συνανάκειμαι	sit at table with	vb	συν-ἀνα-[√]-μι

μητηρ μητρ   88
mother
Memory Aid: maternal, matron, matriarchy [mother: *see Grimm's Law*]

ἀμήτωρ ορος	without a mother	adj	ἀ-[√]-ρ
≥25 μήτηρ τρός	mother	fem	[√]-ρ
μήτρα ας	womb	fem	[√]-α
μητρολῴας ου	mother-murderer	masc	[√]-(ἀλοάω)-ας

πλει πλεον   88
more
Memory Aid: Pliocene [*plenty, plural, plus*]

πλεῖστος η ον	most, large	adj	[√]-ιστος
≥25 πλείων ον	more	adj	[√]-ων
πλεονάζω	increase, grow	vb	[√]-αζω
πλεονεκτέω	take advantage of	vb	[√]-[ἐχ]-εω
πλεονέκτης ου	one who is greedy	masc	[√]-[ἐχ]-της

| ≥10 | πλεονεξία ας | greed (>have more) | fem | [√]-[ἐχ]-ια |
| | ὑπερπλεονάζω | overflow | vb | ὑπερ-[√]-αζω |

φυλακ φυλασσ
guard
88

Memory Aid: phylactery, prophylactic

	γαζοφυλάκιον ου	treasury, offering box	neut	(γάζα)-[√]-ειον
	διαφυλάσσω	protect	vb	δια-[√]-σσω
≥25	φυλακή ῆς	prison	fem	[√]-η
	φυλακίζω	imprison	vb	[√]-ιζω
	φυλακτήριον ου	phylactery	neut	[√]-τηριον
	φύλαξ ακος	guard	masc	[√]-ξ
≥25	φυλάσσω	guard, keep, obey	vb	[√]-σσω

ἀνοιγ
open / start
87

Memory Aid:

≥25	ἀνοίγω	open	vb	[√]-ω
	ἄνοιξις εως	opening	fem	[√]-σις
	διανοίγω	open	vb	δια-[√]-ω

κεφαλ
head / sum
87

Memory Aid: encephalitis [*cap, capital, captain*]

	ἀνακεφαλαιόω	sum up, unite	vb	ἀνα-[√]-οω
	ἀποκεφαλίζω	behead	vb	ἀπο-[√]-ιζω
	κεφάλαιον ου	main point, summary	neut	[√]-ιον
≥25	κεφαλή ῆς	head	fem	[√]-η
	κεφαλιόω	beat over the head	vb	[√]-οω
	περικεφαλαία ας	helmet	fem	περι-[√]-ια
	προσκεφάλαιον ου	pillow	neut	προς-[√]-ιον

πειθ
persuade
87

Memory Aid:

	ἀναπείθω	persuade, incite	vb	ἀνα-[√]-ω
	ἀπείθεια ας	disobedience	fem	ἀ-[√]-εια
≥10	ἀπειθέω	disobey	vb	ἀ-[√]-εω
	ἀπειθής ές	disobedient	adj	ἀ-[√]-ης
	εὐπειθής ές	open to reason	adj	εὐ-[√]-ης
	πειθαρχέω	obey	vb	[√]-[ἀρχ]-εω
	πειθός ή όν	persuasive	adj	[√]-ος
≥25	πείθω	persuade	vb	[√]-ω
	πειθώ οῦς	persuasiveness	fem	ς
	πεισμονή ῆς	persuasion	fem	[√]-η

ἐλπ
hope
86

Memory Aid:

| | ἀπελπίζω | expect in return | vb | ἀπο-[√]-ιζω |

≥25 ἐλπίζω	hope	vb	[√]-ιζω
≥25 ἐλπίς ίδος	hope	fem	[√]-ς
προελπίζω	be the first to hope	vb	προ-[√]-ιζω

ἐντολ ἐνταλ
commandment
Memory Aid: [One must obey the *commandments in total.*]

ἔνταλμα ματος	commandment	neut	[√]-μα
≥10 ἐντέλλομαι	command	vb	[√]-ω
≥25 ἐντολή ῆς	commandment	fem	[√]-η

85

τηρ
keep / observe
Memory Aid:

διατηρέω	keep, treasure up	vb	δια-[√]-εω
παρατηρέω	keep, watch, observe	vb	παρα-[√]-εω
παρατήρησις εως	observation	fem	παρα-[√]-σις
συντηρέω	protect	vb	συν-[√]-εω
≥25 τηρέω	keep, observe	vb	[√]-εω
τήρησις εως	custody, keeping	fem	[√]-σις

85

ὑδρ
water
Memory Aid: hydrant, hydroplane, hydroelectric

ἄνυδρος ον	waterless, desert	adj	ἀ-[√]-ος
ὑδρία ας	water jar	fem	[√]-ια
ὑδροποτέω	drink water	vb	[√]-[πο²]-εω
ὑδρωπικός ή όν	suffering from dropsy	adj	[√]-ικος
≥25 ὕδωρ ὕδατος	water	neut	[√]-ρ

85

σθεν
strong
Memory Aid: asthenia

≥10 ἀσθένεια ας	weakness	fem	ἀ-[√]-εια
≥25 ἀσθενέω	be weak, be sick	vb	ἀ-[√]-εω
ἀσθένημα ματος	weakness	neut	ἀ-[√]-μα
≥25 ἀσθενής ές	weak, sick	adj	ἀ-[√]-ης
σθενόω	strengthen	vb	[√]-οω

84

ἑκασ
each
Memory Aid:

≥25 ἕκαστος η ον	each, every	adj	[√]-τος
ἑκάστοτε	at all times	adv	[√]-[οτε]

82

καρπ
fruit
Memory Aid: pericarp

ἄκαρπος ον	barren, useless	adj	ἀ-[√]-ος
≥25 καρπός οῦ	fruit	masc	[√]-ος

82

| καρποφορέω | be fruitful / productive | vb | [√]-[φερ]-εω |
| καρποφόρος ον | fruitful | adj | [√]-[φερ]-ος |

πιν
drink
82

Memory Aid: symposium

	καταπίνω	swallow (>drink down)	vb	κατα-[√]-ω
≥25	πίνω	drink	vb	[√]-ω
	συμπίνω	drink with	vb	συν-[√]-ω
	συμπόσιον ου	group (>symposium)	neut	συν-[√]-ιον

στομ
mouth
80

Memory Aid: [The *mouth* is the entrance to the *stomach*.]

	ἀποστοματίζω	question (>from mouth)	vb	ἀπο-[√]-ιζω
	ἐπιστομίζω	make silent	vb	ἐπι-[√]-ιζω
≥25	στόμα ματος	mouth	neut	[√]-μα

δεικ δειγ δειξ
show
79

Memory Aid: paradigm, paradigmatic, indicate

	ἀναδείκνυμι	show clearly, appoint	vb	ἀνα-[√]-μι
	ἀνάδειξις εως	public appearance	fem	ἀνα-[√]-σις
	ἀποδείκνυμι	attest, proclaim	vb	ἀπο-[√]-μι
	ἀπόδειξις εως	proof, demonstration	fem	ἀπο-[√]-σις
	δεῖγμα ματος	example, warning	neut	[√]-μα
	δειγματίζω	disgrace, show publicly	vb	μα-[√]-ιζω
≥25	δείκνυμι	show, explain	vb	[√]-μι
	ἔνδειγμα ματος	evidence, proof	neut	ἐν-[√]-μα
≥10	ἐνδείκνυμαι	show, give indication	vb	ἐν-[√]-μι
	ἔνδειξις εως	evidence, indication	fem	ἐν-[√]-σις
	ἐπιδείκνυμι	show	vb	ἐπι-[√]-μι
	παραδειγματίζω	expose to ridicule	vb	παρα-[√]-ιζω
	ὑπόδειγμα τος	example, copy	neut	ὑπο-[√]-μα
	ὑποδείκνυμι	show, warn	vb	ὑπο-[√]-μι

διο
therefore
79

Memory Aid:

≥25	διό	therefore	cj/pt	
	διόπερ	therefore (emphatic)	cj/pt	[√]-περ
≥10	διότι	because, for, therefore	cj/pt	[√]-[ότι]

σταυρ
cross
79

Memory Aid: [Sounds like *star – a cross*.]

	ἀνασταυρόω	crucify, crucify again	vb	ἀνα-[√]-οω
≥25	σταυρός οῦ	cross	masc	[√]-ος
≥25	σταυρόω	crucify	vb	[√]-οω
	συσταυρόομαι	be crucified together	vb	συν-[√]-οω

δαιμ
demon

Memory Aid: demon

≥10 δαιμονίζομαι	be demon possessed	vb	[√]-ιζω
≥25 δαιμόνιον ου	demon, spirit	neut	[√]-ιον
δαιμονιώδης ες	demonic	adj	[√]-ης
δαίμων ονος	demon	masc	[√]-ων

78

ἐλε
mercy

Memory Aid: "Kyrie, eleison."

ἀνελεήμων ον	unmerciful	adj	ἀ-[√]-μων
ἀνέλεος ον	unmerciful	adj	ἀ-[√]-ος
≥25 ἐλεάω (>ἐλεέω)	be merciful	vb	[√]-αω-(εω)
ἐλεεινός ή όν	pitiable	adj	[√]-ινος
≥10 ἐλεημοσύνη ης	charity	fem	[√]-μων-συνη
ἐλεήμων ον	merciful	adj	[√]-μων
≥25 ἔλεος ους	mercy	neut	[√]-ος

78

λιθ
stone

Memory Aid: Paleolithic, lithograph, monolithic, megalith

καταλιθάζω	stone	vb	κατα-[√]-αζω
λιθάζω	stone	vb	[√]-αζω
λίθινος η ον	made of stones	adj	[√]-ινος
λιθοβολέω	stone (>throw stones)	vb	[√]-[βαλ]-εω
≥25 λίθος ου	stone	masc	[√]-ος
λιθόστρωτον ου	pavement	neut	[√]-(στορέννυμι)-ον

78

προσωπ
face

Memory Aid:

εὐπροσωπέω	make a good showing	vb	εὐ-[√]-εω
προσωπολημπτέω	show favoritism	vb	[√]-[λαμβ]-εω
προσωπολήμπτης ου	shower of favoritism	masc	[√]-[λαμβ]-της
προσωπολημψία ας	favoritism	fem	[√]-[λαμβ]-σια
≥25 πρόσωπον ου	face	neut	[√]-ον

78

ἐγγ
near

Memory Aid:

≥25 ἐγγίζω	approach	vb	[√]-ιζω
ἔγγυος ου	guarantor	masc	[√]-ος
≥25 ἐγγύς	near	adv	
ἐγγύτερον	nearer	adv	[√]-τερον
προσεγγίζω	come near	vb	προς-[√]-ιζω

77

μερ
part

Memory Aid: polymer [In a *merger,* different *parts* are brought together.]

77

≥10	διαμερίζω	divide	vb	δια-[√]-ιζω
	διαμερισμός οῦ	division	masc	δια-[√]-ισμος
≥10	μερίζω	divide	vb	[√]-ιζω
	μερίς ίδος	part	fem	[√]-ς
	μερισμός οῦ	distribution, division	masc	[√]-ισμος
	μεριστής οῦ	one who divides	masc	[√]-ιστης
≥25	μέρος ους	part, piece	neut	[√]-ς
	συμμερίζομαι	share with	vb	συν-[√]-ιζω

σοφ
wisdom
77

Memory Aid: philosophy, Sophia, sophomore

	ἄσοφος ον	senseless, foolish	adj	ἀ-[√]-ος
	κατασοφίζομαι	take advantage of	vb	κατα-[√]-ιζω
≥25	σοφία ας	wisdom	fem	[√]-ια
	σοφίζω	give wisdom	vb	[√]-ιζω
≥10	σοφός ή όν	wise, experienced	adj	[√]-ος
	φιλοσοφία ας	philosophy	fem	[φιλ]-[√]-ια
	φιλόσοφος ου	philosopher, teacher	masc	[φιλ]-[√]-ος

βουλ
plan
76

Memory Aid: boule [plan: *see Grimm's Law*]

	βουλεύομαι	plan, consider	vb	[√]-ευω
	βουλευτής οῦ	councillor	masc	[√]-της
≥10	βουλή ῆς	plan, intention	fem	[√]-η
	βούλημα ματος	plan, intention, desire	neut	[√]-μα
≥25	βούλομαι	plan, want	vb	[√]-ω
	ἐπιβουλή ῆς	plot	fem	ἐπι-[√]-η
	συμβουλεύω	advise	vb	συν-[√]-ευω
	συμβούλιον ου	plan, plot	neut	συν-[√]-ιον
	σύμβουλος ου	counselor	masc	συν-[√]-ος

ἐμ
my / mine
76

Memory Aid: Reverse of letters of English *me*.

≥25	ἐμός ή όν	my, mine	adj	[√]-ος

ἐσθι
eat
75

Memory Aid:

≥25	ἐσθίω	eat	vb	[√]-ω
	κατεσθίω	eat up, devour	vb	κατα-[√]-ω
	συνεσθίω	eat with	vb	συν-[√]-ω

ἰσχυ
strong
75

Memory Aid:

	διϊσχυρίζομαι	insist	vb	δια-[√]-ιζω
	ἐνισχύω	strengthen	vb	ἐν-[√]-ω

ἐξισχύω	be fully able	vb	ἐκ-[√]-ω
ἐπισχύω	insist	vb	ἐπι-[√]-ω
≥25 ἰσχυρός ά όν	strong	adj	[√]-ρος
≥10 ἰσχύς ύος	strength	fem	[√]-ς
≥25 ἰσχύω	be able	vb	[√]-ω
κατισχύω	have strength, defeat	vb	κατα-[√]-ω

κραζ κραυγ
shout
Memory Aid: Note shared letters *c-r-y* in the word *cry*.

				75
ἀνακράζω	cry out	vb	ἀνα-[√]-ω	
≥25 κράζω	shout, call out	vb	[√]-ω	
κραυγάζω	shout, call out	vb	[√]-ω	
κραυγή ῆς	shout	fem	[√]-η	

κτειν
kill
Memory Aid:

				74
≥25 ἀποκτείνω	kill	vb	ἀπο-[√]-ω	

μεσο μεσι
middle
Memory Aid: Mesopotamia

				74
μεσιτεύω	mediate	vb	[√]-ευω	
μεσίτης ου	mediator	masc	[√]-της	
μεσονύκτιον ου	midnight	neut	[√]-[νυ](¹)-ιον	
Μεσοποταμία ας	Mesopotamia	fem	[√]-[πο(¹)]-ια	
≥25 μέσος η ον	middle	adj	[√]-ος	
μεσότοιχον ου	dividing wall	neut	[√]-(τεῖχος)-ον	
μεσουράνημα τος	mid-heaven	neut	[√]-[οὐραν]-μα	
μεσόω	be in the middle	vb	[√]-οω	

σωτηρ (≈ σῳζ, p. 59)
salvation
Memory Aid: soteriology, Soter

				74
≥10 σωτήρ ῆρος	savior	masc	[√]-ρ	
≥25 σωτηρία ας	salvation, release	fem	[√]-ια	
σωτήριον ου	salvation	neut	[√]-ιον	
σωτήριος ον	saving	adj	[√]-ιος	

θυ θυσ
sacrifice
Memory Aid:

				73
εἰδωλόθυτον ου	meat offered to idols	neut	[εἰδωλ]-[√]-ον	
≥25 θυσία ας	sacrifice	fem	[√]-ια	
≥10 θυσιαστήριον ου	altar (>place of sacrifice)	neut	[√]-τηριον	
≥10 θύω	sacrifice, kill	vb	[√]-ω	

κηρυξ κηρυγ κηρυσσ
preach
Memory Aid: kerygma

				73

	κήρυγμα ματος	message, kerygma	neut	[√]-μα
	κῆρυξ υκος	preacher	masc	[√]-ξ
≥25	κηρύσσω	preach, proclaim	vb	[√]-σσω
	προκηρύσσω	preach beforehand	vb	προ-[√]-σσω

κοιν κοινων   73
common

Memory Aid: koinonia, koine Greek [*common, community*]

≥10	κοινός ή όν	common, profane	adj	[√]-ος
≥10	κοινόω	defile (>make common)	vb	[√]-οω
	κοινωνέω	share, participate	vb	[√]-εω
≥10	κοινωνία ας	fellowship	fem	[√]-ια
	κοινωνικός ή όν	liberal, generous, sharing	adj	[√]-ικος
≥10	κοινωνός οῦ	partner	masc/fem	[√]-ος
	συγκοινωνέω	take part in	vb	συν-[√]-εω
	συγκοινωνός οῦ	sharer	masc	συν-[√]-ος

πρεσβυ   73
old / elderly

Memory Aid: presbyter

	πρεσβυτέριον ου	body of elders	neut	[√]-τερος-ιον
≥25	πρεσβύτερος ου	elder, presbyter	masc	[√]-τερος
	πρεσβύτης ου	old man	masc	[√]-της
	πρεσβῦτις ιδος	old woman	fem	[√]-ς
	συμπρεσβύτερος ου	fellow-elder	masc	συν-[√]-τερος

φιλ   73
love

Memory Aid: philanthropy, philosophy, Philadelphia

	καταφιλέω	kiss	vb	κατα-[√]-εω
	προσφιλής ές	pleasing	adj	προς-[√]-ης
	φίλαυτος ον	selfish	adj	[√]-[αὐτο]-ος
≥25	φιλέω	love, like, kiss	vb	[√]-εω
	φίλημα ματος	kiss	neut	[√]-μα
	φιλία ας	love, friendship	fem	[√]-ια
≥25	φίλος ου	friend	masc	[√]-ος
	φιλοτιμέομαι	aspire	vb	[φιλ]-[√]-εω

πασχ   72
suffer

Memory Aid: passion, compassion, Paschal lamb

≥25	πάσχα	Passover	neut	
≥25	πάσχω	suffer	vb	[√]-ω
	προπάσχω	suffer previously	vb	προ-[√]-ω
	συμπάσχω	suffer together	vb	συν-[√]-ω

σκ σκοτ   71
dark

Memory Aid: scotoma

	ἀποσκίασμα ματος	shadow, darkness	neut	ἀπο-[√]-μα

ἐπισκιάζω	overshadow	vb	ἐπι-[√]-αζω
σκιά ᾶς	shadow, shade	fem	[√]-α
σκοτεινός ή όν	dark	adj	[√]-ινος
≥10 σκοτία ας	darkness	fem	[√]-ια
σκοτίζομαι	become dark	vb	[√]-ιζω
σκοτόομαι	become dark	vb	[√]-οω
≥25 σκότος ους	darkness, sin	neut	[√]-ς

καλυπτ καλυμ καλυψ
hide
Memory Aid: Apocalypse

70

ἀκατακάλυπτος ον	uncovered	adj	ἀ-κατα-[√]-τος
ἀνακαλύπτω	uncover, unveil	vb	ἀνα-[√]-ω
≥25 ἀποκαλύπτω	reveal	vb	ἀπο-[√]-ω
≥10 ἀποκάλυψις εως	revelation, Apocalypse	fem	ἀπο-[√]-σις
ἐπικάλυμμα ματος	covering, pretext	neut	ἐπι-[√]-μα
ἐπικαλύπτω	cover (sin)	vb	ἐπι-[√]-ω
κάλυμμα ματος	veil	neut	[√]-μα
καλύπτω	cover, hide	vb	[√]-ω
κατακαλύπτομαι	cover one's head	vb	κατα-[√]-ω
παρακαλύπτομαι	be hidden	vb	παρα-[√]-ω
περικαλύπτω	cover, conceal	vb	περι-[√]-ω
συγκαλύπτω	cover up	vb	συν-[√]-ω

πειρ
test
Memory Aid: pirate

69

ἀπείραστος ον	unable to be tempted	adj	ἀ-[√]-τος
ἄπειρος ον	unacquainted	adj	α-[√]-ος
ἐκπειράζω	test, tempt	vb	ἐκ-[√]-αζω
πεῖρα ας	attempt	fem	[√]-α
≥25 πειράζω	test, tempt	vb	[√]-αζω
πειράομαι	try, attempt	vb	[√]-αω
≥10 πειρασμός οῦ	trial, period of testing	masc	[√]-σμος
περιπείρω	pierce through	vb	περι-[√]-ω

πλου
rich
Memory Aid: plutocracy [*plush, plumage*]

69

≥25 πλούσιος α ον	rich	adj	[√]-ιος
πλουσίως	richly	adv	[√]-ως
≥10 πλουτέω	be rich, prosper	vb	[√]-εω
πλουτίζω	make rich	vb	[√]-ιζω
≥10 πλοῦτος ου	wealth	masc	[√]-ος

τεμν τομ
cut
Memory Aid: appendectomy, mastectomy, tome, atom, -tomy

69

| ἀπερίτμητος ον | uncircumcised | adj | ἀ-περι-[√]-τος |

ἀποτομία ας	severity	fem	ἀπο-[√]-ια
ἀποτόμως	severely	adv	ἀπο-[√]-ως
ἄτομος ον	indivisible	adj	ἀ-[√]-ος
δίστομος ον	double-edged	adj	[δευ]-[√]-ος
διχοτομέω	cut in pieces	vb	[δευ]-[√]-εω
καταγομή ῆς	mutilation	fem	κατα-[√]-η
λατομέω	cut, hew (of rock)	vb	[λιθ]-[√]-εω
≥10 περιτέμνω	circumcise	vb	περι-[√]-ω
≥25 περιτομή ῆς	circumcision	fem	περι-[√]-η
συντέμνω	cut short	vb	συν-[√]-ω
τομός ή όν	sharp, cutting	adj	[√]-ος

πο² ποτ ποταμ   68
drink / river (compare πιν)
Memory Aid: Mesopotamia, hippopotamus, symposium

πόσις εως	drink	fem	[√]-σις
≥10 ποταμός οῦ	river	masc	[√]-ος
ποταμοφόρητος ον	swept away	adj	[√]-[φερ]-τος
≥25 ποτήριον ου	cup (>place for water)	neut	[√]-τηριον
≥10 ποτίζω	give to drink, water	vb	[√]-ιζω
πότος ου	drunken orgy	masc	[√]-ος

ἱματ   67
clothe
Memory Aid:

ἱματίζω	clothe, dress	vb	[√]-ιζω
≥25 ἱμάτιον ου	clothes, coat	neut	[√]-ιον
ἱματισμός οῦ	clothing	masc	[√]-ισμος

νυ νυκ νυχ νυσ   67
night
Memory Aid: equinox, nocturnal

διανυκτερεύω	spend the night	vb	δια-[√]-ευω
ἔννυχα	in the night	adv	ἐν-[√]-α
κατάνυξις εως	stupor, numbness	fem	κατα-[√]-ς
≥25 νύξ νυκτός	night	fem	[√]-ξ
νυστάζω	be asleep, drowsy, idle	vb	[√]-αζω
νυχθήμερον ου	a night and a day	neut	[√]-[ἡμερ]-ον

ἄχρι   66
until
Memory Aid:

≥25 ἄχρι (*gen*)	until, to, as, when	cj/prep	
≥10 μέχρι (*gen*)	until, to	cj/prep	

ἑτοιμ   64
ready / prepare
Memory Aid:

≥25 ἑτοιμάζω	prepare, make ready	vb	[√]-αζω
ἑτοιμασία ας	readiness, equipment	fem	[√]-ια

≥10 ἕτοιμος η ον	ready	adj	[√]-ος
ἑτοίμως	readily	adv	[√]-ως
προετοιμάζω	prepare beforehand	vb	προ-[√]-αζω

καυχη καυχα
proud
64

Memory Aid: [A *proud* person is often *cocky*.]

ἐγκαυχάομαι	boast	vb	ἐν-[√]-αω
κατακαυχάομαι	be proud, despise	vb	κατα-[√]-αω
≥25 καυχάομαι	be proud, boast	vb	[√]-αω
≥10 καύχημα ματος	pride, boasting	neut	[√]-μα
≥10 καύχησις εως	pride, boasting	fem	[√]-σις

κληρ
share / choose
64

Memory Aid: clergy

≥10 κληρονομέω	receive, share (in)	vb	[√]-[νομ]-εω
≥10 κληρονομία ας	property	fem	[√]-[νομ]-ια
≥10 κληρονόμος ου	heir	masc	[√]-[νομ]-ος
≥10 κλῆρος ου	lot, share	masc	[√]-ος
κληρόω	choose	vb	[√]-οω
προσκληρόομαι	join	vb	προσ-[√]-οω
συγκληρονόμος ον	sharing	adj	συν-[√]-[νομ]-ος

ὀρ
hill
64

Memory Aid:

ὀρεινή ῆς	hill country	fem	[√]-η
≥25 ὄρος ους	mountain, hill	neut	[√]-ς

θρον
throne
62

Memory Aid: throne

≥25 θρόνος ου	throne	masc	[√]-ος

αἱρ
take / choose
61

Memory Aid: diaresis, heresy

αἵρεσις εως	sect, school	fem	[√]-σις
αἱρετίζω	choose	vb	[√]-ιζω
αἱρετικός η ον	divisive	adj	[√]-τικος
ἀναίρεσις εως	killing, murder	fem	ἀνα-[√]-σις
≥10 ἀναιρέω	do away with, take life	vb	ἀνα-[√]-εω
≥10 ἀφαιρέω	take away	vb	ἀπο-[√]-εω
διαίρεσις εως	variety, difference	fem	δια-[√]-σις
διαιρέω	divide, distribute	vb	δια-[√]-εω
ἐξαιρέω	pull out, rescue	vb	ἐκ-[√]-εω
καθαίρεσις εως	destruction	fem	κατα-[√]-σις
καθαιρέω	take down, destroy	vb	κατα-[√]-εω
περιαιρέω	take away, remove	vb	περι-[√]-εω
προαιρέομαι	decide	vb	προ-[√]-εω

στρατ
army
Memory Aid: strategy

ἀντιστρατεύομαι	war against	vb	ἀντι-[√]-ευω
στρατεία ας	warfare, fight	fem	[√]-εια
στράτευμα ματος	troops, army	neut	[√]-μα
στρατεύομαι	serve as a soldier, battle	vb	[√]-ευω
≥10 στρατηγός οῦ	chief officer	masc	[√]-[ἀγ]-ος
στρατιά ᾶς	army	fem	[√]-ια
≥25 στρατιώτης ου	soldier	masc	[√]-της
στρατολογέω	enlist soldiers	vb	[√]-[λεγ]-εω
στρατοπεδάρχης ου	officer	masc	[√]-[πο¹] [ἀρχ]-ης
στρατόπεδον ου	army	neut	[√]-[πο¹]-ον
συστρατιώτης ου	fellow-soldier	masc	συν-[√]-της

61

ὧδε
here
Memory Aid: See Appendix 2, Chart A.

≥25 ὧδε	here	adv	

61

δε²
bind
Memory Aid: diadem, syndetic

≥25 δέω	bind	vb	[√]-ω
διάδημα ματος	diadem	neut	δια-[√]-μα
καταδέω	bandage, bind up	vb	κατα-[√]-ω
περιδέω	wrap, bind	vb	περι-[√]-ω
συνδέομαι	be in prison with	vb	συν-[√]-ω
ὑποδέομαι	put on shoes	vb	ὑπο-[√]-ω
≥10 ὑπόδημα ματος	sandal	neut	υπο-[√]-μα

60

ἤδη
now / already
Memory Aid:

≥25 ἤδη	now, already	adv	

60

προσκυν
worship
Memory Aid:

≥25 προσκυνέω	worship	vb	[√]-εω
προσκυνητής οῦ	worshiper	masc	[√]-της

60

τρεπ τροπ
turn
Memory Aid: tropic, trophy

ἀνατρέπω	overturn	vb	ἀνα-[√]-ω
ἀποτρέπομαι	avoid (>turn from)	vb	ἀπο-[√]-ω
ἐκτρέπομαι	wander, go astray	vb	ἐκ-[√]-ω
ἐντρέπω	make ashamed	vb	ἐν-[√]-ω

60

ἐντροπή ῆς	shame	fem	ἐν-[√]-η
≥10 ἐπιτρέπω	let, allow	vb	ἐπι-[√]-ω
ἐπιτροπή ῆς	commission	fem	ἐπι-[√]-η
ἐπίτροπος ου	steward, guardian	masc	ἐπι-[√]-ος
μετατρέπω	turn, change	vb	μετα-[√]-ω
περιτρέπω	drive insane	vb	περι-[√]-ω
προτρέπομαι	encourage	vb	προ-[√]-ω
τροπή ῆς	turning, change	fem	[√]-η
≥10 τρόπος ου	way, manner	masc	[√]-ος
τροποφορέω	put up with	vb	[√]-[φερ]-εω

χρον
time
Memory Aid: chronology, synchronize, chronicles, chronic

χρονίζω	delay (>use time)	vb	[√]-ιζω
≥25 χρόνος ου	time	masc	[√]-ος
χρονοτριβέω	spend time	vb	[√]-(τρίβω)-εω

60

ἀξι
worthy
Memory Aid: axiom

ἀνάξιος ον	unworthy	adj	ἀ-[√]-ιος
ἀναξίως	unworthily	adv	ἀν-[√]-ως
≥25 ἄξιος α ον	worthy	adj	[√]-ιος
ἀξιόω	consider / make worthy	vb	[√]-οω
ἀξίως	worthily	adv	[√]-ως
καταξιόω	make / count worthy	vb	κατα-[√]-οω

59

ἐρημ
desert
Memory Aid: hermit, eremite

ἐρημία ας	desert	fem	[√]-ια
ἐρημόομαι	to be made waste	vb	[√]-οω
≥25 ἔρημος ον	lonely, desolate	adj	[√]-ος
ἐρήμωσις εως	desolation	fem	[√]-σις

59

πρασ πραγ
matter / event / something done
Memory Aid: practice, pragmatic

διαπραγματεύομαι	make a profit, earn	vb	δια-[√]-ευω
≥10 πρᾶγμα ματος	matter, event	neut	[√]-μα
πραγματεῖαι ῶν (pl)	affairs	fem	[√]-εια
πραγματεύομαι	trade, do business	vb	[√]-ευω
πρᾶξις εως	deed, practice	fem	[√]-σις
≥25 πράσσω	do	vb	[√]-σσω

59

συν
with
Memory Aid: synonym, sympathy, symphony, synthesis

≥25 σύν (dat)	with	prep	

59

θλιβ θλιψ
trouble / crowd   *58*
Memory Aid: thlipsis

ἀποθλίβω	crowd in upon	vb	ἀπο-[√]-ω
≥10 θλίβω	crush, press	vb	[√]-ω
≥25 θλῖψις εως	trouble	fem	[√]-ς
συνθλίβω	crowd, press upon	vb	συν-[√]-ω

διωκ διωγ
persecute / pursue   *57*
Memory Aid:

≥10 διωγμός οῦ	persecution	masc	[√]-μος
διώκτης ου	persecutor	masc	[√]-της
≥25 διώκω	persecute, pursue	vb	[√]-ω
ἐκδιώκω	persecute harshly	vb	ἐκ-[√]-ω
καταδιώκω	pursue diligently	vb	κατα-[√]-ω

πλαν
error / wandering   *57*
Memory Aid: planet

ἀποπλανάω	mislead, deceive	vb	ἀπο-[√]-αω
≥25 πλανάω	lead astray	vb	[√]-αω
≥10 πλάνη ης	error, deceit	fem	[√]-η
πλανήτης ου	wanderer	masc	[√]-της
πλάνος ον	deceitful	adj	[√]-ος

βλασφημ
blaspheme (compare φα)   *56*
Memory Aid: blaspheme

≥25 βλασφημέω	blaspheme, slander	vb	[√]-εω
>10 βλασφημία ας	blasphemy, slander	fem	[√]-ια
βλάσφημος ον	blasphemous	adj	[√]-ος

γαμ
marriage   *56*
Memory Aid: monogamy, bigamy, polygamy

ἄγαμος ου	unmarried, single	masc/fem	ἀ-[√]-ος
≥25 γαμέω	marry	vb	[√]-εω
γαμίζω	give in marriage	vb	[√]-ιζω
γαμίσκω	give in marriage	vb	[√]-σκω
≥10 γάμος ου	marriage, wedding	masc	[√]-ος
ἐπιγαμβρεύω	marry	vb	ἐπι-[√]-ευω

δοκιμ
examine   *56*
Memory Aid: [One should *examine* legal *documents* closely.]

ἀδόκιμος ον	disqualified, worthless	adj	ἀ-[√]-ος
ἀποδοκιμάζω	reject (after testing)	vb	ἀπο-[√]-αζω
≥10 δοκιμάζω	examine, discern	vb	[√]-αζω

δοκιμασία ας	examination, test	fem	[√]-ια
δοκιμή ῆς	character, evidence	fem	[√]-η
δοκίμιον ου	examination, testing	neut	[√]-ιον
δόκιμος ον	approved, examined	adj	[√]-ος

μακαρ
blessed
55

Memory Aid: macarism

	μακαρίζω	consider blessed	vb	[√]-ιζω
≥25	μακάριος α ον	blessed, happy	adj	[√]-ιος
	μακαρισμός οῦ	blessing, happiness	masc	[√]-ισμος

σεβ
worship / piety / religion
55

Memory Aid: Eusebius

	ἀσέβεια ας	godlessness	fem	ἀ-[√]-εια
	ἀσεβέω	live in an impious way	vb	ἀ-[√]-εω
	ἀσεβής ές	godless	adj	ἀ-[√]-ης
≥10	εὐσέβεια ας	godliness, religion	fem	εὐ-[√]-εια
	εὐσεβέω	worship	vb	εὐ-[√]-εω
	εὐσεβής ές	godly, religious	adj	εὐ-[√]-ης
	εὐσεβῶς	in a godly manner	adv	εὐ-[√]-ως
	σεβάζομαι	worship, reverence	vb	[√]-αζω
	σέβασμα ματος	object / place of worship	neut	[√]-μα
	σεβαστός ή όν	imperial	adj	[√]-τος
≥10	σέβομαι	worship	vb	[√]-ω

δεξ
right (opposite of left)
54

Memory Aid: dexterity, ambidextrous

| ≥25 | δεξιός ά όν | right (opposite of left) | adj | [√]-ιος |

ἐτ
year
54

Memory Aid:

	διετής ές	two years old	adj	[δευ]-[√]-ης
	διετία ας	two-year period	fem	[δευ]-[√]-ια
≥25	ἔτος ους	year	neut	[√]-ς
	τεσσαρακονταετής ές	forty years	adj	[τεσσ]-κοντα-[√]-ης

μακρ μακρο
long
54

Memory Aid: macrocosm, macron

≥10	μακράν	far, at a distance	adv	
≥10	μακρόθεν	far, at a distance	adv	[√]-θεν
≥10	μακροθυμέω	be patient	vb	[√]-[θυμ]-εω
≥10	μακροθυμία ας	patience	fem	[√]-[θυμ]-ια
	μακροθύμως	patiently	adv	[√]-[θυμ]-ως
	μακρός ά όν	long, distant	adj	[√]-ρος
	μακροχρόνιος ον	long-lived	adj	[√]-[χρον]-ιος

ὑψ
high
Memory Aid: hypsography

	ὑπερυψόω	raise to highest position	vb	ὑπερ-[√]-οω
≥10	ὑψηλός ή όν	high	adj	[√]-λος
	ὑψηλοφρονέω	be proud	vb	[√]-[φρ]-εω
≥10	ὕψιστος η ον	highest	adj	[√]-ιστος
	ὕψος ους	height, heaven	neut	[√]-ος
≥10	ὑψόω	exalt (>make high)	vb	[√]-οω
	ὕψωμα ματος	height, stronghold	neut	[√]-μα

54

ἐσχατ
last / final
Memory Aid: eschatology, eschaton

≥25	ἔσχατος η ον	last, final	adj	[√]-τος
	ἐσχάτως	finally	adv	[√]-ως

53

τυφλ
blind
Memory Aid: [*Blindness* is a *tough (tuf) loss*.]

≥25	τυφλός ή όν	blind	adj	[√]-ος
	τυφλόω	make blind	vb	[√]-οω

53

θαυμ
wonder
Memory Aid: thaumaturgy

	ἐκθαυμάζω	be completely amazed	vb	ἐκ-[√]-αζω
	θαυμα ματος	wonder, miracle	neut	[√]-μα
≥25	θαυμάζω	marvel	vb	[√]-αζω
	θαυμάσιος α ον	wonderful	adj	[√]-ιος
	θαυμαστός ή όν	marvelous, astonishing	adj	[√]-τος

52

γλωσσ
tongue
Memory Aid: glossary, glossalalia, gloss

≥25	γλῶσσα ης	tongue, language	fem	[√]-α
	ἐτερόγλωσσος ον	with strange language	adj	[έτερ]-[√]-ος

51

δεσμ
bind / imprison (compare δε²)
Memory Aid:

	δεσμεύω	bind	vb	[√]-ευω
	δέσμη ης	bundle	fem	[√]-η
≥10	δέσμιος ου	prisoner	masc	[√]-ιος
≥10	δεσμός οῦ	bond, chain, jail	masc	[√]-ος
	δεσμοφύλαξ ακος	jailer	masc	[√]-[φυλακ]
	δεσμωτήριον ου	jail, prison	neut	[√]-τηριον
	δεσμώτης ου	prisoner	masc	[√]-της
	σύνδεσμος ου	bond, chain	masc	συν-[√]-ος

51

ἡγ ἡγεμ ἡγεμον
govern (compare with ἀγ)   *51*
Memory Aid: hegemony

ἡγεμονεύω	be governor, rule	vb	[√]-ευω
ἡγεμονία ας	reign, rule	fem	[√]-ια
≥10 ἡγεμών όνος	governor, ruler	masc	[√]-ων
≥25 ἡγέομαι	lead, rule, consider	vb	[√]-εω

καιν
new   *51*
Memory Aid: Cenozoic, Pliocene

ἀνακαινίζω	renew	vb	ἀνα-[√]-ιζω
ἀνακαινόω	renew, remake	vb	ἀνα-[√]-οω
ἀνακαίνωσις εως	renewal	fem	ἀνα-[√]-σις
ἐγκαινίζω	inaugurate, open	vb	ἐν-[√]-ιζω
≥25 καινός ή όν	new	adj	[√]-ος
καινότης ητος	newness	fem	[√]-οτης

οι
such / as   *51*
Memory Aid: See Appendix 2, Chart A.

≥10 οἷος α ον	such, such as	adj	[√]-ος
ὁποῖος α ον	as, such as	adj	[√]-ος
≥25 ποῖος α ον	what, what kind of	pron	[√]-ος

φθαρ φθειρ φθορ
decay   *51*
Memory Aid:

ἀφθαρσία ας	imperishability	fem	ἀ-[√]-ια
ἄφθαρτος ον	imperishable	adj	ἀ-[√]-τος
ἀφθορία ας	integrity	fem	ἀ-[√]-ια
διαφθείρω	decay, destroy	vb	δια-[√]-ω
διαφθορά ᾶς	decay	fem	δια-[√]-α
καταφθείρω	corrupt, ruin	vb	κατα-[√]-ω
φθαρτός ή όν	perishable, mortal	adj	[√]-τος
φθείρω	corrupt, ruin	vb	[√]-ω
φθινοπωρινός ή όν	of late autumn	adj	[√]-(ὀπώρα)-ινος

ψευδ
false   *51*
Memory Aid: pseudonym, Pseudepigrapha

ἀψευδής ές	trustworthy, non-lying	adj	ἀ-[√]-ης
ψευδάδελφος ου	false brother	masc	[√]-[ἀδελφ]-ος
ψευδαπόστολος ου	false apostle	masc	[√]-[στελ]-ος
ψευδής ές	false	adj	[√]-ης
ψευδοδιδάσκαλος ου	false teacher	masc	[√]-[διδασκ]-ος
ψευδολόγος ου	liar	masc	[√]-[λεγ]-ος
≥10 ψεύδομαι	lie	vb	[√]-ω
ψευδομαρτυρέω	give false witness	vb	[√]-[μαρτυρ]-εω

ψευδομαρτυρία ας	false witness	fem	[√]-[μαρτυρ]-ια
ψευδόμαρτυς υρος	false witness	masc	[√]-[μαρτυρ]-ς
≥10 ψεῦδος ους	lie, imitation	neut	[√]-ς
ψεῦσμα ματος	lie, untruthfulness	neut	[√]-μα
≥10 ψεύστης ου	liar	masc	[√]-της

ἀσχημ αἰσχ
shame
50

Memory Aid: Sounds something like *ashamed*.

αἰσχροκερδής ές	greedy (>shameful gain)	adj	[√]-[κερδ]-ης
αἰσχροκερδῶς	greedily	adv	[√]-[κερδ]-ως
αἰσχρολογία ας	obscene speech	fem	[√]-[λεγ]-ια
αἰσχρός ά όν	disgraceful	adj	[√]-ρος
αἰσχρότης ητος	shameful behavior	fem	[√]-οτης
αἰσχύνη ης	shame, shameful thing	fem	[√]-η
αἰσχύνομαι	be ashamed	vb	[√]-υνω
ἀνεπαίσχυντος ον	unashamed	adj	ἀ-ἐπι-[√]-τος
ἀσχημονέω	act improperly	vb	[√]-εω
ἀσχημοσύνη ης	shameless act	fem	[√]-συνη
ἀσχήμων ον	unpresentable, shameful	adj	[√]-ων
≥10 ἐπαισχύνομαι	be ashamed	vb	ἐπι-[√]-υνω
≥10 καταισχύνω	put to shame	vb	κατα-[√]-υνω

δυ
clothe
50

Memory Aid: endue

ἀπεκδύομαι	disarm, discard	vb	ἀπο-ἐκ-[√]-ω
ἀπέκδυσις εως	putting off	fem	ἀπο-ἐκ-[√]-σις
ἐκδύω	strip	vb	ἐκ-[√]-ω
ἐνδιδύσκω	dress in	vb	ἐν-[√]-σκω
ἔνδυμα ματος	clothing	neut	ἐν-[√]-μα
ἔνδυσις εως	wearing	fem	ἐν-[√]-σις
≥25 ἐνδύω	clothe, wear (>endue)	vb	ἐν-[√]-ω
ἐπενδύομαι	put on	vb	ἐπι-ἐν-[√]-ω
ἐπενδύτης ου	outer garment	masc	ἐπι-ἐν-[√]-της

κοπ
work
50

Memory Aid: [Some people find it hard to *cope* at *work*.]

εὐκοπώτερος α ον	easier	adj	εὐ-[√]-τερος
κοπή ῆς	slaughter, defeat	fem	[√]-η
≥10 κοπιάω	work, grow tired	vb	[√]-αω
≥10 κόπος ου	work, trouble	masc	[√]-ος
προκοπή ῆς	progress	fem	προ-[√]-η
προκόπτω	advance, progress	vb	προ-[√]-ω

ὀφειλ
debt
50

Memory Aid:

| ὀφειλέτης ου | debtor, offender | masc | [√]-της |

ὀφειλή ῆς	debt	fem	[√]-η
ὀφείλημα ματος	debt	neut	[√]-μα
≥25 ὀφείλω	owe, ought	vb	[√]-ω
προσοφείλω	owe	vb	προς-[√]-ω
χρεοφειλέτης ου	debtor	masc	[χρ]-[√]-της

ἀγορ   49
market / place of business transactions
Memory Aid: agora, agoraphobia

≥10 ἀγορά ᾶς	market place	fem	[√]-α
≥25 ἀγοράζω	buy, redeem	vb	[√]-αζω
ἀγοραῖος ου	loafer, court session	masc	[√]-ιος
ἀλληγορέω	speak allegorically	vb	[ἀλλ]-[√]-εω
δημηγορέω	make a speech	vb	[δημ]-[√]-εω
ἐξαγοράζω	set free	vb	ἐκ-[√]-αζω

κρυπτ κρυφ   49
hide
Memory Aid: crypt, cryptic, cryptography, Apocrypha

ἀποκρύπτω	hide, keep secret	vb	ἀπο-[√]-ω
ἀπόκρυφος ον	hidden, secret	adj	ἀπο-[√]-ος
ἐγκρύπτω	place / mix / hide in	vb	ἐν-[√]-ω
κρύπτη ης	hidden place, cellar	fem	[√]-η
≥10 κρυπτός ή όν	hidden, secret	adj	[√]-ος
≥10 κρύπτω	hide, cover	vb	[√]-ω
κρυφαῖος α ον	hidden, secret	adj	[√]-ιος
κρυφῇ	secretly	adv	[√]-η
περικρύβω	keep in seclusion	vb	περι-[√]-ω

παυ   49
stop / rest
Memory Aid: pause, menopause, pose, repose

ἀκατάπαυστος ον	unceasing	adj	ἀ-κατα-[√]-τος
ἀνάπαυσις εως	relief, rest	fem	ἀνα-[√]-σις
≥10 ἀναπαύω	relieve, rest, refresh	vb	ἀνα-[√]-ω
ἐπαναπαύομαι	rest / rely upon	vb	ἐπι-ἀνα-[√]-ω
κατάπαυσις εως	place of rest, rest	fem	κατα-[√]-σις
καταπαύω	cause to rest, prevent	vb	κατα-[√]-ω
≥10 παύω	stop	vb	[√]-ω
συναναπαύομαι	have a time of rest with	vb	συν-ἀνα-[√]-ω

θηρ   48
wild animal
Memory Aid:

θήρα ας	trap	fem	[√]-α
θηρεύω	catch	vb	[√]-ευω
θηριομαχέω	fight wild beasts	vb	[√]-[μαχ]-εω
≥25 θηρίον ου	animal	neut	[√]-ιον

μειζ
greater
Memory Aid:

≥25 μείζων ον	greater	adj	[√]-ων

48

ὀργ
anger
Memory Aid: [*Ogres* are usually *angry*.]

≥25 ὀργή ῆς	anger, punishment	fem	[√]-η
ὀργίζομαι	be angry	vb	[√]-ιζω
ὀργίλος η ον	quick-tempered	adj	[√]-λος
παροργίζω	make angry	vb	παρα-[√]-ιζω
παροργισμός οῦ	anger	masc	παρα-[√]-μος

48

πεντ
five
Memory Aid: Pentecost, Pentagon, Pentateuch

πεντάκις	five times	adv	[√]-κις
πεντακισχίλιοι	five thousand	adj	[√]-κις-χιλιοι
πεντακόσιοι αι α	five hundred	adj	[√]-κοσιοι
≥25 πέντε	five	adj	
πεντεκαιδέκατος	fifteenth	adj	[√]-[και]-[δεκ]-τος
πεντήκοντα	fifty		[√]-κοντα

48

βιβλ
book
Memory Aid: Bible, bibliography, bibliotheca

βιβλαρίδιον ου	little book	neut	[√]-αριον
≥25 βιβλίον ου	book, scroll	neut	[√]-ιον
≥10 βίβλος ου	book, record	fem	[√]-ος

47

θεραπ
healing / service
Memory Aid: therapeutic, therapy, chemotherapy

θεραπεία ας	healing, house servants	fem	[√]-εια
≥25 θεραπεύω	heal, serve	vb	[√]-ευω
θεράπων οντος	servant	masc	[√]-ων

47

κλαι κλαυ
weep
Memory Aid:

≥25 κλαίω	weep	vb	[√]-ω
κλαυθμός οῦ	bitter crying	masc	[√]-μος

47

λυπ
pain
Memory Aid: lupus

ἀλυπότερος α ον	freed from pain / sorrow	adj	ἀ-[√]-τερος
≥25 λυπέω	pain, grieve, be sad	vb	[√]-εω
≥10 λύπη ης	pain, grief	fem	[√]-η

47

| περίλυπος ον | very sad | adj | περι-[√]-ος |
| συλλυπέομαι | feel sorry for | vb | συν-[√]-εω |

θερ θερμ   46
warm / harvest
Memory Aid: thermal, thermometer, thermos, hypothermia

≥10	θερίζω	harvest, gather	vb	[√]-ιζω
≥10	θερισμός οῦ	harvest, crop	masc	[√]-μος
	θεριστής οῦ	reaper	masc	[√]-ιστης
	θερμαίνομαι	warm oneself	vb	[√]-αινω
	θέρμη ης	heat	fem	[√]-η
	θέρος ους	summer	neut	[√]-ς

μικρ   46
small
Memory Aid: microscope, microfilm, micrometer

| ≥10 | μικρόν | a little while | adv | [√]-ον |
| ≥25 | μικρός ά όν | small, insignificant | adj | [√]-ρος |

θυρ   45
door
Memory Aid: [door: *see Grimm's Law*]

≥25	θύρα ας	door	fem	[√]-α
	θυρίς ίδος	window	fem	[√]-ς
	θυρωρός οῦ	doorkeeper	masc/fem	[√]-[ώρ]-ος

κλα   45
break
Memory Aid: iconoclastic

	ἐκκλάω	break off	vb	ἐκ-[√]-ω
	κατακλάω	break in pieces	vb	κατα-[√]-ω
≥10	κλάδος ου	branch	masc	[√]-ος
	κλάσις εως	breaking (of bread)	fem	[√]-σις
	κλάσμα ματος	fragment, piece	neut	[√]-μα
≥10	κλάω	break	vb	[√]-ω
	κλῆμα ματος	branch	neut	[√]-μα

να   45
temple
Memory Aid:

| ≥25 | ναός οῦ | temple | masc | [√]-ος |

νε νεο νεω νεα   45
new
Memory Aid: neophyte, new [French: *nouveau*]

	ἀνανεόω	renew, make new	vb	ἀνα-[√]-οω
	νεανίας ου	young man	masc	[√]-ας
≥10	νεανίσκος ου	young man	masc	[√]-ος
	νεομηνία ας	new moon	fem	[√]-[μην]-ια
≥10	νέος α ον	new, young	adj	[√]-ος
	νεότης ητος	youth	fem	[√]-οτης

| νεόφυτος ον | new convert (>neophyte) | masc | [√]-[φυσ]-τος |
| νεωτερικός ή όν | youthful | adj | [√]-τερος-ικος |

οὐαι
woe
45
Memory Aid:

| ≥25 οὐαί | woe | interj | |

φυ φυσ φυτ
natural / growth / planted
45
Memory Aid: physical, physics, physiology, neophyte

	ἐκφύω	sprout	vb	ἐκ-[√]-ω
	ἐμφυσάω	breathe on (>infuse)	vb	ἐν-[√]-αω
	ἔμφυτος ον	implanted, planted	adj	ἐν-[√]-τος
	συμφύομαι	grow up with	vb	συν-[√]-ω
	σύμφυτος ον	sharing in	adj	συν-[√]-τος
	φυσικός ή όν	natural	adj	[√]-ικος
	φυσικῶς	naturally	adv	[√]-ικως
	φυσιόω	make conceited	vb	[√]-οω
≥10	φύσις εως	nature	fem	[√]-σις
	φυσίωσις εως	conceit	fem	[√]-σις
	φυτεία ας	plant	fem	[√]-εια
≥10	φυτεύω	plant	vb	[√]-ευω
	φύω	grow	vb	[√]-ω

χρυσ
gold
45
Memory Aid: chrysanthemum, John Chrysostom

≥10	χρυσίον ου	gold	neut	[√]-ιον
	χρυσοδακτύλιος ον	wearing a gold ring	adj	[√]-(δάκτυλος)-ιος
	χρυσόλιθος ου	chrysolite	masc	[√]-[λιθ]-ος
	χρυσόπρασος ου	chrysoprase (gem)	masc	[√] ος
	χρυσός οῦ	gold	masc	[√]-ος
≥10	χρυσοῦς ῆ οῦν	golden	adj	[√]-ος
	χρυσόω	make golden	vb	[√]-οω

κλιν
recline / incline / turn
44
Memory Aid: incline, recline (as at dinner)

ἀκλινής ές	firm (not turned)	adj	ἀ-[√]-ης
ἀνακλίνω	seat at table, put to bed	vb	ἀνα-[√]-ω
ἀρχιτρίκλινος ου	head steward	masc	[ἀρχ]-[τρι]-[√]-ος
ἐκκλίνω	turn out / away	vb	ἐκ-[√]-ω
κατακλίνω	cause to recline, dine	vb	κατα-[√]-ω
κλινάριον ου	small bed	neut	[√]-αριον
κλίνη ης	bed	fem	[√]-η
κλινίδιον ου	bed	neut	[√]-ιον
κλίνω	lay, put to flight	vb	[√]-ω
κλισία ας	group	fem	[√]-ια

προσκλίνομαι	join	vb	προς-[√]-ω
πρόσκλισις εως	favoritism	fem	προς-[√]-σις
πρωτοκλισία ας	place of honor	fem	[προ]-[√]-ια

σκανδαλ   44
scandal
Memory Aid: scandal

≥25 σκανδαλίζω	scandalize	vb	[√]-ιζω
≥10 σκάνδαλον ου	scandal	neut	[√]-ον

φευγ φυγ   44
flee
Memory Aid: fugitive

ἀποφεύγω	escape	vb	ἀπο-[√]-ω
διαφεύγω	escape	vb	δια-[√]-ω
ἐκφεύγω	escape, flee	vb	ἐκ-[√]-ω
καταφεύγω	flee	vb	κατα-[√]-ω
≥25 φεύγω	flee	vb	[√]-ω
φυγή ῆς	flight	fem	[√]-η

ἁπτ   43
light / touch
Memory Aid:

ἀνάπτω	kindle	vb	ἀνα-[√]-ω
≥25 ἅπτω	kindle, ignite	vb	[√]-ω
καθάπτω	fasten on	vb	κατα-[√]-ω
περιάπτω	kindle	vb	περι-[√]-ω

ἀστρ ἀστηρ ἀστερ   43
star
Memory Aid: star, astronomy, asterisk

≥10 ἀστήρ έρος	star	masc	[√]-ρ
ἀστήρικτος ον	unsteady	adj	[√]-τος
ἀστραπή ῆς	lightning, ray	fem	[√]-η
ἀστράπτω	flash, dazzle	vb	[√]-ω
ἄστρον ου	star, constellation	neut	[√]-ον
ἐξαστράπτω	flash (like lightning)	vb	ἐκ-[√]-ω
περιαστράπτω	flash around	vb	περι-[√]-ω

δωρ   43
gift
Memory Aid: Dorothy

≥10 δωρεά ᾶς	gift	fem	[√]-α
δωρεάν	without cost	adv	
δωρέομαι	give	vb	[√]-εω
δώρημα ματος	gift	neut	[√]-μα
≥10 δῶρον ου	gift, offering	neut	[√]-ον

ἱκαν   43
able
Memory Aid: [Sounds like "*I can*" (i.e., I am *able*).]

≥25	ἱκανός ή όν	able, worthy	adj	[√]-ος
	ἱκανότης ητος	capability, capacity	fem	[√]-οτης
	ἱκανόω	make able, make fit	vb	[√]-οω

κοπτ   43
cut

Memory Aid: [The *Copts* were cut off from the Greeks.]

	ἀποκόπτω	cut off (midmasc castrate)	vb	ἀπο-[√]-ω
	ἀπρόσκοπος ον	blameless	adj	ἀ-προς-[√]-ος
	ἐγκοπή ῆς	obstacle (>cutting in)	fem	ἐν-[√]-η
	ἐγκόπτω	prevent (>cut in)	vb	ἐν-[√]-ω
≥10	ἐκκόπτω	cut off, remove	vb	ἐκ-[√]-ω
	κατακόπτω	cut badly, beat	vb	κατα-[√]-ω
	κόπτω	cut (midmasc mourn)	vb	[√]-ω
	προσκοπή ῆς	obstacle, offense	fem	προς-[√]-η
	προσκόπτω	stumble, be offended	vb	προς-[√]-ω

μισθ   43
pay

Memory Aid:

	ἀντιμισθία ας	recompense, punishment	fem	ἀντι-[√]-ια
	μισθαποδοσία ας	reward, punishment	fem	[√]-[πο[1]]-ια
	μισθαποδότης ου	rewarder	masc	[√]-[πο[1]]-της
	μίσθιος ου	hired man, laborer	masc	[√]-ιος
	μισθόομαι	hire (>make a payee)	vb	[√]-οω
≥25	μισθός οῦ	pay	masc	[√]-ος
	μίσθωμα ματος	expense, rent	neut	[√]-μα
	μισθωτός οῦ	hired man, laborer	masc	[√]-ος

ὀλιγ   43
little / few

Memory Aid: oligarchy

≥25	ὀλίγος η ον	little, few	adj	[√]-ος
	ὀλιγόψυχος ον	faint-hearted	adj	[√]-[ψυχ]-ος
	ὀλιγωρέω	think lightly of	vb	[√]-[ὠρ]-εω
	ὀλίγως	barely, just	adv	[√]-ως

ἀγρ   42
field / wild

Memory Aid: agriculture

	ἀγραυλέω	be out of doors	vb	[√]-[αὐλ]-εω
	ἀγρεύω	trap	vb	[√]-ευω
	ἀγριέλαιος ου	wild olive tree	fem	[√]-[ἐλαι]-ος
	ἄγριος α ον	wild	adj	[√]-ιος
≥25	ἀγρός οῦ	field, farm	masc	[√]-ος

ἐλευθερ   42
free

Memory Aid:

| | ἀπελεύθερος ου | freedman | masc | ἀπο-[√]-ος |

≥10 ἐλευθερία ας	freedom	fem	[√]-ια
≥10 ἐλεύθερος α ον	free	adj	[√]-ος
ἐλευθερόω	set / make free	vb	[√]-οω

ὀπισ   42
behind / after
Memory Aid:

ὄπισθεν	behind	cj/pt	[√]-θεν
≥25 ὀπίσω	behind, after	cj/pt	[√]-ω

ζηλ   41
zealous / jealous
Memory Aid: zeal, zealous

ζηλεύω	be zealous	vb	[√]-ευω
≥10 ζῆλος ου	zeal, jealousy	masc	[√]-ος
≥10 ζηλόω	be jealous	vb	[√]-οω
ζηλωτής οῦ	someone zealous	masc	[√]-της
παραζηλόω	make jealous	vb	παρα-[√]-οω

ἡλι   41
sun
Memory Aid: heliocentric, helium

ἡλικία ας	age, years	fem	[√]-ια
≥25 ἥλιος ου	sun	masc	[√]-ος
συνηλικιώτης ου	contemporary	masc	συν-[√]-ικος-της

μαχ   40
fight
Memory Aid: Sounds like *match*, as in *boxing match*.

ἄμαχος ον	peaceable	adj	ἀ-[√]-ος
διαμάχομαι	protest violently	vb	δια-[√]-ω
≥25 μάχαιρα ης	sword	fem	[√]-α
μάχη ης	fight	fem	[√]-η
μάχομαι	fight	vb	[√]-ω

προβατ   40
sheep
Memory Aid:

προβατικός ή όν	pertaining to sheep	adj	[√]-ικος
προβάτιον ου	lamb, sheep	neut	[√]-ιον
≥25 πρόβατον ου	sheep	neut	[√]-ον

ὑσ   40
last / lack
Memory Aid: hysteria

≥10 ὑστερέω	lack, need	vb	[√]-τερος-εω
ὑστέρημα ματος	what is lacking	neut	[√]-τερος-μα
υστέρησις εως	lack, need	fem	[√]-τερος σις
≥10 ὕστερον	later, afterwards, then	adv	[√]-τερον
ὕστερος α ον	later, last	adj	[√]-τερος

φυλ
tribe
Memory Aid: phylogeny, phylum [file]

	ἀλλόφυλος ον	foreign	adj	[ἀλλ]-[√]-ος
	δωδεκάφυλον ον	the Twelve Tribes	neut	[δεκ]-[√]-ον
	συμφυλέτης ου	fellow countryman	masc	συν-[√]-της
≥25	φυλή ῆς	tribe, nation	fem	[√]-η
	φύλλον ου	leaf	neut	[√]-ον

40

κτισ
create (Two of the consonantal sounds [k and t] are shared.)
Memory Aid:

≥10	κτίζω	create, make	vb	[√]-ω
≥10	κτίσις εως	creation	fem	[√]-σις
	κτίσμα ματος	creation	neut	[√]-μα
	κτίστης ου	creator	masc	[√]-της

39

μισ
hate
Memory Aid: misanthropy

≥25	μισέω	hate, be indifferent to	vb	[√]-εω

39

οἰν
wine
Memory Aid: Sounds something like *wine*.

	οἰνοπότης ου	drinker, drunkard	masc	[√]-[πο²]-της
≥25	οἶνος ου	wine	masc	[√]-ος
	οἰνοφλυγία ας	drunkenness	fem	[√]-(φλέω)-ια
	πάροινος ου	drunkard	masc	παρα-[√]-ος

39

παθ ποθ
feel / desire
Memory Aid: pathology, sympathy, pathetic, psychopath, pathos

	ἐπιποθέω	desire	vb	ἐπι-[√]-εω
	ἐπιπόθησις εως	longing	fem	ἐπι-[√]-σις
	ἐπιπόθητος ον	longed for	adj	ἐπι-[√]-τος
	ἐπιποθία ας	desire	fem	ἐπι-[√]-ια
	μετριοπαθέω	be gentle with	vb	[μετρ]-[√]-εω
≥10	πάθημα ματος	suffering, passion	neut	[√]-μα
	παθητός ή όν	subject to suffering	adj	[√]-τος
	πάθος ους	lust, passion	neut	[√]-ς
	συγκακοπαθέω	share in hardship	vb	συν-[κακ]-[√]-εω
	συμπαθέω	sympathize	vb	συν-[√]-εω
	συμπαθής ές	sympathetic	adj	συν-[√]-ης

39

ποιμ ποιμν
sheep
Memory Aid: [David wrote *poems* while tending *sheep*.]

≥10	ποιμαίνω	tend, rule	vb	[√]-αινω
≥10	ποιμήν ένος	shepherd	masc	[√]-ην

39

ποίμνη ης	flock	fem	[√]-η
ποίμνιον ου	flock	neut	[√]-ιον

σκην
tent
Memory Aid: scene, scenario

				39
	ἐπισκηνόω	rest upon, live in	vb	ἐπι-[√]-οω
	κατασκηνόω	nest, live, dwell	vb	κατα-[√]-οω
	κατασκήνωσις εως	nest	fem	κατα-[√]-σις
≥10	σκηνή ῆς	tent	fem	[√]-η
	σκηνοπηγία ας	Feast of Tabernacles	fem	[√]-(πήγνυμι)-ια
	σκηνοποιός οῦ	tent-maker	masc	[√]-[ποι]-ος
	σκῆνος ους	tent	neut	[√]-ς
	σκηνόω	live, dwell	vb	[√]-οω
	σκήνωμα ματος	body, dwelling place	neut	[√]-μα

ἀν²
up / again
Memory Aid: Anabaptist, anatomy, analysis, anabolism

				38
≥10	ἀνά (>*acc*)	up, each	prep	[√]-ἀνα
	ἄνω	above, up	adv	[√]-ω
≥10	ἄνωθεν	from above, again	adv	ἀνα-[√]-θεν
	ἀνωτερικός ή όν	upper, inland	adj	[√]-τερος-ικος
	ἀνώτερον	first, above	adj	[√]-τερον

ἐχθρ
enemy
Memory Aid:

				38
	ἔχθρα ας	hostility, hatred	fem	[√]-α
≥25	ἐχθρός ά όν	hated (*as noun:* enemy)	adj	[√]-ος

ἰα ἰατρ
heal
Memory Aid: psychiatric, psychiatry, pediatrics

				38
	ἴαμα ματος	healing	neut	[√]-μα
≥25	ἰάομαι	heal	vb	[√]-ω
	ἴασις εως	healing	fem	[√]-σις
	ἰατρός οῦ	physician, healer	masc	[√]-ος

πτωχ
poor
Memory Aid:

				38
	πτωχεία ας	poverty	fem	[√]-εια
	πτωχεύω	become poor	vb	[√]-ευω
≥25	πτωχός ή όν	poor	adj	[√]-ος

σκευ
prepare
Memory Aid:

				38
	ἀνασκευάζω	disturb	vb	ἀνα-[√]-αζω

ἀπαρασκεύαστος ον	unprepared	adj	ἀ-παρα-[√]-τος
ἐπισκευάζομαι	prepare, make ready	vb	ἐπι-[√]-αζω
κατασκευάζω	prepare, make ready	vb	κατα-[√]-αζω
παρασκευάζω	prepare, make ready	vb	παρα-[√]-αζω
παρασκευή ῆς	day of preparation	fem	παρα-[√]-η
σκευή ῆς	gear	fem	[√]-η
≥10 σκεῦος ους	thing, container	neut	[√]-ς

ταχ²
quick
Memory Aid: tachometer

≥10 ταχέως	quickly	adv	[√]-ως
ταχινός ή όν	soon, swift	adj	[√]-ινος
τάχιον	quickly	adv	[√]-ον
τάχιστα	as soon as possible	adv	[√]-ιστος
τάχος ους	speed	neut	[√]-ς
≥10 ταχύ	quickly	adv	
ταχύς εῖα ύ	quick	adj	[√]-ς

38

φον
murder
Memory Aid: [phoenix]

φονεύς έως	murderer	masc	[√]-ευς
≥10 φονεύω	murder, put to death	vb	[√]-ευω
≥10 φόνος ου	murder, killing	masc	[√]-ος

38

ἐπει
since
Memory Aid:

≥25 ἐπεί	since, because, as	cj/pt	
≥10 ἐπειδή	since, because, for, when	cj/pt	
ἐπειδήπερ	inasmuch as, since	cj/pt	[√]-περ

37

λατρ
worship
Memory Aid: idolatry, bibliolatry, mariolatry

εἰδωλολάτρης ου	idol worshipper	masc	[εἰδωλ]-[√]-ης
εἰδωλολατρία ας	idolatry	fem	[εἰδωλ]-[√]-ια
λατρεία ας	worship, service	fem	[√]-εια
≥10 λατρεύω	worship, serve	vb	[√]-ευω

37

σπευδ σπουδ
speed / eagerness
Memory Aid: Sounds something like *speed.*

σπεύδω	hurry	vb	[√]-ω
≥10 σπουδάζω	do one's best, work hard	vb	[√]-αζω
σπουδαῖος α ον	earnest	adj	[√]-ιος
σπουδαίως	eagerly	adv	[√]-ως
≥10 σπουδή ῆς	earnestness, zeal	fem	[√]-η

37

ἀναγκ **necessity**			36
Memory Aid:			
ἀναγκάζω	force (>make necessary)	vb	[√]-αζω
ἀναγκαῖος α ον	necessary, forced	adj	[√]-ιος
ἀναγκαστῶς	under compulsion	adv	[√]-ως
≥10 ἀνάγκη ης	necessity, distress	fem	[√]-η
ἐπάναγκες	necessarily	adv	ἐπι-[√]

ἀρτι **now**			36
Memory Aid:			
≥25 ἄρτι	now, at once	adv	

οὖς ὠτ **ear**			36
Memory Aid: otology			
≥25 οὖς ὠτός	ear	neut	[√]-ς

περα **far / end**			35
Memory Aid: [far: *see Grimm's Law*]			
ἀπέραντος ον	endless	adj	ἀ-[√]-τος
διαπεράω	cross, cross over	vb	δια-[√]-αω
περαιτέρω	further	adv	[√]-τερος-ω
≥10 πέραν	beyond, across	prep	
πέρας ατος	end, boundary	neut	[√]-ς

τρεφ τροφ **feed / support**			35
Memory Aid: atrophy: Sounds like *trough*—where animals *feed*.			
ἀνατρέφω	bring up, train	vb	ἀνα-[√]-ω
διατροφή ῆς	food	fem	δια-[√]-η
ἐκτρέφω	feed, raise	vb	ἐκ-[√]-ω
ἐντρέφομαι	live on, feed oneself on	vb	ἐν-[√]-ω
σύντροφος ου	close friend	masc	συν-[√]-ος
τρέφω	feed, support	vb	[√]-ω
≥10 τροφή ῆς	food, keep	fem	[√]-η
τροφός οῦ	nurse	fem	[√]-ος
τροφοφορέω	care for	vb	[√]-[φερ]-εω

ἀργυρ **money / silver**			34
Memory Aid: Argentina [Couples sometimes *argue* over *money*.]			
≥10 ἀργύριον ου	silver coin, money	neut	[√]-ιον
ἀργυροκόπος ου	silversmith	masc	[√]-[κοπ]-ος
ἄργυρος ου	silver, coin	masc	[√]-ος
ἀργυροῦς ᾶ οῦν	made of silver	adj	[√]-ους
ἀφιλάργυρος ον	not money-loving	adj	ἀ-[φιλ]-[√]-ος

| φιλαργυρία ας | love of money | fem | [φιλ]-[√]-ια |
| φιλάργυρος ον | money-loving | adj | [φιλ]-[√]-ος |

Ἑλλα Ἑλλην   34
Greek
Memory Aid: hellenistic

	Ἑλλάς άδος	Greece	fem	[√]-ς
≥25	Ἑλλην ηνος	Greek person, non-Jew	masc	[√]-ην
	Ἑλληνικός ή όν	hellenistic, Greek	adj	[√]-ικος
	Ἑλληνίς ίδος	Greek / Gentile woman	fem	[√]-ς
	Ἑλληνιστής οῦ	Hellenist	masc	[√]-της
	Ἑλληνιστί	in the Greek language	adv	

μελ²   34
part
Memory Aid: melody [*melee:* confused mixture of *parts*]

| ≥25 | μέλος ους | part, member | neut | [√]-ς |

ναι   34
yes
Memory Aid:

| ≥25 | ναί | yes | cj/pt | |

νικ   34
victory
Memory Aid: Nike

≥25	νικάω	conquer	vb	[√]-αω
	νίκη ης	victory	fem	[√]-η
	νῖκος ους	victory	neut	[√]-ς
	ὑπερνικάω	be completely victorious	vb	ὑπερ-[√]-αω

ταπειν   34
humble (compare πειν)
Memory Aid:

	ταπεινός ή όν	humble, poor	adj	[√]-ινος
	ταπεινοφροσύνη ης	(false) humility	fem	[√]-[φρ]-συνη
	ταπεινόφρων ον	humble	adj	[√]-[φρ]-ων
≥10	ταπεινόω	make humble	vb	[√]-οω
	ταπείνωσις εως	humble state	fem	[√]-σις

χιλι   34
thousand
Memory Aid: chiliasm

| ≥10 | χιλιάς άδος | a thousand | fem | [√]-ς |
| ≥10 | χίλιοι αι α | thousand | adj | [√]-οι |

ἀμπελ   33
grapevine
Memory Aid: [Jesus made *ample wine* for the wedding.]

	ἄμπελος ου	grapevine	fem	[√]-ος
	ἀμπελουργός οῦ	vinedresser, gardener	masc	[√]-[ἐργ]-ος
≥25	ἀμπελών ῶνος	vineyard	masc	[√]-ων

εἰδωλ
image / idol
   Memory Aid: idol, idolatry

εἰδωλεῖον ου	idol's temple	neut	[√]-ειον
εἰδωλόθυτον ου	idol-meat	neut	[√]-[θυ]-τον
εἰδωλολάτρης ου	idolater	masc	[√]-[λατρ]-ης
εἰδωλολατρία ας	idolatry	fem	[√]-[λατρ]-ια
≥10 εἴδωλον ου	idol, image	neut	[√]-ον
κατείδωλος ον	full of idols	adj	κατα-[√]-λος

33

παλαι
old
   Memory Aid: paleontology, paleolithic

ἔκπαλαι	for a long time	adv	ἐκ-[√]
πάλαι	long ago, formerly	adv	
≥10 παλαιός ά όν	old, former	adj	[√]-ιος
παλαιότης ητος	age	fem	[√]-οτης
παλαιόω	make old	vb	[√]-οω

33

τρεχ τροχ
run
   Memory Aid: track, trek

εἰστρέχω	run in	vb	εἰς-[√]-ω
ἐπισυντρέχω	gather rapidly, close in	vb	ἐπι-συν-[√]-ω
κατατρέχω	run down	vb	κατα-[√]-ω
περιτρέχω	run about	vb	περι-[√]-ω
προστρέχω	run up (to someone)	vb	προς-[√]-ω
προτρέχω	run on ahead	vb	προ-[√]-ω
συντρέχω	run together, join with	vb	συν-[√]-ω
≥10 τρέχω	run	vb	[√]-ω
τροχιά ᾶς	path	fem	[√]-ια
τροχός οῦ	wheel, cycle	masc	[√]-ος
ὑποτρέχω	run under the shelter of	vb	ὑπο-[√]-ω

33

ἀνεμ
wind
   Memory Aid: anemometer, animate

ἀνεμίζομαι	be driven by wind	vb	[√]-ιζω
≥25 ἄνεμος ου	wind	masc	[√]-ος

32

κλεπτ κλοπ κλεμ
steal
   Memory Aid: kleptomaniac

κλέμμα ματος	theft	neut	[√]-μα
≥10 κλέπτης ου	thief	masc	[√]-της
≥10 κλέπτω	steal	vb	[√]-ω
κλοπή ῆς	theft	fem	[√]-η

32

ξεν
strange / guest
   Memory Aid: xenophobia

32

ξενία ας	place of lodging, room	fem	[√]-ια
≥10 ξενίζω	entertain strangers	vb	[√]-ιζω
ξενοδοξέω	be hospitable	vb	[√]-[δεχ]-εω
≥10 ξένος η ον	strange, foreign	adj	[√]-ος
φιλοξενία ας	hospitality	fem	[φιλ]-[√]-ια
φιλόξενος ον	hospitable	adj	[φιλ]-[√]-ος

σφραγι
seal *32*
Memory Aid:

κατασφραγίζω	seal	vb	κατα-[√]-ιζω
≥10 σφραγίζω	seal, acknowledge	vb	[√]-ιζω
≥10 σφραγίς ῖδος	seal, evidence	fem	[√]-ς

αὐρ
tomorrow *31*
Memory Aid: aurora borealis

| ≥10 αὔριον | tomorrow, soon | adv | [√]-ιον |
| ≥10 ἐπαύριον | next day | adv | ἐπι-[√]-ιον |

γε²
particle adding emphasis *31*
Memory Aid: Slang *gee!* is used to add emphasis in English.

| ≥25 γέ | (used to add emphasis) | cj/pt | |

κλει
lock / close *31*
Memory Aid: Note *cl* in words *close* and *exclude*.

ἀποκλείω	lock, close	vb	ἀπο-[√]-ω
ἐκκλείω	exclude (>lock out)	vb	ἐκ-[√]-ω
κατακλείω	lock up (in prison)	vb	κατα-[√]-ω
κλείς κλειδός	key	fem	[√]-ς
≥10 κλείω	lock, shut, close	vb	[√]-ω
συγκλείω	make / keep a prisoner	vb	συν-[√]-ω

πλην
but *31*
Memory Aid:

| ≥25 πλήν | but, nevertheless | cj/pt | |

σκοπ σκεπ
view *31*
Memory Aid: scope, stethoscope, periscope, skeptic

ἀλλοτριεπίσκοπος	busybody	masc	[ἀλλ]-ἐπι-[√]-ος
≥10 ἐπισκέπτομαι	visit, care for	vb	ἐπι-[√]-ω
ἐπισκοπέω	see to it, take care	vb	ἐπι-[√]-εω
ἐπισκοπή ῆς	visitation, episcopate	fem	ἐπι-[√]-η
ἐπίσκοπος ου	overseer, bishop	masc	ἐπι-[√]-ος
κατασκοπέω	spy on	vb	κατα-[√]-εω
κατάσκοπος ου	spy	masc	κατα-[√]-ος

| σκοπέω | pay attention to | vb | [√]-εω |
| σκοπός οῦ | goal | masc | [√]-ος |

στερε στηρε — 31
firm / solid

Memory Aid: stereotype, cholesterol, steroids

ἀποστερέω	defraud, deny	vb	ἀπο-[√]-εω
ἐπιστηρίζω	strengthen	vb	ἐπι-[√]-ιζω
στερεός ά όν	firm, solid	adj	[√]-ος
στερεόω	make strong	vb	[√]-οω
στερέωμα ματος	firmness	neut	[√]-μα
στηριγμός οῦ	firm footing	masc	[√]-μος
≥10 στηρίζω	strengthen	vb	[√]-ιζω

τεν τειν τιν¹ τον — 31
extend / stretch

Memory Aid: extend, tension, tone, intonation, catatonic, intense

≥10 ἐκτείνω	stretch out, extend	vb	ἐκ-[√]-ω
ἐκτένεια ας	earnestness	fem	ἐκ-[√]-εια
ἐκτενέστερον	more earnestly	adv	ἐκ-[√]-τερον
ἐκτενής ές	constant, unfailing	adj	ἐκ-[√]-ης
ἐκτενῶς	earnestly, constantly	adv	ἐκ-[√]-ως
ἐκτινάσσω	shake off	vb	ἐκ-[√]-σσω
ἐπεκτείνομαι	stretch toward	vb	ἐπι-ἐκ-[√]-ω
παρατείνω	prolong	vb	παρα-[√]-ω
προτείνω	tie up	vb	προ-[√]-ω
ὑπερεκτείνω	go beyond	vb	ὑπερ-ἐκ-[√]-ω
χειροτονέω	appoint, choose	vb	[χειρ]-[√]-εω

χορτ — 31
food

Memory Aid:

≥10 χορτάζω	feed, satisfy	vb	[√]-αζω
χόρτασμα ματος	food	neut	[√]-μα
≥10 χόρτος ου	grass, vegetation	masc	[√]-ος

αἰν — 30
praise

Memory Aid: paean

αἴνεσις εως	praise	fem	[√]-σις
αἰνέω	praise	vb	[√]-εω
αἶνος ου	praise	masc	[√]-ος
ἐπαινέω	praise, commend	vb	ἐπι-[√]-εω
≥10 ἔπαινος ου	praise, approval	masc	ἐπι-[√]-ος
παραινέω	advise	vb	παρα-[√]-εω

ἁρπ ἁρπαγ — 30
seize

Memory Aid: [harpoon]

| ἁρπαγή ῆς | greed, seizure | fem | [√]-η |

ἁρπαγμός οῦ	booty, prize	masc	[√]-μος
≥10 ἁρπάζω	seize	vb	[√]-αζω
ἅρπαξ αγος	robber (one who seizes)	masc	[√]-ξ
διαρπάζω	plunder	vb	δια-[√]-αζω
συναρπάζω	seize, drag	vb	συν-[√]-αζω

θυγατηρ θυγατρ
daughter
    Memory Aid: [daughter: *see Grimm's Law*]

30

≥25 θυγάτηρ τρός	daughter, woman	fem	[√]-ρ
θυγάτριον ου	little daughter	neut	[√]-ιον

λαμπ
lamp
    Memory Aid: lamp

30

ἐκλάμπω	shine (out)	vb	ἐκ-[√]-ω
λαμπάς άδος	lamp	fem	[√]-ς
λαμπρός ά όν	bright, fine	adj	[√]-ρος
λαμπρότης ητος	brightness	fem	[√]-οτης
λαμπρῶς	splendidly	adv	[√]-ως
λάμπω	shine	vb	[√]-ω
περιλάμπω	shine around	vb	περι-[√]-ω

μετρ
measure
    Memory Aid: meter, odometer

30

ἄμετρος ον	immeasurable	adj	ἀ-[√]-ος
ἀντιμετρέω	measure out in return	vb	ἀντι-[√]-εω
≥10 μετρέω	measure, give	vb	[√]-εω
μετρητής οῦ	measure	masc	[√]-της
μετρίως	greatly	adv	[√]-ως
≥10 μέτρον ου	measure, quantity	neut	[√]-ον

πω
yet
    Memory Aid:

30

οὐδέπω	not yet	adv	[οὐ]-[δέ]-[√]
≥25 οὔπω	not yet	adv	[οὐ]-[√]

συνειδη
conscience
    Memory Aid:

30

≥25 συνείδησις εως	conscience	fem	[√]-σις

βαστ
carry / bear
    Memory Aid: Note common letters in *basket:* b-a-s-(k-e)-t

29

ἀδυσβάστακτος ον	not difficult to bear	adj	ἀ-δυσ-[√]-τος
≥25 βαστάζω	carry, bear	vb	[√]-αζω
δυσβάστακτος ον	difficult to bear	adj	δυσ-[√]-τος

βρω
food
Memory Aid: ambrosia [German: *brot*, meaning *bread* or *food*.]

≥10 βρῶμα ματος	food	neut	[√]-μα
βρώσιμος ον	edible	adj	[√]-ιμος
≥10 βρῶσις εως	food, eating	fem	[√]-σις

29

δημ δομ
people / home
Memory Aid: demographics, democracy, epidemic, demagogue

ἀποδημέω	leave home, go away	vb	ἀπο-[√]-εω
ἀπόδημος ον	away from home	adj	ἀπο-[√]-ος
δῆμος ου	people, crowd	masc	[√]-ος
δημόσιος α ον	public	adj	[√]-ιος
ἐκδημέω	leave home	vb	ἐκ-[√]-εω
ἐνδημέω	be at home, be present	vb	ἐν-[√]-εω
ἐπιδημέω	visit, live	vb	ἐπι-[√]-εω
παρεπίδημος ου	refugee	masc	παρα-ἐπι-[√]-ος
συνέκδημος ου	travelling companion	masc	συν-ἐκ-[√]-ος
συνοικοδομέω	build together	vb	συν-ὀικ-[√]-εω

29

μοιχ
adultery
Memory Aid:

μοιχαλίς ίδος	adulteress	fem	[√]-ς
μοιχάομαι	commit adultery	vb	[√]-αω
μοιχεία ας	adultery	fem	[√]-εια
≥10 μοιχεύω	commit adultery	vb	[√]-ευω
μοιχός οῦ	adulterer	masc	[√]-ος

29

ἥκ
be present
Memory Aid:

ἀνήκει	it is proper	vb	ἀνα-[√]-ω
≥25 ἥκω	have come, be present	vb	[√]-ω

28

κωμ
town
Memory Aid: community, common, commerce, communal

≥25 κώμη ης	small town	fem	[√]-η
κωμόπολις εως	town	fem	[√]-[πολ]-ς

28

μελ[1]
concern / care
Memory Aid: melodramatic

ἀμελέω	disregard, neglect	vb	ἀ-[√]-εω
ἀμεταμέλητος ον	free from care	adj	ἀ-μετα-[√]-τος
ἐπιμέλεια ας	care, attention	fem	ἐπι-[√]-εια
ἐπιμελέομαι	take care of	vb	ἐπι-[√]-εω
ἐπιμελῶς	carefully	adv	ἐπι-[√]-ως

28

≥10 μέλει	it concerns (impersonal)	vb	[√]-ω	
μεταμέλομαι	regret	vb	μετα-[√]-ω	
προμελετάω	prepare ahead of time	vb	προ-[√]-αω	

μεριμν
worry   28
  Memory Aid:
ἀμέριμνος ον	free from worry	adj	ἀ-[√]-ος	
μέριμνα ης	worry, care	fem	[√]-α	
≥10 μεριμνάω	worry	vb	[√]-αω	
προμεριμνάω	worry beforehand	vb	προ-[√]-αω	

νυμφ
bride   28
  Memory Aid: nymph, nuptial
νύμφη ης	bride, daughter-in-law	fem	[√]-η	
≥10 νυμφίος ου	groom	masc	[√]-ιος	
νυμφών ῶνος	wedding hall	neut	[√]-ων	

πυλ
gate / door   28
  Memory Aid: Thermopylae: [One *pulls* a *gate* or *door*.]
≥10 πύλη ης	gate, door	fem	[√]-η	
≥10 πυλών ῶνος	gate, entrance, porch	masc	[√]-ων	

ἐλαι
olive / oil   27
  Memory Aid: oil, petroleum, linoleum
≥10 ἐλαία ας	olive, olive tree	fem	[√]-α	
≥10 ἔλαιον ου	olive oil, oil	neut	[√]-ον	
ἐλαιών ῶνος	olive orchard	masc	[√]-ων	
καλλιέλαιος ου	cultivated olive tree	fem	[καλ[1]]-[√]-ος	

μυστηρ
mystery   27
  Memory Aid: mystery
≥25 μυστήριον ου	secret, mystery	neut	[√]-ιον	

νηστ
hunger   27
  Memory Aid: [Young birds in a *nest* are *hungry*.]
νηστεία ας	hunger, fasting	fem	[√]-εια	
≥10 νηστεύω	fast	vb	[√]-ευω	
νῆστις ιδος	hungry	masc/fem	[√]-ς	

σει
quake   27
  Memory Aid: seismic, seismograph
ἀνασείω	incite, stir up	vb	ἀνα-[√]-ω	
διασείω	take money by force	vb	δια-[√]-ω	
ἐπισείω	urge on, stir up	vb	ἐπι-[√]-ω	

κατασείω	move, make a sign	vb	κατα-[√]-ω
≥10 σεισμός οῦ	earthquake, storm	masc	[√]-μος
σείω	shake, excite	vb	[√]-ω

αὐξ
grow
26

Memory Aid: auction, auxiliary

≥10 αὐξάνω	grow / increase	vb	[√]-ανω
αὔξησις εως	growth	fem	[√]-σις
συναυξάνομαι	grow together	vb	συν-[√]-ανω
ὑπεραυξάνω	grow abundantly	vb	ὑπερ-[√]-ανω

βαρ
burden / weight
26

Memory Aid: baritone, barium, barometer, burden

ἀβαρής ές	burdenless	adj	ἀ-[√]-ης
βαρέω	burden, overcome	vb	[√]-εω
βαρέως	with difficulty	adv	[√]-ως
βάρος ους	burden, weight	neut	[√]-ς
βαρύς εῖα ύ	heavy, weighty, hard	adj	[√]-υς
ἐπιβαρέω	be a burden	vb	ἐπι-[√]-εω
καταβαρέω	be a burden to	vb	κατα-[√]-εω
καταβαρύνομαι	be very heavy	vb	κατα-[√]-υνω

ἐνεκ
because of
26

Memory Aid:

| ≥25 ἕνεκα (*gen*) | because of | prep | |

ἑορτ
feast
26

Memory Aid:

| ἑορτάζω | observe a festival | vb | [√]-αζω |
| ≥25 ἑορτή ῆς | festival, feast | fem | [√]-η |

ζυμ
yeast
26

Memory Aid: enzyme, zymogenic

ἄζυμος ον	without yeast	adj	ἀ-[√]-ος
≥10 ζύμη ης	yeast	fem	[√]-η
ζυμόω	make / cause to rise	vb	[√]-οω

θησαυρ
treasure
26

Memory Aid: thesaurus

ἀποθησαυρίζω	acquire as a treasure	vb	ἀπο-[√]-ιζω
θησαυρίζω	save, store up	vb	[√]-ιζω
≥10 θησαυρός οῦ	treasure, storeroom	masc	[√]-ος

κελευ
command
26

Memory Aid:

	κέλευσμα ματος	command	neut	[√]-μα
≥25	κελεύω	command	vb	[√]-ω

λευκ
white
Memory Aid: leukemia

	λευκαίνω	make white	vb	[√]-αινω
≥10	λευκός ή όν	white, shining	adj	[√]-ος

26

λυχν
lamp
Memory Aid: lux [*lucent*]

≥10	λυχνία ας	lampstand	fem	[√]-ια
≥10	λύχνος ου	lamp	masc	[√]-ος

26

νεφ
cloud
Memory Aid:

≥25	νεφέλη ης	cloud	fem	[√]-η
	νέφος ους	cloud	neut	[√]-ς

26

ὀμ ὀμν
swear
Memory Aid:

≥25	ὀμνύω	swear, vow	vb	[√]-ω

26

πληγ πλασσ πλησσ
plague / strike
Memory Aid: plague, paraplegic, apoplexy

	ἐκπλήσσομαι	be amazed	vb	ἐκ-[√]-ω
	ἐπιπλήσσω	reprimand	vb	ἐπι-[√]-σσω
≥10	πληγή ῆς	plague, blow	fem	[√]-η
	πλήκτης ου	violent person	masc	[√]-της
	πλήσσω	strike	vb	[√]-σσω

26

χηρ
widow
Memory Aid: [*Widows* often needed *charity* in the early church.]

≥25	χήρα ας	widow	fem	[√]-α

26

ὠφελ ὀφελ
gain
Memory Aid:

	ἀνωφελής ές	useless	adj	ἀ-[√]-ης
	ὄφελος ους	gain, benefit	neut	[√]-ς
	ὠφέλεια ας	advantage, benefit	fem	[√]-εια
≥10	ὠφελέω	gain, help	vb	[√]-εω
	ὠφέλιμος ον	valuable, beneficial	adj	[√]-ιμος

26

βο βοηθ
shout
Memory Aid: [A person sometimes *shouts boo!*]

	ἀναβοάω	cry out	vb	ἀνα-[√]-αω

25

≥10 βοάω	call, shout	vb	[√]-αω
βοή ῆς	shout, outcry	fem	[√]-η
βοήθεια ας	help, aid	fem	[√]-εια
βοηθέω	help	vb	[√]-εω
βοηθός οῦ	helper	masc	[√]-ος

δενδρ   25
tree
Memory Aid: rhododendron

| ≥25 δένδρον ου | tree | neut | [√]-ον |

κωλυ   25
hinder
Memory Aid:

ἀκωλύτως	unhindered	adv	ἀ-[√]-ως
διακωλύω	prevent	vb	δια-[√]-ω
≥10 κωλύω	hinder	vb	[√]-ω

πολεμ   25
war
Memory Aid: polemic

| πολεμέω | fight, be at war | vb | [√]-εω |
| ≥10 πόλεμος | war, conflict, polemic | masc | [√]-ος |

σπλαγχν   25
pity
Memory Aid:

εὔσπλαγχνος ον	kind	adj	εὐ-[√]-ος
≥10 σπλαγχνίζομαι	have pity	vb	[√]-ιζω
≥10 σπλάγχνον ου	compassion, feeling	neut	[√]-ον

τελων   25
tax
Memory Aid: toll

ἀρχιτελώνης ου	tax superintendent	masc	[ἀρχ]-[√]-ης
≥10 τελώνης ου	tax-collector	masc	[√]-ης
τελώνιον ου	tax (office)	neut	[√]-ιον

γυμν   24
exercise / naked (sports were done in the nude by the Greeks)
Memory Aid: gymnastics, gym

γυμνάζω	train, discipline, exercise	vb	[√]-αζω
γυμνασία ας	training	fem	[√]-ια
γυμνιτεύω	be dressed in rags	vb	[√]-ευω
≥10 γυμνός ή όν	naked	adj	[√]-ος
γυμνότης ητος	nakedness, poverty	fem	[√]-οτης

ἐξ   24
six
Memory Aid: hexameter, hex key, six

| ≥10 ἕξ | six | adj | |
| ἑξακόσιοι αι α | six hundred | adj | [√]-κοσοι |

ἑξήκοντα	sixty	adj	[√]-κοντα

κενο
empty 24
Memory Aid: cenotaph, kenosis

≥10	κενός ή όν	empty, senseless	adj	[√]-ος
	κενόω	make empty / powerless	vb	[√]-οω
	κενῶς	in vain	adv	[√]-ως

πειν
hunger (compare ταπειν) 24
Memory Aid: hunger *pains*

≥10	πεινάω	be hungry	vb	[√]-αω
	πρόσπεινος ον	hungry	adj	προς-[√]-ος

σαλπ
trumpet 24
Memory Aid:

≥10	σάλπιγξ ιγγος	trumpet	fem	[√]-ξ
≥10	σαλπίζω	sound a trumpet	vb	[√]-ιζω
	σαλπιστής οῦ	trumpeter	masc	[√]-ιστης

τυγχ τυχ
obtain 24
Memory Aid: [A groom *obtains* a *tux* for his wedding.]

	ἐντυγχάνω	intercede, plead, appeal	vb	ἐν-[√]-ανω
	ἐπιτυγχάνω	obtain	vb	ἐπι-[√]-ανω
	παρατυγχάνω	happen to be present	vb	παρα-[√]-ανω
	συντυγχάνω	reach	vb	συν-[√]-ανω
≥10	τυγχάνω	obtain	vb	[√]-ανω
	ὑπερεντυγχάνω	intercede	vb	ὑπερ-ἐν-[√]-ανω

ἀριθμ
number 23
Memory Aid: arithmetic

	ἀναρίθμητος ον	innumerable	adj	ἀ-[√]-τος
	ἀριθμέω	number, count	vb	[√]-εω
≥10	ἀριθμός οῦ	number, total	masc	[√]-ος
	καταριθμέω	number	vb	κατα-[√]-εω

γεμ γομ
full 23
Memory Aid:

	γεμίζω	fill	vb	[√]-ιζω
≥10	γέμω	be full	vb	[√]-ω
	γόμος ου	cargo	masc	[√]-ος

κοιλ
stomach 23
Memory Aid:

≥10	κοιλία ας	stomach, appetite	fem	[√]-ια

ξηρ
dry
Memory Aid: xerox

≥10 ξηραίνω	dry up	vb	[√]-αινω
ξηρός ά όν	dry, withered	adj	[√]-ος

23

ὀψ
late
Memory Aid: [Letters "P.S." — used to add ideas too *late* for main text.]

ὀψέ	late in the day, after	adv/prep	
≥10 ὀψία ας	evening	fem	[√]-ια
ὄψιμος ου	late rain, spring rain	masc	[√]-ος
ὀψώνιον ου	pay (>given late in day)	neut	[√]-ιον

23

σιτ
food / fat
Memory Aid: parasite

ἀσιτία ας	lack of appetite	fem	ἀ-[√]-ια
ἄσιτος ον	without food	adj	ἀ-[√]-ος
ἐπιστιτισμός οῦ	food	masc	ἐπι-[√]-μος
σιτευτός ή όν	fattened	adj	[√]-τος
σιτίον ου	grain / food (*pl*)	neut	[√]-ιον
σιτιστός ή όν	fattened	adj	[√]-ιστος
σιτομέτριον ου	ration (>measured food)	neut	[√]-[μετρ]-ιον
≥10 σῖτος ου	grain	masc	[√]-ος

23

ὑγι
health
Memory Aid: hygiene

≥10 ὑγιαίνω	be healthy, be sound	vb	[√]-αινω
≥10 ὑγιής ές	healthy, whole	adj	[√]-ης

23

ὑπηρετ
serve
Memory Aid: Sounds something like *helper*.

ὑπηρετέω	serve	vb	ὑπο-[√]-εω
≥10 ὑπηρέτης ου	attendant, helper	masc	ὑπο-[√]-της

23

χε χυ
pour
Memory Aid:

ἀνάχυσις εως	flood, excess	fem	ἀνα-[√]-σις
≥10 ἐκχέω	pour out, shed	vb	ἐκ-[√]-ω
ἐπιχέω	pour on	vb	ἐπι-[√]-ω
καταχέω	pour over	vb	κατα-[√]-ω
συγχέω	confound	vb	συν-[√]-ω
σύγχυσις εως	confusion	fem	συν-[√]-σις
ὑπερεκχύννομαι	run over	vb	ὑπερ-ἐκ-[√]-υννω

23

αὐλ
flute / courtyard
Memory Aid:

αὐλέω	play a flute	vb	[√]-εω
≥10 αὐλή ῆς	courtyard, house	fem	[√]-η
αὐλητής οῦ	flute player	masc	[√]-της
αὐλίζομαι	spend the night	vb	[√]-ιζω
αὐλός οῦ	flute	masc	[√]-ος
ἔπαυλις εως	house (>on the court)	fem	ἐπι-[√]-ς
προαύλιον ου	gateway, forecourt	neut	προ-[√]-ιον

22

εὐδ
sleep
Memory Aid:

≥10 καθεύδω	sleep	vb	κατα-[√]-ω

22

ζων
fasten / bind
Memory Aid: zone

ἀναζώννυμι	bind up	vb	ἀνα-[√]-μι
διαζώννυμι	wrap around	vb	δια-[√]-μι
ζώνη ης	belt	fem	[√]-η
ζώννυμι	fasten	vb	[√]-μι
περιζώννυμι	wrap around	vb	περι-[√]-μι
ὑποζώννυμι	strengthen, brace	vb	ὑπο-[√]-μι

22

θεμελι
foundation
Memory Aid: theme

θεμέλιον ου	foundation	neut	[√]-ον
≥10 θεμέλιος ου	foundation	masc	[√]-ος
θεμελιόω	establish (>make firm)	vb	[√]-οω

22

ἰχθυ
fish
Memory Aid: ΙΧΘΥΣ (early Christian acronym for Jesus)

ἰχθύδιον ου	small fish, fish	neut	[√]-ιον
≥10 ἰχθύς ύος	fish	masc	[√]-ς

22

μωρ
foolish
Memory Aid: moron, sophomore

μωραίνω	make foolish	vb	[√]-αινω
μωρία ας	foolishness	fem	[√]-ια
μωρολογία ας	foolish talk	fem	[√]-[λεγ]-ια
≥10 μωρός ά όν	foolish	adj	[√]-ρος

22

ξυλ
wood
Memory Aid: xylophone

22

| | ξύλινος η ον | wooden | adj | [√]-ινος |
| ≥10 | ξύλον ου | wood, tree, club | neut | [√]-ον |

πωλ   22
sell
Memory Aid: monopoly

| ≥10 | πωλέω | sell | vb | [√]-εω |

ῥιζ   22
root
Memory Aid: licorice

	ἐκριζόω	uproot (>make rootless)	vb	ἐκ-[√]-οω
≥10	ῥίζα ης	root, descendant, source	fem	[√]-α
	ῥιζόομαι	be firmly rooted	vb	[√]-οω

σι σιγ   22
silence
Memory Aid: Same initial syllable: *si.*

≥10	σιγάω	keep silent	vb	[√]-αω
	σιγή ῆς	silence	fem	[√]-η
≥10	σιωπάω	be silent	vb	[√]-αω

συκ   22
fig
Memory Aid: sycamore

	συκάμινος ου	mulberry tree	fem	[√]-ος
≥10	συκῆ ῆς	fig tree	fem	[√]-η
	συκομορέα ας	sycamore tree	fem	[√]-(μόρον)α
	σῦκον ου	fig	neut	[√]-ον

ταρασσ ταραχ   22
trouble
Memory Aid: Sounds something like harass (i.e., *trouble*).

	διαταράσσομαι	be deeply troubled	vb	δια-[√]-σσω
	ἐκταράσσω	stir up trouble	vb	ἐκ-[√]-σσω
≥10	ταράσσω	trouble, disturb	vb	[√]-σσω
	ταραχή ῆς	disturbance, trouble	fem	[√]-η
	τάραχος ου	confusion	masc	[√]-ος

ἁλ ἁλι   21
salt / fish
Memory Aid: halite, halibut

	ἅλας ατος	salt	neut	[√]-ς
	ἁλιεύς έως	fisherman	masc	[√]-ευς
	ἁλιεύω	fish	vb	[√]-ευω
	ἁλίζω	salt	vb	[√]-ιζω
	ἅλς ἁλός	salt	neut	[√]-ς
	ἁλυκός ή όν	salty	adj	[√]-ος
	ἄναλος ον	without salt	adj	ἀ-[√]-ος
	ἐνάλιον ου	sea creature	neut	ἐν-[√]-ιον
	παράλιος ου	coastal district	fem	παρα-[√]-ιος

ἀρεσκ ἀρεστ
please

21

Memory Aid: [Most people are *pleased* to take *a rest*.]

ἀνθρωπάρεσκος ον	people-pleasing	adj	[√]-ος
ἀρεσκεία ας	desire to please	fem	[√]-εια
ἀρέσκω	(try to) please	vb	[√]-σκω
ἀρεστός ή όν	pleasing	adj	[√]-τος
εὐαρεστέω	please, be pleasing to	vb	εὐ-[√]-εω
εὐάρεστος ον	pleasing	adj	εὐ-[√]-τος
εὐαρέστως	pleasingly	adv	εὐ-[√]-ως

βασαν
torture

21

Memory Aid:

≥10 βασανίζω	torment, disturb	vb	[√]-ιζω
βασανισμός οῦ	torture	masc	[√]-ισμος
βασανιστής οῦ	torturer, jailer	masc	[√]-ιστης
βάσανος ου	torment, pain	fem	[√]-ος

βεβαι βεβαιο
reliable / firm

21

Memory Aid:

βέβαιος α ον	reliable, firm	adj	[√]-ιος
βεβαιόω	confirm (>make firm)	vb	[√]-οω
βεβαίωσις εως	confirmation	fem	[√]-σις
διαβεβαιόομαι	speak confidently	vb	δια-[√]-οω

δευ
place to / hither

21

Memory Aid:

δεῦρο	hither (place to)	adv	
≥10 δεῦτε	come hither (place to)	vb	

νιπτ
wash

21

Memory Aid:

ἄνιπτος ον	not (ritually) washed	adj	ἀ-[√]-ος
ἀπονίπτω	wash	vb	ἀπο-[√]-ω
νιπτήρ ῆρος	washbasin	masc	[√]-ρ
≥10 νίπτω	wash	vb	[√]-ω

ὀρκ
oath

21

Memory Aid: exorcism

ἐνορκίζω	place under oath	vb	ἐν-[√]-ιζω
ἐξορκίζω	place under oath	vb	ἐκ-[√]-ιζω
ἐξορκιστής ου	exorcist	masc	ἐκ-[√]-της
ἐπιορκέω	break an oath	vb	ἐπι-[√]-εω

ἐπίορκος ου	oath-breaker, perjurer	masc	ἐπι-[√]-ος
ὁρκίζω	place under oath	vb	[√]-ιζω
≥10 ὅρκος ου	oath	masc	[√]-ος
ὁρκωμοσία ας	oath	fem	[√]-ια (ὄμνυμι)

στεφαν
crown / reward
Memory Aid: Stephen

| ≥10 στέφανος ου | crown | masc | [√]-ος |
| στεφανόω | crown, reward | vb | [√]-οω |

21

ἀρτ²
qualified / complete
Memory Aid: An *artist* is a *qualified* performer.

ἀπαρτισμός ού	completion	masc	ἀπο-[√]-ισμος
ἄρτιος α ον	fully qualified	adj	[√]-ιος
ἐξαρτίζω	be completed	vb	ἐκ-[√]-ιζω
καταρτίζω	mend, make adequate	vb	κατα-[√]-ιζω
κατάρτισις εως	adequacy	fem	κατα-[√]-σις
καταρτισμός οῦ	adequacy	masc	κατα-[√]-ισμος
προκαταρτίζω	prepare in advance	vb	προ-κατα-[√]-ιζω

20

δειπν
dine
Memory Aid: [Except for *p*, sounds something like *dine* and *dinner*.]

| δειπνέω | eat, dine | vb | [√]-εω |
| ≥10 δεῖπνον ου | feast, supper | neut | [√]-ον |

20

ἱππ
horse
Memory Aid: hippodrome, hippopotamus

ἱππεύς έως	horseman	masc	[√]-ευς
ἱππικόν οῦ	cavalry	neut	[√]-ικος
≥10 ἵππος ου	horse	masc	[√]-ος

20

κερδ
gain
Memory Aid: [One *gains* access with a membership *card*.]

| ≥10 κερδαίνω | gain, profit | vb | [√]-αινω |
| κέρδος ους | gain | neut | [√]-ς |

20

λανθαν λαθ
forget
Memory Aid:

ἐκλανθάνομαι	forget completely	vb	ἐκ-[√]-ανω
ἐπιλανθάνομαι	forget, overlook	vb	ἐπι-[√]-ανω
λανθάνω	be hidden, ignore	vb	[√]-ανω
λάθρα	secretly, quietly	adv	[√]-α
λήθη ης	forgetfulness	fem	[√]-η

20

τυπ   *20*

type / example

Memory Aid: type, typical, typify

ἀντίτυπος ον	corresponding (copy)	adj	ἀντι-[√]-ος
ἐντυπόω	engrave, carve	vb	ἐν-[√]-οω
τυπικῶς	by way of example	adv	[√]-ικως
≥10 τύπος ου	example, pattern	masc	[√]-ος
ὑποτύπωσις εως	example	fem	ὑπο-[√]-σις

3

Explanation of Greek Prefixes and Suffixes

In the following list, Greek prefixes and suffixes (listed in the far right column of the main Cognate List) are compared with English prefixes and suffixes to demonstrate the ways that a prefix or suffix can alter the meaning of a root. By learning how particular Greek prefixes and suffixes affect the meaning, the student often will be able to determine the meaning of new words simply by paying attention to the attached prefixes and suffixes.

The prefixes and suffixes are listed in alphabetical order. Suffixes apply only to a particular part of speech (e.g., to a verb). That restriction is noted. Prefixes are not restricted in this manner. The general sense of the prefix or suffix is then given in bold letters. Then follow, in most cases, examples of comparable use of suffixes or prefixes in English. The suffix or prefix will first be given, followed by |, which is followed by actual English words that employ the suffix or prefix. Sometimes rather than adding a suffix or prefix, English uses a separate word. In such cases, examples are given. The final part of each entry consists of qualifying comments, where necessary.

One further note on prefixes: they are used extensively in compound words, much more so than in English. And they affect the meaning of the compound in a number of ways. Although sometimes prefixes add nothing to the meaning of the main root, more often there is some change. Prefixes often add emphasis to the main root. Often they add the full impact of a prefixed preposition. Sometimes, though, a change takes place for which no good explanation is possible. In summary, then, prefixes can affect the compound in the following ways:

(1) they produce no change in the meaning;
(2) the root is emphasized or intensified;
(3) the full impact of the preposition is added to the root;
(4) the meaning is changed, but the change cannot be explained by the added prefix.

The effect of verbal endings sometimes is quite specific, though for the larger classes of verbs, generally no useful rule can be offered. There is, however, one somewhat regular pattern: *if a verbal ending can mean both "to do" and "to be," the "to be" form will usually be a deponent* (i.e., middle or passive, rather than active, even though the meaning is active).

Endings of prepositions, conjunctions, particles, and often adverbs contribute nothing to the meaning. Such endings are not included in column five of the Cognate Groups section. The space for suffixes is left blank.

Some words listed as nouns in the Cognate Groups section actually have adjectival endings. This happens when an adjective is used as a noun. English often uses adjectives as nouns too (e.g., *poor: the poor; blind: the blind*).

The list below is intended only as a tool for remembering Greek vocabulary. Any detailed study of cognates requires a more technical work.

ἀ [ἀν] – prefix – **negation** (e.g., *a-* | atheist; *an-* | anarchy; *non-* | nonproductive; un- | unable, undo; -less | reckless, spotless). [Note: when ἀ is prefixed to a word that begins with a vowel, the form will be lengthened to ἀν, as in "anarchy" above. The form will be identical to ἀν (shortened from ἀνα), which occurs when ἀνα is prefixed to a word that begins with a vowel. They do not mean the same thing.]

α – noun feminine first declension – (gen ης or ας) [Since English does not indicate gender, no examples can be given here.]

α – adverb – no specified meaning.

ᾳ – adverb – no specified meaning.

αζω – verb – **to do / to cause / to be** (e.g., *-ize* | terrorize, memorize). If deponent, it usually means "to be." [Note: *z* is common to both English and Greek in the examples given. Usually, however, English does not use the *-ize* form to express this kind of intention.]

αινω – verb – **to cause**; at times, **to be.** If deponent, it usually means to be (e.g., *-en* | frighten; *en-* | enable; *em-* | empower; make | make wide). [Note: *n* (*m*) is common to both Greek and English.]

ακος – adjective – **characteristic of; pertaining to; like** (e.g., *-ac* | cardiac) [Note: *-ac* is common to both Greek and English. Drop the case endings to see this more clearly. This form is for roots ending in ι. Otherwise ικος is used.]

αλος – adjective – **like / of *x* kind of character** (e.g., *-al* | ethical, magical). [Note: *-al* is common to both Greek and English. Drop the case endings to see this more clearly.]

αμφι – prefix – **around** (e.g., *amphi-* | amphitheatre).

ἀνα [ἀν] – prefix – **up / again / back / intensifier** (e.g., *ana-* | anabaptist, analysis [a loosing up]; *re-* | repay, redo; up* | tie up, give up). *As in English, this prefix sometimes does not add much to the meaning of the root. [Note: when ἀνα is prefixed to a word that begins with a vowel, the form will be shortened to ἀν. This must be distinguished from ἀν (lengthened from ἀ) that occurs when ἀ is prefixed to a word that begins with a vowel.]

ἀντι [ἀντ / ἀνθ] – prefix – **against / opposition / replacement** (e.g., *anti-* | antidote, antiaircraft, Antichrist, Antarctic).

ανω – verb – frequently a sense of **gain / increase / getting**, primarily because most words in this group are based on λαμβάνω.

ἀπο [ἀπ ἀφ] – prefix – **from / back / again / intensifier** (e.g., *apo-* | apostasy) sometimes in English with the prefix *re-*.

αριον – noun – (αριδιον) – **small** (e.g., *-let* | booklet; *-y* | puppy).

ας – noun masculine first declension – (gen ου).

αω – **to do / to be**: "to do" is the more frequent.

δια [δι] – prefix – **completion / intensifier / distribution / division:** but often does not affect the meaning of the root (e.g., *dia-* | diagnosis [as in complete / full]; *dia-* | diaspora [as in distribution]; *dia-* | diameter [as in division]).

δυσ – prefix – **bad / hard** (e.g., *dys-* | dystentery, lit., "bad entrails").

εια – noun feminine first declension – **abstract** (e.g., *-ity* | purity; | *-ion* | starvation; *-ness* | truthfulness; *-ence* | disobedience; *-ance* | forbearance). Although often this ending indicates "quality," the only safe rule is that it will be an abstract noun.

ειον – noun neuter second declension – **place** (gen ειου).

εἰς – prefix – **into / to.**

ἐκ [ἐξ] – prefix – **from / intensifier:** but quite often no effect on the meaning of the root.

ἐν [ἐμ / ἐγ / ἐλ] – prefix – **in; into:** but often this prefix does not alter the meaning of the root (e.g., *en-* | enclose; *em-* | employ; *in-* | inaugurate; *im-* | implant; in | live in, stay in). [Note: this Greek prefix never negates, unlike the English prefix *in-* (*im-*), as in "impossible" or "inadmissible."]

ἐπι [ἐπ / ἐφ] – prefix – **on / upon / intensifier** (e.g., *epi-* | epidermis, epidemic, epicenter; "upon" | come upon). This is a lightweight prefix and often does not alter the meaning of the root (e.g., καλέω and ἐπικαλέω both mean "name").

εὐ | prefix – **well / good / full** (e.g., *eu-* | euthanasia, eugenics, euphony; *-ful* | cheerful, useful; well | well known; good | goodwill).

ευς – noun masculine third declension – **profession / position / doer** (e.g., *-eus* | masseuse; *-er* | teacher; *-or* | actor).

ευω – verb – **to be / to do:** like εω below, though ευω verbs are far fewer. Often with τ, as in τευω.

εω – verb –**to be / to do:** Even when the "to be" form is not the normal expression in English, frequently a "be" form can be substituted so that the meaning is retained (e.g., grieve / be sad; love / be a friend; fear / be afraid; do / be active). But this is not the case often enough to be generally useful.

η – noun feminine first declension (gen ης). The most common feminine noun ending, with no meaning reflected often enough to offer a useful rule.

η – adverb – **manner / location.**

ἡμι – prefix – **half** (e.g., *hemi-* | hemisphere).

ην / ενος (ηνος) – noun – see ς.

ης / ες – adjective – **quality.**

ης – noun masculine first declension (gen ου) – **agent** see της.

ητος – see τος.

θεν – adverb – **place from where** (e.g., from | from home). [This is opposite to the English suffix *-ward,* as in homeward.]

ια – noun feminine first declension – frequently **quality,** often an abstract idea (e.g., *-ia* | *-y* | *-ness* |). With σ (σια) often indicates action.

ιζω – verb – **to do / to cause / to be** (e.g., *-ize* | symbolize, characterize). Often the English equivalent will contain the suffix *-ize,* or an intelligible new English word could be created by using the related adjective or noun combined with the suffix *-ize.* About one half the deponent forms are translated as "to be."

ικος / ικη / ικον – adjective – **characteristic of / pertaining to / like:** Adjectival ending (e.g., *-ic* | metallic, plastic, despotic; *-ly* | worldly; *-al* | spiritual; pertaining to | pertaining to nature (i.e., natural). [Note: *-ic* is common to both Greek and English. Drop the case endings to see this more clearly. Also see τικος. Sometimes these forms are used as nouns.]

ικως – adverb – combination of endings ικος and ως.

ιμος / ιμη / ιμον – adjective – **fitness / ability** (e.g., *-able* | *-ed* | *-ful*).

ινος / ινη / ινον – adjective – **source** / **material** (e.g., *-in* | toxin; *-ine* | chlorine; *-en* | wooden, ethylene; of | of wood). [Note: *in* is common to both Greek and English. Drop the case endings to see this more clearly.]

ιον – noun neuter second declension (gen ιου) – **diminutive** / **general.**

ιος / ια / ιον – adjective – **related to.**

ισμος – see μος.

ισσα – feminine noun ending: **profession** / **position** (e.g., *-ess* | goddess). [Note: vowel *i* / *e* plus double *ss* is common to both Greek and English. Drop the case ending to see this more clearly.]

ιστα – adverb – **superlative**: neuter plural used as adverb.

ιστης – see της.

ιστος / ιστη / ιστον – adjective – **superlative** (e.g., *-est* | fast > fastest). [Note: *-ist* / *-est* is common to both Greek and English. Drop the case endings to see this more clearly.]

κατα [κατ / καθ] – prefix – **down** / **against** / **order** / **destructive.** This is the most negative of the Greek prefixes (except for the rare δυσ), though it does not always imply something negative.

κις – one times indicator.

κοντα – ten times indicator.

λος / λη / λον – adjective – **characterized by** (e.g., *-ful* | sinful.

μα – noun neuter third declension – **object** / often **result of action** (gen ματος; e.g., *-ma* | drama, enigma; *-ion* | *-ing* | *-ment* | "something + past participle" | something spoken [i.e., a word] or something obscurely spoken [i.e., enigma]). This is the most common neuter nominal ending.

μετα [μετ / μεθ] – prefix – **after** / **with** / **change** (e.g., *meta-* | metaphysics; metamorphosis).

μι – verb – **general.**

μος – noun masculine second declension (gen μου) – **action** (e.g., *-ing* | Running is healthy, the dividing; *-ion* | the division; often σμος or ισμος.

μων / μον – adjective – **having quality of** *x* (e.g., *-ful*).

ξ – noun – see ς.

ον – noun neuter second declension – frequently an **object** (gen ου) no general rule is adequate.

ον – adverb – from neuter singular adjective.

ος – noun masculine second declension (gen ου, more rarely, feminine)

ος – noun neuter third declension – **object** / **concept.**

ος / η / ον – adjective – most common ending for adjectives; note two variations: (1) if the root ends in ρ, the form will be ος α ον; (2) for some words, the neuter singular form is simply ο rather than ον.

οτης – noun feminine third declension (gen ητος) – **quality.**

ου – adverb – but not always an adverb.

ους / α / ουν – adjective – (= ε + ος) see ος η ον.

οω – verb – **to cause** (e.g., *en-* | widen; *en-* | enrich, enable; *em-* | empower; make | make rich, make able). Often best translated as "make" + adjective (e.g., strengthen / make strong). A few times, must be translated as "to be."

παρα [παρ] – prefix – **beside** / **disordered** / **negative** (e.g., *para-* | parallel, paramedic).

περ – emphasis, but often no observable change.

περι [περ] – prefix – **around** / **about** / **beyond** / **excessive**: almost always means one of the first two (e.g., *peri* | perimeter; around | circumcise (i.e., cut around).

προ – prefix – **before** (e.g., *pro-* | prologue; before).

προς – **toward** / **to** (e.g., *pros-* | prosthesis).

ρ – noun (similar to ς below).

ρος – adjective – **quality.**

ς – noun third declension – many third declension nouns end in ς or a blank in the nominative, and a genitive (of various forms) with an ending of ος ους ως.

σια – see ια.

σις – noun feminine third declension (gen εως) – **action or something that results from action** (e.g., -*ing* | the educating, the forming; or the related -*tion* | formation, education.

σκω – verb – point at which something **begins** or **changes;** often with mental actions.

σμος – see μος.

σσω – verb – **to do.**

συν / συ / συγ / συλ / συμ / συσ – prefix – **with / completely** almost always with sense of "with" in the NT; otherwise probably means completely (e.g., *syn-* | synonym; *sym-* | sympathy; with | with the same meaning; up | break up; break completely).

συνη – noun feminine first declension – **quality.**

τερος / τερα / τερον – adjective – **comparative form er** (e.g., -*er* | small > smaller). [Note: this is roughly equivalent to English, where -*er* indicates comparative forms. Drop the case endings to see this more clearly.]

τερον – adverb – from neuter singular adjective above.

τηρ – **agent / doer** (e.g., -*er* | teacher, mover, player; -*or* | actor). It can be translated as a relative clause (e.g., teacher = the one who teaches). [Note: -*er* is common to both Greek and English.]

τηριον – noun neuter second declension – **place.**

της – noun masculine first declension (gen ου) – **agent / instrument.**

της – noun masculine – **member of class / doer** (as in τηρ above).

της – see οτης.

τικος / τικη / τικον – adjective – **characteristic of / pertaining to / like** (e.g., -*tic* | semantic, therapeutic). [Note: -*tic* is common to both Greek and English. Drop the case endings to see this more clearly.] Also see ικος.

τικως – combination of τικος and ως.

τος / τη / τον – adjective – **possibility / actuality** (e.g., -*able* | believable; -*ible* | incredible; -*ing* | pleasing) (often: ητος).

τρια – noun feminine – **agent** (e.g., -*ess* | actress).

τρον – noun neuter second declension – **instrument** (e.g., -*tron* | cyclotron). [Note: *tron* is common to both Greek and English.]

τωρ – noun – **agent / doer** (e.g., -*or* | mediator, actor, arbitrator; -*er* | teacher, mover, player). It can be translated as a relative clause (e.g., teacher = the one who teaches). [Note: -*or* is common to both Greek and English.]

υνω – verb – **to cause** / at times: **to be;** especially as deponent (e.g., -*en* |widen, enlighten, frighten; *en-* | enrich, enable; *em-* | empower; make | make rich, make able). [Note: *n* (*m*) is common to both Greek and English.]

ὑπερ – prefix – **over / excessive** (e.g., *hyper-* | hyperactive).

ὑπο [ὑπ / ὑφ] – prefix – **under / inferior** (e.g., *hypo-* | hypodermic).

υς εια υ – adjective – **quality.**

ω – verb – **the most common verbal ending.**

ω – adverb – **from / place.**

ων – noun third declension (generally; masculine gen ωνος or οντος; neuter gen ονος) – **object.**

ων ον – adjective (neuter singular is sometimes used as an adverb) – **comparative / quality.**

ως – adverb – **manner** (e.g., -*ly* | slowly) almost always with an English equivalent ending in -*ly.*

Identical Greek/English Prefixes and Suffixes

Greek	English	General Meaning	Example
ἀ-	a-	negation	*a*theist
-ακος*	-ac	pertaining to	cardi*ac*
-αλος*	-al	of *x* character	magic*al*
ἀμφι-	amphi-	around	*amphi*theatre
ἀνα-	ana-	up / back / again	*Ana*baptist
ἀντι-	anti-	against / opposition	*Anti*christ
ἀπο-	apo-	from	*apo*stasy
δια-	dia-	divided	*dia*meter
δυσ-	dys-	bad	*dys*function
ἐν-	en-	in / into	*en*close
ἐπι-	epi-	on / upon	*epi*dermis
εὐ-	eu-	well / good	*eu*thanasia
-ια	-ia	quality (abstract)	euthanas*ia*
-ιζω	-ize	do something to	terror*ize*
-ικος*	-ic	characteristic of	metall*ic*
-ινος*	-in	material / source	tox*in*
-ισμος*	-ism	belief in	Marx*ism*
-ιστης*	-ist	one who does	art*ist*
-ιστος*	-est	superlative	fast*est*
κατα-	cata-	down	*cata*ract
-μα	-ma	object (result)	enig*ma*
μετα-	meta-	after / change	*meta*morphosis
παρα-	para-	beside	*para*llel
περι-	peri-	around / about	*peri*meter
προ-	pro-	before	*pro*logue
προσ-	pros-	to / toward	*pros*thesis

A fuller discussion of Prefixes and Suffixes can be found in Section 3.

*Delete case ending (ος or ης) to see the Greek / English parallel more clearly.

-σις	-sis	action	metamorpho*sis*
συν-	syn-	with	*syn*onym
-τερος*	-er	comparative	small*er*
-τηρ	-er	doer	teach*er*
-τικος*	-tic	pertaining to	therapeu*tic*
-τρον	-tron	instrument	cyclo*tron*
-τωρ	-or	doer	act*or*
ὑπερ-	hyper-	over / excessive	*hyper*active
ὑπο-	hypo-	under	*hypo*dermic

5

Derived English Words

Most of the words offered as examples in the Memory Aid section of the main lists are included here. Some words do not appear, however. Exceptions were made wherever a word matched closely the spelling and meaning of the root. For example, the memory aid "lamp" is given for the cognate λαμπ, but is not included in this section. The connection is obvious; no explanation is necessary.

Primarily, it is compound words that are included here, and for these the Greek roots are given. If the word is already a compound in ancient Greek, the word is marked with the symbol ♦. (But note: the meaning of the Greek compound is often not the same as that of the modern English compound.)

Rare technical vocabulary has generally been avoided as being of little help as a memory aid. The exception is technical *theological* vocabulary. It is more likely that students of Greek will have a larger vocabulary in this area.

One should note that certain prefixes have several meanings. The entries below suggest the most likely meaning for the word in question. The user should refer to the section on prefixes and suffixes for a more complete presentation of these elements.

acolyte: one who assists (follows) a priest, performing minor parts of the ritual.

acoustic: anything having to do with sound or hearing; suffix *-ic* is the same as the Greek adjectival suffix ικος.

acrobat: ♦ (top + walk – ἀκρ + βατ [βαιν]) one who walks a tight rope or high wire.

agape: one of several words for love used in the early church as the technical term for a common meal, which was misunderstood by outsiders as something immoral (from the idea of a love-feast).

agent: from root to lead or drive, thus *agent* for something capable of bringing about an effect: e.g., "an agent of change."

agnostic: ♦ (not + knowing – ἀ + γνο) one who believes that it is not possible to know whether God exists.

agora: term used widely in the ancient world for the local marketplace; often used in compounds with the sense of speak (e.g., *allegory*) because public discussion and town meetings were usually carried out in the market.

agoraphobia: ♦ (market [public space] + fear + quality – ἀγορ + φοβ + ια) the fear of public places.

agriculture: (field + culture) English word comes from the Latin, but the first word of the compound is from Greek ἀγρ; *acre* comes from Greek too (see Grimm's Law).

allegory: ♦ (other + speak – ἀλλ + ἀγορ) *speak* is from the word for *marketplace,* where the local assembly met to discuss and make decisions; thus *allegory* for something spoken about one thing but meant for some other thing (see *agora* above).

allotrope: ♦ (other + turn – ἀλλ + τροπ [τρεπ]) general meaning: strangeness, variety; in chemistry: different forms of elements or compounds without a change in the chemical composition.

ambidextrous: ♦ (both + right – αμφἰ + δεξ) skilled with both hands.

ambrosia: food of the gods.

amnesia: ♦ (no + memory – ἀ + μνη [μιμν]) the condition of having lost one's memory; suffix *-ia* is common Greek suffix.

amnesty: ♦ (not + remember – ἀ + μνη [μιμν]) the granting of a pardon by forgetting acts that had brought condemnation. Compare with *amnesia* above.

Anabaptist: (re + baptize – ἀνα + βαπτ) polemical term given to a group in the Protestant Reformation who held to "believer's baptism" and who required rebaptism of those who had been baptized as children; suffix *-ist* is from Greek suffix ιστος.

Anabasis: ♦ (up + to – ἀνα + βασ [βαιν]) from the title of Greek work by Xenophon about the retreat of a Greek army back up to the Black Sea; σις is common Greek suffix.

analysis: ♦ (up + loose – ἀνα + λυ) studying the whole by considering its individual parts; *-sis* is from the suffix σις.

anarchy: ♦ (no + rule – ἀ + ἀρχ) a breakdown of normal structures of authority. [Note: ν (English *n*) is usual between ἀ and a word that begins with a vowel.]

Anatolia: ♦ (up + far – ἀνα + τολ) the land of Turkey, which from the perspective of the Greek was the distant land where the sun came up.

anatomy: ♦ (up + cut – ἀνα + τομ [τεμν]) a view of the body cut up into distinctive parts.

anchorite: ♦ (back + place – ἀνα + χωρ) meaning *withdraw* or *retire;* term for the form of monasticism that is solitary, in contrast to communal (or cenobite) monasticism.

androgynous: ♦ (male + female – ἀνδρ [ἀνηρ] + γυνη) something with both male and female characteristics.

android: ♦ (man + form – ἀνδρ [ἀνηρ] + οἰδ) an automaton with human form.

anemia: ♦ (no + blood – ἀ + αἰμ) deficiency in the red blood corpuscles. [Note: ν (English *n*) is usual between ἀ and a word that begins with a vowel.]

anemometer: (wind + measure – ἀνεμ + μετρ) instrument for measuring the velocity of the wind.

angel: *angel* is simply a transliteration of the Greek word ἄγγελος, meaning messenger. A divine messenger came to be called an *angel.*

anomaly: ♦ (not + law – ἀ + νομ) something that is not according to custom.

anonymous: ♦ (not + name – ἀ + ὀνομ) without a name, unknown.

antarctic: the land mass that is opposite to the Arctic.

anthropology: (man + study – ἀνθρωπ + λογ) the broad study of human culture and society.

anthropomorphic: (man + form – ἀνθρωπ + μορφ) often used for a description of God in terms of human attributes: *-ic* is from Greek suffix ικος.

antibiotic: (against + life – ἀντι + βι) against the life of a virus, which is really in aid of human life; *-tic* is from Greek suffix τικος.

Antichrist: ♦ word used in the Johannine letters to describe the chief source of opposition to the Christian church.

antidote: ♦ (against + give – ἀντι + δο [διδ]) something given against the effects of a poison; a remedy.

antinomian: ◆ (against + law – ἀντι + νομ) used for theological positions similar to Paul's, in which the Law is depreciated.

aphorism: ◆ (from + limit – ἀπο + ὁρ) brief statement of truth; a short definition; suffix *-ism* is from Greek ισμος.

Apocalypse: ◆ (from + cover – ἀπο + καλυψ [καλυπτ]) thus something revealed, as in the last book of the Bible – the Apocalypse or the Revelation.

Apocrypha: (from + hide – ἀπο + κρυφ [κρυπτ]) used for those books that church leaders believed should be hidden from the faithful (i.e., non-canonical).

Apollyon: destroying angel of the bottomless pit.

apoplexy: ◆ (utterly + strike – ἀπο + πλησσ [πλαγ]) ἀπο here has a sense of intensifier; thus, a crippling stroke.

apostle: ◆ (from + send – ἀπο + στελ) one sent from another to serve as representative of the sender.

apostrophe: ◆ (from + turn – ἀπο + στροφ [στρεφ]) sign that shows where some letters have been "turned away from" their place in a word.

appendectomy: (appendix + out + cut – appendix + ἐκ + τομ [τεμν]) *appendix* is from Latin base; the suffix is ἐκ + word for cut (i.e., cut out), thus to remove the appendix. Suffix *-ectomy* is often used in medical terminology for *removal by surgery.*

archaeology: ◆ (old + study – ἀρχ + λογ) a study of ancient things.

archangel: ◆ (chief + messenger – ἀρχ + ἀγγελ) an angel of the highest rank.

archbishop: (chief + bishop – ἀρχ + bishop) chief bishop of a province; *bishop* is Old English.

archetype: ◆ (beginning + example – ἀρχ + τυπ) an original model; a prototype.

Argentina: (silver + land) more closely from the Latin, but note the Greek root ἀργυρ.

arithmetic: the science of numbers.

asterisk: a little star; *-isk* is from Greek suffix ισκος.

asthenia: ◆ (not + strong + quality – ἀ + σθεν + ια) weakness (the quality of not being strong).

astronomy: ◆ (star + law – ἀστρ + νομ) study of the laws by which the regular courses of astral bodies may be determined.

atheist: ◆ (no + god – ἀ + θε) one who does not believe in God; *-ist* is from the Greek suffix ιστος.

atom: ◆ (not + cut – ἀ + τομ [τεμν]) named for the part of matter that could not be divided – until the twentieth century showed otherwise.

atrophy: (not + support – ἀ + τροφ [τρεφ]) medical condition in which the body wastes away.

auction: a method of sale in which the price increases through bidding; more directly from the Latin.

aurora borealis: (light/dawn + north) more closely from the Latin, but note the Greek root αὐρ, dawn/day.

autistic: condition of being completely withdrawn from all others but oneself; *-tic* is from Greek suffix τικος.

autobiography: (self + life + writing – αὐτο + βι + γραφ) a biography written by the subject.

autocratic: ◆ (self + power – αὐτο + κρατ) not "self-rule" in the sense of national independence, but the opposite – rule by one individual; others have no voice.

autograph: ◆ (self + writing – αὐτο + γραφ) technical term for the manuscript penned by the author personally, in contrast to all manuscripts copied from the original by scribes.

automatic: on one's own power.

autopsy: (self + see – αὐτο + οπ) to examine for oneself. (The synonym for a post-mortem examination is a more technical use of the word.)

auxiliary: more closely from the Latin, but note the Greek root αὐξ (*to grow*).

axiom: established principle; something worthy of universal acceptance.

ballistic: of anything *thrown;* suffix *-ic* comes from the Greek suffix ικος.

baritone: ♦ (heavy + tone – βαρ + τον [τεν]) male singing voice between bass and tenor; bass is used for the lowest voice, since the lowest part of anything is its *base* (from βασις).

barium: element found primarily in heavy spar.

barometer: (heavy + measure – βαρ + μετρ) instrument for measuring atmospheric pressure.

basilica: originally meant a royal hall.

Bible: plural of βιβλιον, meaning *book,* thus *Bible* for a collection of books.

bibliography: ♦ (book + writing – βιβλ + γραφ) a list of books.

biblioatry: (book + worship – βιβλ + λατρ) used to describe attitude of various religious groups to their Scriptures (as with Muslims and fundamentalist Christians).

bibliotheca: (book + place – βιβλιο + θη [τιθ]) a place for books; a library.

bigamy: (two + marriage) prefix *bi-* is Latin prefix; for state in which one person is married while legally married to another.

boule: technical term widely used for the town council in Greek society.

cacography: (bad + writing – κακ + γραφ) bad writing (cf. *calligraphy*).

cacophony: ♦ (bad + sound – κακ + φων) discordant sound.

calisthenics: (beautiful + strength – καλ + σθεν) gymnastics to promote grace and strength.

calligraphy: ♦ (beautiful + writing – καλ + γραφ) the art of writing, for which medieval monks and Muslims are famous.

cardiac: pertaining to the heart.

cataclysm: ♦ (down + wash – κατα + κλυσμ) κατα often has a negative sense in a compound, thus the sense here of destruction.

catacomb: underground cemetery; the first part, κατα, is Greek; the second part, *comb,* is from Latin root, and the compound itself is late Latin.

catapult: ♦ (against + hurl – κατα + παλλ) instrument designed to hurl heavy stones at fortified walls.

cataract: ♦ (down + dash – κατα + ἀρα) waterfall.

catastrophe: ♦ (down + turn – κατα + στροφ [στρεφ]) an overturning.

catatonic: ♦ (down + stretch – κατα + τον [τεν]) stretching down, as in a depression.

Cathar: medieval Christan group who judged material to be evil and who, by asceticism, hoped to purify themselves.

catharsis: cleansing; *sis* is common noun ending.

cathedral: from Greek for *seat;* means the *seat* of the bishop.

catholic: (according to + the whole – κατα + ὁλ) the belief that is held by all the churches (i.e., universal).

cemetery: a place where the dead lie; more directly from Latin.

cenotaph: ♦ (empty + tomb – κεν + ταφ) monument to dead who are buried elsewhere.

Cenozoic: (recent + life) term for present geological system.

charismatic: gifted; suffix *-tic* is from Greek τικος.

charity: gift.

chemotherapy: (chemical + healing – chemical + θεραπ) a process of attempted healing by the use of chemicals; *chemical* is from the word *alchemy*, derived from Latin.

chiliasm: the theological position that focuses on a thousand-year golden age at the end of world history; from Greek for *thousand.*

chiropractic: (hand + practice – χειρ + πρασ) a method of curing that depends primarily on the use of the physician's hands.

cholesterol: (gall + solid – χολη + στερε) fatty substance, so-called because it was originally found in gall stones.

chronology: (time + study – χρον + λογ) the part of any study that deals with the time (sequence) of events.

chrysanthemum: ♦ (gold + flower – χρυσ + ἀνθ) a flower.

clergy: apparently so named from the Greek word for portion, because God was their portion.

comma: a mark that cuts into the flow of a sentence.

cosmetic: ordered; suffix *-tic* is from Greek suffix τικος.

cosmopolitan: ♦ (world + citizen – κοσμ + πολ) citizen of the world.

cosmos: the world as ordered.

creosote: a wood preservative.

crime: from the Latin, though sharing elements with Greek root κρι.

crisis: a time of decision or judgment.

critic: one who judges.

critique: judgment.

crypt: vault for burial or hiding.

cryptic: secret; hidden; *-ic* is from Greek suffix ικος.

cryptography: (hide + write – κρυπτ + γραφ) secret writing.

deacon: lower church office, for which the common term for servant was used.

decade: ten-year period.

decalogue: ♦ (ten + word – δεκ + λογ) the "Ten Words," another name for the Ten Commandments.

decimate: more directly from the Latin, meaning to kill off a large number (lit., to kill a tenth).

demagogue: ♦ (people + leader – δημ + ἀγ) a leader whose power is based on popular support among the people.

democracy: ♦ (people + power – δημ + κρατ) a system of government in which the government is in the hands of the people, often through elected representatives.

demographics: (people + writing – δημ + γραφ) statistics of births, deaths, diseases of human populations.

Deuteronomy: ♦ (second + law – δευ + νομ) name for the fifth book of the Pentateuch, in which the Law is repeated (see suffix τερος).

dexterity: skilful; originally associated with right-handedness; more directly from Latin.

diabolical: ♦ (across + throw – δια + βολ [βαλ]) from Greek word διάβολος, meaning *devil* or *slanderer.*

diadem: ♦ (through + bind – δια + δε) δια here intensifies the binding, thus the sense of to bind fully (as in a circle), thus diadem or crown.

diaeresis: ♦ (through + take – δια + αἱρ) δια is used here in the sense of division. Two vowels standing together in Greek are usually pronounced together (called a diphthong). If they are pronounced separately, two dots (··) are placed over the second vowel, and the vowels are pronounced separately. The mark to indicate this separation is called a diaeresis.

diagnostic: ♦ (through + know – διὰ + γνο) διὰ here is an intensifier, as in a thorough examination.

diagonal: ♦ (though + angle – διὰ + γων) a line that cuts through the corner angles.

dialect: ♦ (through + say – διὰ + λεκτ [λεγ]) a variety of speech distinguished by particular idioms, pronunciation, etc., but which is understood by persons who speak another form of the primary language; διὰ may have a sense of division here.

diarrhea: ♦ (through + flow – διὰ + ῥη) no other term so adequately describes this disorder.

Didache: a translation of the Greek word for *teaching*. The term is used as a shortened title for one of the works of the Apostolic Fathers called *The Teaching of the Twelve*.

didactic: transliteration of the Greek word διδακτικος; suffix *-tic* is the same as Greek τικος. Greek, of course, reflects a case ending too.

dilemma: ♦ (two + receive – δι + λημ [λαμβ]) a choice between two equally undesirable alternatives.

diocese: (through + dwell – διὰ + οἰκ) the churches under a bishop; διὰ here is used in the sense of "complete."

Docetic: a heretical group in the early second century distinguished by the belief that Jesus only *seemed* to have human form.

Dorothy: ♦ (gift + God – δωρ + θε) this personal name means "a gift of God."

doxology: ♦ (glory + word – δοξ + λογ) a hymn (*word*) of *praise*.

dynamic: characterized by energy or power; suffix *-ic* is from the Greek suffix ικος.

dynamo: see *dynamic* above.

dynamite: see *dynamic* above.

dynasty: from δυναστεια, which has the same root as *dynamic* above.

ecclesiastical: ♦ (out + call – ἐκ + κλη [καλ]) ἐκκλησία was the technical name chosen by the early Christians to describe their assemblies.

eclipse: ♦ (out + leave – ἐκ + λειπ) as when the sun is *eclipsed* by the moon.

ecology: (house + study – οἰκ + λογ) study of the environment (i.e., living space; house) of plants and animals.

economy: ♦ (house + law – οἰκ + νομ) related to the management of a household, or some larger household; the Greek root νομ (mainly pertaining to law in the New Testament) is related to the root νεμ, which means to *deal out* or *distribute;* the νεμ / νομ complex in Greek has a wide variety of meanings.

ecosystem: see *ecology* and *system*.

ecstasy: ♦ (out + stand – ἐκ + στα [ἰστη]) a behaviour that stands outside the normal.

ecumenical: ♦ a movement including all inhabitants.

eisegesis: ♦ (into + lead – εἰς + ἠγε) theological term for bad exegesis; exegesis is reading (*leading*) "out of" the text what is in the text; eisegesis is reading "into" the text what is not intended by the text.

emporium: ♦ (in + journey – ἐν + πορ) a market; the word for *commerce* is ἐμπορία, reflecting the fact that travel was regularly involved in commerce.

encephalitis: (in + head – ἐν + κεφαλ) inflammation of the brain; Greek had already created the compound ἐγκέφαλος (*in the head*) to indicate the *brain*.

enchiridion: ♦ (in + hand – ἐν + χειρ) a handbook or manual (i.e., something *in the hand*).

encyclopaedia: ♦ (in + circle + training – ἐν + κυκλο + παιδεια) lit., *training in a circle* (i.e., general education).

endemic: ♦ (in + people – ἐν + δεμ) native to a particular people.

energy: ♦ (in + work – ἐν + ἐργ) something that is present in work.

enzyme: (in + leaven – ἐν + ζυμ) a chemical ferment.

ephemeral: ♦ (on + day – ἐπι + ἡμερ) short-lived (lit., *on a day*).

epicentre: ♦ (on + centre – ἐπι + κεντρ) the point at which an earthquake is the strongest.

epidemic: ♦ (on + people – ἐπι + δημ) disease that has spread widely on a population.

epidermis: ♦ (on + skin – ἐπι + δερμ) the outer skin (lit., *on the skin*).

epiphany: ♦ (on + appear – ἐπι + φαν) appearance of a god.

epistemic: ♦ (on + stand – ἐπι + στη [ἱστη]) pertaining to knowledge; suffix -*ic* is from Greek suffix ικος.

epistemology: see *epistemic* above.

epitaph: ♦ (on + tomb – ἐπι + ταφ) what is written on a tomb.

epithet: ♦ (on + place – ἐπι + θη [τιθ]) a descriptive word used in place of the usual name.

equinox: (equal + night – Latin *equal* + νυκ) time at which days and nights are of equal length at the equator.

ergonomic: (work + law – ἐργ + νομ) something that conforms to appropriate rules (or laws) related to working.

eremite: hermit; more directly from the Latin, but related to Greek root ἐρημ, meaning desert.

eschatology: (last + study – ἐσκατ + λογ) a study of final things.

eschaton: the last days.

esophagus: ♦ (inside + eat – ἐσω [εἰς] + φαγ) a tube that carries eaten food inside the body.

esoteric: for the initiated only; for those on the inside (see suffix τερος).

essence: the real nature or being.

ethnarch: ♦ (nation + rule – ἐθν + ἀρχ) a ruler of a nation.

etiology (aetiology): ♦ (cause + study – αἰτ + λογ) the science of causes or reasons.

eucharist: ♦ (good + gift – εὐ + χαρι) as a compound, means *thanks* or *thanksgiving;* used as a technical term for a primary Christian sacrament.

eulogy: ♦ (good + word – εὐ + λογ) praise.

euphemistic: ♦ (good + say – εὐ + φη) pertaining to the use of a mild word in place of a harsh word.

euphony: ♦ (good + sound – εὐ + φων) a pleasing sound.

euphoria: ♦ (well + bear – εὐ + φορ [φερ]) sense of well-being (lit., a bearing well).

eureka: this word was supposedly shouted by Archimedes on his discovery of a method for determining the purity of gold; it means *I have found it!*

euthanasia: (good + death – εὐ + θαν) death that is not the result of a disease, but is done intentionally to avoid death by disease or old age; -*ia* is from Greek suffix ια.

evangelist: ♦ (good + messenger – εὐ + ἀγγελ) one who announces the good news.

ex cathedra: (from + chair – ἐκ + καθεδρ [καθ]) for those proclamations by the pope when he speaks from his position as bishop of Rome.

excommunicate: from the Latin, which Latin shares with Greek *ex-* (ἐκ [ἐξ]) to mean *out.*

exegesis: ♦ (out + lead – ἐξ [ἐκ] + ἠγε) theological term for good interpretation (a reading or *leading out of* the text what is in the text; cf. *eisegesis* above).

exile: from the Latin, but shares with the Greek the sense of *ex* (ἐκ [ἐξ]) as *out.*

exodus: ♦ (out + way – ἐξ [ἐκ] + ὁδ) the way out.

exorcise: ♦ (out + oath – ἐκ + ὁρκ) to cast out by incantations and prayer. In the New Testament, ἐκβάλλω is more commonly used for "exorcize."

extend: ♦ (out + stretch – ἐκ + τεν) more directly from the Latin.

fugitive: one who is fleeing.

genealogy: ◆ (family + study – γεν + λογ) a study of family roots.

generation: more directly from Latin, but *gen-* is shared with Greek (see *genealogy* above).

genesis: a beginning; *-sis* is a common Greek suffix.

genetic: related to origin and development; *-tic* is from the Greek suffix τικος.

genocide: from the Latin, but Latin shares the meaning of the root *gen-* with Greek; means the *killing* (Latin: *cidere*) *of a race*.

genre: kind; family; more directly from Latin (see *generation* above).

geography: ◆ (earth + write – γη + γραφ) description of the earth.

George: (earth + worker – γη + οὐργ [ἐργ]) the personal name George means *farmer.*

gloss: from Greek γλωσσα, meaning language or tongue; this comes to mean any marginal or explanatory notes in a text.

glossalalia: (tongues + speak – γλωσσ + λαλ) term for religious phenomenon in which a person speaks a language – normally unintelligible – by divine inspiration. If the unlearned language spoken were identifiable, it would be an instance of xenolalia.

glossary: a collection of glosses; dictionary of foreign words (see *gloss* above).

gnosis: transliterated directly from Greek; means *knowledge.*

gnosticism: see *gnosis* above; *-ism* is from Greek suffix ισμος.

grammar: the art of writing.

graphite: the material used in pencils.

gym – gymnastics: exercise; since exercise was done in the nude, both meanings can be conveyed by γυμν.

gynecology: (woman + study – γυνη + λογ) field of medicine that deals with the physical health of women.

Hagia Sophia: name of a church built by Justinian in the sixth century in Istanbul; means *Holy Wisdom.*

hagiology: (holy + study – ἁγι + λογ) literature dealing with the lives of saints.

halibut: a saltwater fish.

halite: rock salt.

hamartiology: the part of theology that deals with sin.

hegemony: leadership.

heliocentric: (sun + centre – ἑλι + κεντρ) any view having the sun as center; suffix *-ic* is from Greek suffix ικος.

helium: name of gaseous element, so called because this element was first observed during an eclipse of the sun in 1868.

hellenistic: from Greek word for *Greek; -ic* is from Greek suffix ικος.

hemoglobin: the pigment in the red blood cells; *hemo-* is from the Greek word for blood; *globin* is from the Latin for ball or mass.

hemophilia: (blood + love – αἱμ + φιλ) used to describe the condition of excessive bleeding.

hemorrhage: ◆ (blood + flow – αἱμ + ῥη) discharge of blood from ruptured blood vessel.

henotheism: (one + god – ἑν + θε) a kind of polytheism in which one god has priority.

Heptateuch: ◆ (seven + book : ἑπτ + τευχ) τευχ can mean *book,* thus *Heptateuch:* the first seven books of the Old Testament.

hermit: from Greek word meaning *desert,* a place where monastic hermits generally lived.

heterodox: (different + belief – ἑτερ + δοξ) different belief, usually used with negative overtones; similar to the word *heresy.*

heterosexual: (different + sex – ἑτερ + Latin *sex*) having the desire for the opposite sex.

heuristic: related to discovering or finding out; suffix -*ic* is from the Greek suffix ικος.

hex key: also called Allen wrench; it has six sides.

hexameter: ♦ (six + measure – ἑξ + μετρ) a verse of six metrical feet.

hierarchy: ♦ (priest + rule – ἱερ + ἀρχ) a graded system of officials, especially of sacred persons.

hieroglyph: ♦ (priest + carve – ἱερ + γλυφ) picture writing used by the ancient Egyptians and done by the priestly class.

hippodrome: ♦ (horse + run – ἱππ + δρομ) place where horses are raced.

hippopotamus: ♦ (horse + river – ἱππ + ποταμ [πο²]) an animal that spends much of its time in the water.

Holocaust: ♦ (whole + burnt – ὁλ + καυστ) whole burnt offering; primarily used since World War II for the wide-scale destruction of Jews.

homogeneous: (same + kind – ὁμο + γεν) for material that is the same throughout.

homogenize: (same + kind) as above, but with suffix -*ize* meaning, as in Greek, "to do, to make."

homonym: ♦ (same + name – ὁμο + ὀνομ) but not really meaning same name; rather, it is a term for a word that sounds the same as another word, though it has a different meaning; thus *same sound* is the real meaning of *homonym.*

homoiousion: ♦ (similar + substance – ὁμοι [ὁμο] + ουσ [εἰμι]), used in the Arian debate to distinguish between the view that the Son was of *similar* substance with the Father or whether the Son was of the *same* substance (*homoousion*) as the Father.

horizon: the *bounds* or *limits* of vision.

horoscope: ♦ (hour + watch – ὡρ + σκοπ) a chart of the zodiac, which people use to have insight into the future on the basis of a scheme related to the time of one's birth.

hydrant: device for the delivery of water; suffix -*ant* is from the Latin.

hydro-electric: use of water to produce electricity.

hydroplane: vehicle used to travel over the water.

hygiene: the science of health.

hyperactive: excessively active.

hyperbole: ♦ (excessive + throw : ὑπερ + βολ [βαλ]) an overstatement.

hypersensitive: *hyper* is from Greek ὑπερ; *sensitive* from Latin.

hypodermic: (under + skin – ὑπο + δερμ) anything pertaining to the area under the skin.

hypothermia: (under + heat – ὑπο + θερμ) a condition of low body heat.

hypsography: (high + write – ὑψ + γραφ) a description (graphing) of the earth's surface.

hysteria: from the word for *womb;* it was originally thought that hysteria in a woman was caused by some disorder of the womb.

iconoclastic: ♦ (image + break – ἰκον + κλασ) term applied to the smashing of images, especially in the controversies in the eastern church during the eighth and ninth centuries.

idiomatic: of language: expressions peculiar to a particular language or group of languages (e.g., a *Semitic* idiom).

idiosyncratic: ♦ (own + with + mix – ἰδι + συν + κρασ) of mannerisms peculiar to an individual; similar to *syncretism,* which means a *mixing together,* but in this case, only of one individual.

idolatry: ♦ (idol + worship – εἰδωλ + λατρ) worship of idols.

intonation: more directly from the Latin *intonatus,* but related to Greek τειν / τον.

irenic: peaceful.

isotope: (equal + place – ἰσο + τοπ) two or more forms of an element having the same atomic number but different atomic weights.

John Chrysostom: ◆ (John + gold + mouth – χρυσ + στομ) John, Bishop of Antioch and Constantinople, nicknamed *Golden-Mouth* for his preaching ability.

kenosis: a term to express the *emptying* of divinity in the incarnation; from Philippians 2:5–11.

kerygma: preaching (merely transliterated as a technical term for the gospel).

kleptomaniac: (steal + maniac – κλεπτ + μαν) one who is controlled by the urge to steal.

koine Greek: common or vernacular Greek.

koinonia: merely transliterated from the Greek; often used in Christian circles today in place of the word *fellowship*.

kyrie, eleison: (lord + mercy + imperatival ending – κυρ + ἐλει + σον) an old liturgical prayer.

kyrios: term for Lord, in theological works, often transliterated.

laity: the *people* (Greek λαός), in contrast to the *clergy*.

lexicon: dictionary.

leukemia: (white + blood – λευκ + αἱμ) a disease characterized by a marked increase in the number of white blood corpuscles.

licorice: ◆ (sweet + root – γλυκ + ῥιζ) note that the initial γ is dropped in the English transliteration.

lithograph: (stone + write – λιθ + γραφ) a method of printing from stone or metal plates.

liturgy: ◆ (public + work – λειτ + οὐργ [ἐργ]) originally used for any public service; now with religious sense.

lupus: painful disease of the skin.

lux: in physics, a unit of light.

macarcism: beatitude; blessing (the more common *beatitude* is from the Latin).

macrocosm: (far + world – μακρ + κοσμ) the universe (lit., the *long* or *large world*).

macron: an accent that indicates a long vowel, marked by a short horizontal line placed over the vowel.

mariolatry: (Mary + worship – Μαρι + λατρ) an elevation of Mary, the mother of Jesus, to a position of worship and devotion.

martyr: originally meant *witness*, but came to mean *martyr*, as one who has witnessed to the death.

mastectomy: (breast + out + cut – μαστ + ἐκ + τομ [τεμν]) see *appendectomy* above.

maternal: from the Latin *maternus*, meaning *pertaining to a mother*, but related to Greek word for mother: μήτηρ.

math: originally meant learning generally.

matriarchy: (mother + rule – μητρ [μητηρ] + ἀρχ) term for a society in which the women hold the chief power.

matron: more directly from the Latin *matrona*, meaning *a married woman*, but related to the Greek word for mother: μήτηρ.

megalomania: (great + madness – μεγαλ [μεγ] + μαν) delusion of greatness.

megaphone: (great + sound – μεγ + φων) an instrument that magnifies (makes greater) the voice.

megaton: explosive power of a million tons of T.N.T.; the prefix *mega-* is used in the metric system for one million.

menopause: (month + stop – μην + παυσ) the period in life during which the monthly menstrual cycle stops.

Mesopotamia: ◆ (middle + river – μεσο + ποταμ [πο²]) land that lies between the Tigris and Euphrates Rivers.

metamorphosis: ◆ (change + form – μετα + μορφη) change of form; transformation.

metaphysics: ◆ (after + physics – μετα + φυσ) the section of Aristotle's writings that followed his section on physics.

metropolis: ◆ (mother + city – μητρ [μητηρ] + πολ) a capital city or a large urban area.

microfilm: greatly reduced photographic reproduction on film; *film* is from Old English.

micrometer: (small + measure – μικρ + μετρ) instrument used to measure small units.

microscope: (small + look – μικρ + σκοπ) an instrument used to look at small things.

misanthropy: ◆ (hate + man – μισ + ἀνθρωπ) a hatred of humans.

mnemonic: pertaining to the memory; suffix *-ic* is from the Greek suffix ικος.

monarch: ◆ (one + rule – μον + ἀρχ) one who is sole ruler.

monogamy: ◆ (one + marriage – μον + γαμ) being married to one wife or one husband at any one time.

monolithic: ◆ (one + stone – μον + λιθ) any large object viewed as being made of one mass.

monologue: ◆ (alone + speak – μον + λογ) a speech by a single person.

monopoly: ◆ (alone + sell – μονο + πωλ) exclusive right to sell a commodity.

monothelite: (one + will – μον + θελ) a christological controversy arising out of the monophysite debate; the monothelite position was orthodox in that it spoke of two natures but heretical in that it spoke of only one will.

monotone: ◆ (one + tone – μον + τον [τεν]) unvarying tone, either of sound or colour.

mystery: lit., place where one closes the eyes (i.e., secret); from suffix for place (τηριον).

necropolis: ◆ (dead + city – νεκρ + πολ) synonym for cemetery.

neophyte: ◆ (new + plant – νεο + φυτ [φυσ]) used of a recent convert to a religion or a beginner in an activity.

Nike: Greek goddess of victory; identified in Roman mythology with the goddess Victoria.

nominal: existing in name only, as a nominal ruler.

nomos: law; often not translated in theological writings; words in English that end with the suffix *-onomy* or *-nomy* come from this root.

nous: the intellect.

nuptial: pertaining to marriage; more directly from the Latin *nuptialis*, but clearly related to the Greek word νυμφη (directly below).

nymph: bride, maiden; from the Greek word for a class of minor female deities inhabiting the sea, wells, woods, etc.

ochlacracy: (crowd + power – ὀχλο + κρατ) mob rule.

odometer: ◆ (way + measure – ὁδ + μετρ) an instrument for measuring distance travelled.

oligarchy: ◆ (few + rule – ὀλιγ + ἀρχ) rule by a small group.

onomatopoeia: ◆ (name + make – ὀνομ + ποι) a literary term for a word that is pronounced like the natural sound it represents.

ontological: (being + study – ὀντ [εἰμι] + λογ) of things pertaining to the branch of metaphysics dealing with reality or *being.*

ophthalmology: (eye + study – ὀφθαλμ + λογ) the branch of medicine that deals with the eye.

orator: more directly from the Latin *oratio,* but related to the Greek ῥήτωρ, from which comes the closer English cognate *rhetoric.*

organ: instrument; an object that *works.*

otology: (ear + study – ὠτ [οὐς] + λογ) the branch of medicine that deals with the ear.

paleolithic: (old + stone – παλαι + λιθ) a period of human culture characterized by the use of flaked stone implements.

paleontology: (old + being + study – παλαι + ὀντ [εἰμι] + λογ) science that deals with ancient forms of life.

palimpsest: (again + rub – παλ + ψα) the paper or parchment of a manuscript that has been reused by rubbing out the old letters and writing the new text over it.

palindrome: (again + run – παλ + δρομ) a word or sentence that reads the same backwards as forwards (e.g., *Madam, I'm Adam*).

Pan America: any organization represented throughout the Americas.

panacea: (all + cure – παν + ἀκ) a cure-all.

pandemic: ♦ (all + people – πας + δεμ) affecting the whole people.

panorama: (all + sight – παν + ὁρα) a complete view in all directions.

pantheon: ♦ (all + god – παν + θε) all the gods of a particular religion (e.g., the Olympic Pantheon), or a temple dedicated to all the gods.

Paraclete: ♦ (beside + call – παρα + κλη [καλ]) a synonym for the Holy Spirit, who is called alongside to serve as a comforter.

paradigm: ♦ (beside + show – παρα + δειγ [δεικ]) pattern.

paradox: ♦ (beside/beyond/disordered + think – παρα + δοκ) thought that seems absurd but true.

parallel: ♦ (beside + one another – παρα + ἀλλ) pertaining to two things that run beside each other.

paralysis: ♦ (beside + loose – παρα + λυ) a loss of motor function; here the negative side of the suffix παρα appears.

paramedic: one who works alongside a doctor; prefix *para-* is from Greek, *med* is a Latin root for healing.

paranoia: ♦ (beside + mind – παρα + νο) a mental disorder; here the negative side of the prefix παρα appears.

paraphernalia: ♦ (beside + carry – παρα + φερ) personal effects; more directly from the Latin.

paraplegic: ♦ (beside + strike – παρα + πληγ) here the negative side of the suffix παρα appears.

parasite: ♦ (beside + food – παρα + σιτ) an organism that lives off another animal.

paratactic: (beside + arrange – παρα + τακ [ταγ]) grammatical term for a sentence in which clauses are attached by the word και, contrasted to *hypotactic* arrangement, where clauses are subordinated.

parousia: ♦ (beside + being – παρα + οὐσ) an appearing; becomes a technical term in Christianity for the Second Coming of Christ.

paternity: more directly from the Latin *paternitas,* but related to the Greek πατήρ.

pathetic: something that arouses pity.

pathology: (suffer + study – παθ + λογ) the branch of medicine that deals with the origin and treatment of diseases (or *suffering*).

pathos: the quality that arouses feelings of pity or sorrow.

patriarch: ♦ (family + rule – πατρι + ἀρχ) a leader (ruler) of a family; one might also connect the ending *-arch* to the other meaning of the Greek word ἀρχή (old), thus *patriarch* as one of the old persons in a family.

patristics: pertaining to the Fathers of the early church; suffix *-ic* is from Greek compound suffix ικος.

pause: to stop.

pedagogy: ♦ (child + lead – παιδ + ἀγωγ [ἀγ]) education.

pedantic: one who makes needless display of learning.

pedestrian: more directly from the Latin, but related to the Greek word ποδ, for *foot*.

pediatrics: (child + heal – παιδ + ἰατρ) the branch of medicine that treats children.

pentagon: ♦ (five + angle – πεντ + γων) a five-sided (or five-angled) figure, as is the shape of the building that houses the U.S. Department of Defense.

Pentateuch: (five + book – πεντε + τευχ) τευχ can mean book, thus the term for the first five books of the Bible.

Pentecost: ♦ (five + suffix κοστ) used to indicate *ten times*, thus 5 x 10 or 50; for a Jewish festival that was to follow an earlier festival by fifty days.

pericarp: ♦ (around + fruit – περι + καρπ) the wall of fruit.

perimeter: ♦ (around + measure – περι + μετρ) the distance around an object; a border.

peripatetic: ♦ (about + walk – περι + πατ) applied to the philosophy of Aristotle, who lectured while walking around.

peripheral: ♦ (around + carry – περι + φερ) that which is related to the edge (perimeter) rather than the center.

periscope: (around + see – περι + σκοπ) an instrument (as on a submarine) that rotates and extends so that one can see around the ocean's surface.

phantom: an apparition.

phenomenon: neuter passive participle (ομενον) of *show*, thus something that is shown or seen.

Philadelphia: (love + brother – φιλ + ἀδελφ) new world Quaker city founded by William Penn where religious toleration was practised, thus its name "City of Brotherly Love."

philanthropy: ♦ (love + man – πιλ + ἀνθρωπ) a love of people (cf. *misanthropy*).

philosophy: (love + wisdom – φιλ + σοφ) the literal meaning of *philosophy* is the "love of wisdom."

Phoenix: a fabled bird that killed itself, only to be reborn.

phoneme: a sound in human speech.

phonetics: branch of linguistics dealing with sounds.

phosphorus: ♦ (light + bring – φως + φορ [φερ]) an element that emits light; the morning star was so named.

photogenic: (light + generating – φωτ [φως] + γεν) here *photo* refers primarily to *photograph*, thus *photogenic* for what produces good photographs.

photograph: (light + writing – φωτ [φως]) + γραφ) an image made by light being reflected onto a negative.

photosynthesis: the process by which plants combine elements into food by means of sunlight; *photo* is from Greek word for *light;* for the other part of the compound, see *synthesis* below.

phylactery: ♦ in Judaism, leather case in which Scripture verses are kept; from the word *guard* and the Greek suffix τηριον, used to indicate place where something is done.

phylogeny: (tribe + generation – φυλ + γεν) the history of a tribe.

phylum: a biological division.

physics: the branch of science that deals with features of the natural world.

physiology: ♦ (nature + study – φυσ + λογ) the branch of science that deals with the function of living organisms.

pirate: roughly from the word meaning "attempt"; perhaps to attempt an attack on a ship.

plague: calamity; something that attacks or strikes.

planet: From the perspective of ancient astronomers, planets appeared in the heavens like stars, yet they did not follow the expected courses of the stars, thus the use of the Greek word for *wandering* for these astral bodies.

plenary: full; complete.

Pleroma: gnostic word for the primary realm, the *Fullness*.

plethora: excessive fullness; superfluity.

Pliocene: examine a Geological Time Scale; a few of the names derived from the Greek are: Archeozoic, Proterozoic, Paleozoic, Mesozoic, Cenozoic, Pleistocene, Pliocene, Oligocene.

plutocracy: ♦ (wealth + rule – πλου + κρατ) rule by the wealthy.

pneumatic: related to air, as a pneumatic tool.

pneumonia: ♦ inflammation of the lungs.

podiatry: (foot + heal – ποδ [πο¹] + ιατρ) the branch of medicine that deals with feet.

podium: a stand with legs or feet.

poem: something made or constructed.

polemic: war.

polis: suffix *-polis* indicates *city*.

political: pertaining to the activities of citizens.

polygamy: ♦ (many + marriage – πολυ [πολλ] + γαμ) the practice of one individual being legally married to more than one person at a time.

polygyny: ♦ (many + women – πολυ [πολλ] + γυν) the practice of one man having more than one wife at one time.

polymer: ♦ (many + part – πολ + μερ) compound of many parts.

polytheistic: ♦ (man + god – πολυ [πολλ] + θε) religion that worships more than one divine being.

pore: a small passage through the skin.

pornographic: (sexually immoral + writing – πορν + γραφ) related to the portrayal of sexually explicit scenes.

practice: to do again and again.

pragmatic: practical (see *practice* above).

presbyter: at first simply meant older man, but came to be employed for a specific office in the church in which age was probably a criterion.

problem: ♦ (before + throw – προ + βλη) something thrown before one.

progeny: more directly from the Latin; *gen* is common to Latin and Greek.

prognosis: ♦ (before + knowledge – προ + γνο) foreknowledge.

program: ♦ (before + writing – προ + γραφ) something written before the performance that it describes.

prologue: (before + word) the part of a book included before the main body of the text, as a brief introduction to the work.

prophecy: ♦ (before + say – προ + φη) something spoken about an event before it happens.

prophet: ♦ see *prophecy* above.

prophylactic: ♦ (before + guard – προ + φυλακ) something to guard against (i.e., to take precautions before the danger).

prosthesis: ♦ (to + place – προς + θη [τιθ]) an artificial limb attached to the body.

prototype: ♦ (first + type – πρωτ [προ] + τυπ) the first draft or sample.

protozoa: ♦ (first + life – πρωτ [προ] + ζω) name for the simplest organisms of the animal kingdom.

prow: fore of a ship.

Pseudepigrapha: ♦ (false + upon + writing – ψευδ + ἐπι + γραφ) collective name for Jewish writings with authors falsely attributed.

pseudonym: ♦ (false + name – ψευδ + ὀνομ) pen name (i.e., not one's real name).

psyche: soul.

psychiatric: see *psychiatry* below.

psychiatry: (psyche + heal – ψυχ + ἰατρ) the branch of medicine that deals with the treatment of the psyche.

psychology: ♦ (psyche + study – ψυχ + λογ) the study of the psyche.

psychopath: (psyche + suffer – ψυχ + παθ) one suffering from a mental disease.

prye: pile of combustible material.

Pyrex: a trade name for a glass that is heat resistant.

pyromaniac: (fire + madness – πυρ + μαν) one who has a madness about fire.

recline: more directly from the Latin but related to Greek root κλιν.

rheostat: (flow + stand – ῥη + στα [ἱστη]) a device used to control the current (flow) of a circuit; in other words, it causes the flow to stand.

rheumatism: medical condition; as a memory aid, note that rheumatism prevents the flowing movement of joints and muscles.

rhododendron: (rose + tree – ῥοδ + δενδρ) lit., rose-tree.

sarcastic: to tear flesh like a dog or to bite one's lips in rage; used for bitter or harsh speaking.

sarcophagus: (flesh + eat – σαρχ + φαγ) a coffin (lit., an eater of flesh).

scenario: an outline of a dramatic work.

scene: tent from where actors prepared; later applied to where they performed.

schizophrenia: (divide + mind – σχιζ + φρεν) a disease characterized by a split in the personality.

scotoma: dimness of vision.

seismic: related to earthquakes.

seismograph: (shake + write – σει + γραφ) instrument used to measure the movement of the earth during an earthquake (i.e., something that records [writes] movement).

semaphore: (sign + bear – σημ + φορ [φερ]) an apparatus used for signalling.

semantics: serving as a sign or warning; suffix *-ic* is from the Greek suffix ικος.

somatic: related to the body.

Sophia: in Gnosticism, Wisdom.

sophomore: (wise + fool – σοφ + μορ) a second-year student.

Soter: saviour; an epithet for Zeus and later used by Christians for Jesus.

soteriology: (saviour + study – σωτηρ + λογ) branch of theology that deals with salvation.

sperm: seed.

sporadic: scattered.

static: stationary.

status: standing; position (more directly from the Latin).

Stephen: personal name meaning *crown*.

stereotype: (firm + type – στερε + τυπ) a pattern.

steroids: as a memory aid, note that steroids are used to make a person firm or solid.

stethoscope: (breast + see – στηθο + σκοπ) an instrument for hearing (note: not *seeing*) the breast.

strategy: ◆ (army + lead – στρατ + ἀγ) to *lead* an *army*, though used more widely without a military sense.

surgery: ◆ (hand + work – χειρ + ἐργ) the word for *hand* has become very abbreviated; the root *urg* for work remains unaffected.

sycamore: a fig tree.

syllable: ◆ (together + take – συν + λαβ [λαμβ]) letters taken together to produce one sound.

sympathy: ◆ (with + suffer – συν + παθ) the sharing in the suffering of others.

symphony: ◆ (together + sound – συν + φων) agreeable mixing of sounds.

symposium: ◆ (together + drink – συν + ποσ [πο²]) a meeting to discuss a particular topic; originally associated with a meal.

symptom: ◆ (with + fall – συν + πτομ [πιπτ]) any condition that occurs (falls) with a disease and thus can be used to indicate the presence of the disease.

synagogue: ◆ (together + lead – συν + ἀγ) place where Jews were led together by a common interest.

synchronize: ◆ (with + time – συν + χρον) to set watches so that each one has the same time; *-ize* is like the Greek suffix ιζω; originally, to be contemporary with.

syndetic: ◆ (together + bind – συν + δε) uniting.

syndicate: ◆ (with + judge – συν + δικ) a group that decides (judges) together what course of action should be taken.

synod: ◆ (together + way – συν + ὁδ) an ecclesiastical council.

synonym: ◆ (with + name – συν + ὀνομ) does not really mean "with the same name" but "with the same (similar) meaning."

synoptic: ◆ (together + see – συν + ὀπτ) as the Synoptic Gospels, which are viewed together, thus giving a full view.

syntax: ◆ (together + arrange – συν + ταξ [ταγ]) the branch of linguistics dealing with the relationships among parts of a sentence.

synthesis: ◆ (together + place – συν + θη [τιθ]) act of placing together things once apart; *-sis* is Greek suffix.

synthetic: see *synthesis* above; *-ic* is from the Greek ending ικος.

system: ◆ (together + stand – συν + θη [τιθ]) something that *stands together*.

tachometer: (speed + measure – ταχ + μετρ) instrument for measuring speed.

tactics: (arrange + adjectival ending – ταξ [ταγ] + ικος) science of troop arrangement. [Note: English word *tactics* (a noun) is simply a transliteration of a Greek adjective.]

tautology: (same + word – ταυτ + λογ) unnecessary repetition of the same idea in different words.

taxidermist: (arrange + skin – ταχ + δερμ) one who stuffs and mounts animal skins.

taxidermy: (order + skin – ταξ [ταγ] + δερμ) bringing order to the skin of an animal, so that the original shape is restored.

taxonomy: (arrangement + law – ταξ [ταγ] + νομ) systematic arrangement according to established criteria.

teleology: (end + study – τελ + λογ) the branch of cosmology that deals with final causes.

telephone: (far + voice – τελ + φων) an instrument that carries the voice over a distance.

telescope: (far + sight – τελ + σκοπ) an instrument that permits one to *see* things that are far away.

television: from the Latin (far + see), though the first part of the compound is shared with Greek.

tension: more directly from the Latin, meaning the condition of being stretched tight; but see τειν.

tetrahedron: ♦ (four + base – τετρα + ἑδρον) a four-sided object.

tetrarch: ♦ (four + rule – τετρ + ἀρχ) ruler of small territory (a fourth part); title given to one of Herod the Great's sons after his kingdom was divided.

tetris: a game with various shapes of four-piece squares.

thallassic: (sea + characteristic of – θαλλασ + ικος) pertaining to the sea.

thaumaturgy: ♦ (wonder + work – θαυμ + ὑργ [ἐργ]) magic; the *working* of *wonders* or miracles.

theatre: ♦ place for seeing performances, from the word *sight* (θεα) and the suffix τηριον, used to indicate place where something is done.

theme: from τιθημι, for thing placed.

theology: ♦ (god + study – θε + λογ) study of divine matters.

theophany: ♦ (god + appear – θε + φαν [φαιν]) a term used for various appearances by gods, often in human form.

theory: something viewed (or speculated) about a phenomenon.

Theotokos: (God + bear – θε + τοκ [τεκν]) means the *bearer of God*, and used of Mary in the Nestorian debate.

therapeutic: transliterated from Greek for healing; the ending *-ic* is from the Greek ικος.

therapy: simply transliterated from the Greek; any practice or service directed toward the process of healing.

thermal: from Greek word for *warm;* the ending *-al* is the same as the Greek suffix αλος.

thermometer: (hot + measure – θερμ + μετρ) an instrument that measures the temperature.

Thermopylae: (warm + gates – θερμ + πυλ) site of famous battle in 480 B.C.E., where the Greeks tried to check the advance of the Persians in a narrow pass.

thermos: a container used to keep liquids warm.

thesaurus: storehouse; treasure.

thesis: something put forward as an explanation; a proposition.

thlipsis: pressure on blood vessels.

tome: one of a series of volumes (i.e., something cut from a larger series to form a distinct volume).

tone: a sound that changes depending on tension.

topography: ♦ (place + write – τοπ + γραφ) the representing (graphing) on a map of the physical features of a place.

track: more directly from Old French, but with close similarity to Greek τρεχ.

trek: more directly from culture of South Africa, meaning to *travel* by wagon.

triangle: ♦ (three + angle – τρι + γων): the form is more directly Latin but is also close to the Greek.

trilogy: ♦ (three + word – τρι + λογ) any three-part production considered together.

trinity: (three + one) the form is Latin, as is the root *one,* but *tri-* is common to Greek and Latin.

triumvirate: from the Latin meaning ruling body of three people; *tri* is both Greek and Latin.

tripod: ♦ (three + foot – τρι + ποδ [πο¹]) device with three feet or legs.

trophy: originally, a memorial erected by the victorious army at the place of battle where they routed (turned) the enemy.

tropic: lines between the poles and the equator at which point the sun turns back toward the equator.

Uranus: the sky god in Greek mythology.

Utopia: (no + place – οὐ + τοπ) coined in 1516 by Thomas More to describe an ideal country; prefix is from οὐ, not from the normal negating prefix ἀ.

xenophobia: (strange + fear – ξεν + φοβ) fear of foreign people or things.

xerox: a method of dry printing that uses light, electricity, and powder rather than ink.

xylophone: (wood + sound – ξυλ + φων) instrument constructed from strips of wood which, when hit, vibrate, producing musical sounds.

zodiac: diminutive of ζῷον (animal); a scheme in which animals (living things) are key symbols.

zone: something that girds or binds.

zoo: place for keeping live animals, as opposed to a museum.

zoology: (life + study – ζω + λογ) branch of science that studies animal life.

6

Mini Greek/English Cognate Dictionary

Greek = basic cognate stem
English plain text = basic meaning
Italics = English cognate
[in square brackets] = useful memory aid

ἀγ ἀγωγ   bring/lead *demagogue; agent; synagogue*
ἀγαπ   love *agape*
ἀγγελ   message *angel, evangelism*
ἁγι ἁγν   holy/sacred *hagiography*
ἀγορ   market *agora; agoraphobia*
ἀγρ   field/wild *agriculture; acre*
ἀδελφ   brother/sister *Philadelphia*
αἱμ   blood *hemoglobin; hemophilia; hemorrhage; anemic*
αἰν   praise *paean*
αἱρ   take/choose *heresy*
αἰτ   reason/cause/accusation *etiology*
αἰων   age *eon*
ἀκο   hear *acoustic*
ἀκολουθ   follow *acolyte*
ἁλ ἁλι   salt/fish *[halibut]*
ἀλλ   other/change *alien; alias; allegory*
ἀμην   truly *amen*
ἀν   up/again *anatomy; Anabaptist*
ἀνεμ   wind/movement *animation; anemometer*
ἀνηρ ἀνδρ   man *android; androgynous*
ἀνθρωπ   man *anthropomorphic; anthropology*
ἀντι   oppose/replace *antichrist; antibiotic; antidote; anti-*
ἀξι   worthy *axiom*
ἀπ ἀπο   from/away *apostate; apostle*
ἀργυρ   money/silver *Argentina*
ἀριθμ   number *arithmetic*

ἁρπαγ ἁρπαζ   seize *[harpoon]*
ἀρχ   begin/old/rule/chief *archaic, archaeology; monarch; anarchy*
ἀστρ ἀστηρ ἀστερ   star *star; astronomy; asterisk*
ἀσχημ αἰσχ   shame *[a shame]*
αὐξ   grow *auction; auxiliary*
αὐρ   tomorrow *aurora borealis*
αὐτο   self *autobiography; autocrat; autistic; auto-*
βαιν βα βη βασ   go/foot *acrobat; base*
βαλ βολ βλη   throw *ball; ballistic; problem*
βαπτ   baptize/dip *baptize*
βαρ   burden/weight *barometer; baritone*
βασιλ   royal *basilica*
βιβλ   book *Bible; bibliography*
βλασφημ   blaspheme *blaspheme*
βο   shout *[boo!]*
βουλ   plan *boule*
βρω   food *ambrosia; German: brot*
γαμ   marriage *bigamy; polygamy*
γεν γιν γον   family/birth *genetic; generation; genealogy*
γη γε   earth *geography*
γλωσσα   tongue *glossary; glossalalia*
γνο γνω γινω   know *gnostic; diagnosis; knowledge*
γραφ γραπ γραμ   write *monograph; grammar; -graph*
γυμν   exercise/naked *gymnasium*
γυνη γυναικ   woman *gynecology; polygyny; androgynous*
δαιμ   demon *demon; pandemonium*
δε   bind *diadem*
δεικ δειγ δειξ   show/example *paradigm; indicate*

δεκα   ten *decade; Decalogue; decimate*
δενδρ   tree *rhododendron*
δεξ   right *dexterity; ambidextrous*
δευτερ δυο   two *duet, duo; duplex; Deuteronomony*
δημ   people/home *democracy; domestic; demagogue; pandemic*
δια   through *diarrhea; diameter; dia-*
διακον   serve *deacon*
διδ δο δω   give *antidote; dose*
διδασκ διδακ διδαχ   teach *didactic; Didache*
δικ   just/judgment *syndicate*
δοκ   think/seem *docetic; paradox; dogma*
δοξ   glory *doxology*
δυ   clothe *endue*
δυνα δυναμ   power/ability *dynamic; dynamite*
δωρ   gift *Dorothy*
ἐγω   I *ego, egocentric*
ἐθν   nation/Gentile *ethnic; ethnography*
εἰδωλ   image/idol *idol*
εἰμι εἰ ἐσ οὐσ ὀντ   be/exist *essence; ontological; parousia*
εἰρην   peace *irenic*
εἰ μια ἑν   one *henotheism*
εἰ ἐσω   into *eisegesis; esophagus*
ἐκ ἐξ   out/from *exit; exodus; exhale*
ἐλαι   olive/oil *oil; petroleum*
ἐλει   mercy *Kyrie eleison*
ἐλλ   Greek *hellenistic*
ἐν   in *in; in-; endemic; en-*
ἐξ   six *hex key; hexameter; [six]*
ἐπι   on *epicenter; epidermis*
ἑπτ   seven *Heptateuch*
ἐργ οὐργ   work *energy; erg; ergonomic; -urgy*
ἐρημ   desert *hermit*
ἐσχατ   last/final *eschaton; eschatology*
ἑτερ   other/different *heterodoxy; heterosexual*
εὐ   well, good, *euphemism; eulogy; euthanasia*
εὐρ   find *eureka!; heuristic*
ζηλ   zealous/jealous *zeal*
ζυμ   yeast *enzyme*
ζω ζα   life *zoo; zodiac*
ζων   fasten/bind *zone*
ἡγε   lead/govern *hegemony*
ἡλι   sun *heliocentric*
ἡμερ   day *ephemeral*
θαλασ   sea *thalassic*
θαν θνη   death *euthanasia*
θαυμ   wonder *thaumaturgy*
θε θεο   god *theism, theology; atheist*
θεα θεωρ   see *theatre; theory*
θελ   will *monothelite*
θεμελι   foundation *theme*

θερ   warm/harvest *thermal; thermos; therometer*
θεραπ   healing/service *theraputic*
θησαυρ   treasure *thesaurus*
θρον   throne *throne*
θυγατηρ θυγατρ   daughter *daughter*
θυρ   door *door*
ἰα ἰατρ   heal *psychiatry; pediatrics*
ἰδ   see *idea; idol*
ἰδι   own *idiosyncratic; idiom*
ἰερ   priest *hierarchy; hieroglyph*
ἰκαν   able *["I can . . ."]*
ἰππ   horse *hippopotamus; hippodrome*
ἰστη στα στη   stand *static; ecstasy; status; stamina; system*
ἰχθυ   fish *IXΘΥΣ*
καθ καθεδρ   sit *cathedral*
καθαρ καθαιρ   clean *cathartic; Cathar*
καιν   new *Cenozoic*
κακ   bad *cacophony; caca*
καλ¹   good/proper *calligraphy*
καλ² κλη   call *call; paraclete*
καλυπτ καλυμ καλυψ   hide *apocalyptic*
καρδ   heart *cardiac*
καρπ   fruit *pericarp*
κατ καθ   down/according to *catacomb; catastrophe*
κει   lie *cemetery*
κενο   empty *cenotaph; kenosis*
κεφαλ   head/sum *encephalitis*
κηρυξ κηρυγ κηρυσσ   preach *kerygma*
κλα   break *iconoclastic*
κλει   lock/close *[close]*
κλεπτ κλοπ κλεμ   steal *kleptomaniac*
κληρ   share *clergy*
κλιν   recline/incline/turn *recline*
κοιν κοινων   common *koine; koinonia*
κοσμ   world/order *cosmic; cosmetics*
κρατ   strong/power *autocratic; democratic*
κρι   judge *critique; crime*
κρυπτ κρυφ   hide *crypt; cryptic; Apocrypha*
κυρι   lord/power *Kyrie eleison; czar; Caesar*
κωμ   town *common; community*
λα   people *laity*
λαλ   speak *glossolalia*
λαμβ λημ λαβ   take/receive *syllable; dilemma*
λαμπ   lamp *lamp*
λατρ   worship *idolatry; Mariolatry*
λεγ λογ λεκτ   say/word *dialogue; dialect; lectern*
λειπ λοιπ λειμ λιμ   leave/lack *eclipse*
λειτουργ   worship (compare with ἐργ) *liturgy*
λευκ   white *leukemia*
λιθ   stone *lithograph; megalith*
λυ λυτρ   loose/redeem *analysis*
λυπ   pain *lupus*

λυχν   lamp *lux*
μαθ μανθ   learn *math*
μακαρ   blessed *macarism*
μακρ μακρο   long *macro-*
μαρτυρ   witness *martyr*
μεγ μεγαλ   great *megaphone; megalith*
μειζ   greater
μελ[1]   concern/care *melodramatic*
μελ[2]   part *melody*
μεν μον   wait/remain *remain*
μερ   part *polymer; merit*
μεσο μεσι   middle *Mesopotamia*
μετα   with/after/change *metabolism; meta-phor; metamorphosis*
μετρ   measure *meter*
μητηρ μητρ   mother *maternal*
μικρ   small *microscopic; micro-*
μιμν μν μνη μνημ   remember *amnesia; mnemonic*
μισ   hate *misanthropy*
μονο   only *monopoly; mono-*
μυστηρ   mystery *mystery*
μωρ   foolish *moron; sophomore*
νεκρ   death *necropolis*
νε νεα νεο   new *new; neophyte; Fr. nouveau*
νικ   victory *Nike*
νο   mind *paranoia*
νομ   law *astronomy; anomoly; Deuteronomy*
νυ νυκ νυχ   night *nocturnal; equinox*
νυμφ   bride *nuptial; nymph*
ξεν   strange/guest *xenophobia*
ξυλ   wood *xylophone*
ξηρ   dry *Xerox*
ὁδ   way/travel *odometer; exodus; synod*
ὁικ   house *economy*
ὁλ   whole/all *holocaust; holistic; catholic; whole*
ὀλιγ   little/few *oligarchy*
ὀλλ   destroy *Apollyon*
ὁμο ὁμοι   same/like *homogenous; homonym; homo-*
ὀνομ   name *name; synonym; pseudonym; anonymous*
ὀπ ὀπτ   see *optics; optical; autopsy*
ὁρ   boundary *horizon; aphorism*
ὁρα   see *panorama*
ὁρκ   oath *exorcism*
ου   where *[French: où]*
οὐραν   heaven *Uranus*
οὐς ὠτ   ear *otology*
ὀφθαλμ   eye *ophthalmology*
ὀχλ   crowd/mob *ochlocracy*
παθ ποθ   feel/desire *pathos; sympathy; apathay*
παι παιδ   child/education *pediatrician; ency-clopedia; pedophile*

παλ   again *palindrome; palimpsest*
παλαι   old *paleontology*
παν πας παντ   all *pantheistic; pandemic; panacea; pantheon*
παρα   by *paragraph; parasite; parenthesis*
πασχ   suffer *passion; paschal*
πατ   walk *peripatetic*
πατηρ πατρ   father *patriarchy; paternal*
παυ   stop *pause; menopause*
πειρ   test/attempt *pirate*
πεμπ   send *pomp; pompous*
πεντ   five *pentagon; Pentateuch*
περι   around *perimeter; periscope; peripheral*
περα   far *far (Grimm's Law) [see πορ]*
πιπτ πεσ πεπτ   fall *symptom*
πιστ   belief/faith *epistemology*
πλαν   error/wandering *planet: a wandering star*
πλει πλεον   more *Pliocene [plural; plus]*
πλη   full *plethora; plenary; plenty*
πληγ πλασσ πλησσ   plague/strike *plague; ap-oplexy; paraplegic*
πλου   rich *plutocrat*
πν πνευ   spirit/wind/breath *pneumatic; pneumonia*
πο[1] ποδ πεδ πεζ   foot *pedestrian; podiatrist; tripod; orthopedic*
πο[2] ποτ ποταμ   drink/river *potable; symposium*
πολι   city *metropolis; politics; police*
πολεμ   war *polemical*
πολλ πολυ   much/many *polytheism*
πορ   journey *emporium, far [see περα]*
πορν πονηρ   evil *pornography*
πρασσ πραγ   matter/event/something done *pragmatic*
πρεσβυ   old/elderly *presbyter*
προ πρω πρωτ   before/first *program; proto-type; prognosis*
προσ   to/toward *prosthetic; proselyte*
πυλ   gate/door *Thermopylae*
πυρ   fire *Pyrex; pyre; pyromaniac*
πωλ   sell *monopoly*
ῥε ῥη[1]   flow *diarrhea; rheumatism*
ῥη[2] ῥητ   word *rhetoric; orator*
ῥιζ   root *rhizome*
σαρξ σαρκ   flesh *sarcophagus*
σεβ   worship *Eusebius*
σει   quake *seismograph; seismic*
σημ   sign/indication *semaphore; semantics*
σιτ   food/fat *parasite*
σθεν   strong / ασθεν weak *asthma; asthenia*
σκ σκοτ   dark *scotoma*
σκανδαλ   scandal *scandal*
σκην   tent *scene; scenario*

σκοπ σκεπ   view *scope; microscopic; skeptical*
σοφ   wisdom *philosophy; sophomore*
σπερ σπειρ σπορ   scatter/seed *sporatic; diaspora; sperm*
σπευδ σπουδ   speed/eagerness *[speed]*
σταυρ   cross [compare ἀστρ *star*]
στελ στολ   send *apostle*
στερε στηρε   firm/solid *steroid; stereotype; cholesterol*
στεφαν   crown/reward *Stephan*
στομ   mouth *John Chrysostom; stomach*
στρατ   army *strategy*
στρεφ στροφ   turn *apostrophe; catastrophic*
συκ   fig *sycamore*
συν   with *synonyn; synchronize; syn-*
σωζ   save *creosote*
σωμα   body/physical *psychosomatic; somatic*
σωτηρ   salvation *soteriology*
ταγ τακ ταξ ταχ[1] τασσ   order *taxonomy; tactic; taxidermist*
ταχ[2]   quick *tachometer*
τεκν τικ τοκ   child *[tike]*
τελ   end/far *telephone; teleology*
τελων   tax *toll*
τεμν τομ   cut *anatomy; atom; appendectomy; -tomy*
τεν τειν τιν τον   extend/stretch *extend; tension; tendon*
τεσσαρ τεταρ τετρα   four *tetrarch Diatessaron; tetris; trapezoid*
τιθ θε θη   put/place *synthesis; antithesis; bibliotheca; epithet*
τιμ   honor *Timothy*
τοπ   place *topography; Utopia*
τρεπ τροπ   turn *trophy; trope; tropics*
τρεφ τρε τραμ   feed/support *atrophy*

τρεχ τροχ   run *track; trek*
τρι   three *trinity; tri-*
τυπ   type/example *type; typical*
ὑγι   health *hygiene*
ὑδρ   water *hydrant; hydro*
ὑπερ   over *hypersensitive; hyperbole; hyper-*
ὑπο   under / by means of *hypothermia; hypodermic; hypo-*
ὑσ ὑστερ   last/lack *hysteria*
ὑψ   high *hypsography*
φα φη φημ   say/report *fame; prophet; euphemism*
φαν φαιν   display/appear *phantom; fantasy*
φερ φορ   bring/bear/carry *periphery; ferry; transfer; semaphore; phosphorus*
φευγ φυγ   flee *fugitive*
φιλ   love *Philadelphia; philanthrophy*
φοβ   fear *claustrophobia; -phobia*
φρ φρο φρον   think *schizophrenia*
φυ φυσ φυτ   natural/growth/planted *physical; neophyte*
φυλ   tribe *phylum; phylogeny; [file]*
φυλακ φυλασσ   guard *phylactery; prophylactic*
φων   voice *telephone; phonics*
φως φωτ   light *photograph; phosphorus*
χαρι χαριστ   gift *charity; charismatic; eucharist*
χειρ   hand *chiropractor*
χιλι   thousand *chiliasm*
χρι   anoint *Christ; christen*
χρον   time *chronology; chronic*
χρυσ   gold *John Chrysostom; chrysanthemum*
χωρ   place *anchorite*
ψευδ   false *pseudonym; pseudo-*
ψυχ   self/spirit *psyche*
ὡρ   time/hour *hour; horoscope*

7

Prepositions and Cases

PREPOSITIONS:

Prepositions are words that relate one noun or pronoun (**A**) to another noun or pronoun (**B**), usually in some way that expresses a physical location or position of object **A** in relation to object **B** (e.g., **A** *is* on, in, over, or under **B**), or the movement of object **A** in relation to object **B** (e.g., **A** *walks* to, into, from, or through **B**, where *walks* represents any verb that supplies the idea of movement). The noun whose position or movement is being described (**A**) usually stands before the preposition, and can take any case, depending on its use in the sentence. The other noun (**B**), which represents the stationary object in reference to which the location or movement of noun **A** is specified, will be in one of three cases (accusative, dative, or genitive).

DETERMINING THE CASE:

Students often have difficulty remembering which case noun **B** requires. In the examples below, prepositions expressing motion or position (location) are illustrated. As a general rule, prepositions expressing *motion to* take a noun in the accusative case, prepositions expressing *motion or separation from* take a noun in the genitive case, and prepositions expressing *location or lack of motion* take a noun in the dative case.

> accusative — motion *to*
> genitive — motion *from* or separation *from*
> dative — mere position or absence of motion

With a little imagination, the illustrations can be made to work for many prepositions. The diagrams use the following logic:

- The case is being determined for noun **B** only.
- The **X** or the arrow represents noun **A**. **X** indicates noun **A** at rest; the arrow indicates noun **A** in motion.

- The dark circle represents noun **B**.
- The *left* side of the diagram represents the *accusative* case for noun **B** (expressing the motion of object **A** *to* object **B**).
- The *right* side of the diagram represents the *genitive* case for noun **B** (expressing the motion of object **A** *from* object **B**).
- Motion generally moves from left to right.
- *Wherever the motion arrow ends* (accusative or genitive for motion), the case for that location is to be used.
- Generally if there is no motion, there will be an **X** within or by the circle (in the middle of the diagram), and in these cases, the dative case is used.
- Where a case other than the dative case is used for a diagram using an **X**, the appropriate case required by the situation will be visually clear. In many of these cases, some degree of separation is indicated by the preposition. In such instances, the genitive case is usually used.
- From left to right, the order of the cases is alphabetical: **A** (accusative), **D** (dative), and **G** (genitive). *Remember this. It is a key to remembering the required cases.*
- RE: ἀνά. Think of *up* (ἀνά) as opposite of *down* (κατά), and of ἀνά in compounds meanings *back*, thus in the UP ARROW illustration, the motion runs from right to left, *back* from the usual left to right direction used in most of the diagrams.
- RE: κατά. When meaning *against*, κατά takes the genitive. In the diagram, the arrow runs from right to left, *against* the usual direction used in the diagrams.

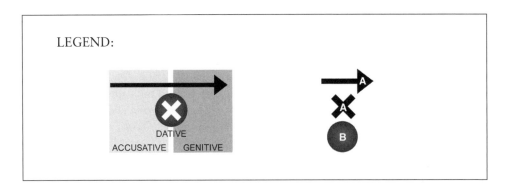

ACCUSATIVE	DATIVE	GENITIVE

εἰς into, to

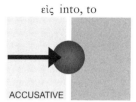

σύν with

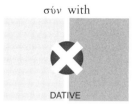

ἐκ from out of

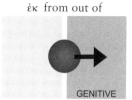

περί around

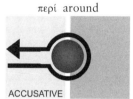

διά through

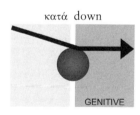

παρά to beside, beside

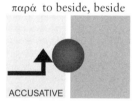

παρά beside, with

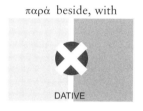

παρά from beside, from

ἀνά up

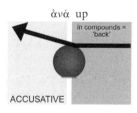

κατά down

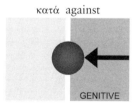

ὑπέρ above

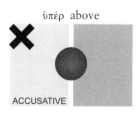

κατά against

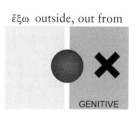

ὑπό under

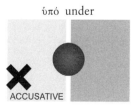

ἔξω outside, out from

ACCUSATIVE	DATIVE	GENITIVE

χωρίς apart from

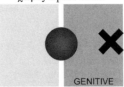

ἄχρι until, as far as

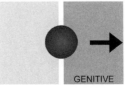

ὀπίσω after, behind

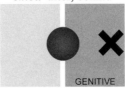

APPENDIX 1: GRIMM'S LAW

From one of the brothers of German fairy-tale fame, Grimm's Law is a list of rules that helps to explain some of the relations between words of Indo-European languages and their Greek roots where there is not a direct letter-for-letter correspondence. In order to understand this "law," one needs first to learn a particular subdivision of consonants. In this case, we distinguish between SOFT, HARD, and ASPIRATE consonants. The rule is that where there is not an equivalent letter in an English word derived from the Greek, there may be a substitution of a related letter. The substitution, from Greek to English, is: (1) SOFT (voiced); (2) HARD (voiceless); (3) ASPIRATED; (4) SOFT (voiced), as illustrated on the chart below. Simply find on the chart the letter from the Greek word and replace it with the letter to the immediate right on the chart to find its English equivalent.

	1	2	3	4
GUTTURAL	γ → k	κ → h	χ → g	
LABIAL	β → p	π → f	φ → b	
DENTAL	δ → t	τ → th	θ → d	

Examples from the vocabulary list:

ἀργ – acre
γεν – kind; kin
γνο – know
δε – tie
δεκα – ten
δυ – two
ἐργ οὐργ – work
θυγατηρ – daughter
θυρ – door
καρδ – heart

μητηρ – mother
πατηρ – father
πιστ – faith
ποδ – foot
πολ – full
πορν – fornication
πυρ – fire
τρι – three
φερ – bear
χαρ – grace

APPENDIX 2: COMMON PRONOUNS, ADJECTIVES, AND ADVERBS

CHART A

	Key Syllable ὁ	Relative ὁ	Interrogative π	Indefinite* π	Indefinite Relative o + indefinite	Demonstrative τ for π or δε
Place Where	ου	οὗ where	ποῦ where?	που somewhere	ὅπου wherever/whither	ὧδε here
Time When	οτε	ὅτε when	πότε when?	ποτε sometime	ὁπότε whenever	τότε then
Manner How	ως	ὡς as	πῶς how?	πως somehow	ὅπως that/in order that	οὕτως thus/so
Quantity** How much	οσ	ὅσος as much as	πόσος how much?	ποσος of some quantity	ὁπόσος of however much	τοσοῦτος so much
Quality** What kind	οι	οἷος such as	ποῖος what kind?	ποιος of some kind	ὁποῖος of whatever kind	τοιοῦτος such

CHART B

	Relative ὁ	Interrogative τ	Indefinite* τ	Indefinite Relative o + indefinite	Demonstrative often δε
Person** Who	ὅς who	τίς who?	τις someone	ὅστις whoever	οὗτος/ὅδε this
Thing** What	ὅς what	τίς what?	τις something	ὅστις whatever	οὗτος/ὅδε this

---

* English translation: "some" or "any"

** Only the masculine form is given on the chart.

INDEX 1: WORDS OCCURRING
10–19 TIMES

ἀλέκτωρ ορος	rooster	masc	[√]-ρ
ἅλυσις εως	chain, imprisonment	fem	[√]-σις
ἅμα (>acc)	together / together with	adv/prep	[√]-α
ἀμφότεροι αι α	both, all	adj	(ἀμφι)-τερος
ἅπαξ	once	adv	
ἀπαρνέομαι	disown	vb	ἀπο-[√]-ω
ἀσέλγεια ας	vice, indecency	fem	[√]-α
ἀσκός οῦ	wineskin	masc	[√]-ος
ἀτενίζω	look at, stare	vb	ἀ-[τειν]-ιζω
βροντή ῆς	thunder	fem	[√]-η
γέεννα ης	hell (gehenna)	fem	[√]-α
γεύομαι	taste	vb	[√]-ω
γόνυ γόνατος	knee (Grimm's Law)	neut	
δάκρυον ου	tear (as in crying)	neut	[√]-ον
δέρω	beat	vb	[√]-ω
δηνάριον ου	denarius	neut	[√]-ιον
δίκτυον ου	net for fishing	neut	[√]-ον
διψάω	thirst	vb	[√]-αω
δόλος οω	deceit	masc	[√]-ος
δράκων οντος	dragon	masc	[√]-ων
εἴκοσι	twenty	adj	
εἰκών όνος	likeness (>ıcon)	fem	[√]-ων
ἑκατόν	hundred (>prefix hec/hect)	adj	[√]-ον
ἐλάξιστος η ον	least	adj	[√]-ιστος
ἐλέγχω	show error, convince	vb	[√]-ω
ἔνατος η ον	ninth	adj	[√]-τος
ἐνιαυτός οῦ	year	masc	(ἔνος)-[αὐτ]-ος
ἐξουθενέω	despise	vb	[√]-εω
ἔπειτα	then, next	adv	[√]-α
θάπτω	bury	vb	[√]-ω
θρίξ τριχός	hair (>tress)	fem	[√]-ξ
καίω	light, burn	vb	[√]-ω
καπνός οῦ	smoke	masc	[√]-ων
κατακαίω	burn, consume	vb	κατα-[√]-ω
κέρας ατος	horn, power	neut	[√]-ς
κοιμάομαι	sleep, die (>coma)	vb	[√]-αω

This index includes only words that are not listed in Section 2: Cognate Groups.

κολλάομαι	unite with, associate	vb	[√]-αω
κομίζω	bring, buy (>commerce)	vb	[√]-ιζω
κράβαττος ου	bed	masc	[√]-ος
κρείσσων ον	better, greater	adj	[√]-ων
κωφός ή όν	mute	adj	[√]-ος
ληστής οῦ	robber	masc	[√]-της
λίαν	greatly	adv	
λίμνη ης	lake	fem	[√]-η
λιμός οῦ	famine	masc/fem	[√]-ος
μήν μηνός	month	masc	
μύρον ου	myrrh	neut	[√]-ον
νήπιος α ον	infant	adj	[√]-ιος
νόσος ου	disease	fem	[√]-ος
ὀδούς ὀδόντος	tooth (>dental, orthodontist)	masc	[√]-ς
ὅθεν	where, from where	adv	[ὁ]-θεν
ὄφις εως	snake (>Ophites)	masc	[√]-ς
παρθένος ου	virgin (>Parthenon)	fem	[√]-ος
πατάσσω	strike, touch	vb	[√]-σσω
πενθέω	mourn (>penitence)	vb	[√]-εω
πετεινόν οῦ	bird (>petrel)	neut	[√]-ον
πέτρα ας	rock (>petrify)	fem	[√]-α
πηγή ῆς	spring, well	fem	[√]-η
πιάζω	seize	vb	[√]-αζω
πλησίον (>gen)	near (as noun: neighbor)	prep	[√]-ιον
ποικίλος η ον	varied, diverse	adj	[√]-λος
πραΰς, πραεῖα, πραΰ	humble	adj	[√]-υς
προσκαρτερέω	devote onself to	vb	προς-[√]-εω
πυνθάνομαι	ask	vb	[√]-ω
πῶλος ου	colt	masc	[√]-ος
ῥαββί	rabbi	masc	
ῥάβδος ου	stick (>rod)	fem	[√]-ος
ῥύομαι	rescue	vb	[√]-ω
σαλεύω	shake	vb	[√]-ευω
σφόδρα	very much	adv	[√]-α
σχίζω	split (>schism)	vb	[√]-ιζω
τάλαντον ου	talent (coin)	neut	[√]-ον
τέρας ατος	wonder, omen	neut	[√]-ς
τολμάω	dare	vb	[√]-αω
τύπτω	beat, hit	vb	[√]-ω
ὑμέτερος α ον	your	adj	[√]-ος
φείδομαι	spare	vb	[√]-ω
φιάλη ης	bowl (Grimm's Law)	fem	[√]-η
χείρων ον	worse	adj	[√]-ων
χιτών ῶνος	tunic	masc	[√]-ων
χοῖρος ου	pig	masc	[√]-ος
χωλός ή όν	lame	adj	[√]-ος
ὦ	O!	interj	

INDEX 2: GREEK WORD ENDINGS

This index of word endings has been compiled *solely* to make it quick and easy for the reader of a Greek text to identify the ending of a puzzling word. The index can be used with any Greek text, unlike many reading or translation aids that are focused on a particular corpus, particularly the New Testament. Indeed, readers can much more easily explore the Church Fathers or the Septuagint, for example, with this index at their side. But remember, the index is not intended as an analysis of Greek word formation. Other parts of this volume offer assistance in that regard.

Greek words can end with any vowel (α, ε, η, ι, o, υ, or ω). They can also end with the consonants ν and ς. In a few nouns, the nominative singular forms may end with ξ, ρ, ψ. Prepositions sometimes end with letters other than these, such as κ. In English, a word can end with any letter of the alphabet. The reason for the fewer letters with which a Greek word can end is that Greek words take a set of standard endings specific to the kind of word it is. By far, verbs have the greatest number of distinctive endings.

In the index that follows, all Koine and most classical Greek word endings are listed. The unique feature of this index is that the endings are listed in *reverse alphabetical order,* working from the last letter of the ending backward. Thus rather than having all words that *begin* with the letter "A" listed together (as one would have in a normal dictionary), in this index all endings that *end* with "A" are listed together. The importance of this somewhat unusual arrangement is that the user does not need to know where the ending of a particular word begins to find the proper parsing for that form. To use the index, work backwards from the last letter of the word to the longest ending listed in the index that fits the word you are trying to parse. In nearly all cases, the longest ending in the list is the correct ending. The full description of that form is then given.

The one exception to the reverse alphabetical arrangement is that endings having all but the farthest left letter in common are listed in *normal alphabetical order,* followed by the ending this group shares in common. For example, ξαμεθα is listed in normal alphabetical order before σαμεθα and ψαμεθα, followed by the shorter common ending, αμεθα. This exception is designed to help avoid the pitfall of selecting the shorter of the listed endings before considering whether one of the longer options also fits the word in question.

Be careful to distinguish between nominals (nouns and adjectives primarily) and all other words. Nominals appear far more frequently in a sentence than anything else, though there are far fewer distinctive forms for nominals. They can often quickly be identified by the presence of an article or by surrounding nominal modifiers with the same ending as the word in question. Note, too, that the nominative singular form of a noun is often irregular, but fortunately this is the form we encounter in vocabulary lists, making it a simple matter to look up such words in a lexicon.

Endings appear in the index as illustrated in the example below. Note that the numbers in parentheses do not appear in the index. These numbers indicate each part of the entry, explained in detail following the example.

σομεν (1)

V • fut ind act 1 pl • ★

(2)   (3)   (4)

---

(1)   The boldface Greek entry is the ending. The line or lines that follow lists all the possible forms for that ending. These lines are divided into three parts, separated by small bullets (•).
(2)   The first part is the letter V (verb), P (participle), I (infinitive), or N (nominal).
(3)   The second part lists the full description of the ending.
(4)   The third part lists a code or codes, describing for what kind of word that ending applies.

In the example above, σομεν is a verb ending for the future indicative active first person plural. The ★ indicates the code for the specific kind of word that the ending applies to. (See specific codes below.)

CODES:

αω   α–contract verb
εω   ε–contract verb
οω   o–contract verb
αμι   αμι verb
εμι   εμι verb
ομι   ομι verb
νυμι νυμι verb
★   Regular Verb: These are the most basic forms of the verb; other forms are modified or contracted from these. The forms of a verb a student first learns are the regular forms. This entry includes irregular verbs that follow the regular form at this point.
☆   Strong Tense, such as the Second Aorist. These omit the tense format letter, such as σ in aorists and κ in perfect and use primary endings. Both thematic and athematic verbs may take these forms. Although most verbs have first aorist endings, many of the common verbs use second aorist endings.
A   Nominals: First declension.
C   Nominals: Third declension consonant stems. In these lists, we have included the basic form, as well as longer entries that include part of the root, wherever that would assist in identifying the form.
D   Dental: The stem of the verb ends in a dental letter (δ, τ, ς).
G   Guttural: The stem of the verb ends in a guttural (palatal) letter (γ, κ, χ).
L   Labial: The stem of the verb ends in a labial letter (β, π, φ).
MI   μι Verbs: This form applies to all μι verbs.
O   Nominals: Second declension.

Q   Liquid: The stem of the verb ends in a liquid letter (λ, μ, ν, ρ)
1   Root Aorists (sometimes called third aorists): These omit the tense format letter (as in ☆) , but have a long vowel at the end of the root and use secondary endings.
2   Many words omit or modify the tense format letter, such as the σ in future forms. This is particularly true of liquid verbs. Some verbs of the μι ending have a κ-aorist form, replacing the expected σ of the aorist with a κ.
3   A few αω contract verbs present unusual vowel contraction in many of their forms.
4   A few common words have retained primitive endings, such as εἰμί, εἶμι, and φημί. Often, these stems are short. We have included, as well, longer entries that include part of the root, where that assists in identifying the form.

NOTE:
• Future Perfects do not occur in the New Testament and are rare in classical literature. Such forms are not included in the following lists. They occur only in the passive and they are identical in their endings with the future middle forms. They have, however, a reduplicated prefix, thus distinguishing them from the future middle forms. To find future perfect forms in this index: (1) find the ending, then in the descriptions (2) replace "future" with "future perfect," (3) replace "middle" with "passive."
• In μι verbs, the distinctive vowel technically belongs to the root rather than the ending. Both forms (with the vowel and without the vowel) are listed as endings in these lists in order to assist as much as possible in distinguishing between similar forms.
• Vocative endings usually are the same as the nominative form; otherwise, they often end in ε. To find such an ending that is not in the index, replace ε with ος.

General Rules for Word Endings

Since endings are highly standardized in Greek, some general rules can be offered.
ε   Most words ending in ε have either τε of θε as their final letters. Almost all words ending in ε are verbs in the second person plural form.
θε   Verbs ending in θε are always middle or passive voice.
τε   Verbs ending in τε are almost always active voice.
η   Words ending in η are almost always singular (exception in a third declension noun).
θ   Verbs with θ in the ending are almost always middle or passive.
μι   Words ending in μι are always active first person singular
ο   Verbs ending in ο are middle or passive voice. Except for the two cases below (ντο and το), words ending in ο are second person singular.
ντο Verbs ending in ντο are third person plural.
το   Verbs ending simply in το are third person singular.
ς   Verbs ending in ς are always second person singular.
υ   Verbs ending in υ are usually second person singular or middle or passive participles.
θω   Verbs ending simply in θω are third person singular.
ω   Verbs ending in ω are always singular.

α

————ξαμεθα

V • aor ind mid 1 pl • G

————σαμεθα

V • aor ind mid 1 pl • ★

————ψαμεθα

V • aor ind mid 1 pl • L

————αμεθα

V • pres ind mid/pass 1 pl • αμι
V • impf ind mid/pass 1 pl • αμι
V • 2 aor ind mid 1 pl • αμι
V • aor ind mid 1 pl • 2

————γμεθα

V • perf ind mid pass 1 pl • G
V • plup ind mid pass 1 pl • G

————εμεθα

V • pres ind mid/pass 1 pl • εμι
V • impf ind mid/pass 1 pl • εμι
V • 2 aor ind mid 1 pl • εμι

————ξαιμεθα

V • aor opt mid 1 pl • G

————σαιμεθα

V • aor opt mid 1 pl • ★

————ψαιμεθα

V • aor opt mid 1 pl • L

————αιμεθα

V • pres opt mid/pass 1 pl • αμι
V • 2 aor opt mid 1 pl • αμι
V • aor opt mid 1 pl • 2

————ειμεθα

V • pres opt mid/pass 1 pl • εμι
V • 2 aor opt mid 1 pl • εμι

————ξοιμεθα

V • fut opt mid 1 pl • G

————θησοιμεθα

V • fut opt pass 1 pl • ★

————ησοιμεθα

V • 2 fut opt pass 1 pl • ☆

————σοιμεθα

V • fut opt mid 1 pl • ★

————ψοιμεθα

V • fut opt mid 1 pl • L

————οιμεθα

V • pres opt mid/pass 1 pl • ★
V • fut opt mid 1 pl • 2
V • 2 aor opt mid 1 pl • ☆

————μμεθα

V • perf ind mid/pass 1 pl • L
V • plup ind mid/pass 1 pl • L

————ξομεθα

V • fut ind mid 1 pl • G

————θησομεθα

V • fut ind pass 1 pl • ★

————ησομεθα

V • 2 fut ind pass 1 pl • ☆

————σομεθα

V • fut ind mid 1 pl • ★

————ψομεθα

V • fut ind mid 1 pl • L

————ομεθα

V • pres ind mid/pass 1 pl • ★
V • impf ind mid/pass 1 pl • ★
V • 2 aor ind mid 1 pl • ☆

————σμεθα

V • perf ind mid/pass 1 pl • D
V • plup ind mid/pass 1 pl • D

————νυμεθα

V • pres ind mid/pass 1 pl • νυμι
V • impf ind mid/pass 1 pl • νυμι

————ουμεθα

V • pres ind mid/pass 1 pl • εω οω
V • impf ind mid/pass 1 pl • εω οω
V • fut ind mid 1 pl • 2

————ξωμεθα

V • aor subj mid 1 pl • G

————σωμεθα

V • aor subj mid 1 pl • ★

————ψωμεθα

V • aor subj mid 1 pl • L

————ωμεθα

V • pres opt mid/pass 1 pl • αω

————ωμεθα

V • pres subj mid/pass 1 pl • ★
V • pres ind mid/pass 1 pl • αω
V • impf ind mid/pass 1 pl • αω
V • aor subj mid 1 pl • 2
V • 2 aor subj mid 1 pl • ☆

—————μεθα

V • perf ind mid/pass 1 pl • ★
V • plup ind mid/pass 1 pl • ★

—————ειοθα

V • impf ind act 2 sg • 4

—————σθα

V • impf ind act 2 sg • 4

—————κυια

P • perf act dat fem sg • ★

—————κυια

P • perf act nom fem sg • ★

—————υια

P • 2 perf act dat fem sg • ☆

—————υια

P • 2 perf act nom fem sg • ☆

—————κα

V • perf ind act 1 sg • ★
V • aor ind act 1 sg • MI 2

—————μα

N • nom/voc/acc sg neut • C

—————ξαμενα

P • aor mid nom/acc neut pl • G

—————σαμενα

P • aor mid nom/acc neut pl • ★

—————ψαμενα

P • aor mid nom/acc neut pl • L

—————αμενα

P • pres mid/pass nom/acc neut pl • αμι
P • 2 aor mid nom/acc neut pl • αμι
P • aor mid nom/acc neut pl • 2

—————γμενα

P • perf mid/pass nom/acc neut pl • G

—————εμενα

P • pres mid/pass nom/acc neut pl • εμι
P • 2 aor mid nom/acc neut pl • εμι

—————μμενα

P • perf mid/pass nom/acc neut pl • L

—————ξομενα

P • fut mid nom/acc neut pl • G

—————θησομενα

P • fut pass nom/acc neut pl • ★

—————ησομενα

P • 2 fut pass nom/acc neut pl • ☆

—————σομενα

P • fut mid nom/acc neut pl • ★

—————ψομενα

P • fut mid nom/acc neut pl • L

—————ομενα

P • pres mid/pass nom/acc neut pl • ★
P • 2 aor mid nom/acc neut pl • ☆

—————σμενα

P • perf mid/pass nom/acc neut pl • D

—————νυμενα

P • pres mid/pass nom/acc neut pl • νυμι

—————ουμενα

P • pres mid/pass nom/acc neut pl • εω οω
P • fut mid nom/acc neut pl • 2

—————ωμενα

P • pres mid/pass nom/acc neut pl • αω

—————μενα

P • perf mid/pass nom/acc neut pl • ★

—————ενα

N • acc sg masc/fem • C

—————ηνα

N • acc sg masc/fem • C

—————ονα

N • acc sg masc/fem • C

—————ωνα

N • acc sg masc/fem • C

—————ξα

V • aor ind act 1 sg • G

—————ρα

N • acc sg masc/fem • C

—————ξασα

P • aor act nom fem sg • G

—————σασα

P • aor act nom fem sg • ★

—————ψασα

P • aor act nom fem sg • L

—————ασα

P • pres act nom fem sg • αμι
P • 2 aor act nom fem sg • αμι 1
P • aor act nom fem sg • 2

—————θεισα

P • aor pass nom fem sg • ★

—————εισα
P • pres act nom fem sg • εμι
P • 2 aor act nom fem sg • εμι
P • 2 aor pass nom fem sg • ☆

—————νυσα
P • pres act nom fem sg • νυμι

—————ξουσα
P • fut act nom fem sg • G

—————σουσα
P • fut act nom fem sg • ★

—————ψουσα
P • fut act nom fem sg • L

—————ουσα
P • pres act nom fem sg • ★
P • 2 aor act nom fem sg • ☆
P • fut act nom fem sg • 2

—————ωσα
P • pres act nom fem sg • αω

—————σα
V • aor ind act 1 sg • ★
P • pres act nom fem sg • MI
P • 2 aor act nom fem sg • MI

—————ματα
N • nom/voc/acc pl neut • C

—————ατα
N • nom/voc/acc pl neut • C

—————ξαντα
P • aor act nom/acc neut pl • G
P • aor act acc masc sg • G

—————σαντα
P • aor act nom/acc neut pl • ★
P • aor act acc masc sg • ★

—————ψαντα
P • aor act nom/acc neut pl • L
P • aor act acc masc sg • L

—————αντα
P • pres act nom/acc neut pl • αμι
P • pres act acc masc sg • αμι
P • 2 aor act nom/acc neut pl • αμι 1
P • 2 aor act acc masc sg • αμι 1
P • aor act nom/acc neut pl • 2
P • aor act acc masc sg • 2
N • acc sg masc • C

—————θεντα
P • aor pass nom/acc neut pl • ★
P • aor pass acc masc sg • ★

—————εντα
P • pres act nom/acc neut pl • εμι
P • pres act acc masc sg • εμι
P • 2 aor act nom/acc neut pl • εμι
P • 2 aor act acc masc sg • εμι
P • 2 aor pass nom/acc neut pl • ☆
P • 2 aor pass acc masc sg • ☆

—————ξοντα
P • fut act nom/acc neut pl • G
P • fut act acc masc sg • G

—————σοντα
P • fut act nom/acc neut pl • ★
P • fut act acc masc sg • ★

—————ψοντα
P • fut act nom/acc neut pl • L
P • fut act acc masc sg • L

—————οντα
P • pres act nom/acc neut pl • ★
P • pres act acc masc sg • ★
P • 2 aor act nom/acc neut pl • ☆
P • 2 aor act acc masc sg • ☆
N • acc sg masc • C

—————νυντα
P • pres act nom/acc neut pl • νυμι
P • pres act acc masc sg • νυμι

—————ουντα
P • pres act nom/acc neut pl • εω οω
P • pres act acc masc sg • εω οω
P • fut act nom/acc neut pl • 2
P • fut act acc masc sg • 2

—————ωντα
P • pres act nom/acc neut pl • αω
P • pres act acc masc sg • αω

—————ντα
P • pres act nom/acc neut pl • MI
P • pres act acc masc sg • MI
P • 2 aor act nom/acc neut pl • MI
P • 2 aor act acc masc sg • MI

—————κοτα
P • perf act nom/acc neut pl • ★
P • perf act acc masc sg • ★

—————οτα
P • 2 perf act nom/acc neut pl • ☆
P • 2 perf act acc masc sg • ☆

—————τα
N • nom/acc neut pl • C

——————ψα

V • aor ind act 1 sg • L

——————ᾳ

V • pres ind act 3 sg • αω
V • pres ind mid/pass 2 sg • αω
V • pres subj act 3 sg • αω
V • pres subj mid/pass 2 sg • αω
V • 2 aor subj act 3 sg • 1
N • dat sg fem/masc • A

——————α

V • pres impv act 2 sg • αω
V • impf ind act 3 sg • αω
V • impf ind act 1 sg • 4
V • aor ind act 1 sg • 2
V • 2 aor ind act 3 sg • 1
V • 2 aor impv act 2 sg • αμι
V • 2 perf ind act 1 sg • ☆
N • nom/voc sg fem • A
N • voc sg masc • A
N • nom/acc/voc pl neut • O
N • acc sg masc/fem • C
N • nom/acc sg neut • C
N • nom/acc/voc pl neut • C

ε

——————ξασθε

V • aor ind mid 2 pl • G
V • aor impv mid 2 pl • G

——————σασθε

V • aor ind mid 2 pl • ★
V • aor impv mid 2 pl • ★

——————ψασθε

V • aor ind mid 2 pl • L
V • aor impv mid 2 pl • L

——————ασθε

V • pres ind mid/pass 2 pl • αω αμι
V • pres subj mid/pass 2 pl • αω
V • pres impv mid/pass 2 pl • αω αμι
V • impf ind mid/pass 2 pl • αω αμι
V • aor ind mid 2 pl • 2
V • aor impv mid 2 pl • 2
V • 2 aor ind mid 2 pl • αμι
V • 2 aor impv mid 2 pl • αμι

——————ξεσθε

V • fut ind mid 2 pl • G

——————θησεσθε

V • fut ind pass 2 pl • ★

——————ησεσθε

V • 2 fut ind pass 2 pl • ☆

——————σεσθε

V • fut ind mid 2 pl • ★

——————ψεσθε

V • fut ind mid 2 pl • L

——————εσθε

V • pres ind mid/pass 2 pl • ★
V • pres impv mid/pass 2 pl • ★
V • impf ind mid/pass 2 pl • ★
V • 2 aor ind mid 2 pl • ☆
V • 2 aor impv mid 2 pl • ☆

——————ξησθε

V • aor subj mid 2 pl • G

——————σησθε

V • aor subj mid 2 pl • ★

——————ψησθε

V • aor subj mid 2 pl • L

——————ησθε

V • pres subj mid/pass 2 pl • ★
V • 2 aor subj mid 2 pl • ☆
V • pres ind mid/pass 2 pl • 3
V • pres impv mid/pass 2 pl • 3
V • impf ind mid/pass 2 pl • 3
V • aor subj mid 2 pl • 2

——————ξαισθε

V • aor opt mid 2 pl • G

——————σαισθε

V • aor opt mid 2 pl • ★

——————ψαισθε

V • aor opt mid 2 pl • L

——————αισθε

V • pres opt mid/pass 2 pl • αμι
V • aor opt mid 2 pl • 2
V • 2 aor opt mid 2 pl • αμι

——————εισθε

V • pres ind mid/pass 2 pl • εω
V • pres impv mid/pass 2 pl • εω
V • impf ind mid/pass 2 pl • εω
V • pres opt mid/pass 2 pl • εμι
V • 2 aor opt mid 2 pl • εμι
V • fut ind mid 2 pl • 2

——————ξοισθε

V • fut opt mid 2 pl • G

——————θησοισθε

V • fut opt pass 2 pl • ★

——————ησοισθε

V • 2 fut opt pass 2 pl • ☆

——————σοισθε

V • fut opt mid 2 pl • ★

——————ψοισθε

V • fut opt mid 2 pl • L

——————οισθε

V • pres opt mid/pass 2 pl • ★
V • 2 aor opt mid 2 pl • ☆
V • fut opt mid 2 pl • 2

——————οσθε

V • pres ind mid/pass 2 pl • ομι
V • pres impv mid/pass 2 pl • ομι
V • impf ind mid/pass 2 pl • ομι
V • 2 aor ind mid 2 pl • ομι
V • 2 aor impv mid 2 pl • ομι

——————νυσθε

V • pres ind mid/pass 2 pl • νυμι
V • pres impv mid/pass 2 pl • νυμι
V • impf ind mid/pass 2 pl • νυμι

——————ουσθε

V • pres ind mid/pass 2 pl • οω
V • pres impv mid/pass 2 pl • οω
V • impf ind mid/pass 2 pl • οω

——————ῳσθε

V • pres opt mid/pass 2 pl • αω

——————ωσθε

V • pres subj mid/pass 2 pl • οω ομι
V • 2 aor subj mid 2 pl • ομι

——————σθε

V • perf ind mid/pass 2 pl • ★
V • perf impv mid/pass 2 pl • ★
V • plup ind mid/pass 2 pl • ★

——————φθε

V • perf ind mid/pass 2 pl • L
V • perf impv mid/pass 2 pl • L
V • plup ind mid/pass 2 pl • L

——————χθε

V • perf ind mid/pass 2 pl • G
V • perf impv mid/pass 2 pl • G
V • plup ind mid/pass 2 pl • G

——————θε

V • perf ind mid/pass 2 pl • Q
V • perf impv mid/pass 2 pl • Q

V • plup ind mid/pass 2 pl • Q

——————ξειε

V • aor opt act 3 sg • G

——————σειε

V • aor opt act 3 sg • ★

——————ψειε

V • aor opt act 3 sg • L

——————ειε

V • aor opt act 3 sg • 2

——————κε

V • perf ind act 3 sg • ★
V • perf impv act 2 sg • ★
V • aor ind act 3 sg • 2

——————ξε

V • aor ind act 3 sg • G

——————σε

V • aor ind act 3 sg • ★

——————κατε

V • perf ind act 2 pl • ★
V • aor ind act 2 pl • 2

——————ξατε

V • aor ind act 2 pl • G
V • aor impv act 2 pl • G

——————σατε

V • aor ind act 2 pl • ★
V • aor impv act 2 pl • ★

——————ψατε

V • aor ind act 2 pl • L
V • aor impv act 2 pl • L

——————ατε

V • pres ind act 2 pl • αω αμι
V • pres subj act 2 pl • αω
V • pres impv act 2 pl • αω αμι
V • impf ind act 2 pl • αω αμι
V • aor ind act 2 pl • 2
V • aor impv act 2 pl • 2
V • 2 aor ind act 2 pl • 1
V • 2 aor subj act 2 pl • 1
V • 2 aor impv act 2 pl • 1
V • 2 perf ind act 2 pl • ☆

——————κετε

V • perf impv act 2 pl • ★
V • plup ind act 2 pl • ★

——————ξετε

V • fut ind act 2 pl • G

—————σετε

V • fut ind act 2 pl • ★

—————ψετε

V • fut ind act 2 pl • L

—————ετε

V • pres ind act 2 pl • ★
V • pres impv act 2 pl • ★
V • impf ind act 2 pl • ★
V • 2 aor ind act 2 pl • ☆
V • 2 aor impv act 2 pl • ☆
V • 2 perf impv act 2 pl • ☆
V • 2 plup ind act 2 pl • ☆

—————θητε

V • aor ind pass 2 pl • ★
V • aor subj pass 2 pl • ★
V • aor impv pass 2 pl • ★

—————αιητε

V • pres opt act 2 pl • αμι
V • 2 aor opt act 2 pl • αμι

—————θειητε

V • aor opt pass 2 pl • ★

—————ειητε

V • pres opt act 2 pl • εμι
V • 2 aor opt act 2 pl • εμι
V • 2 aor opt pass 2 pl • ☆

—————οιητε

V • pres opt act 2 pl • εω οω ομι
V • 2 aor opt act 2 pl • ομι
V • fut opt act 2 pl • 2

—————κητε

V • perf subj act 2 pl • ★

—————ξητε

V • aor subj act 2 pl • G

—————σητε

V • aor subj act 2 pl • ★

—————ψητε

V • aor subj act 2 pl • L

—————ωητε

V • pres opt act 2 pl • αω

—————ητε

V • pres subj act 2 pl • ★
V • 2 aor subj act 2 pl • ☆
V • 2 aor impv act 2 pl • αμι 1
V • 2 aor ind act 2 pl • αμι 1
V • pres ind act 2 pl • 3
V • pres impv act 2 pl • 3

V • impf ind act 2 pl • 3
V • aor subj act 2 pl • 2
V • 2 aor ind pass 2 pl • ☆
V • 2 aor subj pass 2 pl • ☆
V • 2 perf subj act 2 pl • ☆
V • 2 aor impv pass 2 pl • ☆

—————ξαιτε

V • aor opt act 2 pl • G

—————σαιτε

V • aor opt act 2 pl • ★

—————ψαιτε

V • aor opt act 2 pl • L

—————αιτε

V • pres opt act 2 pl • αμι
V • 2 aor opt act 2 pl • αμι 1
V • aor opt act 2 pl • 2

—————θειτε

V • aor opt pass 2 pl • ★

—————κειτε

V • plup ind act 2 pl • ★

—————ειτε

V • pres ind act 2 pl • εω
V • pres impv act 2 pl • εω
V • impf ind act 2 pl • εω
V • pres opt act 2 pl • εμι
V • 2 aor opt act 2 pl • εμι
V • fut ind act 2 pl • 2

—————κοιτε

V • perf opt act 2 pl • ★

—————ξοιτε

V • fut opt act 2 pl • G

—————σοιτε

V • fut opt act 2 pl • ★

—————ψοιτε

V • fut opt act 2 pl • L

—————οιτε

V • pres opt act 2 pl • ★
V • 2 aor opt act 2 pl • ☆
V • 2 perf opt act 2 pl • ☆
V • fut opt act 2 pl • 2

—————οτε

V • pres ind act 2 pl • ομι
V • pres impv act 2 pl • ομι
V • impf ind act 2 pl • ομι
V • 2 aor ind act 2 pl • ομι
V • 2 aor impv act 2 pl • ομι

———στε
V • impf ind act 2 pl • 4

———νυτε
V • pres ind act 2 pl • νυμι
V • pres impv act 2 pl • νυμι
V • impf ind act 2 pl • νυμι

———ουτε
V • pres ind act 2 pl • οω
V • pres impv act 2 pl • οω
V • impf ind act 2 pl • οω

———υτε
V • 2 aor ind act 2 pl • νυμι
V • 2 aor impv act 2 pl • νυμι

———ωτε
V • pres opt act 2 pl • αω
V • 2 aor opt act 2 pl • 1

———ωτε
V • pres subj act 2 pl • οω ομι
V • 2 aor subj act 2 pl • ομι 1
V • 2 aor ind act 2 pl • 1
V • 2 aor impv act 2 pl • 1

———τε
V • pres ind act 2 pl • 4
V • impf ind act 2 pl • 4
V • pres impv act 2 pl • 4

———ψε
V • aor ind act 3 sg • L

———ε
V • pres impv act 2 sg • ★
V • impf ind act 3 sg • ★
V • aor ind act 3 sg • 2
V • 2 aor ind act 3 sg • ☆
V • 2 aor impv act 2 sg • ☆
V • 2 perf ind act 3 sg • ☆
V • 2 perf impv act 2 sg • ☆
N • voc sg masc/fem • O
N • acc sg [personal pronoun ending]

η

———θη
V • aor subj pass 3 sg • ★

———θη
V • aor ind pass 3 sg • ★

———αιη
V • pres opt act 3 sg • αμι

V • 2 aor opt act 3 sg • αμι 1

———θειη
V • aor opt pass 3 sg • ★

———ειη
V • pres opt act 3 sg • εμι
V • 2 aor opt act 3 sg • εμι
V • 2 aor opt pass 3 sg • ☆

———κοιη
V • perf opt act 3 sg • ★

———οιη
V • pres opt act 3 sg • εω οω ομι
V • 2 aor opt act 3 sg • ομι 1
V • fut opt act 3 sg • 2
V • 2 perf opt act 3 sg • ☆

———κη
V • perf subj act 3 sg • ★

———κη
V • plup ind act 1 sg • ★

———ξαμενη
P • aor mid dat fem sg • G

———ξαμενη
P • aor mid nom fem sg • G

———σαμενη
P • aor mid dat fem sg • ★

———σαμενη
P • aor mid nom fem sg • ★

———ψαμενη
P • aor mid dat fem sg • L

———ψαμενη
P • aor mid nom fem sg • L

———αμενη
P • pres mid/pass dat fem sg • αμι
P • 2 aor mid dat fem sg • αμι
P • aor mid dat fem sg • 2

———αμενη
P • pres mid/pass nom fem sg • αμι
P • 2 aor mid nom fem sg • αμι
P • aor mid nom fem sg • 2

———γμενη
P • perf mid/pass dat fem sg • G

———γμενη
P • perf mid/pass nom fem sg • G

———εμενη
P • pres mid/pass dat fem sg • εμι

P • 2 aor mid dat fem sg • εμι

—————εμενη

P • pres mid/pass nom fem sg • εμι
P • 2 aor mid nom fem sg • εμι

—————μμενη

P • perf mid/pass dat fem sg • L

—————μμενη

P • perf mid/pass nom fem sg • L

—————ξομενη

P • fut mid dat fem sg • G

—————ξομενη

P • fut mid nom fem sg • G

—————θησομενη

P • fut pass dat fem sg • ★

—————θησομενη

P • fut pass nom fem sg • ★

—————ησομενη

P • 2 fut pass dat fem sg • ☆

—————ησομενη

P • 2 fut pass nom fem sg • ☆

—————σομενη

P • fut mid dat fem sg • ★

—————σομενη

P • fut mid nom fem sg • ★

—————ψομενη

P • fut mid dat fem sg • L

—————ψομενη

P • fut mid nom fem sg • L

—————ομενη

P • pres mid/pass dat fem sg • ★
P • 2 aor mid dat fem sg • ★

—————ομενη

P • pres mid/pass nom fem sg • ★
P • 2 aor mid nom fem sg • ★

—————σμενη

P • perf mid/pass dat fem sg • D

—————σμενη

P • perf mid/pass nom fem sg • D

—————νυμενη

P • pres mid/pass dat fem sg • νυμι

—————νυμενη

P • pres mid/pass nom fem sg • νυμι

—————ουμενη

P • pres mid/pass dat fem sg • εω οω
P • fut mid dat fem sg • 2

—————ουμενη

P • pres mid/pass nom fem sg • εω οω
P • fut mid nom fem sg • 2

—————ωμενη

P • pres mid/pass dat fem sg • αω

—————ωμενη

P • pres mid/pass nom fem sg • αω

—————μενη

P • perf mid/pass dat fem sg • ★

—————μενη

P • perf mid/pass nom fem sg • ★

—————ξη

V • fut ind mid 2 sg • G
V • aor subj act 3 sg • G
V • aor subj mid 2 sg • G

—————ξαση

P • aor act dat fem sg • G

—————σαση

P • aor act dat fem sg • ★

—————ψαση

P • aor act dat fem sg • L

—————αση

P • pres act dat fem sg • αμι
P • 2 aor act dat fem sg • 1 αμι
P • aor act dat fem sg • 2

—————θηση

V • fut ind pass 2 sg • ★

—————ηση

V • 2 fut ind pass 2 sg • ☆

—————θειση

P • aor pass dat fem sg • ★

—————ειση

P • pres act dat fem sg • εμι
P • 2 aor act dat fem sg • εμι
P • 2 aor pass dat fem sg • ☆

—————νυση

P • pres act dat fem sg • νυμι

—————σουση

P • fut act dat fem sg • ★

—————ουση

P • pres act dat fem sg • ★

P • 2 aor act dat fem sg • ☆
P • fut act dat fem sg • 2

—————ωση

P • pres act dat fem sg • αω

—————ση

V • fut ind mid 2 sg • ★
V • aor subj act 3 sg • ★
V • aor subj mid 2 sg • ★
P • pres act dat fem sg • MI
P • 2 aor act dat fem sg • MI

—————ψη

V • fut ind mid 2 sg • L
V • aor subj act 3 sg • L
V • aor subj mid 2 sg • L

—————ῳη

V • pres opt act 3 sg • αω
V • 2 aor opt act 3 sg • ομι 1

—————η

V • pres ind mid/pass 2 sg • ★
V • pres subj act 3 sg • ★
V • pres subj mid/pass 2 sg • ★
V • pres ind act 3 sg • 3
V • fut ind mid 2 sg • 2
V • aor subj act 3 sg • 2
V • aor subj mid 2 sg • 2
V • 2 aor subj act 3 sg • ☆
V • 2 aor subj mid 2 sg • ☆
V • 2 aor subj pass 3 sg • ☆
V • 2 perf subj act 3 sg • ☆
N • dat sg fem/masc • A

—————η

V • pres impv act 2 sg • αμι 3
V • impf ind act 3 sg • αμι 3
V • 2 aor ind act 3 sg • αμι 1
V • 2 aor ind pass 3 sg • ☆
V • 2 plup ind act 1 sg • ☆
N • nom/voc sg fem • A
N • nom/acc/voc pl neut • C
N • acc sg masc/fem • C

ι

—————ξασθαι

I • aor mid • G

—————σασθαι

I • aor mid • ★

—————ψασθαι

I • aor mid • L

—————ασθαι

I • pres mid/pass • αω αμι
I • 2 aor mid • αμι
I • aor mid • 2

—————ξεσθαι

I • fut mid • G

—————θησεσθαι

I • fut pass • ★

—————ησεσθαι

I • 2 fut pass • ☆

—————σεσθαι

I • fut mid • ★

—————ψεσθαι

I • fut mid • L

—————εσθαι

I • pres mid/pass • ★
I • 2 aor mid • ☆

—————ησθαι

I • pres mid/pass • 3

—————εισθαι

I • pres mid/pass • εω
I • fut mid • 2

—————οσθαι

I • pres mid/pass • ομι
I • 2 aor mid • ομι

—————νυσθαι

I • pres mid/pass • νυμι

—————ουσθαι

I • pres mid/pass • οω

—————σθαι

I • perf mid/pass • ★ D

—————φθαι

I • perf mid/pass • L

—————χθαι

I • perf mid/pass • G

—————θαι

I • perf mid/pass • Q

—————κυιαι

P • perf act nom fem pl • ★

—————υιαι

P • 2 perf act nom fem pl • ☆

—————αμαι

V • pres ind mid/pass 1 sg • αμι

—————γμαι

V • perf ind mid/pass 1 sg • G

—————εμαι

V • pres ind mid/pass 1 sg • εμι

—————μμαι

V • perf ind mid/pass 1 sg • L

————ξομαι

V • fut ind mid 1 sg • G

———θησομαι

V • fut ind pass 1 sg • ★

—————ησομαι

V • 2 fut ind pass 1 sg • ☆

—————σομαι

V • fut ind mid 1 sg • ★

—————ψομαι

V • fut ind mid 1 sg • L

—————ομαι

V • pres ind mid/pass 1 sg • ★

—————σμαι

V • perf ind mid/pass 1 sg • D

—————νυμαι

V • pres ind mid/pass 1 sg • νυμι

—————ουμαι

V • pres ind mid/pass 1 sg • εω οω
V • fut ind mid 1 sg • ?

————ξωμαι

V • aor subj mid 1 sg • G

—————σωμαι

V • aor subj mid 1 sg • ★

—————ψωμαι

V • aor subj mid 1 sg • L

—————ωμαι

V • pres subj mid/pass 1 sg • ★
V • pres ind mid/pass 1 sg • αω
V • aor subj mid 1 sg • 2
V • 2 aor subj mid 1 sg • ☆

—————μαι

V • perf ind mid/pass 1 sg • ★

—————αναι

I • pres act • αμι
I • 2 aor act • 1

—————κεναι

I • perf act • ★

————ξαμεναι

P • aor mid nom fem pl • G

————σαμεναι

P • aor mid nom fem pl • ★

————ψαμεναι

P • aor mid nom fem pl • L

—————αμεναι

P • pres mid/pass nom fem pl • αμι
P • 2 aor mid nom fem pl • αμι
P • aor mid nom fem pl • 2

————γμεναι

P • perf mid/pass nom fem pl • G

————εμεναι

P • pres mid/pass nom fem pl • εμι
P • 2 aor mid nom fem pl • εμι

————μμεναι

P • perf mid/pass nom fem pl • L

————ξομεναι

P • fut mid nom fem pl • G

———θησομεναι

P • fut pass nom fem pl • ★

————ησομεναι

P • 2 fut pass nom fem pl • ☆

————σομεναι

P • fut mid nom fem pl • ★

————ψομεναι

P • fut mid nom fem pl • L

————ομεναι

P • pres mid/pass nom fem pl • ★
P • 2 aor mid nom fem pl • ★

————σμεναι

P • perf mid/pass nom fem pl • D

————νυμεναι

P • pres mid/pass nom fem pl • νυμι

————ουμεναι

P • pres mid/pass nom fem pl • εω οω
P • fut mid nom fem pl • 2

————ωμεναι

P • pres mid/pass nom fem pl • αω

————μεναι

P • perf mid/pass nom fem pl • ★

———εναι
I • pres act • ειμι
I • 2 perf act • ☆

———θηναι
I • aor pass • ★

———ηναι
I • 2 aor act • αμι 1
I • 2 aor pass • ☆

———ειναι
I • 2 aor act • ειμι

———οναι
I • pres act • ομι

———υυναι
I • pres act • νυμι
I • 2 aor act • νυμι 1

———ουναι
I • 2 aor act • ομι

———ωναι
I • 2 aor act • 1

———ναι
I • pres act • 4

———ξαι
V • aor opt act 3 sg • G
V • aor impv mid 2 sg • G
V • perf ind mid/pass 2 sg • G
I • aor act • G

———ξασαι
P • aor act nom fem pl • G

———σασαι
P • aor act nom fem pl • ★

———ψασαι
P • aor act nom fem pl • L

———ασαι
V • pres ind mid/pass 2 sg • αω αμι
P • pres mid/pass nom fem pl • αμι
P • 2 aor act nom fem pl • αμι 1
P • aor act nom fem pl • 2

———εσαι
V • pres ind mid/pass 2 sg • εμι

———θεισαι
P • aor pass nom fem pl • ★

———εισαι
P • pres act nom fem pl • εμι
P • 2 aor act nom fem pl • εμι
P • 2 aor pass nom fem pl • ☆

———οσαι
V • pres ind mid/pass 2 sg • ομι

———υυσαι
V • pres ind mid/pass 2 sg • νυμι
P • pres act nom fem pl • νυμι

———σουσαι
P • fut act nom fem pl • ★

———ουσαι
P • pres act nom fem pl • ★
P • 2 aor act nom fem pl • ☆ ομι 1
P • fut act nom fem pl • 2

———ωσαι
P • pres act nom fem pl • αω

———σαι
V • aor opt act 3 sg • ★
V • aor impv mid 2 sg • ★
V • perf ind mid/pass 2 sg • ★
P • pres act nom fem pl • MI
P • 2 aor act nom fem pl • MI 1
I • aor act • ★

———αται
V • pres ind mid/pass 3 sg • αω αμι
V • pres subj mid/pass 3 sg • αω

———ξεται
V • fut ind mid 3 sg • G

———θησεται
V • fut ind pass 3 sg • ★

———ησεται
V • 2 fut ind pass 3 sg • ☆

———σεται
V • fut ind mid 3 sg • ★

———ψεται
V • fut ind mid 3 sg • L

———εται
V • pres ind mid/pass 3 sg • ★

———ξηται
V • aor subj mid 3 sg • G

———σηται
V • aor subj mid 3 sg • ★

———ψηται
V • aor subj mid 3 sg • L

———ηται
V • pres subj mid/pass 3 sg • ★
V • aor subj mid 3 sg • 2
V • 2 aor subj mid 3 sg • αμι εμι ☆

———ειται

V • pres ind mid/pass 3 sg • εω
V • fut ind mid 3 sg • 2

———κται

V • perf ind mid/pass 3 sg • G

———ανται

V • pres ind mid/pass 3 pl • αμι

———ενται

V • pres ind mid/pass 3 pl • εμι

———ξονται

V • fut ind mid 3 pl • G

———θησονται

V • fut ind pass 3 pl • ★

———ησονται

V • 2 fut ind pass 3 pl • ☆

———σονται

V • fut ind mid 3 pl • ★

———ψονται

V • fut ind mid 3 pl • L

———ονται

V • pres ind mid/pass 3 pl • ★

———νυνται

V • pres ind mid/pass 3 pl • νυμι

———ουνται

V • pres ind mid/pass 3 pl • εω οω
V • fut ind mid 3 pl • 2

———ξωνται

V • aor subj mid 3 pl • G

———σωνται

V • aor subj mid 3 pl • ★

———ψωνται

V • aor subj mid 3 pl • L

———ωνται

V • pres subj mid/pass 3 pl • ★
V • pres ind mid/pass 3 pl • αω
V • aor subj mid 3 pl • 2
V • 2 aor subj mid 3 pl • ☆

———νται

V • perf ind mid/pass 3 pl • ★

———οται

V • pres ind mid/pass 3 sg • ομι

———πται

V • perf ind mid/pass 3 sg • L

———σται

V • perf ind mid/pass 3 sg • D

———νυται

V • pres ind mid/pass 3 sg • νυμι

———ουται

V • pres ind mid/pass 3 sg • οω

———ωται

V • pres subj mid/pass 3 sg • οω ομι
V • 2 aor subj mid 3 sg • ομι

———ται

V • perf ind mid/pass 3 sg • ★

———ψαι

V • aor opt act 3 sg • L
V • aor impv mid 2 sg • L
V • perf ind mid/pass 2 sg • L
I • aor act • L

———αι

V • aor opt act 3 sg • 2
V • aor impv mid 2 sg • 2
I • aor act • 2
N • nom/voc pl fem/masc • A
N • dat sg neut • C

———κει

V • plup ind act 3 sg • ★

———ξει

V • fut ind act 3 sg • G
V • fut ind mid 2 sg • G

———θησει

V • fut ind pass 2 sg • ★

———ησει

V • 2 fut ind pass 2 sg • ☆

———σει

V • fut ind act 3 sg • ★
V • fut ind mid 2 sg • ★

———ψει

V • fut ind act 3 sg • L
V • fut ind mid 2 sg • L

———ει

V • pres ind act 3 sg • ★
V • pres ind mid/pass 2 sg • ★
V • pres impv act 2 sg • εω εμι
V • fut ind act 3 sg • 2
V • fut ind mid 2 sg • 2
V • impf ind act 3 sg • εω εμι
V • 2 plup ind act 3 sg • ☆
N • dat sg masc/fem/neut • C

——**αθι**

V • 2 aor impv act 2 sg • 1

——**ηθι**

V • 2 aor impv act 2 sg • αμι 1
V • 2 aor impv pass 2 sg • ☆

——**υθι**

V • 2 aor impv act 2 sg • νυμι

——**ωθι**

V • 2 aor impv act 2 sg • 1

——**θι**

V • 2 aor impv act 2 sg • αμι

——**ημι**

V • pres ind act 1 sg • αμι εμι

——**ξαιμι**

V • aor opt act 1 sg • G

——**σαιμι**

V • aor opt act 1 sg • ★

——**ψαιμι**

V • aor opt act 1 sg • L

——**αιμι**

V • aor opt act 1 sg • 2

——**κοιμι**

V • perf opt act 1 sg • ★

——**ξοιμι**

V • fut opt act 1 sg • G

——**σοιμι**

V • fut opt act 1 sg • ★

——**ψοιμι**

V • fut opt act 1 sg • L

——**οιμι**

V • pres opt act 1 sg • ★
V • fut opt act 1 sg • 2
V • 2 aor opt act 1 sg • ☆
V • 2 perf opt act 1 sg • ☆

——**νυμι**

V • pres ind act 1 sg • νυμι

——**ωμι**

V • pres opt act 1 sg • αω

——**ωμι**

V • pres ind act 1 sg • ομι

——**μι**

V • pres ind act 1 sg • 4

——**ενι**

N • dat sg masc/fem • C

——**ηνι**

N • dat sg masc/fem • C

——**ονι**

N • dat sg masc/fem • C

——**ωνι**

N • dat sg masc/fem • C

——**ξι**

N • dat pl masc/fem • C

——**κοι**

V • perf opt act 3 sg • ★

——**ξαμενοι**

P • aor mid nom masc pl • G

——**σαμενοι**

P • aor mid nom masc pl • ★

——**ψαμενοι**

P • aor mid nom masc pl • L

——**αμενοι**

P • pres mid/pass nom masc pl • αμι
P • 2 aor mid nom masc pl • αμι
P • aor mid nom masc pl • 2

——**γμενοι**

P • perf mid/pass nom masc pl • G

——**εμενοι**

P • pres mid/pass nom masc pl • εμι
P • 2 aor mid nom masc pl • εμι

——**μμενοι**

P • perf mid/pass nom masc pl • L

——**ξομενοι**

P • fut mid nom masc pl • G

——**θησομενοι**

P • fut pass nom masc pl • ★

——**ησομενοι**

P • 2 fut pass nom masc pl • ☆

——**σομενοι**

P • fut mid nom masc pl • ★

——**ψομενοι**

P • fut mid nom masc pl • L

——**ομενοι**

P • pres mid/pass nom masc pl • ★
P • 2 aor mid nom masc pl • ☆

—————σμενοι

P • perf mid/pass nom masc pl • D

—————νυμενοι

P • pres mid/pass nom masc pl • νυμι

—————ουμενοι

P • pres mid/pass nom masc pl • εω οω
P • fut mid nom masc pl • 2

—————ωμενοι

P • pres mid/pass nom masc pl • αω

—————μενοι

P • perf mid/pass nom masc pl • ★

—————ξοι

V • fut opt act 3 sg • G

—————σοι

V • fut opt act 3 sg • ★

—————ψοι

V • fut opt act 3 sg • L

—————οι

V • pres opt act 3 sg • ★
V • pres ind act 3 sg • οω
V • pres ind mid/pass 2 sg • οω
V • pres subj act 3 sg • οω ομι
V • pres subj mid/pass 2 sg • οω
V • fut opt act 3 sg • 2
V • 2 aor opt act 3 sg • ☆
V • 2 perf opt act 3 sg • ☆
N • nom/voc pl masc/fem • O

—————ρι

N • dat sg masc/fem • C

—————εασι

V • pres ind act 3 pl • εμι

—————ιασι

V • pres ind act 3 pl • εμι

—————κασι

V • perf ind act 3 pl • ★

—————μασι

N • dat pl neut • C

—————ξασι

P • aor act dat masc/neut pl • G

—————οασι

V • pres ind act 3 pl • ομι

—————ρασι

N • dat pl masc/fem • C

—————σασι

P • aor act dat masc/neut pl • ★

—————νυασι

V • pres ind act 3 pl • νυμι

—————υασι

N • dat sg masc • C

—————ψασι

P • aor act dat masc/neut pl • L

—————ασι

V • pres ind act 3 pl • αμι
P • pres act dat masc/neut pl • αμι
P • 2 aor act dat masc/neut pl • αμι 1
P • aor act dat masc/neut pl • 2
N • dat pl masc/fem/neut • C

—————εσι

N • dat pl masc/fem/neut • C

—————ησι

V • pres ind act 3 sg • αμι εμι
N • dat pl masc/fem • C

—————θεισι

P • aor pass dat masc/neut pl • ★

—————εισι

P • pres act dat masc/neut pl • εμι
P • 2 aor act dat masc/neut pl • εμι
P • 2 aor pass dat masc/neut pl • ☆

—————κοσι

P • perf act dat masc/neut pl • ★

—————οσι

P • 2 perf act dat masc/neut pl • ☆
N • dat pl masc/fem • C

—————ροσι

N • dat pl masc/fem • C

—————ευσι

N • dat pl masc • C

—————νυσι

V • pres ind act 3 sg • νυμι
P • pres act dat masc/neut pl • νυμι

—————ξουσι

V • fut ind act 3 pl • G

—————σουσι

V • fut ind act 3 pl • ★
P • fut act dat masc/neut pl • ★

—————ψουσι

V • fut ind act 3 pl • L

————ουσι

V • pres ind act 3 pl • ★
V • fut ind act 3 pl • 2
P • pres act dat masc/neut pl • ★
P • 2 aor act dat masc/neut pl • ☆
P • fut act dat masc/neut pl • 2
N • dat pl masc/fem • C

————υσι

N • dat pl masc/fem/neut • C

————θωσι

V • aor subj pass 3 pl • ★

————κωσι

V • perf subj act 3 pl • ★

————ξωσι

V • aor subj act 3 pl • G

————σωσι

V • aor subj act 3 pl • ★

————ψωσι

V • aor subj act 3 pl • L

————ωσι

V • pres subj act 3 pl • ★
V • pres ind act 3 sg • ομι
V • pres ind act 3 pl • αω
V • aor subj act 3 pl • 2
V • 2 aor subj act 3 pl • ☆
V • 2 aor subj pass 3 pl • ☆
V • 2 perf subj act 3 pl • ☆
P • pres act dat masc/neut pl • 3
N • dat pl masc/fem • C

————σι

V • 2 perf ind act 3 pl • MI
V • pres ind act 3 pl • 4
P • pres act dat masc/neut pl • MI
P • 2 aor act dat masc/neut pl • MI 1
N • dat pl masc/fem • C

————ματι

N • dat sg neut • C

————ατι

N • dat sg neut • C

————θητι

V • aor impv pass 2 sg • ★

————ητι

V • 2 aor impv pass 2 sg • ☆

————ξαντι

P • aor act dat masc/neut sg • G

————σαντι

P • aor act dat masc/neut sg • ★

————ψαντι

P • aor act dat masc/neut sg • L

————αντι

P • pres act dat masc/neut sg • αμι
P • 2 aor act dat masc/neut sg • αμι
P • aor act dat masc/neut sg • 2
N • dat sg masc/fem • C

————θεντι

P • aor pass dat masc/neut sg • ★

————εντι

P • pres act dat masc/neut sg • εμι
P • 2 aor act dat masc/neut sg • εμι
P • 2 aor pass dat masc/neut sg • ☆

————ξοντι

P • fut act dat masc/neut sg • G

————σοντι

P • fut act dat masc/neut sg • ★

————ψοντι

P • fut act dat masc/neut sg • L

————οντι

P • pres act dat masc/neut sg • ★
P • 2 aor act dat masc/neut sg • ☆
N • dat sg masc/fem • C

————νυντι

P • pres act dat masc/neut sg • νυμι

————ουντι

P • pres act dat masc/neut sg • εω οω
P • fut act dat masc/neut sg • 2

————ωντι

P • pres act dat masc/neut sg • αω

————ντι

P • pres act dat masc/neut sg • MI
P • 2 aor act dat masc/neut sg • MI

————κοτι

P • perf act dat masc/neut sg • ★

————οτι

P • 2 perf act dat masc/neut sg • ☆

————τι

V • pres ind act 3 sg • 4
N • dat sg neut • C

————υι

N • dat sg masc • C

————ψι

N • dat pl masc/fem • C

————ι

N • dat sg masc/fem/neut • C
N • voc sg masc/fem • C

ν

————ξειαν

V • aor opt act 3 pl • G

————σειαν

V • aor opt act 3 pl • ★

————ψειαν

V • aor opt act 3 pl • L

————ειαν

V • aor opt act 3 pl • 2

————κυιαν

P • perf act acc fem sg • ★

————υιαν

P • 2 perf act acc fem sg • ☆

————καν

V • aor ind act 3 pl • 2

————ξαν

V • aor ind act 3 pl • G
P • aor act nom/acc neut sg • G

————ξασαν

P • aor act acc fem sg • G

————σασαν

P • aor act acc fem sg • ★

————ψασαν

P • aor act acc fem sg • L

————ασαν

V • impf ind act 3 pl • αμι
V • 2 aor ind act 3 pl • 1
P • pres act acc fem sg • αμι
P • 2 aor act acc fem sg • αμι 1
P • aor act acc fem sg • 2

————κεσαν

V • plup ind act 3 pl • ★

————εσαν

V • impf ind act 3 pl • εμι
V • 2 aor ind act 3 pl • εμι
V • 2 plup ind act 3 pl • ☆

————θησαν

V • aor ind pass 3 pl • ★

————αιησαν

V • pres opt act 3 pl • αμι
V • 2 aor opt act 3 pl • αμι

————θειησαν

V • aor opt pass 3 pl • ★

————ειησαν

V • pres opt act 3 pl • εμι
V • 2 aor opt act 3 pl • εμι
V • 2 aor opt pass 3 pl • ☆

————οιησαν

V • pres opt act 3 pl • εω οω ομι
V • 2 aor opt act 3 pl • ομι

————ῳησαν

V • pres opt act 3 pl • αω

————ησαν

V • 2 aor ind act 3 pl • αμι 1
V • 2 aor ind pass 3 pl • ☆

————θεισαν

P • aor pass acc fem sg • ★

————κεισαν

V • plup ind act 3 pl • ★

————εισαν

V • 2 plup ind act 3 pl • ☆
P • pres act acc fem sg • εμι
P • 2 aor act acc fem sg • εμι
P • 2 aor pass acc fem sg • ☆

————οσαν

V • impf ind act 3 pl • ομι
V • 2 aor ind act 3 pl • ομι

————νυσαν

V • impf ind act 3 pl • νυμι
P • pres act acc fem sg • νυμι
P • 2 aor act acc fem sg • νυμι

————σουσαν

P • fut act acc fem sg • ★

————ουσαν

P • pres act acc fem sg • ★
P • 2 aor act acc fem sg • ☆
P • fut act acc fem sg • 2

————υσαν

V • 2 aor ind act 3 pl • νυμι
P • 2 aor act acc fem sg • νυμι

————**ξασθωσαν**
V • aor impv mid 3 pl • G

————**σασθωσαν**
V • aor impv mid 3 pl • ★

————**ψασθωσαν**
V • aor impv mid 3 pl • L

————**ασθωσαν**
V • pres impv mid/pass 3 pl • αω αμι
V • 2 aor impv mid 3 pl • αμι
V • aor impv mid 3 pl • 2

————**εσθωσαν**
V • pres impv mid/pass 3 pl • ★
V • 2 aor impv mid 3 pl • ☆

————**ησθωσαν**
V • pres impv mid/pass 3 pl • 3

————**εισθωσαν**
V • pres impv mid/pass 3 pl • εω

————**οσθωσαν**
V • pres impv mid/pass 3 pl • ομι οω
V • 2 aor impv mid 3 pl • ομι

————**νυσθωσαν**
V • pres impv mid/pass 3 pl • νυμι

————**ουσθωσαν**
V • pres impv mid/pass 3 pl • οω

————**σθωσαν**
V • perf impv mid/pass 3 pl • ★

————**ξατωσαν**
V • aor impv act 3 pl • G

————**σατωσαν**
V • aor impv act 3 pl • ★

————**ψατωσαν**
V • aor impv act 3 pl • L

————**ατωσαν**
V • pres impv act 3 pl • αω αμι
V • aor impv act 3 pl • 2

————**κετωσαν**
V • perf impv act 3 pl • ★

————**ετωσαν**
V • pres impv act 3 pl • ★
V • 2 aor impv act 3 pl • ☆

————**θητωσαν**
V • aor impv pass 3 pl • ★

————**ητωσαν**
V • pres impv act 3 pl • 3

V • 2 aor impv act 3 pl • αμι
V • 2 aor impv pass 3 pl • ☆

————**ειτωσαν**
V • pres impv act 3 pl • εω

————**οτωσαν**
V • pres impv act 3 pl • ομι
V • 2 aor impv act 3 pl • ομι

————**νυτωσαν**
V • pres impv act 3 pl • νυμι

————**ουτωσαν**
V • pres impv act 3 pl • οω

————**υτωσαν**
V • 2 aor impv act 3 pl • νυμι

————**ωτωσαν**
V • 2 aor impv act 3 pl • 1

————**ωσαν**
V • 2 aor ind act 3 pl • 1
P • pres act acc fem sg • αω

————**σαν**
V • aor ind act 3 pl • ★
V • 2 plup ind act 3 pl • MI
V • impf ind act 3 pl • 4
P • aor act nom/acc neut sg • ★
P • pres act acc fem sg • MI
P • 2 aor act acc fem sg • MI

————**ψαν**
V • aor ind act 3 pl • L
P • aor act nom/acc neut sg • L

————**αν**
V • aor ind act 3 pl • 2
V • 2 aor ind act 1 sg • 1
I • pres act • αω
P • pres act nom/acc neut sg • αμι
P • 2 aor act nom/acc neut sg • αμι 1
P • aor act nom/acc neut sg • 2
N • acc sg fem/masc • A
N • acc/voc sg masc • C

————**θεν**
P • aor pass nom/acc neut sg • ★

————**ξαιεν**
V • aor opt act 3 pl • G

————**σαιεν**
V • aor opt act 3 pl • ★

————**ψαιεν**
V • aor opt act 3 pl • L

———αιεν

V • pres opt act 3 pl • αμι
V • 2 aor opt act 3 pl • αμι 1
V • aor opt act 3 pl • 2

———θειεν

V • aor opt pass 3 pl • ★

———ξειεν

V • aor opt act 3 sg • G

———σειεν

V • aor opt act 3 sg • ★

———ψειεν

V • aor opt act 3 sg • L

———ειεν

V • pres opt act 3 pl • εμι
V • 2 aor opt act 3 pl • εμι
V • aor opt act 3 sg • 2
V • 2 aor opt pass 3 pl • ☆

———κοιεν

V • perf opt act 3 pl • ★

———ξοιεν

V • fut opt act 3 pl • G

———σοιεν

V • fut opt act 3 pl • ★

———ψοιεν

V • fut opt act 3 pl • L

———οιεν

V • pres opt act 3 pl • ★
V • fut opt act 3 pl • 2
V • 2 aor opt act 3 pl • ☆
V • 2 perf opt act 3 pl • ☆

———κεν

V • perf ind act 3 sg • ★

———καμεν

V • perf ind act 1 pl • ★
V • aor ind act 1 pl • 2

———ξαμεν

V • aor ind act 1 pl • G

———σαμεν

V • aor ind act 1 pl • ★

———ψαμεν

V • aor ind act 1 pl • L

———αμεν

V • pres ind act 1 pl • αμι
V • impf ind act 1 pl • αμι
V • aor ind act 1 pl • 2

V • 2 aor ind act 1 pl • 1
V • 2 perf ind act 1 pl • ☆

———κεμεν

V • plup ind act 1 pl • ★

———εμεν

V • pres ind act 1 pl • εμι
V • impf ind act 1 pl • εμι
V • 2 aor ind act 1 pl • εμι
V • 2 plup ind act 1 pl • ☆

———θημεν

V • aor ind pass 1 pl • ★

———αιημεν

V • pres opt act 1 pl • αμι
V • 2 aor opt act 1 pl • αμι

———θειημεν

V • aor opt pass 1 pl • ★

———ειημεν

V • pres opt act 1 pl • εμι
V • 2 aor opt act 1 pl • εμι
V • 2 aor opt pass 1 pl • ☆

———οιημεν

V • pres opt act 1 pl • εω οω ομι
V • 2 aor opt act 1 pl • ομι

———ωημεν

V • pres opt act 1 pl • αω

———ημεν

V • 2 aor ind act 1 pl • αμι 1
V • 2 aor ind pass 1 pl • ☆

———ξαιμεν

V • aor opt act 1 pl • G

———σαιμεν

V • aor opt act 1 pl • ★

———ψαιμεν

V • aor opt act 1 pl • L

———αιμεν

V • pres opt act 1 pl • αμι
V • 2 aor opt act 1 pl • αμι 1
V • aor opt act 1 pl • 2

———θειμεν

V • aor opt pass 1 pl • ★

———κειμεν

V • plup ind act 1 pl • ★

———ειμεν

V • pres opt act 1 pl • εμι
V • 2 aor opt act 1 pl • εμι

V • 2 aor opt pass 1 pl • ☆
V • 2 plup ind act 1 pl • ☆

——————κοιμεν

V • perf opt act 1 pl • ★

——————ξοιμεν

V • fut opt act 1 pl • G

——————σοιμεν

V • fut opt act 1 pl • ★

——————ψοιμεν

V • fut opt act 1 pl • L

——————οιμεν

V • pres opt act 1 pl • ★
V • fut opt act 1 pl • 2
V • 2 aor opt act 1 pl • ☆
V • 2 perf opt act 1 pl • ☆

——————ξομεν

V • fut ind act 1 pl • G

——————σομεν

V • fut ind act 1 pl • ★

——————ψομεν

V • fut ind act 1 pl • L

——————ομεν

V • pres ind act 1 pl • ★
V • impf ind act 1 pl • ★
V • 2 aor ind act 1 pl • ☆

——————νυμεν

V • pres ind act 1 pl • νυμι
V • impf ind act 1 pl • νυμι

——————ουμεν

V • pres ind act 1 pl • εω οω
V • impf ind act 1 pl • εω οω
V • fut ind act 1 pl • 2

——————θωμεν

V • aor subj pass 1 pl • ★

——————κωμεν

V • perf subj act 1 pl • ★

——————ξωμεν

V • aor subj act 1 pl • G

——————σωμεν

V • aor subj act 1 pl • ★

——————νυωμεν

V • pres subj act 1 pl • νυμι

——————ψωμεν

V • aor subj act 1 pl • L

——————ωμεν

V • pres opt act 1 pl • αω
V • 2 aor opt act 1 pl • 1

——————ωμεν

V • pres subj act 1 pl • ★
V • pres ind act 1 pl • αω
V • impf ind act 1 pl • αω
V • aor subj act 1 pl • 2
V • 2 aor ind act 1 pl • 1
V • 2 aor subj act 1 pl • ☆
V • 2 aor subj pass 1 pl • ☆
V • 2 perf subj act 1 pl • ☆

——————μεν

V • 2 perf ind act 1 pl • MI
V • 2 plup ind act 1 pl • MI
V • pres ind act 1 pl • 4
V • impf ind act 1 pl • 4

——————ξεν

V • aor ind act 3 sg • G

——————σεν

V • aor ind act 3 sg • ★

——————ψεν

V • aor ind act 3 sg • L

——————ωεν

V • pres opt act 3 pl • αω

——————εν

V • impf ind act 3 sg • ★
V • aor ind act 3 sg • 2
V • 2 aor ind act 3 sg • ☆
V • 2 perf ind act 3 sg • ☆
P • pres act nom/acc neut sg • εμι
P • 2 aor act nom/acc neut sg • ☆
P • 2 aor pass nom/acc neut sg • ☆

——————θην

V • aor ind pass 1 sg • ★

——————αιην

V • pres opt act 1 sg • αμι
V • 2 aor opt act 1 sg • αμι 1

——————θειην

V • aor opt pass 1 sg • ★

——————ειην

V • pres opt act 1 sg • εμι
V • 2 aor opt act 1 sg • εμι
V • 2 aor opt pass 1 sg • ☆

——————κοιην

V • perf opt act 1 sg • ★

————οιην

V • pres opt act 1 sg • εω οω ομι
V • 2 aor opt act 1 sg • ομι 1
V • fut opt act 1 sg • 2
V • 2 perf opt act 1 sg • ☆

————ξαμην

V • aor ind mid 1 sg • G

————σαμην

V • aor ind mid 1 sg • ★

————ψαμην

V • aor ind mid 1 sg • L

————αμην

V • impf ind mid/pass 1 sg • αμι
V • 2 aor ind mid 1 sg • αμι
V • aor ind mid 1 sg • 2

————γμην

V • plup ind mid/pass 1 sg • G

————εμην

V • impf ind mid/pass 1 sg • εμι
V • 2 aor ind mid 1 sg • εμι

————ξαιμην

V • aor opt mid 1 sg • G

————σαιμην

V • aor opt mid 1 sg • ★

————ψαιμην

V • aor opt mid 1 sg • L

————αιμην

V • pres opt mid/pass 1 sg • αμι
V • 2 aor opt mid 1 sg • αμι
V • aor opt mid 1 sg • 2

————ειμην

V • pres opt mid/pass 1 sg • εμι
V • 2 aor opt mid 1 sg • εμι

————ξοιμην

V • fut opt mid 1 sg • ★

————θησοιμην

V • fut opt pass 1 sg • ★

————ησοιμην

V • 2 fut opt pass 1 sg • ☆

————σοιμην

V • fut opt mid 1 sg • ★

————ψοιμην

V • fut opt mid 1 sg • L

————οιμην

V • pres opt mid/pass 1 sg • ★
V • 2 aor opt mid 1 sg • ☆
V • fut opt mid 1 sg • 2

————μμην

V • plup ind mid/pass 1 sg • L

————ομην

V • impf ind mid/pass 1 sg • ★
V • 2 aor ind mid 1 sg • ☆

————σμην

V • plup ind mid/pass 1 sg • D

————νυμην

V • impf ind mid/pass 1 sg • νυμι

————ουμην

V • impf ind mid/pass 1 sg • εω οω

————ῳμην

V • pres opt mid/pass 1 sg • αω

————ωμην

V • impf ind mid/pass 1 sg • αω

————μην

V • plup ind mid/pass 1 sg • ★

————ξαμενην

P • aor mid acc fem sg • G

————σαμενην

P • aor mid acc fem sg • ★

————ψαμενην

P • aor mid acc fem sg • L

————αμενην

P • pres mid/pass acc fem sg • αμι
P • 2 aor mid acc fem sg • αμι
P • aor mid acc fem sg • 2

————γμενην

P • perf mid/pass acc fem sg • G

————εμενην

P • pres mid/pass acc fem sg • εμι
P • 2 aor mid acc fem sg • εμι

————μμενην

P • perf mid/pass acc fem sg • L

————ξομενην

P • fut mid acc fem sg • G

————θησομενην

P • fut pass acc fem sg • ★

————ησομενην

P • 2 fut pass acc fem sg • ☆

————σομενην
P • fut mid acc fem sg • ★

————ψομενην
P • fut mid acc fem sg • L

————ομενην
P • pres mid/pass acc fem sg • ★
P • 2 aor mid acc fem sg • ★

————σμενην
P • perf mid/pass acc fem sg • D

————νυμενην
P • pres mid/pass acc fem sg • νυμι

————ουμενην
P • pres mid/pass acc fem sg • εω οω
P • fut mid acc fem sg • 2

————ωμενην
P • pres mid/pass acc fem sg • αω

————μενην
P • perf mid/pass acc fem sg • ★

————ῳην
V • pres opt act 1 sg • αω
V • 2 aor opt act 1 sg • 1

————ην
V • impf ind act 1 sg • αμι εμι
V • 2 aor ind act 1 sg • αμι 1
V • 2 aor ind pass 1 sg • ☆
I • pres act • 3
N • acc sg fem/masc • A
N • nom/voc sg masc/fem • C

————κειν
V • plup ind act 1 sg • ★
V • plup ind act 3 sg • ★

————ξειν
I • fut act • G

————σειν
I • fut act • ★

————ψειν
I • fut act • L

————ειν
V • 2 plup ind act 1 sg • ☆
V • 2 plup ind act 3 sg • ☆
V • impf ind act 1 sg • 4
V • impf ind act 3 sg • 4
I • pres act • ★
I • fut act • 2
I • 2 aor act • ☆

————ξιν
N • dat pl masc/fem/neut • C

————εασιν
V • pres ind act 3 pl • εμι

————ιασιν
V • pres ind act 3 pl • εμι

————κασιν
V • perf ind act 3 pl • ★

————μασιν
N • dat pl neut • C

————ξασιν
P • aor act dat masc/neut pl • G

————οασιν
V • pres ind act 3 pl • ομι

————ρασιν
N • dat pl masc/fem • C

————σασιν
P • aor act dat masc/neut pl • ★

————νυασιν
V • pres ind act 3 pl • νυμι

————ψασιν
P • aor act dat masc/neut pl • L

————ασιν
V • pres ind act 3 pl • αμι εμι
V • 2 perf ind act 3 pl • ☆
P • pres act dat masc/neut pl • αμι
P • 2 aor act dat masc/neut pl • αμι 1
P • aor act dat masc/neut pl • 2
N • dat pl masc/fem/neut • C

————εσιν
N • dat pl masc/fem/neut • C

————ησιν
V • pres ind act 3 sg • αμι εμι
N • dat pl masc/fem • C

————θεισιν
P • aor pass dat masc/neut pl • ★

————εισιν
P • pres act dat masc/neut pl • εμι
P • 2 aor act dat masc/neut pl • εμι
P • 2 aor pass dat masc/neut pl • ☆

————κοσιν
P • perf act dat masc/neut pl • ★

————οσιν
P • 2 perf act dat masc/neut pl • ☆

N • dat pl masc/fem • C

—————ρσιν

N • dat pl masc/fem • C

—————ευσιν

N • dat pl masc • C

—————νυσιν

V • pres ind act 3 sg • νυμι
P • pres act dat masc/neut pl • νυμι

—————ξουσιν

V • fut ind act 3 pl • G

—————σουσιν

V • fut ind act 3 pl • ★
P • fut act dat masc/neut pl • ★

—————ψουσιν

V • fut ind act 3 pl • L

—————ουσιν

V • pres ind act 3 pl • ★
V • fut ind act 3 pl • 2
P • pres act dat masc/neut pl • ★
P • 2 aor act dat masc/neut pl • ☆
P • fut act dat masc/neut pl • 2

—————υσιν

N • dat pl masc/fem • C

—————θωσιν

V • aor subj pass 3 pl • ★

—————κωσιν

V • perf subj act 3 pl • ★

—————ξωσιν

V • aor subj act 3 pl • G

—————σωσιν

V • aor subj act 3 pl • ★

—————ψωσιν

V • aor subj act 3 pl • L

—————ωσιν

V • pres subj act 3 pl • ★
V • pres ind act 3 sg • ομι
V • pres ind act 3 pl • αω
V • aor subj act 3 pl • 2
V • 2 aor subj act 3 pl • ☆
V • 2 aor subj pass 3 pl • ☆
V • 2 perf subj act 3 pl • ☆
P • pres act dat masc/neut pl • αω
N • dat pl masc/fem • C

—————σιν

V • pres ind act 3 pl • 4

P • pres act dat masc/neut pl • MI
P • 2 aor act dat masc/neut pl • MI
N • dat pl masc/fem/neut • C

—————τιν

V • pres ind act 3 sg • 4

—————ψιν

N • dat pl masc/fem/neut • C

—————ιν

N • acc sg masc/fem • C

—————ξαμενον

P • aor mid nom/acc neut sg • G
P • aor mid acc masc sg • G

—————σαμενον

P • aor mid nom/acc neut sg • ★
P • aor mid acc masc sg • ★

—————ψαμενον

P • aor mid nom/acc neut sg • L
P • aor mid acc masc sg • L

—————αμενον

P • pres mid/pass nom/acc neut sg • αμι
P • 2 aor mid nom/acc neut sg • αμι
P • aor mid nom/acc neut sg • 2
P • pres mid/pass acc masc sg • αμι
P • 2 aor mid acc masc sg • αμι
P • aor mid acc masc sg • 2

—————γμενον

P • perf mid/pass nom/acc neut sg • G
P • perf mid/pass acc masc sg • G

—————εμενον

P • pres mid/pass nom/acc neut sg • εμι
P • 2 aor mid nom/acc neut sg • εμι
P • pres mid/pass acc masc sg • εμι
P • 2 aor mid acc masc sg • εμι

—————μμενον

P • perf mid/pass nom/acc neut sg • L
P • perf mid/pass acc masc sg • L

—————ξομενον

P • fut mid nom/acc neut sg • G
P • fut mid acc masc sg • G

—————θησομενον

P • fut pass nom/acc neut sg • ★
P • fut pass acc masc sg • ★

—————ησομενον

P • 2 fut pass nom/acc neut sg • ☆
P • 2 fut pass acc masc sg • ☆

——σομενον

P • fut mid nom/acc neut sg • ★
P • fut mid acc masc sg • ★

——ψομενον

P • fut mid nom/acc neut sg • L
P • fut mid acc masc sg • L

——ομενον

P • pres mid/pass nom/acc neut sg • ★
P • 2 aor mid nom/acc neut sg • ★
P • pres mid/pass acc masc sg • ★
P • 2 aor mid acc masc sg • ★

——μμενον

P • perf mid/pass nom/acc neut sg • D
P • perf mid/pass acc masc sg • D

——νυμενον

P • pres mid/pass nom/acc neut sg • νυμι
P • pres mid/pass acc masc sg • νυμι

——ουμενον

P • pres mid/pass nom/acc neut sg • εω οω
P • fut mid nom/acc neut sg • 2
P • pres mid/pass acc masc sg • εω οω
P • fut mid acc masc sg • 2

——ωμενον

P • pres mid/pass nom/acc neut sg • αω
P • pres mid/pass acc masc sg • αω

——μενον

P • perf mid/pass nom/acc neut sg • ★
P • perf mid/pass acc masc sg • ★

——ξον

V • aor impv act 2 sg • G
P • fut act nom/acc neut sg • G

——σον

V • aor impv act 2 sg • ★
P • fut act nom/acc neut sg • ★

——ψον

V • aor impv act 2 sg • L
P • fut act nom/acc neut sg • L

——ον

V • impf ind act 1 sg • ★
V • impf ind act 3 pl • ★
V • aor impv act 2 sg • 2
V • 2 aor ind act 1 sg • ☆
V • 2 aor ind act 3 pl • ☆
P • pres act nom/acc neut sg • ★
P • 2 aor act nom/acc neut sg • ☆
N • acc sg masc/fem/neut • O
N • nom/acc/voc sg neut • O

——νυν

V • impf ind act 1 sg • νυμι
P • pres act nom/acc neut sg • νυμι

——ουν

V • impf ind act 1 sg • εω οω ομι
V • impf ind act 3 pl • εω οω ομι
I • pres act • οω
P • pres act nom/acc neut sg • εω οω
P • fut act nom/acc neut sg • 2
N • acc sg masc • O
N • nom/acc/voc sg neut • O

——υν

V • 2 aor ind act 1 sg • νυμι
P • 2 aor act nom/acc neut sg • νυμι
N • acc sg masc/fem • C

——εων

N • gen pl masc/fem • C

——ξασθων

V • aor impv mid 3 pl • G

——σασθων

V • aor impv mid 3 pl • ★

——ψασθων

V • aor impv mid 3 pl • L

——ασθων

V • pres impv mid/pass 3 pl • αω αμι
V • 2 aor impv mid 3 pl • αμι
V • aor impv mid 3 pl • 2

——εσθων

V • pres impv mid/pass 3 pl • ★
V • 2 aor impv mid 3 pl • ☆

——ησθων

V • pres impv mid/pass 3 pl • 3

——εισθων

V • pres impv mid/pass 3 pl • εω

——οσθων

V • pres impv mid/pass 3 pl • ομι
V • 2 aor impv mid 3 pl • ομι

——νυσθων

V • pres impv mid/pass 3 pl • νυμι

——ουσθων

V • pres impv mid/pass 3 pl • οω

——σθων

V • perf impv mid/pass 3 pl • ★

——φθων

V • perf impv mid/pass 3 pl • L

————χθων

V • perf impv mid/pass 3 pl • G

————θων

V • perf impv mid/pass 3 pl • Q

————κυιων

P • perf act gen fem pl • ★

————υιων

P • 2 perf act gen fem pl • ☆

————ξαμενων

P • aor mid gen masc/fem/neut pl • G

————σαμενων

P • aor mid gen masc/fem/neut pl • ★

————ψαμενων

P • aor mid gen masc/fem/neut pl • L

————αμενων

P • pres mid/pass gen masc/fem/neut pl • αμι
P • 2 aor mid gen masc/fem/neut pl • αμι
P • aor mid gen masc/fem/neut pl • 2

————γμενων

P • perf mid/pass gen masc/fem/neut pl • G

————εμενων

P • pres mid/pass gen masc/fem/neut pl • εμι
P • 2 aor mid gen masc/fem/neut pl • εμι

————μμενων

P • perf mid/pass gen masc/fem/neut pl • L

————ξομενων

P • fut mid gen masc/fem/neut pl • G

————θησομενων

P • fut pass gen masc/fem/neut pl • ★

————ησομενων

P • 2 fut pass gen masc/fem/neut pl • ☆

————σομενων

P • fut mid gen masc/fem/neut pl • ★

————ψομενων

P • fut mid gen masc/fem/neut pl • L

————ομενων

P • pres mid/pass gen masc/fem/neut pl • ★
P • 2 aor mid gen masc/fem/neut pl • ★

————σμενων

P • perf mid/pass gen masc/fem/neut pl • D

————νυμενων

P • pres mid/pass gen masc/fem/neut pl • νυμι

————ουμενων

P • pres mid/pass gen masc/fem/neut pl • εω οω
P • fut mid gen masc/fem/neut pl • 2

————ωμενων

P • pres mid/pass gen masc/fem/neut pl • αω

————μενων

P • perf mid/pass gen masc/fem/neut pl • ★

————ενων

N • gen pl masc/fem • C

————ηνων

N • gen pl masc/fem • C

————ονων

N • gen pl masc/fem • C

————ωνων

N • gen pl masc/fem • C

————ξων

P • fut act nom masc sg • G

————ρων

N • gen pl masc/fem • C

————ξασων

P • aor act gen fem pl • G

————σασων

P • aor act gen fem pl • ★

————ψασων

P • aor act gen fem pl • L

————ασων

P • pres act gen fem pl • αμι
P • 2 aor act gen fem pl • αμι 1
P • aor act gen fem pl • 2

————θεισων

P • aor pass gen fem pl • ★

————εισων

P • pres act gen fem pl • εμι
P • 2 aor act gen fem pl • εμι
P • 2 aor pass gen fem pl • ☆

————νυσων

P • pres act gen fem pl • νυμι

————σουσων

P • fut act gen fem pl • ★

————ουσων

P • pres act gen fem pl • ★
P • 2 aor act gen fem pl • ☆
P • fut act gen fem pl • 2

——————ωσων

P • pres act gen fem pl • αω

——————σων

P • fut act nom masc sg • ★
P • pres act gen fem pl • MI
P • 2 aor act gen fem pl • MI

——————ματων

N • gen pl neut • C

——————ατων

N • gen pl neut • C

——————ετων

V • 2 perf impv act 3 pl • ☆

——————ξαντων

V • aor impv act 3 pl • G
P • aor act gen masc/neut pl • G

——————σαντων

V • aor impv act 3 pl • ★
P • aor act gen masc/neut pl • ★

——————ψαντων

V • aor impv act 3 pl • L
P • aor act gen masc/neut pl • L

——————αντων

V • pres impv act 3 pl • αμι
V • 2 aor impv act 3 pl • αμι 1
V • aor impv act 3 pl • 2
P • pres act gen masc/neut pl • αμι
P • 2 aor act gen masc/neut pl • αμι
P • aor act gen masc/neut pl • 2
N • gen pl masc/fem • C

——————θεντων

V • aor impv pass 3 pl • ★
P • aor pass gen masc/neut pl • ★

——————εντων

V • pres impv act 3 pl • εμι
V • 2 aor impv act 3 pl • εμι
V • 2 aor impv pass 3 pl • ☆
P • pres act gen masc/neut pl • εμι
P • 2 aor act gen masc/neut pl • εμι
P • 2 aor pass gen masc/neut pl • ☆

——————κοντων

V • perf impv act 3 pl • ★

——————σοντων

P • fut act gen masc/neut pl • ★

——————οντων

V • pres impv act 3 pl • ★
V • 2 aor impv act 3 pl • ☆

P • pres act gen masc/neut pl • ★
P • 2 aor act gen masc/neut pl • ☆

——————νυντων

V • pres impv act 3 pl • νυμι
P • pres act gen masc/neut pl • νυμι

——————ουντων

V • pres impv act 3 pl • εω οω
P • pres act gen masc/neut pl • εω οω
P • fut act gen masc/neut pl • 2

——————υντων

V • 2 aor impv act 3 pl • νυμι
P • 2 aor act gen masc/neut pl • νυμι

——————ωντων

V • pres impv act 3 pl • αω
P • pres act gen masc/neut pl • αω

——————ντων

V • 2 perf impv act 3 pl • MI
P • pres act gen masc/neut pl • MI
P • 2 aor act gen masc/neut pl • MI

——————κοτων

P • perf act gen masc/neut pl • ★

——————οτων

P • 2 perf act gen masc/neut pl • ☆

——————τον

V • pres impv act 3 pl • 4

——————υων

N • gen pl masc • C

——————ψων

P • fut act nom masc sg • L

——————ων

V • impf ind act 1 sg • αω
V • impf ind act 3 pl • αω
V • 2 aor ind act 1 sg • 1
P • pres act nom masc sg • ★
P • pres act nom/acc neut sg • αω
P • 2 aor act nom masc sg • ☆
P • fut act nom masc sg • 2
N • gen pl masc/fem/neut • A O C
N • acc sg masc • C
N • nom/voc sg masc/fem • C

——————ν

V • impf ind act 1 sg • 4
V • impf ind act 3 sg • 4
P • pres act nom/acc neut sg • MI
P • 2 aor act nom/acc neut sg • MI
N • acc sg masc/fem • C

ξ

—————ξ

N • nom/voc sg masc/fem • C

o

—————ξαιο

V • aor opt mid 2 sg • G

—————σαιο

V • aor opt mid 2 sg • ★

—————ψαιο

V • aor opt mid 2 sg • L

—————αιο

V • pres opt mid/pass 2 sg • αμι
V • 2 aor opt mid 2 sg • αμι
V • aor opt mid 2 sg • 2

—————ειο

V • pres opt mid/pass 2 sg • εμι
V • 2 aor opt mid 2 sg • εμι

—————ξοιο

V • fut opt mid 2 sg • G

—————θησοιο

V • fut opt pass 2 sg • ★

—————ησοιο

V • 2 fut opt pass 2 sg • ☆

—————σοιο

V • fut opt mid 2 sg • ★

—————ψοιο

V • fut opt mid 2 sg • L

—————οιο

V • pres opt mid/pass 2 sg • ★
V • fut opt mid 2 sg • 3
V • 2 aor opt mid 2 sg • ομι

—————ξο

V • plup ind mid/pass 2 sg • G
V • perf impv mid/pass 2 sg • G

—————ασο

V • pres impv mid/pass 2 sg • αμι
V • impf ind mid/pass 2 sg • αμι

—————εσο

V • pres impv mid/pass 2 sg • εμι
V • impf ind mid/pass 2 sg • εμι

—————οσο

V • pres impv mid/pass 2 sg • ομι
V • impf ind mid/pass 2 sg • ομι

—————νυσο

V • pres impv mid/pass 2 sg • νυμι
V • impf ind mid/pass 2 sg • νυμι

—————σο

V • perf impv mid/pass 2 sg • ★
V • plup ind mid/pass 2 sg • ★

—————ξατο

V • aor ind mid 3 sg • G

—————σατο

V • aor ind mid 3 sg • ★

—————ψατο

V • aor ind mid 3 sg • L

—————ατο

V • impf ind mid/pass 3 sg • αω αμι
V • 2 aor ind mid 3 sg • αμι
V • aor ind mid 3 sg • 2

—————ετο

V • impf ind mid/pass 3 sg • ★
V • 2 aor ind mid 3 sg • ☆

—————ητο

V • impf ind mid/pass 3 sg • 3

—————ξαιτο

V • aor opt mid 3 sg • G

—————σαιτο

V • aor opt mid 3 sg • ★

—————ψαιτο

V • aor opt mid 3 sg • L

—————αιτο

V • pres opt mid/pass 3 sg • αμι
V • 2 aor opt mid 3 sg • αμι
V • aor opt mid 3 sg • 2

—————ειτο

V • pres opt mid/pass 3 sg • εμι
V • 2 aor opt mid 3 sg • εμι
V • impf ind mid/pass 3 sg • εω

—————ξοιτο

V • fut opt mid 3 sg • G

—————θησοιτο

V • fut opt pass 3 sg • ★

—————ησοιτο

V • 2 fut opt pass 3 sg • ☆

——————σοιτο
V • fut opt mid 3 sg • ★

——————ψοιτο
V • fut opt mid 3 sg • L

——————οιτο
V • pres opt mid/pass 3 sg • ★
V • 2 aor opt mid 3 sg • ομι ☆
V • fut opt mid 3 sg • 2

——————κτο
V • plup ind mid/pass 3 pl • G

——————ξαντο
V • aor ind mid 3 pl • G

——————σαντο
V • aor ind mid 3 pl • ★

——————ψαντο
V • aor ind mid 3 pl • L

——————αντο
V • impf ind mid/pass 3 pl • αμι
V • 2 aor ind mid 3 pl • αμι
V • aor ind mid 3 pl • 2

——————εντο
V • impf ind mid/pass 3 pl • εμι
V • 2 aor ind mid 3 pl • εμι

——————ξαιντο
V • aor opt mid 3 pl • G

——————σαιντο
V • aor opt mid 3 pl • ★

——————ψαιντο
V • aor opt mid 3 pl • L

——————αιντο
V • pres opt mid/pass 3 pl • αμι
V • 2 aor opt mid 3 pl • αμι
V • aor opt mid 3 pl • 2

——————ειντο
V • pres opt mid/pass 3 pl • εμι
V • 2 aor opt mid 3 pl • εμι

——————ξοιντο
V • fut opt mid 3 pl • G

——————θησοιντο
V • fut opt pass 3 pl • ★

——————ησοιντο
V • 2 fut opt pass 3 pl • ☆

——————σοιντο
V • fut opt mid 3 pl • ★

——————ψοιντο
V • fut opt mid 3 pl • L

——————οιντο
V • pres opt mid/pass 3 pl • ★
V • 2 aor opt mid 3 pl • ☆
V • fut opt mid 3 pl • 2

——————οντο
V • impf ind mid/pass 3 pl • ★
V • 2 aor ind mid 3 pl • ☆

——————νυντο
V • impf ind mid/pass 3 pl • νυμι

——————ουντο
V • impf ind mid/pass 3 pl • εω οω

——————ῳντο
V • pres opt mid/pass 3 pl • αω

——————ωντο
V • impf ind mid/pass 3 pl • αω

——————ντο
V • plup ind mid/pass 3 pl • ★

——————οτο
V • impf ind mid/pass 3 sg • ομι
V • 2 aor ind mid 3 sg • ομι

——————πτο
V • plup ind mid/pass 3 sg • L

——————στο
V • plup ind mid/pass 3 sg • D

——————νυτο
V • impf ind mid/pass 3 sg • νυμι

——————ουτο
V • impf ind mid/pass 3 sg • οω

——————ῳτο
V • pres opt mid/pass 3 sg • αω

——————το
V • plup ind mid/pass 3 sg • ★

——————ψο
V • plup ind mid/pass 2 sg • L
V • perf impv mid/pass 2 sg • L

——————ῳο
V • pres opt mid/pass 2 sg • αω

——————ο
N • nom/acc sg neut • O [pronominal ending]

ρ

——————ρ

N • nom/voc sg masc/fem • C
N • nom/acc/voc sg neut • C

ς

——————ξειας

V • aor opt act 2 sg • G

——————σειας

V • aor opt act 2 sg • ★

——————ψειας

V • aor opt act 2 sg • L

——————ειας

V • aor opt act 2 sg • 2

——————κυιας

P • perf act gen fem sg • ★
P • perf act acc fem pl • ★

——————υιας

P • 2 perf act gen fem sg • ☆
P • 2 perf act acc fem pl • ☆

——————κας

V • perf ind act 2 sg • ★
V • aor ind act 2 sg • 2 MI

——————ξαμενας

P • aor mid acc fem pl • G

——————σαμενας

P • aor mid acc fem pl • ★

——————ψαμενας

P • aor mid acc fem pl • L

——————αμενας

P • pres mid/pass acc fem pl • αμι
P • 2 aor mid acc fem pl • αμι
P • aor mid acc fem pl • 2

——————γμενας

P • perf mid/pass acc fem pl • G

——————εμενας

P • pres mid/pass acc fem pl • εμι
P • 2 aor mid acc fem pl • εμι

——————μμενας

P • perf mid/pass acc fem pl • L

——————ξομενας

P • fut mid acc fem pl • G

——————θησομενας

P • fut pass acc fem pl • ★

——————ησομενας

P • 2 fut pass acc fem pl • ☆

——————σομενας

P • fut mid acc fem pl • ★

——————ψομενας

P • fut mid acc fem pl • L

——————ομενας

P • pres mid/pass acc fem pl • ★
P • 2 aor mid acc fem pl • ★

——————σμενας

P • perf mid/pass acc fem pl • D

——————νυμενας

P • pres mid/pass acc fem pl • νυμι

——————ουμενας

P • pres mid/pass acc fem pl • εω οω
P • fut mid acc fem pl • 2

——————ωμενας

P • pres mid/pass acc fem pl • αω

——————μενας

P • perf mid/pass acc fem pl • ★

——————ενας

N • acc pl masc/fem • C

——————ηνας

N • acc pl masc/fem • C

——————ονας

N • acc pl masc/fem • C

——————ωνας

N • acc pl masc/fem • C

——————ξας

V • aor ind act 2 sg • G
P • aor act nom masc sg • G

——————ρας

N • acc pl masc/fem • C

——————ξασας

P • aor act acc fem pl • G

——————σασας

P • aor act acc fem pl • ★

——————ψασας

P • aor act acc fem pl • L

——————ασας

P • pres act acc fem pl • αμι

P • 2 aor act acc fem pl • αμι 1
P • aor act acc fem pl • 2

———θεισας

P • aor pass acc fem pl • ★

———εισας

P • pres act acc fem pl • εμι
P • 2 aor act acc fem pl • εμι
P • 2 aor pass acc fem pl • ☆

———νυσας

P • pres act acc fem pl • νυμι

———σουσας

P • fut act acc fem pl • ★

———ουσας

P • pres act acc fem pl • ★
P • 2 aor act acc fem pl • ☆
P • fut act acc fem pl • 2

———ωσας

P • pres act acc fem pl • αω

———σας

V • aor ind act 2 sg • ★
P • aor act nom masc sg • ★
P • pres act acc fem pl • MI
P • 2 aor act acc fem pl • MI

———ξαντας

P • aor act acc masc pl • G

———σαντας

P • aor act acc masc pl • ★

———ψαντας

P • aor act acc masc pl • L

———αντας

P • pres act acc masc pl • αμι
P • 2 aor act acc masc pl • αμι 1
P • aor act acc masc pl • 2
N • acc pl masc • C

———θεντας

P • aor pass acc masc pl • ★

———εντας

P • pres act acc masc pl • εμι
P • 2 aor act acc masc pl • εμι
P • 2 aor pass acc masc pl • ☆

———ξοντας

P • fut act acc masc pl • G

———σοντας

P • fut act acc masc pl • ★

———ψοντας

P • fut act acc masc pl • L

———οντας

P • pres act acc masc pl • ★
P • 2 aor act acc masc pl • ☆
N • acc pl masc • C

———νυντας

P • pres act acc masc pl • νυμι

———ουντας

P • pres act acc masc pl • εω οω
P • fut act acc masc pl • 2

———ωντας

P • pres act acc masc pl • αω

———ντας

P • pres act acc masc pl • MI
P • 2 aor act acc masc pl • MI

———κοτας

P • perf act acc masc pl • ★

———οτας

P • 2 perf act acc masc pl • ☆

———υας

N • acc pl masc • C

———ψας

V • aor ind act 2 sg • L
P • aor act nom masc sg • L

———ας

V • pres ind act 2 sg • αω
V • pres subj act 2 sg • αω
V • 2 aor subj act 2 sg • 1

———ας

V • impf ind act 2 sg • αω
V • aor ind act 2 sg • 2
V • 2 aor ind act 2 sg • 1
V • 2 perf ind act 2 sg • ☆
P • pres act nom masc sg • αμι
P • 2 aor act nom masc sg • αμι 1
P • aor act nom masc sg • 2
N • acc pl fem/masc • A
N • gen sg fem • A
N • nom sg masc • A
N • acc pl masc/fem • C
N • nom sg masc • C
N • nom/acc/voc sg neut • C

———ενες

N • nom pl masc/fem • C

——ηνες
N • nom pl masc/fem • C

——ονες
N • nom pl masc/fem • C

——ωνες
N • nom pl masc/fem • C

——ρες
N • nom pl masc/fem • C

——ξαντες
P • aor act nom masc pl • G

——σαντες
P • aor act nom masc pl • ★

——ψαντες
P • aor act nom masc pl • L

——αντες
P • pres act nom masc pl • αμι
P • 2 aor act nom masc pl • αμι 1
P • aor act nom masc pl • 2
N • nom pl masc • C

——θεντες
P • aor pass nom masc pl • ★

——εντες
P • pres act nom masc pl • εμι
P • 2 aor act nom masc pl • εμι
P • 2 aor pass nom masc pl • ☆

——ξοντες
P • fut act nom masc pl • G

——σοντες
P • fut act nom masc pl • ★

——ψοντες
P • fut act nom masc pl • L

——οντες
P • pres act nom masc pl • ★
P • 2 aor act nom masc pl • ☆
N • nom pl masc • C

——ντες
P • pres act nom masc pl • MI
P • 2 aor act nom masc pl • MI

——νυντες
P • pres act nom masc pl • νυμι

——ουντες
P • pres act nom masc pl • εω οω
P • fut act nom masc pl • 2

——ωντες
P • pres act nom masc pl • αω

——κοτες
P • perf act nom masc pl • ★

——οτες
P • 2 perf act nom masc pl • ☆

——υες
N • nom/voc pl masc • C

——ες
V • impf ind act 2 sg • ★
V • 2 aor ind act 2 sg • ☆
V • 2 aor impv act 2 sg • εμι
N • nom/voc pl masc/fem/neut • C

——θης
V • aor subj pass 2 sg • ★

——θης
V • aor ind pass 2 sg • ★

——αιης
V • pres opt act 2 sg • αμι
V • 2 aor opt act 2 sg • αμι 1

——θειης
V • aor opt pass 2 sg • ★

——ειης
V • pres opt act 2 sg • εμι
V • 2 aor opt act 2 sg • εμι
V • 2 aor opt pass 2 sg • ☆

——κοιης
V • perf opt act 2 sg • ★

——οιης
V • pres opt act 2 sg • εω οω ομι
V • 2 aor opt act 2 sg • ομι 1
V • 2 perf opt act 2 sg • ☆
V • fut opt act 2 sg • 2

——κης
V • perf subj act 2 sg • ★

——κης
V • plup ind act 2 sg • ★

——ξαμενης
P • aor mid gen fem sg • G

——σαμενης
P • aor mid gen fem sg • ★

——ψαμενης
P • aor mid gen fem sg • L

——αμενης
P • pres mid/pass gen fem sg • αμι
P • 2 aor mid gen fem sg • αμι
P • aor mid gen fem sg • 2

——γμενης
P • perf mid/pass gen fem sg • G

——εμενης
P • pres mid/pass gen fem sg • εμι
P • 2 aor mid gen fem sg • εμι

——μμενης
P • perf mid/pass gen fem sg • L

——ξομενης
P • fut mid gen fem sg • G

——θησομενης
P • fut pass gen fem sg • ★

——ησομενης
P • 2 fut pass gen fem sg • ☆

——σομενης
P • fut mid gen fem sg • ★

——ψομενης
P • fut mid gen fem sg • L

——ομενης
P • pres mid/pass gen fem sg • ★
P • 2 aor mid gen fem sg • ★

——σμενης
P • perf mid/pass gen fem sg • D

——νυμενης
P • pres mid/pass gen fem sg • νυμι

——ουμενης
P • pres mid/pass gen fem sg • εω οω
P • fut mid gen fem sg • 2

——ωμενης
P • pres mid/pass gen fem sg • αω

——μενης
P • perf mid/pass gen fem sg • ★

——ξης
V • aor subj act 2 sg • G

——ξασης
P • aor act gen fem sg • G

——σασης
P • aor act gen fem sg • ★

——ψασης
P • aor act gen fem sg • L

——ασης
P • pres act gen fem sg • αμι
P • 2 aor act gen fem sg • αμι 1
P • aor act gen fem sg • 2

——θεισης
P • aor pass gen fem sg • ★

——εισης
P • pres act gen fem sg • εμι
P • 2 aor act gen fem sg • εμι
P • 2 aor pass gen fem sg • ☆

——νυσης
P • pres act gen fem sg • νυμι

——ξουσης
P • fut act gen fem sg • G

——σουσης
P • fut act gen fem sg • ★

——ψουσης
P • fut act gen fem sg • L

——ουσης
P • pres act gen fem sg • ★
P • 2 aor act gen fem sg • ☆
P • fut act gen fem sg • 2

——ωσης
P • pres act gen fem sg • αω

——σης
V • aor subj act 2 sg • ★

——σης
P • pres act gen fem sg • MI
P • 2 aor act gen fem sg • MI

——νυης
V • pres subj act 2 sg • νυμι

——ψης
V • aor subj act 2 sg • L

——ωης
V • pres opt act 2 sg • αω

——ης
V • pres subj act 2 sg • ★
V • pres ind act 2 sg • 3
V • aor subj act 2 sg • 2
V • 2 aor subj act 2 sg • ☆
V • 2 aor subj pass 2 sg • ☆
V • 2 perf subj act 2 sg • ☆

——ης
V • pres ind act 2 sg • αμι εμι
V • impf ind act 2 sg • αμι 3

V • 2 aor ind act 2 sg • αμι 1
V • 2 aor ind pass 2 sg • ☆
V • 2 plup act indictive 2 sg • ☆
N • gen sg fem • A
N • nom sg masc • A
N • nom sg masc/fem • C

————κυιαις

P • perf act dat fem pl • ★

————υιαις

P • 2 perf act dat fem pl • ☆

————ξαμεναις

P • aor mid dat fem pl • G

————σαμεναις

P • aor mid dat fem pl • ★

————ψαμεναις

P • aor mid dat fem pl • L

————αμεναις

P • pres mid/pass dat fem pl • αμι
P • 2 aor mid dat fem pl • αμι
P • aor mid dat fem pl • 2

————γμεναις

P • perf mid/pass dat fem pl • G

————εμεναις

P • pres mid/pass dat fem pl • εμι
P • 2 aor mid dat fem pl • εμι

————μμεναις

P • perf mid/pass dat fem pl • L

————ξομεναις

P • fut mid dat fem pl • G

————θησομεναις

P • fut pass dat fem pl • ★

————ησομεναις

P • 2 fut pass dat fem pl • ☆

————σομεναις

P • fut mid dat fem pl • ★

————ψομεναις

P • fut mid dat fem pl • L

————ομεναις

P • pres mid/pass dat fem pl • ★
P • 2 aor mid dat fem pl • ★

————σμεναις

P • perf mid/pass dat fem pl • D

————νυμεναις

P • pres mid/pass dat fem pl • νυμι

————ουμεναις

P • pres mid/pass dat fem pl • εω οω
P • fut mid dat fem pl • 2

————ωμεναις

P • pres mid/pass dat fem pl • αω

————μεναις

P • perf mid/pass dat fem pl • ★

————ξαις

V • aor act opt 2 sg • G

————ξασαις

P • aor act dat fem pl • G

————σασαις

P • aor act dat fem pl • ★

————ψασαις

P • aor act dat fem pl • L

————ασαις

P • pres act dat fem pl • αμι
P • 2 aor act dat fem pl • αμι 1
P • aor act dat fem pl • 2

————θεισαις

P • aor pass dat fem pl • ★

————εισαις

P • pres act dat fem pl • εμι
P • 2 aor act dat fem pl • εμι
P • 2 aor pass dat fem pl • ☆

————νυσαις

P • pres act dat fem pl • νυμι

————σουσαις

P • fut act dat fem pl • ★

————ουσαις

P • pres act dat fem pl • ★
P • 2 aor act dat fem pl • ☆
P • fut act dat fem pl • 2

————ωσαις

P • pres act dat fem pl • αω

————σαις

V • aor opt act 2 sg • ★
P • pres act dat fem pl • MI
P • 2 aor act dat fem pl • MI

————ψαις

V • aor opt act 2 sg • L

————αις

V • aor opt act 2 sg • 2
N • dat pl fem/masc • A

————θεις

P • aor pass nom masc sg • ★

————κεις

V • plup ind act 2 sg • ★

————ξεις

V • fut ind act 2 sg • G

————σεις

V • fut ind act 2 sg • ★

————ψεις

V • fut ind act 2 sg • L

————εις

V • pres ind act 2 sg • ★
V • impf ind act 2 sg • εω εμι
V • fut ind act 2 sg • 2
V • 2 plup ind act 2 sg • ☆
P • pres act nom masc sg • εμι
P • 2 aor act nom masc sg • εμι
P • 2 aor pass nom masc sg • ☆
N • nom/acc pl masc/fem • C
N • nom/voc pl masc • C

————κοις

V • perf opt act 2 sg • ★

————ξαμενοις

P • aor mid dat masc/neut pl • G

————σαμενοις

P • aor mid dat masc/neut pl • ★

————ψαμενοις

P • aor mid dat masc/neut pl • L

————αμενοις

P • pres mid/pass dat masc/neut pl • αμι
P • 2 aor mid dat masc/neut pl • αμι
P • aor mid dat masc/neut pl • 2

————γμενοις

P • perf mid/pass dat masc/neut pl • G

————εμενοις

P • pres mid/pass dat masc/neut pl • εμι
P • 2 aor mid dat masc/neut pl • εμι

————μμενοις

P • perf mid/pass dat masc/neut pl • L

————ξομενοις

P • fut mid dat masc/neut pl • G

————θησομενοις

P • fut pass dat masc/neut pl • ★

————ησομενοις

P • 2 fut pass dat masc/neut pl • ☆

————σομενοις

P • fut mid dat masc/neut pl • ★

————ψομενοις

P • fut mid dat masc/neut pl • L

————ομενοις

P • pres mid/pass dat masc/neut pl • ★
P • 2 aor mid dat masc/neut pl • ★

————σμενοις

P • perf mid/pass dat masc/neut pl • D

————νυμενοις

P • pres mid/pass dat masc/neut pl • νυμι

————ουμενοις

P • pres mid/pass dat masc/neut pl • εω οω
P • fut mid dat masc/neut pl • 2

————ωμενοις

P • pres mid/pass dat masc/neut pl • αω

————μενοις

P • perf mid/pass dat masc/neut pl • ★

————ξοις

V • fut opt act 2 sg • G

————σοις

V • fut opt act 2 sg • ★

————νυοις

V • pres opt act 2 sg • νυμι

————ψοις

V • fut opt act 2 sg • L

————οις

V • pres opt act 2 sg • ★
V • pres ind act 2 sg • οω
V • pres subj act 2 sg • οω
V • 2 aor opt act 2 sg • ☆
V • 2 perf opt act 2 sg • ☆
V • fut opt act 2 sg • 2
N • dat pl masc /neut • O

————ις

N • nom sg fem • C
N • voc sg fem • C

————εος

N • dat sg masc/neut • C
N • gen sg masc • C

————κος

P • perf act nom/acc neut sg • ★

————ξαμενος

P • aor mid nom masc sg • G

——————σαμενος
P • aor mid nom masc sg • ★

——————ψαμενος
P • aor mid nom masc sg • L

——————αμενος
P • pres mid/pass nom masc sg • αμι
P • 2 aor mid nom masc sg • αμι
P • aor mid nom masc sg • 2

——————γμενος
P • perf mid/pass nom masc sg • G

——————εμενος
P • pres mid/pass nom masc sg • εμι
P • 2 aor mid nom masc sg • εμι

——————μμενος
P • perf mid/pass nom masc sg • L

——————ξομενος
P • fut mid nom masc sg • G

——————θησομενος
P • fut pass nom masc sg • ★

——————ησομενος
P • 2 fut pass nom masc sg • ☆

——————σομενος
P • fut mid nom masc sg • ★

——————ψομενος
P • fut mid nom masc sg • L

——————ομενος
P • pres mid/pass nom masc sg • ★
P • 2 aor mid nom masc sg • ★

——————σμενος
P • perf mid/pass nom masc sg • D

——————νυμενος
P • pres mid/pass nom masc sg • νυμι

——————ουμενος
P • pres mid/pass nom masc sg • εω οω
P • fut mid nom masc sg • 2

——————ωμενος
P • pres mid/pass nom masc sg • αω

——————μενος
P • perf mid/pass nom masc sg • ★

——————ενος
N • gen sg masc/fem • C

——————ηνος
N • gen sg masc/fem • C

——————ονος
N • gen sg masc/fem • C

——————ωνος
N • gen sg masc/fem • C

——————ρος
N • gen sg masc/fem • C

——————ματος
N • gen sg neut • C

——————ατος
N • gen sg neut • C

——————ξαντος
P • aor act gen masc/neut sg • G

——————σαντος
P • aor act gen masc/neut sg • ★

——————ψαντος
P • aor act gen masc/neut sg • L

——————αντος
P • pres act gen masc/neut sg • αμι
P • 2 aor act gen masc/neut sg • αμι
P • aor act gen masc/neut sg • 2
N • gen sg masc • C

——————θεντος
P • aor pass gen masc/neut sg • ★

——————εντος
P • pres act gen masc/neut sg • εμι
P • 2 aor act gen masc/neut sg • εμι
P • 2 aor pass gen masc/neut sg • ☆

——————ξοντος
P • fut act gen masc/neut sg • G

——————σοντος
P • fut act gen masc/neut sg • ★

——————ψοντος
P • fut act gen masc/neut sg • L

——————οντος
P • pres act gen masc/neut sg • ★
P • 2 aor act gen masc/neut sg • ☆
N • gen sg masc • C

——————νυντος
P • pres act gen masc/neut sg • νυμι

——————ουντος
P • pres act gen masc/neut sg • εω οω
P • fut act gen masc/neut sg • 2

——————ωντος
P • pres act gen masc/neut sg • αω

————ντος

P • pres act gen masc/neut sg • MI
P • 2 aor act gen masc/neut sg • MI

————κοτος

P • perf act gen masc/neut sg • ★

————οτος

P • 2 perf act gen masc/neut sg • ☆

————τος

N • gen sg masc/neut • C

————υος

N • gen sg masc/fem • C

————ος

V • 2 aor impv act 2 sg • ομι
P • 2 perf act nom/acc neut sg • ☆
N • nom sg masc/fem • O
N • gen sg masc/fem/neut • C
N • nom/acc sg neut • C

————αυς

N • nom sg fem • C
N • acc pl fem • C

————ευς

N • nom sg masc • C

————νυς

V • pres ind act 2 sg • νυμι
V • impf ind act 2 sg • νυμι
P • pres act nom masc sg • νυμι

————ξαμενους

P • aor mid acc masc pl • G

————σαμενους

P • aor mid acc masc pl • ★

————ψαμενους

P • aor mid acc masc pl • L

————αμενους

P • pres mid/pass acc masc pl • αμι
P • 2 aor mid acc masc pl • αμι
P • aor mid acc masc pl • 2

————γμενους

P • perf mid/pass acc masc pl • G

————εμενους

P • pres mid/pass acc masc pl • εμι
P • 2 aor mid acc masc pl • εμι

————μμενους

P • perf mid/pass acc masc pl • L

————ξομενους

P • fut mid acc masc pl • G

————θησομενους

P • fut pass acc masc pl • ★

————ησομενους

P • 2 fut pass acc masc pl • ☆

————σομενους

P • fut mid acc masc pl • ★

————ψομενους

P • fut mid acc masc pl • L

————ομενους

P • pres mid/pass acc masc pl • ★
P • 2 aor mid acc masc pl • ★

————σμενους

P • perf mid/pass acc masc pl • D

————νυμενους

P • pres mid/pass acc masc pl • νυμι

————ουμενους

P • pres mid/pass acc masc pl • εω οω
P • fut mid acc masc pl • 2

————ωμενους

P • pres mid/pass acc masc pl • αω

————μενους

P • perf mid/pass acc masc pl • ★

————ους

V • impf ind act 2 sg • οω ομι
P • pres act nom masc sg • ομι
P • 2 aor act nom masc sg • ομι
N • acc pl masc • O
N • nom/voc sg masc • O
N • gen sg fem/neut • C
N • nom/voc sg masc/fem • C
N • acc pl masc/fem • C

————υς

V • 2 aor ind act 2 sg • νυμι
P • 2 aor act nom masc sg • νυμι
N • nom sg masc/fem • C
N • acc pl masc/fem • C

————εως

N • gen sg masc/fem • C

————κως

P • perf act nom masc sg • ★

————ῳς

V • pres subj act 2 sg • ομι
V • 2 aor subj act 2 sg • ομι 1
V • pres opt act 2 sg • αω
N • dat pl masc • O

————ως

V • pres ind act 2 sg • ομι
V • 2 aor ind act 2 sg • 1
P • 2 perf act nom masc sg • ☆
N • nom sg masc • O
N • acc pl masc • O
N • gen sg masc/fem/neut • C

————ς

V • pres ind act 2 sg • 4
N • nom sg masc/fem • C

υ

————αυ

N • voc sg fem • C

————ευ

N • voc sg masc • C

————νυ

V • pres impv act 2 sg • νυμι
V • impf ind act 3 sg • νυμι
V • 2 aor ind act 3 sg • 1

————ξαμενου

P • aor mid gen masc/neut sg • G

————σαμενου

P • aor mid gen masc/neut sg • ★

————ψαμενου

P • aor mid gen masc/neut sg • L

————αμενου

P • pres mid/pass gen masc/neut sg • αμι
P • 2 aor mid gen masc/neut sg • αμι
P • aor mid gen masc/neut sg • 2

————γμενου

P • perf mid/pass gen masc/neut sg • G

————εμενου

P • pres mid/pass gen masc/neut sg • εμι
P • 2 aor mid gen masc/neut sg • εμι

————μμενου

P • perf mid/pass gen masc/neut sg • L

————ξομενου

P • fut mid gen masc/neut sg • G

————θησομενου

P • fut pass gen masc/neut sg • ★

————ησομενου

P • 2 fut pass gen masc/neut sg • ☆

————σομενου

P • fut mid gen masc/neut sg • ★

————ψομενου

P • fut mid gen masc/neut sg • L

————ομενου

P • pres mid/pass gen masc/neut sg • ★
P • 2 aor mid gen masc/neut sg • ★

————σμενου

P • perf mid/pass gen masc/neut sg • D

————νυμενου

P • pres mid/pass gen masc/neut sg • νυμι

————ουμενου

P • pres mid/pass gen masc/neut sg • εω οω
P • fut mid gen masc/neut sg • 2

————ωμενου

P • pres mid/pass gen masc/neut sg • αω

————μενου

P • perf mid/pass gen masc/neut sg • ★

————ου

V • pres impv mid/pass 2 sg • ★
V • impf ind mid/pass 2 sg • ★
V • pres impv act 2 sg • οω ομι
V • impf ind act 3 sg • οω ομι
V • 2 aor ind mid 2 sg • εμι ομι ☆
V • 2 aor impv mid 2 sg • εμι ομι ☆
N • gen sg masc • A
N • gen sg masc/fem/neut • O

————υ

V • 2 aor ind act 3 sg • νυμι
N • nom/acc/voc sg neut • C
N • voc sg masc/fem • C

ψ

————ψ

N • nom/voc sg masc/fem • C

ω

————ξασθω

V • aor impv mid 3 sg • G

————σασθω

V • aor impv mid 3 sg • ★

————ψασθω

V • aor impv mid 3 sg • L

————ασθω

V • pres impv mid/pass 3 sg • αω αμι
V • 2 aor impv mid 3 sg • αμι
V • aor impv mid 3 sg • 2

————εσθω

V • pres impv mid/pass 3 sg • ★
V • 2 aor impv mid 3 sg • ☆

————ησθω

V • pres impv mid/pass 3 sg • 3

————εισθω

V • pres impv mid/pass 3 sg • εω

————οσθω

V • pres impv mid/pass 3 sg • ομι
V • 2 aor impv mid 3 sg • ομι

————νυσθω

V • pres impv mid/pass 3 sg • νυμι

————ουσθω

V • pres impv mid/pass 3 sg • οω

————σθω

V • perf impv mid/pass 3 sg • ★

————φθω

V • perf impv mid/pass 3 sg • L

————χθω

V • perf impv mid/pass 3 sg • G

————θω

V • aor subj pass 1 sg • ★
V • perf impv mid/pass 3 sg • Q

————κω

V • perf subj act 1 sg • ★

————ξαμενῳ

P • aor mid dat masc/neut sg • G

————σαμενῳ

P • aor mid dat masc/neut sg • ★

————ψαμενῳ

P • aor mid dat masc/neut sg • L

————αμενῳ

P • pres mid/pass dat masc/neut sg • αμι
P • 2 aor mid dat masc/neut sg • αμι
P • aor mid dat masc/neut sg • 2

————γμενῳ

P • perf mid/pass dat masc/neut sg • G

————εμενῳ

P • pres mid/pass dat masc/neut sg • εμι
P • 2 aor mid dat masc/neut sg • εμι

————μμενῳ

P • perf mid/pass dat masc/neut sg • L

————ξομενῳ

P • fut mid dat masc/neut sg • G

————θησομενῳ

P • fut pass dat masc/neut sg • ★

————ησομενῳ

P • 2 fut pass dat masc/neut sg • ☆

————σομενῳ

P • fut mid dat masc/neut sg • ★

————ψομενῳ

P • fut mid dat masc/neut sg • L

————ομενῳ

P • pres mid/pass dat masc/neut sg • ★
P • 2 aor mid dat masc/neut sg • ★

————σμενῳ

P • perf mid/pass dat masc/neut sg • D

————νυμενῳ

P • pres mid/pass dat masc/neut sg • νυμι

————ουμενῳ

P • pres mid/pass dat masc/neut sg • εω οω
P • fut mid dat masc/neut sg • 2

————ωμενῳ

P • pres mid/pass dat masc/neut sg • αω

————μενῳ

P • perf mid/pass dat masc/neut sg • ★

————ξω

V • fut ind act 1 sg • G
V • aor ind mid 2 sg • G
V • aor subj act 1 sg • G

————σω

V • fut ind act 1 sg • ★
V • aor ind mid 2 sg • ★
V • aor subj act 1 sg • ★

ξατω

V • aor impv act 3 sg • G

————σατω

V • aor impv act 3 sg • ★

————ψατω

V • aor impv act 3 sg • L

——————ατω

V • pres impv act 3 sg • αω αμι
V • aor impv act 3 sg • 2

——————κετω

V • perf impv act 3 sg • ★

——————ετω

V • pres impv act 3 sg • ★
V • 2 aor impv act 3 sg • ☆
V • 2 perf impv act 3 sg • ☆

——————θητω

V • aor impv pass 3 sg • ★

——————ητω

V • pres impv act 3 sg • 3
V • 2 aor impv act 3 sg • αμι 1
V • 2 aor impv pass 3 sg • ☆

——————ειτω

V • pres impv act 3 sg • εω

——————οτω

V • pres impv act 3 sg • ομι
V • 2 aor impv act 3 sg • ομι

——————νυτω

V • pres impv act 3 sg • νυμι

——————ουτω

V • pres impv act 3 sg • οω

——————υτω

V • 2 aor impv act 3 sg • νυμι

——————ωτω

V • 2 aor impv act 3 sg • 1

——————τω

V • pres impv act 3 sg • 4

——————ψω

V • fut ind act 1 sg • L
V • aor ind mid 2 sg • L
V • aor subj act 1 sg • L

——————ῳ

V • pres subj act 3 sg • ομι
V • pres subj mid/pass 2 sg • ομι
V • 2 aor subj act 3 sg • ομι 1
V • 2 aor subj mid 2 sg • ομι
V • pres opt act 3 sg • αω
N • dat sg masc/fem/neut • O

——————ω

V • pres ind act 1 sg • ★
V • pres subj act 1 sg • ★
V • pres impv mid/pass 2 sg • αω
V • impf ind mid/pass 2 sg • αω
V • fut ind act 1 sg • 2
V • aor ind mid 2 sg • 2
V • aor subj act 1 sg • 2
V • 2 aor subj act 1 sg • ☆
V • 2 aor ind act 3 sg • 1
V • 2 aor subj pass 1 sg • ☆
V • 2 perf subj act 1 sg • ☆
V • 2 aor ind mid 2 sg • αμι
V • 2 aor impv mid 2 sg • αμι
N • gen sg masc • O

Forms of the Verb εἰμί

εἶ
V • pres ind act 2 sg
εἶεν
V • pres opt act 3 pl
εἴη
V • pres opt act 3 sg
εἴημεν
V • pres opt act 1 pl
εἴην
V • pres opt act 1 sg
εἴης
V • pres opt act 2 sg
εἴησαν
V • pres opt act 3 pl
εἴητε
V • pres opt act 2 pl
εἶμεν
V • pres opt act 1 pl
εἰμί
V • pres ind act 1 sg
εἶναι
I • pres act
εἰσί
V • pres ind act 3 pl
εἶτε
V • pres opt act 2 pl
ἔσει
V • fut ind mid 2 sg
ἔσεσθαι
I • fut mid
ἔσεσθε
V • fut ind mid 2 pl
ἔση
V • fut ind mid 2 sg
ἐσμέν
V • pres ind act 1 pl
ἐσοίμεθα
V • fut opt mid 1 pl
ἐσόμεν . . .
P • fut [see note]
ἐσοίμην
V • fut opt mid 1 sg
ἔσοιντο
V • fut opt mid 3 pl

ἔσοιο
V • fut opt mid 2 sg
ἔσοισθε
V • fut opt mid 2 pl
ἔσοιτο
V • fut opt mid 3 sg
ἔσομαι
V • fut ind mid 1 sg
ἐσόμεθα
V • fut ind mid 1 pl
ἔσονται
V • fut ind mid 3 pl
ἔσται
V • fut ind mid 3 sg
ἐστέ
V • pres ind act 2 pl
ἔστε
V • pres impv act 2 pl
ἐστί(ν)
V • pres ind act 3 sg
ἔστω
V • pres impv act 3 sg
ἔστων
V • pres impv act 3 pl
ἔστωσαν
V • pres impv act 3 pl
ἦ
V • impf ind act 1 sg
ᾖ
V • pres subj act 3 sg
ἦμεν
V • impf ind act 1 pl
ἤμεθα
V • impf ind mid 1 pl
ἤμην
V • impf ind mid 1 sg
ἦν
V • impf ind act 3 sg
ἦς
V • impf ind act 2 sg
ᾖς
V • pres subj act 2 sg
ἦσαν
V • impf ind act 3 pl

ἦσθα
V • impf ind act 2 sg
ἦστε
V • impf ind act 2 pl
ἦτε
V • pres subj act 2 pl
V • impf ind act 2 pl
ἤτω
V • pres impv act 3 sg
ἴσθι
V • pres impv act 2 sg
ὄν
P • pres act nom/acc sg neut
ὄντ . . .
P • pres [see note]
ὄντων
V • pres impf act 3 pl
οὖσ . . .
P • pres [see note*]
ὦ
V • pres subj act 1 sg

ὦμεν
V • pres subj act 1 pl
ὤν
P • pres act nom masc
ὦσι(ν)
V • pres subj act 3 pl

NOTE: participle forms:

• For present feminine participles, or for masculine or neuter dative plural forms, use Chart B. Simply combine the ου ending in column 1 with any entry in column 2.

• For present masculine and neuter participles, use Chart C. Simply combine the ο ending in column 1 with any entry in column 2.

• For future participles, use Chart A. Simply combine the σο ending in column 1 with any entry in column 2.

Participle Charts

From the three participle charts that follow, over one thousand participle endings can be determined. Each chart is divided into two columns. By combining any entry from column one with any entry from column two, the full participle form can be determined. A few participle forms that do not fit these three charts are listed in *Index 2: Greek Word Endings*. [Note that the reverse order is used here, as in *Index 2: Greek Word Endings*.]

Participle Chart A

ξα		**μενα**	
G • aor mid		nom/acc neut pl	
σα		**μενη**	
★ • aor mid		dat fem sg	
ψα		**μενη**	
L • aor mid		nom fem sg	
α		**μεναι**	
αμι • pres mid/pass		nom fem pl	
αμι • 2 aor mid		**μενοι**	
2 • aor mid		nom masc pl	
ε		**μενην**	
εμι • pres mid/pass		acc fem sg	
εμι • 2 aor mid		**μενον**	
γ		nom/acc neut sg	
G • perf mid/pass		acc masc sg	
μ		**μενων**	
L • perf mid/pass		gen masc/fem/neut pl	
ξο		**μενας**	
G • fut mid		acc fem pl	
θησο		**μενης**	
★ • fut pass		gen fem sg	
ησο		**μεναις**	
☆ • 2 fut pass		dat fem pl	
σο		**μενοις**	
★ • fut mid		dat masc/neut pl	
ψο		**μενος**	
L • fut mid		nom masc sg	
ο		**μενους**	
ομι ★ • pres mid/pass		acc masc pl	
ομι ★ • 2 aor mid		**μενου**	
σ		gen masc/neut sg	
D • perf mid/pass		**μενῳ**	
ου		dat masc/neut sg	
εω οω • pres mid/pass			
2 • fut mid			

νυ

νυμι • pres mid/pass

ω

αω • pres mid/pass

[blank]

★ • perf mid/pass

Participle Chart B

ξα	**σα**
G • aor act	nom fem sg
σα	**ση**
★ • aor act	dat fem sg
ψα	**σαι**
L • aor act	nom fem pl
α	**σι**
MI • pres mid/pass	dat masc/neut pl
1 αμι • 2 aor act	**σαν**
2 • aor act	acc fem sg
θει	**σιν**
★ • aor pass	dat masc/neut pl
ει	**σων**
εμι • pres act	gen fem pl
εμι • 2 aor act	**σας**
☆ • 2 aor pass	acc fem pl
θει	**σης**
★ • aor pass	gen fem sg
ξου	**σαις**
G • fut act	dat fem pl
σου	
★ • fut act	
ψου	
L • fut act	
ου	
★ • pres act	
☆ • 2 aor act	
3 • fut act	
νυ	
νυμι • pres act	
ω	
αω • pres act	

Participle Chart C

ξα	**ντα**	
G • aor act		nom/acc neut pl
σα		acc masc sing
★ • aor act	**ντι**	
ψα		dat masc/neut sg
L • aor act	**ντων**	
α		gen masc/neut pl
αμι • pres act	**ντας**	
1 αμι • 2 aor act		acc masc pl
2 • aor act	**ντες**	
θε		nom masc pl
★ • aor pass	**ντος**	
ε		gen masc/neut sg
εμι • pres act		
εμι • 2 aor act		
☆ • 2 aor pass		
ξο		
G • fut act		
σο		
★ • fut act		
ψο		
L • fut act		
ο		
★ • pres act		
☆ • 2 aor act		
ου		
★ • pres act		
3 • fut act		
υ		
νυμι • pres act		
ω		
αω • pres act		

INDEX 3: COGNATE GROUP TERMS

Entries in bold type and followed by a dash are cognate roots. All other entries are complete words. The numbers refer to the pages on which each root or word can be found in Section 2 of the book. This index can also be used as a compact dictionary.

ἀβαρής ές burdenless, 104
ἀγ – bring, lead, 24
ἀγαθ – good, 56
ἀγαθοεργέω do good, be generous, 56
ἀγαθοποιέω do good, be helpful, 56
ἀγαθοποιΐα ας good-doing, 56
ἀγαθοποιός οῦ good doer, 56
ἀγαθός ή όν good, useful, 56
ἀγαθουργέω do good, be kind, 56
ἀγαθωσύνη ης goodness, 56
ἄγαμος ου unmarried, single, 81
ἀγαπ – love, 33
ἀγαπάω love, 33
ἀγάπη ης love, 33
ἀγαπητός ή όν beloved, 33
ἀγγελ – message, 23
ἀγγελία ας message, news, 23
ἀγγέλλω tell, 23
ἄγγελος ου angel, messenger, 23
ἀγενεαλότητος ον without genealogy, 14
ἀγενής ές insignificant, inferior, 14
ἀγι – holy, sacred, 34
ἁγιάζω make holy, purify, 34
ἁγιασμός οῦ consecration, 34
ἅγιος α ον holy, consecrated, 34
ἁγιότης ητος holiness, 34
ἁγιωσύνη ης holiness, consecration, 34
ἀγν – holy, sacred, 34
ἁγνεία ας moral purity, 34
ἁγνίζω purify (> holy + ize), 34
ἁγνισμός οῦ purification, 34
ἀγνοέω be ignorant, disregard, 25
ἀγνόημα ματος sin done in ignorance, 25
ἄγνοια ας ignorance, 25
ἁγνός ή όν holy, pure, 34
ἁγνότης ητος purity, sincerity, 34
ἁγνῶς purely, 34
ἀγνωσία ας lack of spiritual insight, 25
ἄγνωστος ον unknown, 25
ἀγορ – market, place of business transactions, 86
ἀγορά ᾶς marketplace, 86

ἀγοράζω buy, redeem, 86
ἀγοραῖος ου loafer, court session, 86
ἀγρ – field, wild, 91
ἀγράμματος ον uneducated, 31
ἀγραυλέω be outdoors, 91
ἀγρεύω trap, 91
ἀγριέλαιος ου wild olive tree, 91
ἄγριος α ον wild, 91
ἀγρός οῦ field, farm, 91
ἄγω lead, 24
ἀγωγ – bring, lead, 24
ἀγωγή ῆς manner of life, 24
ἀδελφ – brother, sister, 29
ἀδελφή ῆς sister, 30
ἀδελφός οῦ brother, countryman, 30
ἀδελφότης ητος brotherhood, 30
ἀδιάκριτος ον without favoritism, 21
ἀδιάλειπτος ον endless, constant, 57
ἀδιαλείπτως constantly, always, 57
ἀδικέω wrong, 33
ἀδίκημα ματος crime, sin, wrong, 33
ἀδικία ας wrongdoing, evil, 33
ἄδικος ον evil, sinful, 34
ἀδίκως unjustly, 34
ἀδόκιμος ον disqualified, worthless, 81
ἀδυνατεῖ it is impossible, 29
ἀδύνατος ον impossible, unable, 29
ἀδυσβάστακτος ον not difficult to bear, 101
ἄζυμος ον without yeast, 104
ἀθανασία ας immortality, 36
ἄθεος ον without God (> atheist), 13
ἄθεσμος ον morally corrupt, lawless, 31
ἀθετέω reject, ignore (> not put), 31
ἀθέτησις εως nullification (> not put), 31
ἀθυμέω become discouraged, 60
αἱμ – blood, 64
αἷμα τος blood, death, 64
αἱματεκχυσία ας shedding of blood, 64
αἱμορροέω hemorrhage, bleed, 64
αἰν – praise, 100
αἴνεσις εως praise, 100
αἰνέω praise, 100

See also Section 1: Identical Greek/English Words, and Index 1: Words Occurring 10–19 Times

αἶνος ου praise, 100
αἱρ – take, 53
αἱρ – take, choose, 78
αἵρεσις εως sect, school, 78
αἱρετίζω choose, 78
αἱρετικός ή όν divisive, 78
αἴρω take, 53
αἰσχ – shame, 85
αἰσχροκερδής ές greedy (> shameful gain), 85
αἰσχροκερδῶς greedily, 85
αἰσχρολογία ας obscene speech, 85
αἰσχρός ά όν disgraceful, 85
αἰσχρότης ητος shameful behavior, 85
αἰσχύνη ης shame, shameful thing, 85
αἰσχύνομαι be ashamed, 85
αἰτ – ask, reason, cause, accusation, 56
αἰτέω ask, require, 56
αἴτημα ματος request, demand, 56
αἰτία ας reason, cause, charge, 56
αἴτιον ου guilt, reason, 56
αἴτιος ου cause, source, 56
αἰτίωμα ματος charge, accusation, 56
αἰων – age, 42
αἰών ῶνος age, eternity, 42
αἰώνιος ον eternal, 42
ἀκαθαρσία ας impurity, 61
ἀκάθαρτος ον unclean, 61
ἀκαιρέομαι be without opportunity, 64
ἀκαίρως untimely, 64
ἄκακος ον innocent, 59
ἄκαρπος ον barren, useless, 70
ἀκατάγνωστος ον above criticism, 25
ἀκατακάλυπτος ον uncovered, 76
ἀκατάκριτος ον uncondemned, 21
ἀκατάλυτος ον indestructible, 46
ἀκατάπαυστος ον unceasing, 86
ἀκαταστασία ας disorder, 20
ἀκατάστατος ον unstable, 20
ἀκλινής ές firm (not turned), 89
ἀκο – hear, 23
ἀκοή ῆς hearing, report, news, 23
ἀκολουθ – follow, 63
ἀκολουθέω follow, be a disciple, 63
ἀκου – hear, 23
ἀκούω hear, understand, 23
ἀκρασία ας lack of self control, 67
ἀκρατής ές uncontrolled, violent, 67
ἀκωλύτως unhindered, 106
ἀλ – salt, fish, 110
ἀλαλάζω wail, 32
ἀλάλητος ον inexpressible, 32
ἄλαλος ον unable to speak, dumb, 32
ἅλας ατος salt, 110
ἀλέκτωρ ορος rooster, 149
ἀληθ – true, 43
ἀλήθεια ας truth, truthfulness, 43
ἀληθεύω be truthful, honest, 44
ἀληθής ές true, truthful, genuine, 44
ἀληθινός ή όν real, true, genuine, 44
ἀληθῶς truly, actually, 44

ἁλι – salt, fish, 110
ἁλιεύς έως fisherman, 110
ἁλιεύω fish, 110
ἁλίζω salt, 110
ἀλλ – other, change, 15
ἀλλά but, 15
ἀλλάσσω change, 15
ἀλλαχόθεν at another place, 15
ἀλλαχοῦ elsewhere, 15
ἀλληγορέω speak allegorically, 86
ἀλλήλων οις ους one another, 16
ἀλλογενής ους foreigner, 16
ἄλλος η ο another, other, 16
ἀλλοτριεπίσκοπος busybody, 99
ἀλλότριος α ον of another, foreign, 16
ἀλλόφυλος ον foreign, 93
ἄλλως otherwise, 16
ἄλογος ον unreasoning, wild, 17
ἅλς ἁλός salt, 110
ἁλυκός ή όν salty, 110
ἀλυπότερος α ον freed from pain / sorrow, 87
ἅλυσις εως chain, imprisonment, 149
ἀλυσιτελής ές of no advantage, no help, 46
ἅμα (> *acc*) together / together with, 149
ἀμαθής ές ignorant, 34
ἁμαρτ – sin, 36
ἁμαρτάνω sin, 36
ἁμάρτημα ματος sin, 36
ἁμαρτία ας sin, 36
ἀμάρτυρος ον without witness, 42
ἁμαρτωλός όν sinful, 36
ἄμαχος ον peaceable, 92
ἀμελέω disregard, neglect, 102
ἀμέριμνος ον free from worry, 103
ἀμετάθετος ον unchangeable, 31
ἀμεταμέλητος ον free from care or regret, 102
ἀμετανόητος ον unrepentant, 52
ἄμετρος ον immeasurable, 101
ἀμην – truly, 55
ἀμήν amen, truly, 55
ἀμήτωρ ορος without a mother, 68
ἀμπελ – grapevine, 97
ἄμπελος ου grapevine, 97
ἀμπελουργός οῦ vinedresser, gardener, 97
ἀμπελών ῶνος vineyard, 97
ἀμφιβάλλω cast a net, 28
ἀμφίβληστρον ου casting net, 28
ἄμφοδον ου street, 53
ἀμφότεροι αι α both, all, 149
ἄν¹ – particle indicating contingency, 43
ἄν² – up, again, 94
ἄν (signals contingency), 43
ἀνά (> *acc*) up, each, 94
ἀναβαίνω go up, ascend, grow, 37
ἀναβάλλομαι postpone, 28
ἀναβιβάζω make to go, draw, drag, 37
ἀναβλέπω look up, regain sight, 43
ἀνάβλεψις εως restoration of sight, 43
ἀναβοάω cry out, 105
ἀναβολή ῆς delay, 28

ἀνάγαιον ου upstairs room, 24
ἀναγγέλλω tell, proclaim, 23
ἀναγεννάω give new birth to, 15
ἀναγινώσκω read, 25
ἀναγκ – necessity, 96
ἀναγκάζω force (> make necessary), 96
ἀναγκαῖος α ον necessary, forced, 96
ἀναγκαστῶς under compulsion, 96
ἀνάγκη ης necessity, distress, 96
ἀναγνωρίζομαι make known again, 25
ἀνάγνωσις εως reading, 25
ἀνάγω lead up, bring up, 24
ἀναδείκνυμι show clearly, appoint, 71
ἀνάδειξις εως public appearance, 71
ἀναδέχομαι receive, welcome, 49
ἀναδίδωμι deliver (i.e., give up), 18
ἀναζάω revive, 34
ἀναζητέω seek after, 47
ἀναζώννυμι bind up, 109
ἀναζωπυρέω stir into flame, 65
ἀνάθεμα ματος cursed, anathematized, 31
ἀναθεματίζω curse, anathematize, 31
ἀναθεωρέω observe closely, 68
ἀνάθημα ματος offering, gift, 32
ἀναίρεσις εως killing, murder, 78
ἀναιρέω do away with, take life, 78
ἀναίτιος ον not guilty (> no charge), 56
ἀνακαθίζω sit up, 48
ἀνακαινίζω renew, 84
ἀνακαινόω renew, remake, 84
ἀνακαίνωσις εως renewal, 84
ἀνακαλύπτω unveil, uncover, 76
ἀνάκειμαι be seated (lie) at a table, 68
ἀνακεφαλαιόω sum up, unite, 69
ἀνακλίνω seat at table, put to bed, 89
ἀνακράζω cry out, 74
ἀνακρίνω question, examine, 21
ἀνάκρισις εως investigation, 21
ἀναλαμβάνω take (up), 27
ἀνάλημψις εως ascension (> taking up), 27
ἀναλογία ας proportion, 17
ἀναλογίζομαι consider closely, 17
ἄναλος ον without salt, 110
ἀνάλυσις εως death (> releasing), 46
ἀναλύω come back, 46
ἀναμάρτητος ον sinless, 36
ἀναμένω wait expectantly, 41
ἀναμιμνῄσκω remind, 55
ἀνάμνησις εως reminder, remembrance, 55
ἀνανεόω renew, make new, 88
ἀναντίρρητος ον undeniable, 60
ἀναντιρρήτως without objection, 60
ἀνάξιος ον unworthy, 80
ἀναξίως unworthily, 80
ἀνάπαυσις εως relief, rest, 86
ἀναπαύω relieve, refresh, rest, 86
ἀναπείθω incite, persuade, 69
ἀναπέμπω send, send back / up, 63
ἀναπίπτω sit, lean, 45
ἀναπληρόω meet requirements, 39

ἀναπολόγητος ον without excuse, 17
ἀνάπτω kindle, 90
ἀναρίθμητος ον innumerable, 107
ἀνασείω incite, stir up, 103
ἀνασκευάζω disturb, 94
ἀνάστασις εως resurrection, 20
ἀναστατόω agitate, incite a revolt, 20
ἀνασταυρόω crucify, crucify again, 71
ἀναστρέφω return (pass live), 52
ἀναστροφή ῆς manner of life, 52
ἀνατάσσομαι compile, draw up, 57
ἀνατέλλω rise, 45
ἀνατίθεμαι lay before, present, 31
ἀνατολή ῆς rising, dawn, east, 45
ἀνατρέπω overturn, 79
ἀνατρέφω bring up, train, 96
ἀναφαίνω come into sight of, 50
ἀναφέρω offer (bring up), 39
ἀναφωνέω call out, 41
ἀνάχυσις εως flood, excess, 108
ἀναχωρέω withdraw, return, 51
ἀνάψυξις εως refreshment, 55
ἀναψύχω refresh (> cooled), 55
ἀνδρ – man, 40
ἀνδραποδιστής οῦ kidnapper, slave dealer, 40
ἀνδρίζομαι act like a man, 40
ἀνδροφόνος ου murderer, 40
ἀνέγκλητος ον beyond reproach, 22
ἀνεκδιήγητος ον indescribable, 24
ἀνεκλάλητος ον inexpressible in words, 32
ἀνέκλειπτος ον never decreasing, 57
ἀνελεήμων ον unmerciful, 72
ἀνέλεος ον merciless, 72
ἀνεμ – wind, 98
ἀνεμίζομαι be driven by wind, 98
ἄνεμος ου wind, 98
ἀνένδεκτος ον impossible, 49
ἀνεξίκακος ον tolerant, 59
ἀνεπαίσχυντος ον unashamed, 85
ἀνεπίλημπτος ον above reproach, 27
ἀνέρχομαι go (come) up, 13
ἄνεσις εως relief (> let up), 44
ἀνεύθετος ον unsuitable (> not well put), 31
ἀνευρίσκω find, 45
ἀνέχομαι tolerate (> hold up under), 16
ἀνήκει it is proper, 102
ἀνήμερος ον fierce, 26
ἀνηρ – man, 40
ἀνήρ ἀνδρός man, husband, 40
ἀνθίστημι resist, oppose, 20
ἀνθομολογέομαι give thanks, 17
ἀνθρωπ – man, 21
ἀνθρωπάρεσκος ον people-pleasing, 111
ἀνθρώπινος η ον human, 21
ἀνθρωποκτόνος ου murderer, 21
ἄνθρωπος ου man, person, 21
ἀνίημι loosen, stop, desert, 44
ἄνιπτος ον not (ritually) washed, 111
ἀνίστημι raise up, appoint, 20
ἀνόητος ον foolish, ignorant, 52

ἄνοια ας stupidity, foolishness, 52
ἀνοιγ – open, start, 69
ἀνοίγω open, 69
ἀνοικοδομέω rebuild, 27
ἄνοιξις εως opening, 69
ἀνομία ας lawlessness, wickedness, 38
ἄνομος ον lawless, 38
ἀνόμως lawlessly, without law, 38
ἀνοχή ῆς tolerance, 16
ἀντάλλαγμα ματος thing in exchange, 16
ἀνταναπληρόω complete (> make full), 39
ἀνταποδίδωμι repay, return, 18
ἀνταπόδομα ματος repayment, 19
ἀνταπόδοσις εως repayment, 19
ἀνταποκρίνομαι reply, 21
ἀντέχομαι be loyal to, hold firmly, 16
ἀντι – oppose, replace, 65
ἀντί (gen) in place of, against, 66
ἀντιβάλλω exchange, 28
ἀντιδιατίθεμαι oppose, 32
ἀντίδικος ου opponent at law, enemy, 34
ἀντίθεσις εως antithesis, contradiction, 32
ἀντικαθίστημι resist, 20
ἀντικαλέω invite in return, 22
ἀντίκειμαι oppose, 68
ἄντικρυς (gen) opposite, off, 66
ἀντιλαμβάνομαι help, 27
ἀντιλέγω object to, 17
ἀντιλημψις εως ability to help, helper, 27
ἀντιλογία ας argument, hatred, 17
ἀντίλυτρον ου ransom, 46
ἀντιμετρέω measure out in return, 101
ἀντιμισθία ας recompense, punishment, 91
ἀντιπαρέρχομαι pass by the other side, 13
ἀντιπέρα (gen) opposite, 66
ἀντιπίπτω resist, fight against, 45
ἀντιστρατεύομαι war against, 79
ἀντιτάσσομαι resist, oppose, 57
ἀντίτυπος ον corresponding (n. copy), 113
ἀντίχριστος ου Antichrist, 21
ἀντοφθαλμέω head into, face, 64
ἄνυδρος ον waterless, desert, 70
ἀνυπόκριτος ον sincere, genuine, 21
ἀνυπότακτος disorderly, 57
ἄνω above, up, 94
ἄνωθεν from above, again, 94
ἀνωτερικός ή όν upper, inland, 94
ἀνώτερον first, above, 94
ἀνωφελής ές useless, 105
αξι – worthy, 80
ἄξιος α ον worthy, 80
ἀξιόω consider / make worthy, 80
ἀξίως worthily, 80
ἀόρατος ον invisible, unseen, 50
ἀπ – from, 18
ἀπαγγέλλω tell, proclaim, 23
ἀπάγω lead away, bring before, 24
ἀπαίδευτος ον ignorant (not learned), 54
ἀπαίρω take away, 53
ἀπαιτέω demand (in return), 56

ἀπαλλάσσω set free, 16
ἅπαν each, all, 13
ἀπαντάω meet, 66
ἀπάντησις εως meeting, 66
ἅπαξ once, 149
ἀπαράβατος ον permanent, 37
ἀπαρασκεύσατος ον unprepared, 95
ἀπαρνέομαι disown, 149
ἀπαρτισμός οῦ completion, 112
ἀπαρχή ῆς first-fruits (> from beginning), 26
ἅπας each, all, 13
ἅπασα each, all, 13
ἀπάτωρ ορος the fatherless, 25
ἀπείθεια ας disobedience, 69
ἀπειθέω disobey, 69
ἀπειθής ές disobedient, 69
ἄπειμι be away, 12
ἀπείραστος ον unable to be tempted, 76
ἄπειρος ον unacquainted, 76
ἀπεκδέχομαι await, 49
ἀπεκδύομαι disarm, discard, 85
ἀπέκδυσις εως putting off, 85
ἀπελεύθερος ου freedman, 91
ἀπελπίζω expect in return, 69
ἀπέναντι (gen) opposite, before, 66
ἀπέραντος ον endless, 96
ἀπερίτμητος ον uncircumcised, 76
ἀπέρχομαι go (away), 13
ἀπέχω receive in full, 16
ἀπιστέω fail to believe, 19
ἀπιστία ας unbelief, 19
ἄπιστος ον unfaithful, unbelieving, 19
ἀπο – from, 18
ἀπό from, 18
ἀποβαίνω get out, go from, 37
ἀποβάλλω throw off, 29
ἀποβλέπω keep one's eyes on, 43
ἀπόβλητος ον rejected, 29
ἀποβολή ῆς loss, rejection, 29
ἀπογίνομαι have no part in, 15
ἀπογραφή ῆς registration, census, 31
ἀπογράφω register, 31
ἀποδείκνυμι attest, proclaim, 71
ἀπόδειξις εως proof, demonstration, 71
ἀποδεκατόω tithe, make one tithe, 54
ἀπόδεκτος ον pleasing, 49
ἀποδέχομαι welcome, receive, 49
ἀποδημέω leave home, go away, 102
ἀπόδημος ον away from home, 102
ἀποδίδωμι give, pay, 19
ἀποδιορίζω cause divisions, 66
ἀποδοκιμάζω reject (after testing), 81
ἀποδοχή ῆς acceptance, 49
ἀπόθεσις εως removal, 32
ἀποθήκη ης barn, 32
ἀποθησαυρίζω acquire as a treasure, 104
ἀποθλίβω crowd in upon, 81
ἀποθνήσκω die, face death, 36
ἀποκαθίστημι reestablish, cure, 20
ἀποκαλύπτω reveal, 76

ἀσύμφωνος ον   in disagreement, 42
ἀσύνετος ον   without understanding, 44
ἀσύνθετος ον   faithless, disloyal, 32
ἀσχημ – shame, 85
ἀσχημονέω   act improperly, 85
ἀσχημοσύνη ης   shameless act, 85
ἀσχήμων ον   unpresentable, shameful, 85
ἀτακτέω   be lazy (not ordered), 57
ἀτακτός ον   lazy (not ordered), 57
ἀτάκτως   lazily, 57
ἄτεκνος ον   childless, 54
ἀτενίζω   look at, stare, 149
ἀτιμάζω   dishonor, 48
ἀτιμία ας   dishonor, shame, 48
ἄτιμος ον   dishonored, despised, 48
ἄτομος ον   indivisible, 77
ἄτοπος ον   improper, 64
αὐλ – flute, courtyard, 109
αὐλέω   play a flute, 109
αὐλή ῆ   courtyard, house, 109
αὐλητής οῦ   flute player, 109
αὐλίζομαι   spend the night, 109
αὐλός οῦ   flute, 109
αὐξ – grow, 104
αὐξάνω   grow / increase, 104
αὔξησις εως   growth, 104
αὐρ – tomorrow, 99
αὔριον   tomorrow, soon, 99
αὐτ – this, 12
αὐτο – self, 11
αὐτοκατάκριτος ον   self-condemned, 21
αὐτόματος η ον   automatic, 11
αὐτός ή ό   self, same, he, she, it, 11
αὐτόχειρ ος   the doer, 43
ἀφ – from, 18
ἀφαιρέω   take away, 78
ἀφανής ές   hidden, 50
ἀφανίζω   ruin, 50
ἀφανισμός οῦ   disappearance, 50
ἄφαντος ον   invisible, 50
ἄφεσις εως   forgiveness, 44
ἀφθαρσία ας   imperishability, 84
ἄφθαρτος ον   imperishable, 84
ἀφθορία ας   integrity, 84
ἀφίημι   cancel, forgive, 44
ἀφιλάγαθος ον   not good-loving, 56
ἀφιλάργυρος ον   not money-loving, 96
ἀφίσταμαι   leave, 20
ἀφόβως   without fear, 48
ἀφομοιόω   be like, 59
ἀφοράω   fix one's eyes on, 50
ἀφορίζω   separate, exclude, 66
ἀφροσύνη ης   folly, 61
ἄφρων ον   foolish, 61
ἄφωνος ον   dumb, silent, 42
ἀχάριστος ον   ungrateful, 36
ἀχειροποίητος ον   not made by hands, 19
ἀχρειόομαι   be worthless, 62
ἀχρεῖος ον   worthless, mere, 62
ἄχρηστος ον   of little use, useless, 62

ἄχρι – until, 77
ἄχρι (*gen*)   until, to, as, when, 77
ἀψευδής ές   trustworthy, non-lying, 84
ἄψυχος ον   inanimate, 55

βα – go, foot, 37
βαθμός οῦ   standing, position, 37
βαιν – go, foot, 37
βαλ – throw, 28
βάλλω   throw, 29
βαπτ – baptize, dip, 58
βαπτίζω   baptize, 58
βάπτισμα ματος   baptism, 58
βαπτισμός οῦ   washing, baptism, 58
βαπτιστής οῦ   Baptist (Baptizer), 58
βάπτω   dip, 58
βαρ – burden, weight, 104
βαρέω   burden, overcome, 104
βαρέως   with difficulty, 104
βάρος ους   burden, weight, 104
βαρύτιμος ον   very expensive, 49
βαρύς εῖα ύ   heavy, weighty, hard, 104
βασ – go, foot, 37
βασαν – torture, 111
βασανίζω   torment, disturb, 111
βασανισμός οῦ   torture, 111
βασανιστής οῦ   torturer, jailer, 111
βάσανος ου   torment, pain, 111
βασιλ – royal, 33
βασιλεία ας   reign, kingdom, 33
βασίλειος ον   royal, 33
βασιλεύς έως   king, 33
βασιλεύω   rule, reign, 33
βασιλικός ή όν   royal, 33
βασίλισσα ης   queen, 33
βάσις εως   foot (> base), 37
βαστ – carry, bear, 101
βαστάζω   carry, bear, 101
βατταλογέω   babble, 17
βεβαι – reliable, firm, 111
βεβαιο – reliable, firm, 111
βέβαιος α ον   reliable, firm, 111
βεβαιόω   confirm (> make firm), 111
βεβαίωσις εως   confirmation, 111
βη – go, foot, 37
βῆμα ματος   judgment bench, 37
βιβλ – book, 87
βιβλαρίδιον ου   little book, 87
βιβλίον ου   book, scroll, 87
βίβλος ου   book, record, 87
βλασφημ – blaspheme (compare φα), 81
βλασφημέω   blaspheme, 81
βλασφημία ας   blasphemy, slander, 81
βλάσφημος ον   blasphemous, 81
βλεμ – see, 43
βλέμμα ματος   what is seen, sight, 43
βλεπ – see, 43
βλέπω   see, look, 43
βλεψ – see, 43
βλη – throw, 28

βλητέος α ον must be put, poured, 29
βο – shout, 105
βοάω call, shout, 106
βοή ῆς shout, outcry, 106
βοηθ – shout, 105
βοήθεια ας help, aid, 106
βοηθέω help, 106
βοηθός οῦ helper, 106
βολ – throw, 28
βολή ῆς throw, 29
βολίζω measure depth, 29
βουλ – plan, 73
βουλεύομαι plan, consider, 73
βουλευτής οῦ councillor, 73
βουλή ῆς plan, intention, 73
βούλημα ματος plan, intention, desire, 73
βούλομαι plan, want, 73
βροντή ῆς thunder, 149
βρω – food, 102
βρῶμα ματος food, 102
βρώσιμος ον edible, 102
βρῶσις εως food, eating, 102

γαζοφυλάκιον ου treasury, offering box, 69
γαμ – marriage, 81
γαμέω marry, 81
γαμίζω give in marriage, 81
γαμίσκω give in marriage, 81
γάμος ου wedding, marriage, 81
γαρ – then, therefore, 14
γάρ for, since, then, 14
γε¹ – earth, 35
γε² – (particle adding emphasis), 99
γέ (used to add emphasis), 99
γέεννα ης hell (gehenna), 149
γεμ – full, 107
γεμίζω fill, 107
γέμω be full, 107
γεν – family, birth, 14
γενεά ᾶς generation, age, family, 15
γενεαλογέομαι to descend from, 15
γενεαλογία ας genealogy, 15
γενέσια ων (pl) birthday party, 15
γένεσις εως birth, lineage, 15
γενετή ῆς birth, 15
γένημα ματος harvest, product, 15
γεννάω be father of, bear, 15
γέννημα ματος offspring, 15
γέννησις εως birth, 15
γεννητός ή όν born, 15
γένος ους family, race, 15
γεύομαι taste, 149
γεωργέω cultivate (work earth), 35
γεώργιον ου field (> worked earth), 35
γεωργός οῦ farmer (> earth-worker), 35
γη – earth, 35
γῆ γῆς earth, land, region, 35
γιν – family, birth, 14
γίνομαι become, be, happen, 15
γινω – know, 25

γινώσκω know, learn, 25
γλωσσ – tongue, 83
γλῶσσα ης tongue, language, 83
γνο – know, 25
γνω – know, 25
γνώμη ης purpose, will, opinion, 25
γνωρίζω make known, know, 25
γνῶσις εως knowledge, 25
γνώστης ου one familiar with, 25
γνωστός ή όν known (acquaintance), 25
γομ – full, 107
γόμος ου cargo, 107
γον – family, birth, 14
γονεύς έως parent, 15
γόνυ γόνατος knee (Grimm's Law), 149
γραμ – write, 31
γράμμα ματος letter, Scripture, account, 31
γραμματεύς έως scribe, 31
γραπ – write, 31
γραπτός ή όν written, 31
γραφ – write, 31
γραφή ῆς Scripture, 31
γράφω write, 31
γρηγορ – raise, rouse, 44
γρηγορέω be awake, watch, 44
γυμν – exercise, naked, 106
γυμνάζω train, discipline, exercise, 106
γυμνασία ας training, 106
γυμνιτεύω be dressed in rags, 106
γυμνός ή όν naked, 106
γυμνότης ητος nakedness, poverty, 106
γυναικ – woman, 41
γυναικάριον ου foolish woman, 41
γυναικεῖος α ον female, 41
γυνη – woman, 41
γυνή αικός woman, wife, 41

δαιμ – demon, 72
δαιμονίζομαι be demon possessed, 72
δαιμόνιον ου demon, spirit, 72
δαιμονιώδης ες demonic, 72
δαίμων ονος demon, 72
δάκρυον ου tear (as in crying), 149
δέ but, rather, 11
δε¹ – but, 11
δε² – bind, 79
δε³ – lack, 51
δέησις εως prayer, request, 51
δεῖ it is necessary, 51
δειγ – show, example, 71
δεῖγμα ματος example, warning, 71
δειγματίζω disgrace, show publicly, 71
δεικ – show, example, 71
δείκνυμι show, explain, 71
δειξ – show, example, 71
δειπν – dine, 112
δειπνέω eat, dine, 112
δεῖπνον ου feast, supper, 112
δεκ – receive, 49
δεκα – ten, 54

δέκα   ten, 54
δεκαοκτώ   eighteen, 54
δεκαπέντε   fifteen, 55
Δεκάπολις εως   Decapolis (ten-city area), 55
δεκάτη ης   tithe, 55
δεκατέσσαρες   fourteen, 63
δέκατος η ον   tenth, 55
δεκατόω   collect (pay) tithes, 55
δεκτός ή όν   acceptable, 49
δενδρ – tree, 106
δένδρον ου   tree, 106
δεξ – right, 82
δεξιός ά όν   right, 82
δέομαι   ask, beg, 51
δέρω   beat, 149
δεσμ – bind, imprison (compare δε²), 83
δεσμεύω   bind, 83
δέσμη ης   bundle, 83
δέσμιος ου   prisoner, 83
δεσμός οῦ   bond, chain, jail, 83
δεσμοφύλαξ ακος   jailer, guard, 83
δεσμωτήριον ου   jail, prison, 83
δεσμώτης ου   prisoner, 83
δεσπότης   despot, lord, 28
δευ – place to, hither, 111
δεῦρο   hither (place to), 111
δεῦτε   come hither (place to), 111
δευτερ – two, 44
δευτεραῖος α ον   in two days, 44
δευτερόπρωτος ον   the next, 44
δεύτερος α ον   second, 44
δεχ – receive, 49
δέχομαι   receive, take, 49
δέω   bind, 79
δημ – people, home, 102
δημηγορέω   make a speech, 86
δημιουργός οῦ   builder, 30
δῆμος ου   people, crowd, 102
δημόσιος α ον   public, 102
δηνάριον ου   denarius, 149
δήποτε   whatever, 22
δήπου   of course, 43
δια – through, 18
διά (*gen, acc*)   through, on account of, 18
διαβαίνω   cross, cross over, 37
διαβάλλω   accuse (> throw against), 29
διαβεβαιόομαι   speak confidently, 111
διαβλέπω   see clearly, 43
διάβολος ον   accusing (falsely), 29
διάβολος ου   devil (the accuser), 29
διαγγέλλω   preach, proclaim, 23
διαγίνομαι   pass (of time), 15
διαγινώσκω   investigate, decide, 25
διάγνωσις εως   decision (> diagnosis), 25
διαγρηγορέω   become fully awake, 44
διάγω   lead, spend (a life), 24
διαδέχομαι   receive possession of, 49
διάδημα ματος   diadem, 79
διαδίδωμι   distribute, 18
διάδοχος ου   successor, 49

διαζώννυμι   wrap around, 109
διαθήκη ης   covenant, 32
διαίρεσις εως   variety, difference, 78
διαιρέω   divide, distribute, 78
διακαθαίρω   clean out, 61
διακαθαρίζω   clean out, 61
διακον – serve, 65
διακονέω   serve, care for, 65
διακονία ας   service, help, 65
διάκονος ου   servant, deacon, 65
διακούω   hear (legal cases), 23
διακρίνω   evaluate (mid doubt), 21
διάκρισις εως   ability to discriminate, 21
διακωλύω   prevent, 106
διαλαλέω   discuss, 32
διαλέγομαι   discuss, 18
διαλείπω   cease, stop, 57
διάλεκτος ου   language (> dialect), 18
διαλιμπάνω   stop, quit, 57
διαλλάσσομαι   be reconciled, 16
διαλογίζομαι   discuss, question, 18
διαλογισμός οῦ   opinion, thought, 18
διαλύω   scatter, 46
διαμαρτύρομαι   declare solemnly, 42
διαμάχομαι   protest violently, 92
διαμένω   remain, stay, 41
διαμερίζω   divide, 73
διαμερισμός οῦ   division, 73
διανόημα ματος   thought, 52
διάνοια ας   mind, understanding, 52
διανοίγω   open, 69
διανυκτερεύω   spend the night, 77
διαπεράω   cross, cross over, 96
διαπλέω   sail across, 66
διαπορεύομαι   go through, 38
διαπραγματεύομαι   make a profit, 80
διαρπάζω   plunder, 101
διασείω   take money by force, 103
διασπείρω   scatter, 61
διασπορά ᾶς   dispersion, 61
διαστέλλομαι   order, 35
διάστημα ματος   interval, 20
διαστολή ῆς   distinction, 36
διαστρέφω   pervert, distort, 52
διασῴζω   rescue, 59
διαταγή ῆς   decree, 57
διάταγμα ματος   order, decree, 57
διαταράσσομαι   be deeply troubled, 110
διατάσσω   command, 57
διατελέω   continue, go, be, 45
διατηρέω   keep, treasure up, 70
διατίθεμαι   make (a covenant), 32
διατροφή ῆς   food, 96
διαφέρω   be superior, carry through, 40
διαφεύγω   escape, 90
διαφημίζω   spread around, 35
διαφθείρω   decay, destroy, 84
διαφθορά ᾶς   decay, 84
διαφυλάσσω   protect, 69
διαχειρίζομαι   seize and kill, 43

διαχωρίζομαι   leave, 51
διδ – give, 18
διδακ – teach, 41
διδακτικός ή όν   able to teach, 41
διδακτός ή όν   taught, 41
διδασκ – teach, 41
διδασκαλία ας   teaching, instruction, 41
διδάσκαλος ου   teacher, 41
διδάσκω   teach, 41
διδαχ – teach, 41
διδαχή ῆς   instruction, 41
δίδωμι   give, 19
διεγείρω   awake, 44
διενθυμέομαι   think over, 60
διέξοδος ου   outlet, passage, 53
διέρχομαι   go, come through, 13
διερωτάω   learn, 58
διετής ές   two years old, 82
διετία ας   two-year period, 82
διηγέομαι   tell fully, 24
διήγησις εως   account, 24
διθάλασσος ον   between the seas, 67
διΐστημι   part, past time, 20
διϊσχυρίζομαι   insist, 73
δικ – just, judgment, 33
δικαιοκρισία ας   just judgment, 34
δίκαιος α ον   just, right, 34
δικαιοσύνη ης   righteousness, justice, 34
δικαιόω   acquit, make righteous, 34
δικαίωμα ματος   judgment, acquittal, 34
δικαίως   justly, 34
δικαίωσις εως   acquittal, 34
δικαστής οῦ   judge, 34
δίκη ης   justice, punishment, 34
δίκτυον ου   net for fishing, 149
δίλογος ον   two-faced, 18
διο – therefore, 71
διό   therefore, 71
διοδεύω   go about, 53
διόπερ   therefore (emphatic), 71
διότι   because, for, therefore, 71
δίστομος ον   double-edged, 77
διχοστασία ας   division, 20
διχοτομέω   cut in pieces, 77
διψάω   thirst, 149
δίψυχος ον   undecided (> two minds), 55
διωγ – persecute, 81
διωγμός οῦ   persecution, 81
διωκ – persecute, 81
διώκτης ου   persecutor, 81
διώκω   persecute, pursue, 81
δο – give, 18
δογ – think, seem, 63
δόγμα ατος   decree, 63
δοκ¹ – receive, 49
δοκ² – think, seem, 63
δοκέω   think, seem, 63
δοκιμ – examine, 81
δοκιμάζω   examine, discern, 81
δοκιμασία ας   examination, test, 82

δοκιμή ῆς   character, evidence, 82
δοκίμιον ου   examination, testing, 82
δόκιμος ον   approved, examined, 82
δόλος οω   deceit, 149
δομ – people, home, 102
δόμα ματος   gift, 19
δοξ – ¹ glory, 39
δοξ – ² think, seem, 63
δόξα ης   glory, power, 39
δοξάζω   praise, honor, 39
δόσις εως   gift, 19
δότης ου   giver, 19
δουλ – slave, 44
δουλαγωγέω   bring under control, 44
δουλεία ας   slavery, 44
δουλεύω   serve, be enslaved, 44
δούλη ης   female servant, 44
δοῦλος η ον   slave-like, 44
δοῦλος ου   servant, slave, 44
δουλόω   enslave (> make a slave), 44
δοχ – receive, 49
δοχή ῆς   reception, 49
δράκων οντος   dragon, 149
δυ – clothe, 85
δυνα – power, ability, 29
δυναμ – power, ability, 29
δύναμαι   be able, 29
δύναμις εως   power, strength, 29
δυναμόω   make strong, 29
δυνάστης ου   ruler, 29
δυνατέω   be able, be strong, 29
δυνατός ή όν   able, possible, strong, 29
δυο – two, 44
δύω   two, 44
δυσβάστακτος ον   difficult to bear, 101
δυσνόητος ον   difficult to understand, 52
δυσφημέω   slander, 35
δυσφημια ας   slander, 35
δω – give, 18
δώδεκα   twelve, 55
δωδέκατος η ον   twelfth, 55
δωδεκάφυλον ου   the Twelve Tribes, 93
δωρ – gift, 90
δωρεά ᾶς   gift, 90
δωρεάν   without cost, 90
δωρέομαι   give, 90
δώρημα ματος   gift, 90
δῶρον ου   gift, offering, 90
δωροφορία ας   a bearing of gifts, 40

ε – let, send, 44
ἐάν   if, even if, though, 16
ἐάνπερ   if only, 16
ἑαυτοῦ ῆς οῦ   himself, herself, itself, 11
ἐγγ – near, 72
ἐγγίζω   approach, 72
ἐγγράφω   write, record, 31
ἔγγυος ου   guarantor, guarantee, 72
ἐγγύς   near, 72
ἐγγύτερον   nearer, 72

ἐγειρ – raise, rouse, 44
ἐγείρω   raise, 44
ἐγερ – raise, rouse, 44
ἔγερσις εως   resurrection, 44
ἐγκάθετος ου   spy, 44
ἐγκαινίζω   inaugurate, open, 84
ἐγκακέω   become discouraged, 59
ἐγκαλέω   accuse, 22
ἐγκαταλείπω   forsake, leave, 57
ἐγκατοικέω   live among, 27
ἐγκαυχάομαι   boast, 78
ἔγκλημα ματος   charge, accusation, 22
ἐγκοπή ῆς   obstacle (> thing cutting in), 91
ἐγκόπτω   prevent (> cut in), 91
ἐγκράτεια ας   self-control, 67
ἐγκρατεύομαι   be self-controlled, 67
ἐγκρατής ές   self-controlled, 67
ἐγκρίνω   class with, 21
ἐγκρύπτω   place / mix / hide in, 86
ἐγχρίω   rub on, 22
ἐγώ   I (first person pronoun), 12
ἐγω – I, 12
ἐθν – nation, Gentile, 47
ἐθνάρχης ου   governor, ethnarch, 47
ἐθνικός ή όν   pagan, Gentile, 47
ἐθνικῶς   like a Gentile, 47
ἔθνος ους   nation, Gentiles, 47
ει¹ – be, exist, 12
ει² – if, 15
εἰ   if, 15
εἰδέα ας   appearance, form, 40
εἶδος ους   visible form, sight, 40
εἰδωλ – image, idol, 98
εἰδωλεῖον ου   idol's temple, 98
εἰδωλόθυτον ου   meat offered to idols, 74, 98
εἰδωλολάτρης ου   idol worshipper, 95, 98
εἰδωλολατρία ας   idolatry, 95, 98
εἴδωλον ου   idol, image, 98
εἴκοσι   twenty, 149
εἰκών όνος   likeness (icon), 149
εἰλικρίνεια ας   sincerity, 21
εἰλικρινής ές   sincere, pure, 21
εἰμι – be, exist, 12
εἰμί   be, exist, 12
εἴπερ   since, if it is true that, 15
εἰρην – peace, 64
εἰρηνεύω   be at peace, 64
εἰρήνη ης   peace, 65
εἰρηνικός ή όν   peaceful, irenic, 65
εἰρηνοποιέω   make peace, 65
εἰρηνοποιός οῦ   peace-maker, 65
εἰς – into, 12
εἰς (acc)   into, to, 12
εἰς μια έν – one, 26
εἰς μία ἕν   one, only, 27
εἰσάγω   lead, bring in, 24
εἰσακούω   hear, obey (> listen to), 23
εἰσδέχομαι   welcome, receive, 49
εἰσέρχομαι   come, enter, share in, 13
εἰσκαλέομαι   invite in, 22

εἴσοδος ου   coming, entrance, 53
εἰσπορεύομαι   go / come in, enter, 38
εἰστρέχω   run in, 98
εἰσφέρω   bring in, 40
εἶτα   then, moreover, 15
εἴτε   if, whether, 15
ἐκ – out, from, 14
ἐκ (gen)   from, out from, 14
ἐκασ – each, 70
ἕκαστος η ον   each, every, 70
ἑκάστοτε   at all times, 70
ἑκατόν   hundred (> prefix hec / hect), 149
ἑκατονάρχης ου   centurion, 26
ἐκβαίνω   leave, go out, 37
ἐκβάλλω   force out, exclude, 29
ἐκβολή ῆς   throwing overboard, 29
ἔκγονον ου   grandchild, 15
ἐκδέχομαι   wait for, expect, 49
ἐκδημέω   leave home, 102
ἐκδίδομαι   let out, lease, 19
ἐκδιηγέομαι   tell fully, 24
ἐκδικέω   avenge, punish, 34
ἐκδίκησις εως   punishment, 34
ἔκδικος ου   one who punishes, 34
ἐκδιώκω   persecute harshly, 81
ἔκδοτος ον   given over, 19
ἐκδοχή ῆς   expectation, 49
ἐκδύω   strip, 85
ἐκει – there, 28
ἐκεῖ   there, 28
ἐκεῖθεν   from there, 28
ἐκειν – there, 28
ἐκείνης   there, 28
ἐκεῖνος η ο   that, 28
ἐκεῖσε   there, 28
ἐκζητέω   seek diligently, 47
ἐκζήτησις εως   speculation, 47
ἐκθαυμάζω   be completely amazed, 83
ἔκθετος ον   abandoned, 32
ἐκκαθαίρω   clean out, 61
ἐκκλάω   break off, 88
ἐκκλείω   exclude (> lock out), 99
ἐκκλησία ας   church, assembly, 22
ἐκκλίνω   turn out / away, 89
ἐκκόπτω   cut off, remove, 91
ἐκλαλέω   tell (> speak out), 32
ἐκλάμπω   shine, 101
ἐκλανθάνομαι   forget completely, 112
ἐκλέγομαι   choose, select (> elect), 18
ἐκλείπω   fail, cease, leave, 57
ἐκλεκτός ή όν   chosen (> elected), 18
ἐκλογή ῆς   election, choosing, 18
ἐκλύομαι   give up, faint, 46
ἔκπαλαι   for a long time, 98
ἐκπειράζω   test, tempt, 76
ἐκπέμπω   send out / away, 63
ἐκπερισσῶς   emphatically, 67
ἐκπίπτω   fall off, lose, 45
ἐκπλέω   sail, 66
ἐκπληρόω   fulfill (> make happen), 39

ἐκπλήρωσις εως   completion, end, 39
ἐκπλήσσομαι   be amazed, 105
ἐκπνέω   die, 26
ἐκπορεύομαι   go / come out, 38
ἐκπορνεύω   live immorally, 47
ἐκριζόω   uproot (> make rootless), 110
ἔκστασις εως   amazement (> ecstasy), 20
ἐκστρέφομαι   be perverted, 52
ἐκσῴζω   save, keep safe, 60
ἐκταράσσω   stir up trouble, 110
ἐκτείνω   stretch out, extend, 100
ἐκτελέω   finish, complete, 45
ἐκτένεια ας   earnestness, 100
ἐκτενέστερον   more earnestly, 100
ἐκτενής ές   constant, unfailing, 100
ἐκτενῶς   earnestly, constantly, 100
ἐκτίθεμαι   explain, expound, 32
ἐκτινάσσω   shake off, 100
ἐκτός (gen)   outside, except, 14
ἐκτρέπομαι   wander, go astray, 79
ἐκτρέφω   feed, raise, 96
ἐκφέρω   carry out, yield, 40
ἐκφεύγω   escape, flee, 90
ἐκφοβέω   frighten, terrify, 48
ἔκφοβος ον   frightened, 48
ἐκφύω   sprout, 89
ἐκχέω   pour out, shed, 108
ἐκχωρέω   leave, 51
ἐκψύχω   die, 55
ἐλαι – olive, oil, 103
ἐλαία ας   olive, olive tree, 103
ἔλαιον ου   olive oil, oil, 103
ἐλαιών ῶνος   olive orchard, 103
ἐλάχιστος η ον   least, 149
ἐλε – mercy, 72
ἐλεάω (> ἐλεέω)   be merciful, 72
ἐλέγχω   show error, convince, 149
ἐλεεινός ή όν   pitiable, 72
ἐλεημοσύνη ης   charity, 72
ἐλεήμων ον   merciful, 72
ἔλεος ους   mercy, 72
ἐλευθερ – free, 91
ἐλευθερία ας   freedom, 92
ἐλεύθερος α ον   free, 92
ἐλευθερόω   set / make free, 92
Ἑλλα – Greek, 97
Ἑλλάς άδος   Greece, 97
Ἑλλην – Greek, 97
Ἕλλην ηνος   Greek person, non-Jew, 97
Ἑλληνικός ή όν   hellenistic, Greek, 97
Ἑλληνίς ίδος   Greek / Gentile woman, 97
Ἑλληνιστής οῦ   Hellenist, 97
Ἑλληνιστί   in the Greek language, 97
ἐλλογέω   record, 18
ἐλπ – hope, 69
ἐλπίζω   hope, 70
ἐλπίς ίδος   hope, 70
ἐμ – my, mine, 73
ἐμαυτοῦ ῆς   myself, my own, 11
ἐμβαίνω   get in, embark, 37

ἐμβάλλω   throw, 29
ἐμβάπτω   dip, 58
ἐμβλέπω   look at, consider, 43
ἐμμένω   remain faithful, 41
ἐμός ή όν   my, mine, 73
ἐμπαιγμονή ῆς   mockery, ridicule, 54
ἐμπαιγμός οῦ   public ridicule, 54
ἐμπαίζω   ridicule, trick, 54
ἐμπαίκτης ου   mocker, 54
ἐμπεριπατέω   live among, 35
ἐμπίμπλημι   fill, satisfy, enjoy, 39
ἐμπίπτω   fall into or among, 46
ἐμπνέω   breathe, 26
ἐμπορεύομαι   be in business, exploit, 38
ἐμπορία ας   business, 38
ἐμπόριον ου   market (> emporium), 38
ἔμπορος ου   merchant, 38
ἔμπροσθεν (gen)   before, 17
ἐμφανής ές   visible, revealed, 50
ἐμφανίζω   inform, reveal, 50
ἔμφοβος ον   full of fear, 48
ἐμφυσάω   breathe on, 89
ἔμφυτος ον   implanted, planted, 89
ἐν – in, 11
ἐν (dat)   in, 11
ἐνάλιον ου   sea creature, 110
ἔναντι (gen)   before (in judgment of), 66
ἐναντίον (gen)   before (in judgment of), 66
ἐναντιόομαι   oppose, contradict, 66
ἐναντίος α ον   against, hostile, 66
ἐνάρχομαι   begin, 26
ἔνατος η ον   ninth, 149
ἐνδεής ές   needy (> in need), 51
ἔνδειγμα ματος   evidence, proof, 71
ἐνδείκνυμαι   show, give indication, 71
ἔνδειξις εως   evidence, indication, 71
ἕνδεκα   eleven, 55
ἑνδέκατος η ον   eleventh, 55
ἐνδέχεται   it is possible, 49
ἐνδημέω   be at home, be present, 102
ἐνδιδύσκω   dress in, 85
ἔνδικος ον   just, deserved, 34
ἐνδοξάζομαι   receive glory, 39
ἔνδοξος ον   glorious, fine, 39
ἔνδυμα ματος   clothing, 85
ἐνδυναμόω   strengthen, 29
ἔνδυσις εως   wearing, 85
ἐνδύω   clothe, wear (> endue), 85
ἔνειμι   be in(side), 12
ἐνεκ – because of, 104
ἕνεκα (gen)   because of, 104
ἐνέργεια ας   work (> energy), 30
ἐνεργέω   work, 30
ἐνέργημα ματος   working, activity, 30
ἐνεργής ές   active, effective, 30
ἐνευλογέω   bless, 18
ἐνέχω   have grudge against, 16
ἐνθάδε   here, in this place, 12
ἔνθεν   from here, 12
ἐνθυμέομαι   think about, think, 60

ἐνθύμησις εως thought, idea, 60
ἐνιαυτός οὖ year, 149
ἐνίστημι be present, 20
ἐνισχύω strengthen, 73
ἔννοια ας attitude, thought, 52
ἔννομος ον legal, subject to law, 38
ἔννυχα in the night, 77
ἐνοικέω live in, 27
ἐνορκίζω place under oath, 111
ἑνότης ητος unity, 27
ἐνοχλέω trouble (> crowd in), 45
ἔνοχος liable, 16
ἐνταλ – commandment, 70
ἔνταλμα ματος commandment, 70
ἐντέλλομαι command, order, 70
ἔντιμος ον valuable, esteemed, 49
ἐντολ – commandment, 70
ἐντολή ῆς commandment, 70
ἐντόπιος α ον local (*pl* residents), 64
ἐντός (*gen*) within, 12
ἐντρέπω make ashamed, 79
ἐντρέφομαι live on, feed oneself on, 96
ἐντροπῆς ῆς shame, 80
ἐντυγχάνω intercede, plead, appeal, 107
ἐντυπόω engrave, carve, 113
ἐνωπ – before, 58
ἐνώπιον (*gen*) before, 58
ἐξ – out, from, 14
ἕξ – six, 106
ἕξ six, 106
ἐξαγγέλλω tell, proclaim, 23
ἐξαγοράζω set free, 86
ἐξάγω lead, bring out, 24
ἐξαιρέω pull out, rescue, 78
ἐξαίρω remove, drive out, 53
ἐξαιτέομαι ask, demand, 56
ἐξακολουθέω follow, be obedient, 63
ἐξακόσιοι αι α six hundred, 106
ἐξανάστασις εως resurrection, 20
ἐξανατέλλω sprout, spring up, 45
ἐξανίστημι have, stand up, 20
ἐξαποστέλλω send off, 36
ἐξαρτίζω be completed, 112
ἐξαστράπτω flash (like lightning), 90
ἐξαυτῆς at once, 11
ἐξεγείρω raise, 44
ἐξέρχομαι come / go out, escape, 13
ἔξεστι it is proper / possible, 12
ἐξηγέομαι tell, explain, 24
ἐξήκοντα sixty, 107
ἐξίστημι be amazed, amaze, 20
ἐξισχύω be fully able, 74
ἔξοδος ου departure (> exodus), 53
ἐξομολογέω agree, consent, admit, 18
ἐξορκίζω put under oath, 111
ἐξορκιστής ου exorcist, 111
ἐξουσ – authority, 62
ἐξουσία ας authority, official, 62
ἐξουσιάζω have power over, 63
ἐξουσιαστικός ή όν authoritative, 63

ἐξουθενέω despise, 149
ἔξω (*gen*) out, outside, 14
ἔξωθεν (*gen*) from outside, 14
ἐξωθέω drive out, run aground, 14
ἐξώτερος α ον outer, 14
ἑορτ – feast, 104
ἑορτάζω observe a festival, 104
ἑορτή ῆς festival, feast, 104
ἐπαγγελία ας promise, decision, 23
ἐπαγγέλλομαι promise, confess, 23
ἐπάγγελμα ματος promise, 23
ἐπάγω bring upon, 24
ἐπαινέω praise, commend, 100
ἔπαινος ου praise, approval, 100
ἐπαίρω raise, lift up, 53
ἐπαισχύνομαι be ashamed, 85
ἐπαιτέω beg, 56
ἐπακολουθέω follow, 63
ἐπακούω hear, listen to, 23
ἐπάν when, 43
ἐπάναγκες necessarily, 96
ἐπανάγω return, put out, 24
ἐπαναμιμνήσκω remind, 55
ἐπαναπαύομαι rest / rely upon, 86
ἐπανέρχομαι return, 13
ἐπανίσταμαι turn against, rebel, 20
ἐπάνω (*gen*) on, above, over, 16
ἐπαρχεία ας province (> thing ruled), 26
ἔπαυλις εως house (> on the court), 109
ἐπαύριον next day, 99
ἐπεγείρω stir up, 44
ἐπει – since, 95
ἐπεί since, because, as, 95
ἐπειδή since, because, for, when, 95
ἐπειδήπερ inasmuch as, since, 95
ἐπεισαγωγή ῆς bringing in, 24
ἐπεισέρχομαι come upon, 13
ἔπειτα then, next, 149
ἐπέκεινα (*gen*) beyond, 28
ἐπεκτείνομαι stretch toward, 100
ἐπενδύομαι put on, 85
ἐπενδύτης ου outer garment, 85
ἐπέρχομαι come, come upon, 13
ἐπερωτάω ask, ask for, 58
ἐπερώτημα ματος promise, answer, 58
ἐπέχω notice, 16
ἐπι – on, 16
ἐπί (*gen, dat, acc*) upon, on, over, 16
ἐπιβαίνω embark, arrive, 37
ἐπιβάλλω lay (hands) on, 29
ἐπιβαρέω be a burden, 104
ἐπιβλέπω look upon (with care), 43
ἐπιβουλή ῆς plot, 73
ἐπιγαμβρεύω marry, 81
ἐπίγειος ον earthly, 35
ἐπιγίνομαι spring up, come on, 15
ἐπιγινώσκω know, perceive, 25
ἐπίγνωσις εως knowledge, 25
ἐπιγραφή ῆς inscription (> epigraph), 31
ἐπιγράφω write on, 31

ἐπιδείκνυμι   show, 71
ἐπιδέχομαι   receive, welcome, 49
ἐπιδημέω   visit, live, 102
ἐπιδιατάσσομαι   add to (a will), 57
ἐπιδίδωμι   deliver, give way, 19
ἐπιζητέω   seek, desire, 47
ἐπιθανάτιος ον   sentenced to death, 36
ἐπίθεσις εως   laying on (of hands), 32
ἐπιθυμέω   desire, covet, lust for, 60
ἐπιθυμητής οῦ   one who desires, 60
ἐπιθυμία ας   desire, lust, 60
ἐπικαθίζω   sit, sit on, 48
ἐπικαλέω   call, name, 22
ἐπικάλυμμα ματος   covering, pretext, 76
ἐπικαλύπτω   cover (sin), 76
ἐπίκειμαι   lie on, crowd, 68
ἐπικρίνω   decide, 21
ἐπιλαμβάνομαι   take, seize, help, 27
ἐπιλανθάνομαι   forget, overlook, 112
ἐπιλέγω   call, name, 18
ἐπιλείπω   run short, 57
ἐπίλοιπος ον   remaining, 57
ἐπίλυσις εως   interpretation, 46
ἐπιλύω   explain, settle, 46
ἐπιμαρτυρέω   witness, declare, 42
ἐπιμέλεια ας   care, attention, 102
ἐπιμελέομαι   take care of, 102
ἐπιμελῶς   carefully, 102
ἐπιμένω   remain, continue, 41
ἐπίνοια ας   intent, purpose, 52
ἐπιορκέω   break an oath, 111
ἐπίορκος ου   oath-breaker, perjurer, 112
ἐπιπίπτω   fall upon, close in on, 46
ἐπιπλήσσω   reprimand, 105
ἐπιποθέω   desire, 93
ἐπιπόθησις εως   longing, 93
ἐπιπόθητος ον   longed for, 93
ἐπιποθία ας   desire, 93
ἐπιπορεύομαι   come to, 38
ἐπισείω   urge on, stir up, 103
ἐπίσημος ον   well known, 67
ἐπισιτισμός οῦ   food, 108
ἐπισκέπτομαι   visit, care for, 99
ἐπισκευάζομαι   prepare, make ready, 95
ἐπισκηνόω   rest upon, live in, 94
ἐπισκιάζω   overshadow, 76
ἐπισκοπέω   see to it, take care, 99
ἐπισκοπή ῆς   visitation, episcopate, 99
ἐπίσκοπος ου   overseer, bishop, 99
ἐπισπείρω   sow in addition, 61
ἐπίσταμαι   know, understand, 20
ἐπίστασις εως   pressure, stirring up, 20
ἐπιστάτης ου   master, 20
ἐπιστέλλω   write, 36
ἐπιστήμων ον   understanding, 20
ἐπιστηρίζω   strengthen, 100
ἐπιστολή ῆς   letter, 36
ἐπιστομίζω   make silent, 71
ἐπιστρέφω   turn back, 52
ἐπιστροφή ῆς   conversion, 52

ἐπισυνάγω   gather, 24
ἐπισυναγωγή ῆς   assembly, 24
ἐπισυντρέχω   gather rapidly, close in, 98
ἐπισχύω   insist, 74
ἐπιταγή ῆς   command, authority, 57
ἐπιτάσσω   order, 57
ἐπιτελέω   complete, 45
ἐπιτίθημι   put on, place, 32
ἐπιτιμάω   order, rebuke, 49
ἐπιτιμία ας   punishment, 49
ἐπιτρέπω   let, allow, 80
ἐπιτροπή ῆς   commission, 80
ἐπίτροπος ου   steward, guardian, 80
ἐπιτυγχάνω   obtain, 107
ἐπιφαίνω   appear, give light, 50
ἐπιφάνεια ας   appearance, coming, 50
ἐπιφανής ές   glorious, 50
ἐπιφέρω   bring upon, inflict, 40
ἐπιφωνέω   shout, 42
ἐπιφώσκω   dawn, draw near, 65
ἐπιχειρέω   undertake, 43
ἐπιχέω   pour on, 108
ἐπιχρίω   smear, 22
ἐποικοδομέω   build on / build up, 27
ἐπονομάζομαι   call oneself, 39
ἐποπτεύω   see, observe, 58
ἐπόπτης ου   observer, eyewitness, 58
ἐπουράνιος ον   heavenly, 34
ἑπτ – seven, 66
ἑπτά   seven, 66
ἑπτάκις   seven times, 66
ἑπτακισχίλιοι αι α   seven thousand, 66
ἑπταπλασίων ον   seven times as much, 66
ἐργ – work, 30
ἐργάζομαι   work, do, 30
ἐργασία ας   gain, doing, 30
ἐργάτης ου   worker, 30
ἔργον ου   work, action, 30
ἐρημ – desert, 80
ἐρημία ας   desert, 80
ἐρημόομαι   to be made waste, 80
ἔρημος ον   lonely, desolate, 80
ἐρήμωσις εως   desolation, 80
ἐρχ – come, 13
ἔρχομαι   come, 13
ἐρωτ – ask, 58
ἐρωτάω   ask, 58
ἐσ – be, exist, 12
ἐσθι – eat, 73
ἐσθίω   eat, 73
ἔσοπτρον ου   mirror, 58
ἐσχατ – last, final, 83
ἔσχατος η ον   last, final, 83
ἐσχάτως   finally, 83
ἐσω – into, 12
ἔσω   inside, 12
ἔσωθεν   from within, 12
ἐσώτερος α ον   inner (adj); behind / in (prep), 12
ἐτ – year, 82

ἕτερ – other, different, 65
ἑτερόγλωσσος ον   with strange language, 83
ἑτεροδιδασκαλέω   teach different doctrine, 41
ἕτερος α ον   other, different, 65
ἑτέρως   otherwise, differently, 65
ἔτι – still, yet, 47
ἔτι   still, yet, 47
ἕτοιμ – ready, prepare, 77
ἑτοιμάζω   prepare, make ready, 77
ἑτοιμασία ας   readiness, equipment, 77
ἕτοιμος η ον   read, 78
ἑτοίμως   readily, 78
ἔτος ους   year, 82
εὐαγγελίζω   evangelize, 23
εὐαγγέλιον ου   good news, gospel, 23
εὐαγγελιστής οῦ   evangelist, 23
εὐαρεστέω   please, be pleasing to, 111
εὐάρεστος ον   pleasing, 111
εὐαρέστως   pleasingly, 111
εὐγενής ές   high born (> eugenics), 15
εὐδ – sleep, 109
εὐδοκέω   be pleased, choose, will, 63
εὐδοκία ας   good will, pleasure, 63
εὐεργεσία ας   service, kind act, 30
εὐεργετέω   do good, 30
εὐεργέτης ου   benefactor, 30
εὐθ – immediate, straight, 64
εὔθετος ον   suitable (> well placed), 32
εὐθέως   immediately, soon, 64
εὐθυμέω   take courage, be happy, 60
εὔθυμος ον   encouraged, 60
εὐθύμως   cheerfully, 60
εὐθύνω   make straight, 64
εὐθύς   immediately, 64
εὐθύς εῖα ύ   straight, (up)right, 64
εὐθύτης ητος   uprightness, justice, 64
εὐκαιρέω   have time, spend time, 64
εὐκαιρία ας   opportune moment, 64
εὔκαιρος ον   suitable, timely, 64
εὐκαίρως   when the time is right, 64
εὐκοπώτερος α ον   easier, 85
εὐλάβεια ας   godly fear, reverence, 27
εὐλαβέομαι   act in reverence, 27
εὐλαβής ές   reverent, 27
εὐλογέω   bless (> eulogize), 18
εὐλογητός ή όν   blessed, praised, 18
εὐλογία ας   blessing (> eulogy), 18
εὐμετάδοτος ον   liberal, generous, 19
εὐνοέω   make friends, 52
εὔνοια ας   good will, eagerness, 52
εὐοδόομαι   have things go well, 53
εὐπειθής ές   open to reason, 69
εὐπερίστατος ον   holding on tightly, 20
εὐποιΐα ας   doing of good, 19
εὐπορέομαι   have financial means, 38
εὐπορία ας   wealth, 38
εὐπρόσδεκτος ον   acceptable, 49
εὐπροσωπέω   make a good showing, 72
εὑρ – find, 45
εὑρίσκω   find, 45

εὐρύχωρος ον   wide, spacious, 51
εὐσέβεια ας   godliness, religion, 82
εὐσεβέω   worship, 82
εὐσεβής ές   godly, religious, 82
εὐσεβῶς   in a godly manner, 82
εὔσημος ον   intelligible, 67
εὔσπλαγχνος ον   kind, 106
εὐφημία ας   good reputation, 35
εὔφημος ον   worthy of praise, 35
εὐφορέω   produce good crops, 40
εὐφραίνω   make glad, 61
εὐφροσύνη ης   gladness, 61
εὐχ – pray, 54
εὐχαριστέω   thank, be thankful, 36
εὐχαριστία ας   thanksgiving eucharist, 36
εὐχάριστος ον   thankful, 37
εὐχή ῆς   prayer, vow, 54
εὔχομαι   pray, 54
εὔχρηστος ον   useful, 62
εὐψυχέω   be encouraged, 55
ἐφευρετής οῦ   inventor, 45
ἐφημερία ας   division, 26
ἐφήμερος ον   daily, 26
ἐφίστημι   come to, approach, 20
ἐφοράω   take notice of, 50
ἐχ – have, hold, 16
ἐχθρ – enemy, 94
ἔχθρα ας   hostility, hatred, 94
ἐχθρός ά όν   hated (*as noun*: enemy), 94
ἔχω   have, 16
ἕως – until, 51
ἕως (*gen*)   until, 51

ζα – life, 33
ζάω   live, 33
ζηλ – zealous, jealous, 92
ζηλεύω   be zealous, 92
ζῆλος ου   zeal, jealousy, 92
ζηλόω   be jealous, 92
ζηλωτής οῦ   someone zealous, 92
ζητ – seek, discuss, 47
ζητέω   seek, try, 47
ζήτημα ματος   question, 47
ζήτησις εως   discussion, 47
ζυμ – yeast, 104
ζύμη ης   yeast, 104
ζυμόω   make / cause to rise, 104
ζω – life, 33
ζωή ῆς   life, 33
ζων – fasten, bind, 109
ζώνη ης   belt, 109
ζώννυμι   fasten, 109
ζωογονέω   save life, 33
ζῷον ου   animal (> living thing), 33
ζωοποιέω   make alive, 33

ἤ – or, than, 31
ἤ   or, than, 31
ἡ – the, 11
ἡγ – govern (compare with ἀγ), 84

ἡγεμ – govern, 84
ἡγεμον – govern, 84
ἡγεμονεύω be governor, rule, 84
ἡγεμονία ας reign, rule, 84
ἡγεμών όνος governor, ruler, 84
ἡγέομαι lead, rule, consider, 84
ἤδη – now, already, 79
ἤδη now, already, 79
ἤκ – be present, 102
ἥκω have come, be present, 102
ἡλι – sun, 92
ἡλικία ας age, years, 92
ἥλιος ου sun, 92
ἡμερ – day, 26
ἡμέρα ας day, 26
ἡμιθανής ές half dead, 36
ἡμίωρον ου half an hour, 62
ἤπερ than, 31
ἤτοι or, 31

θαλλασ – sea, 66
θάλασσα ης sea, 66
θαν – death, 36
θανάσιμον ου deadly poison, 36
θανατηφόρος ον deadly, 36
θάνατος ου death, 36
θανατόω kill (> make dead), 36
θάπτω bury, 149
θαυμ – wonder, 83
θαῦμα ματος wonder, miracle, 83
θαυμάζω marvel, 83
θαυμάσιος α ον wonderful, 83
θαυμαστός ή όν marvelous, astonishing, 83
θε¹ – god, 13
θε² – put, place, 31
θεα – see, 68
θεά ᾶς goddess, 13
θεάομαι see, observe, 68
θεατρίζω expose to public shame, 68
θέατρον ου theatre, spectacle, 68
θει – god, 13
θεῖος α ον divine, 13
θειότης ητος deity, 13
θελ – will, 36
θέλημα ματος will, desire, 36
θέλησις εως will, 36
θέλω wish, want, 36
θεμελι – foundation, 109
θεμέλιον ου foundation, 109
θεμέλιος ου foundation, 109
θεμελιόω establish (> make firm), 109
θεο – god, 13
θεοδίδακτος ον taught by God, 41
θεομάχος ον God-opposing, 13
θεόπνευστος ον God-inspired, 13
θεός οῦ God, 13
θεοσέβεια ας religion, 13
θεοσεβής ές religious, 13
θεοστυγής ές God-hating, 13
θεότης ητος deity, 13

θερ – warm, harvest, 88
θεραπ – healing, service, 87
θεραπεία ας healing, house servants, 87
θεραπεύω heal, serve, 87
θεράπων οντος servant, 87
θερίζω harvest, gather, 88
θερισμός οῦ harvest, crop, 88
θεριστής οῦ reaper, 88
θερμ – warm, harvest, 88
θερμαίνομαι warm oneself, 88
θέρμη ης heat, 88
θέρος ους summer, 88
θεωρ – see, 68
θεωρέω see, observe, 68
θεωρία ας sight, 68
θη – put, place, 31
θήκη ης sheath, 32
θηρ – wild animal, 86
θήρα ας trap, 86
θηρεύω catch, 86
θηριομαχέω fight wild beasts, 86
θηρίον ου animal, 86
θησαυρ – treasure, 104
θησαυρίζω save, store up, 104
θησαυρός οῦ treasure, storeroom, 104
θλιβ – trouble, crowd, 81
θλίβω crush, press, 81
θλιψ – trouble, crowd, 81
θλῖψις εως trouble, 81
θνη – death, 36
θνήσκω die, 36
θνητός ή όν mortal, 36
θρίξ τριχός hair (> tress), 149
θρον – throne, 78
θρόνος ου throne, 78
θυ – sacrifice, 74
θυγατηρ – daughter, 101
θυγάτηρ τρός daughter, woman, 101
θυγατρ – daughter, 101
θυγάτριον ου little daughter, 101
θυμ – feelings (emotions), 60
θυμομαχέω be very angry, 60
θυμόομαι be furious, 60
θυμός οῦ anger, 60
θυρ – door, 88
θύρα ας door, 88
θυρίς ίδος window, 88
θυρωρός οῦ doorkeeper, 88
θυσ – sacrifice, 74
θυσία ας sacrifice, 74
θυσιαστήριον ου altar (> place of sacrifice), 74
θύω sacrifice, kill, 74

ια – heal, 94
ἴαμα ματος healing, 94
ἰάομαι heal, 94
ἴασις εως healing, 94
ιατρ – heal, 94

ἰατρός οὖ   physician, healer, 94
ἰδ – see, 40
ἴδε   Behold! here is, 40
ἰδι – own, 58
ἴδιος α ον   one's own, pesonal, 58
ἰδιώτης ου   untrained person, 58
ἰδού   Behold! here is, 40
ἰερ – priest, 58
ἰερατ – priest, 58
ἰερατεία ας   priestly office, 58
ἰεράτευμα ματος   priesthood, 58
ἰερατεύω   serve as a priest, 58
ἰερεύς έως   priest, 58
ἰερόθυτος ον   sacrificial, 58
ἰερόν οὖ   temple, 58
ἰεροπρεπής ές   reverent, 58
ἰερός ά όν   sacred, 58
ἰεροσυλέω   commit sacrilege, 58
ἰερόσυλος ου   sacrilegious person, 58
ἰερουργέω   work as a priest, 58
ἰερωσύνη ης   priesthood, 58
ἰη – let, send, 44
ἰκαν – able, 90
ἰκανός ή όν   able, worthy, 91
ἰκανότης ητος   capability, capacity, 91
ἰκανόω   make fit, make able, 91
ἰματ – clothe, 77
ἰματίζω   clothe, dress, 77
ἰμάτιον ου   clothing, coat, 77
ἰματισμός οὖ   clothing, 77
ἰνα – in order that, 17
ἴνα   in order that, 17
ἰνατί   why? 16, 17
ἰππ – horse, 112
ἰππεύς έως   horseman, 112
ἰππικόν οὖ   cavalry, 112
ἴππος ου   horse, 112
ἰσάγγελος ον   angel-like, 23
ἰσότιμος ον   equally valuable, 49
ἰσόψυχος ον   sharing same feelings, 55
ἰστη – stand, 20
ἴστημι   set, stand, 20
ἰσχυ – strong, 73
ἰσχυρός ά όν   strong, 74
ἰσχύς ύος   strength, 74
ἰσχύω   be able, 74
ἰχθυ –fish, 109
ἰχθύδιον ου   small fish, 109
ἰχθύς ύος   fish, 109

κἀγώ   and I; I also, 11
καθ¹ – down, according to, 22
καθ² – sit (compare with κατ), 48
καθαιρ – clean, 61
καθαίρεσις εως   destruction, 78
καθαιρέω   take down, destroy, 78
καθαίρω   clean, prune, 61
καθάπερ   as, just as, 22
καθάπτω   fasten on, 90
καθαρ – clean, 61

καθαρίζω   cleanse, 62
καθαρισμός οὖ   cleansing, 62
καθαρός ά όν   clean, pure, 62
καθαρότης ητος   purification, purity, 62
καθεδρ – sit (compare with κατ), 48
καθέδρα ας   chair, 48
καθέζομαι   sit, 48
καθεύδω   sleep, 109
καθηγητής οὖ   teacher, 24
κάθημαι   sit, live, 48
καθημερινός ή όν   daily, 26
καθίζω   sit, 48
καθίημι   let down, 44
καθίστημι   put in charge, 20
καθό   as, according as, 22
καθόλου   completely, altogether, 60
καθοράω   perceive clearly, 50
καθώς   as, just as, 16
καθώσπερ   as, just as, 16
και – and, 11
καί   and, also, but, 11
καιν – new, 84
καινός ή όν   new, 84
καινότης ητος   newness, 84
καίπερ   though, 11
καιρ – time, 64
καιρός οὖ   time, age, 64
καίτοι   yet, though, 11
καίτοιγε   yet, though, 11
καίω   light, burn, 149
κακ – bad, 59
κἀκεῖ   and there, 28
κἀκεῖθεν   from there, 28
κἀκεῖνος η ο   and that one, 28
κακία ας   evil, trouble, 59
κακοήθεια ας   meanness, 59
κακολογέω   speak evil of, curse, 59
κακοπάθεια ας   suffering, endurance, 59
κακοπαθέω   suffer, endure, 59
κακοποιέω   do evil, 59
κακοποιός οὖ   criminal, wrongdoer, 59
κακός ή όν   evil, bad, 59
κακοῦργος ου   criminal, 59
κακουχέομαι   be treated badly, 59
κακόω   treat badly, harm, 59
κακῶς   badly, 59
κάκωσις εως   oppression, suffering, 59
καλ¹ – good, proper, 53
καλ² – call, 22
καλέω   call, name, 22
καλλιέλαιος ου   cultivated olive tree, 103
κάλλιον   very well, 53
καλοδιδάσκαλος ον   teaching what is good, 41
καλοποιέω   do what is good, 53
καλός ή όν   good, proper, 53
καλυμ –hide, 76
κάλυμμα ματος   veil, 76
καλυπτ – hide, 76
καλύπτω   cover, hide, 76
καλυψ – hide, 76

καλῶς   well, 53
κἄν (καὶ ἐάν)   even if, 43
καρδ – heart, 47
καρδία ας   heart, 47
καρδιογνώστης ου   knower of hearts, 48
καρπ – fruit, 70
καρπός οῦ   fruit, 70
καρποφορέω   be fruitful / productive, 71
καρποφόρος ον   fruitful, 71
καπνός οῦ   smoke, 149
κατ – down, according to, 22
κατά (*gen, acc*)   down, according to, 22
καταβαίνω   descend, fall, 37
καταβάλλω   knock down, 29
καταβαπτίζομαι   wash oneself, 58
καταβαρέω   be a burden to, 104
καταβαρύνομαι   be very heavy, 104
κατάβασις εως   descent, slope, 37
καταβολή ῆς   beginning, foundation, 29
καταγγελεύς έως   proclaimer, 23
καταγγέλλω   proclaim, 23
καταγινώσκω   condemn, 25
καταγράφω   write, 31
κατάγω   bring (down), 24
καταδέω   bandage, bind up, 79
καταδικάζω   condemn, 34
καταδίκη ης   sentence, condemnation, 34
καταδιώκω   search for diligently, pursue, 81
καταδουλόω   make a slave of, 44
καταδυναστεύω   oppress, 29
κατάθεμα ματος   God-cursed thing, 13
καταθεματίζω   curse, 32
καταισχύνω   put to shame, 85
κατακαίω   burn, consume, 149
κατακαλύπτομαι   cover one's head, 76
κατακαυχάομαι   be proud, despise, 78
κατάκειμαι   lie, be sick, 68
κατακλάω   break in pieces, 88
κατακλείω   lock up (in prison), 99
κατακλίνω   cause to recline, dine, 89
κατακολουθέω   follow, accompany, 63
κατακόπτω   cut badly, beat, 91
κατάκριμα ματος   condemnation, 21
κατακρίνω   condemn, judge, 21
κατάκρισις εως   condemnation, 21
κατακυριεύω   have power over, 17
καταλαλέω   slander (> speak against), 33
καταλαλιά ᾶς   slander, 33
κατάλαλος ου   slanderer, 33
καταλαμβάνω   obtain, attain, overtake, 27
καταλέγω   enroll (> catalogue), 18
καταλείπω   leave, forsake, 57
καταλιθάζω   stone, 72
καταλλαγή ῆς   reconciliation, 16
καταλλάσσω   reconcile, 16
κατάλοιπος ον   rest, remaining, 57
κατάλυμα ματος   room, guest room, 46
καταλύω   destroy, stop, 46
καταμανθάνω   consider, observe, 34
καταμαρτυρέω   witness against, 42

καταμένω   remain, stay, live, 41
κατανοέω   consider, 52
κατάνταω   come, arrive, 66
κατάνυξις εως   stupor, numbness, 77
καταξιόω   make / count worthy, 80
καταπατέω   trample on, despise, 35
κατάπαυσις εως   place of rest, rest, 86
καταπαύω   cause to rest, prevent, 86
καταπίνω   swallow (> drink down), 71
καταπίπτω   fall (down), 46
καταπλέω   sail, 67
καταργέω   destroy, 30
καταριθμέω   number, 107
καταρτίζω   mend, make adequate, 112
κατάρτισις εως   adequacy, 112
καταρτισμός οῦ   adequacy, 112
κατασείω   move, make a sign, 104
κατασκευάζω   prepare, make ready, 95
κατασκηνόω   nest, live, dwell, 94
κατασκήνωσις εως   nest, 94
κατασκοπέω   spy on, 99
κατάσκοπος ου   spy, 99
κατασοφίζομαι   take advantage of, 73
καταστέλλω   quiet, 36
κατάστημα ματος   behavior, 20
καταστρέφω   overturn, 52
καταστροφή ῆς   ruin (> catastrophe), 52
κατασφραγίζω   seal, 99
κατατίθημι   lay, place, 32
κατατομή ῆς   mutilation, 77
κατατρέχω   run down, 98
καταφέρω   bring against, 40
καταφεύγω   flee, 90
καταφθείρω   corrupt, ruin, 84
καταφιλέω   kiss, 75
καταφρονέω   despise, 61
καταφρονητής οῦ   scoffer, 61
καταχέω   pour over, 108
καταχράομαι   use, use fully, 73
καταψύχω   cool, refresh, 55
κατείδωλος ον   full of idols, 98
κατέναντι (*gen*)   opposite, 66
κατεξουσιάζω   rule over, 63
κατεργάζομαι   do, accomplish, 30
κατέρχομαι   come / go down, 13
κατεσθίω   eat up, devour, 73
κατευθύνω   direct, guide, 64
κατευλογέω   bless, 18
κατεφίστημι   attack, set upon, 20
κατέχω   hold fast, keep, 16
κατηγορέω   accuse (bring against), 24
κατηγορία   accusation, 24
κατήγορος ου   accuser, 24
κατήγωρ ορος   accuser, 24
κατισχύω   have strength, defeat, 74
κατοικέω   live, inhabit, 27
κατοίκησις εως   home, 27
κατοικητήριον ου   house, home, 27
κατοικία ας   place where one lives, 27
κατοικίζω   place, put, 27

κατοπρίζω   behold, 58
κάτω   down, below, 22
κατώτερος α ον   lower, 22
κατωτέρω   under, 22
καυχα – proud, 78
καυχάομαι   be proud, boast, 78
καυχη – proud, 78
καύχημα ματος   pride, boasting, 78
καύχησις εως   pride, boasting, 78
κει – lie, 68
κεῖμαι   lie, be laid, be, 68
κελευ – command, 104
κέλευσμα ματος   command, 105
κελεύω   command, 105
κενο – empty, 107
κενοδοξία ας   conceit (> empty glory), 39
κενόδοξος ον   conceited, 39
κενός ή όν   empty, senseless, 107
κενοφωνία ας   foolish (empty) talk, 42
κενόω   make empty / powerless, 107
κενῶς   in vain, 107
κέρας ατος   horn, power, 149
κερδ – gain, 112
κερδαίνω   gain, profit, 112
κέρδος ους   gain, 112
κεφαλ – head, sum, 69
κεφάλαιον ου   main point, summary, 69
κεφαλή ῆς   head, 69
κεφαλιόω   beat over the head, 69
κηρυγ – preach, 74
κήρυγμα ματος   message, kerygma, 75
κηρυξ – preach, 74
κῆρυξ υκος   preacher, 75
κηρυσσ – preach, 74
κηρύσσω   preach, proclaim, 75
κλα – break, 88
κλάδος ου   branch, 88
κλαι – weep, 87
κλαίω   weep, 87
κλάσις εως   breaking (of bread), 88
κλάσμα ματος   fragment, piece, 88
κλαυ – weep, 87
κλαυθμός οῦ   bitter crying, 87
κλάω   break, 88
κλει – lock, close, 99
κλείς κλειδός   key, 99
κλείω   lock, shut, close, 99
κλεμ – steal, 98
κλέμμα ματος   theft, 98
κλεπτ – steal, 98
κλέπτης ου   thief, 98
κλέπτω   steal, 98
κλη – call, 22
κλῆμα ματος   branch, 88
κληρ – share, choose, 78
κληρονομέω   receive, share (in), 78
κληρονομία ας   property, 78
κληρονόμος ου   heir, 78
κλῆρος ου   lot, share, 78
κληρόω   choose, 78

κλῆσις εως   call, calling, 22
κλητός ή όν   called, invited, 22
κλιν – recline, incline, turn, 89
κλινάριον ου   small bed, 89
κλίνη ης   bed, 89
κλινίδιον ου   bed, 89
κλίνω   lay, put to flight, 89
κλισία ας   group, 89
κλοπ – steal, 98
κλοπή ῆς   theft, 98
κοιλ – stomach, 107
κοιλία ας   stomach, appetite, 107
κοιμάομαι   sleep, die (> coma), 149
κοιν – common, 75
κοινός ή όν   common, profane, 75
κοινόω   defile (> make common), 75
κοινων – common, 75
κοινωνέω   share, participate, 75
κοινωνία ας   fellowship, 75
κοινωνικός ή όν   liberal, generous, sharing, 75
κοινωνός οῦ   partner, 75
κολλάομαι   unite with, associate, 150
κομίζω   bring, buy (> commerce), 150
κοπ – work, 85
κοπή ῆς   slaughter, defeat, 85
κοπιάω   work, grow tired, 85
κόπος ου   work, trouble, 85
κοπτ – cut, 91
κόπτω   cut (mid mourn), 91
κοσμ – world, order, 42
κοσμέω   adorn, put in order, 42
κοσμικός ή όν   worldly, man-made, 42
κόσμιος ον   well-behaved, ordered, 42
κοσμοκράτωρ ορος   world-ruler, 42
κόσμος ου   world, universe, 42
κράβαττος ου   bed, 150
κραζ – shout, 74
κράζω   shout, call out, 74
κρατ – strong, power, 67
κραταιόομαι   become strong, 68
κραταιός ά όν   strong, 68
κρατέω   hold, seize, 68
κράτιστος η ον   most excellent, 68
κράτος ους   strength, power, 68
κραυγ – shout, 74
κραυγάζω   shout, call out, 74
κραυγή ῆς   shout, 74
κρείσσων ον   better, greater, 150
κρι – judge, 21
κρίμα τος   judgment, decision, 21
κρίνω   judge, consider, 21
κρίσις εως   judgment, 21
κριτήριον ου   court (judgment hall), 21
κριτής οῦ   judge, 21
κριτικός ή όν   able to judge, 21
κρυπτ – hide, 86
κρύπτη ης   hidden place, cellar, 86
κρυπτός ή όν   hidden, secret, 86
κρύπτω   hide, cover, 86
κρυφ – hide, 86

μανθ – learn, 34
μανθάνω   learn, discover, 35
μαρτυρ – witness, 42
μαρτυρέω   testify, affirm, 42
μαρτυρία ας   witness, testimony, 42
μαρτύριον ου   witness, testimony, 42
μαρτύρομαι   witness, testify, urge, 42
μάρτυς μάρτυρος   witness, martyr, 42
μαχ – fight, 92
μάχαιρα ης   sword, 92
μάχη ης   fight, 92
μάχομαι   fight, 92
μεγ – great, 40
μεγαλ – great, 40
μεγαλεῖον ου   great / mighty act, 41
μεγαλειότης ητος   greatness, majesty, 41
μεγαλύνω   enlarge, 41
μεγάλως   greatly, 41
μεγαλωσύνη ης   greatness, majesty, 41
μέγας μεγάλη μέγα   great, large, 41
μέγεθος ους   greatness, 41
μεγιστάν ᾶνος   person of high position, 41
μέγιστος η ον   very great, greatest, 41
μεθίστημι   remove, mislead, 20
μεθοδεία ας   trickery, 53
μειζ – greater, 87
μείζων ον   greater, 87
μελ¹ – concern, care, 102
μελ² – part, 97
μέλει   it concerns (impersonal), 103
μελλ – about, 62
μέλλω   be going, be about, 62
μέλος ους   part, member, 97
μέν   (used to show contrast), 42
μεν¹ [particle of contrast], 42
μεν² – wait, remain, 41
μενοῦν   rather, 42
μέντοι   but, 42
μένω   remain, 41
μερ – part, 72
μερίζω   divide, 73
μεριμν – worry, 103
μέριμνα ης   worry, care, 103
μεριμνάω   worry, 103
μερίς ίδος   part, 73
μερισμός οῦ   distribution, division, 73
μεριστής οῦ   one who divides, 73
μέρος ους   part, piece, 73
μεσι – middle, 74
μεσιτεύω   mediate, 74
μεσίτης ου   mediator, 74
μεσο – middle, 74
μεσονύκτιον ου   midnight, 74
Μεσοποταμία ας   Mesopotamia, 74
μέσος η ον   middle, 74
μεσότοιχον ου   dividing wall, 74
μεσουράνημα τος   mid-heaven, 74
μεσόω   be in the middle, 74
μετα – with, after, 24
μετά (*gen, acc*)   with, after, 24

μεταβαίνω   leave, move, 37
μεγαβάλλομαι   change one's mind, 29
μετάγω   guide, direct, 24
μεγαδίδωμι   give, share, 19
μετάθεσις εως   removal, change, 32
μεταίρω   leave, 53
μετακαλέομαι   send for, invite, 23
μεταλαμβάνω   receive, share in, 27
μετάλημψις εως   receiving, accepting, 27
μεταλλάσσω   exchange, 16
μεταμέλομαι   regret, 103
μετανοέω   repent, 52
μετάνοια ας   repentance, 52
μεταξύ (*gen*)   between, among, 24
μεταπέμπομαι   send for, 63
μεταστρέφω   change, alter, 52
μετατίθημι   remove, change, 32
μετατρέπω   turn, change, 80
μετέχω   share in, eat, have, 16
μετοικεσία ας   carrying off, 27
μετοικίζω   deport / send off, 27
μετοχή ῆς   partnership, 17
μέτοχος ου   partner, 17
μετρ – measure, 101
μετρέω   measure, give, 101
μετρητής οῦ   measure, 101
μετριοπαθέω   be gentle with, 93
μετρίως   greatly, 101
μέτρον ου   measure, quantity, 101
μέτωπον ου   forehead, 59
μέχρι (*gen*)   until, to, 77
μη – not, 14
μή   not, 14
μήγε   otherwise, 14
μηδαμῶς   no, by no means, 14
μηδέ   nor, 14
μηδείς μηδεμία μηδέν   no one, 27
μηδέποτε   never, 22
μηκέτι   no longer, 47
μήν μηνός   month, 150
μήποτε   lest, whether, never, 22
μήτε   and not, 14
μητηρ – mother, 68
μήτηρ τρός   mother, 68
μήτι (negative answer), 14
μητρ – mother, 68
μήτρα ας   womb, 68
μητρολῴας ου mother-murderer, 68
μια – one, 27
μικρ – small, 88
μικρόν   a little while, 88
μικρός ά όν   small, insignificant, 88
μιμν – remember, 55
μιμνήσκομαι   remember, 55
μισ – hate, 93
μισέω   hate, be indifferent to, 93
μισθ – pay, 91
μισθαποδοσία ας   reward, punishment, 91
μισθαποδότης ου   rewarder, 91
μίσθιος ου   hired man, laborer, 91

μισθόομαι   hire (> make a payee), 91
μισθός οὗ   pay, 91
μίσθωμα ματος   expense, rent, 91
μισθωτός οὗ   hired man, laborer, 91
μν – remember, 55
μνεία ας   remembrance, mention, 55
μνη – remember, 55
μνημ – remember, 55
μνῆμα ματος   grave, tomb (memorial), 55
μνημεῖον ου   grave, monument, 55
μνήμη ης   remembrance, memory, 55
μνημονεύω   remember, 55
μνημόσυνον ου   memorial, 55
μογιλάλος ον   mute, dumb, 33
μοιχ – adultery, 102
μοιχαλίς ίδος   adulteress, 102
μοιχάομαι   commit adultery, 102
μοιχεία ας   adultery, 102
μοιχεύω   commit adultery, 102
μοιχός οὗ   adulterer, 102
μον – wait, remain, 41
μονή ῆς   room, 41
μονο – only, 56
μονογενής ές   only begotten, unique, 15, 56
μόνον   only, alone, 56
μονόομαι   be left alone, 57
μόνος η ον   only, alone, 57
μύρον ου   myrrh, 150
μυστηρ – mystery, 103
μυστήριον ου   secret, mystery, 103
μυωπάζω   be shortsighted, 59
μωρ – foolish, 109
μωραίνω   make foolish, 109
μωρία ας   foolishness, 109
μωρολογία ας   foolish talk, 109
μωρός ά όν   foolish, 109

να – temple, 88
ναι – yes, 97
ναί   yes, 97
ναός οὗ   temple, 88
νε – new, 88
νεα – new, 88
νεανίας ου   young man, 88
νεανίσκος ου   young man, 88
νεκρ – death, 54
νεκρός ά όν   dead, 54
νεκρόω   put to death, make dead, 54
νέκρωσις εως   death, barrenness, 54
νεο – new, 88
νεομηνία ας   new moon, 88
νέος α ον   new, young, 88
νεότης ητος   youth, 88
νεόφυτος ον   new convert (neophyte), 89
νεφ – cloud, 105
νεφέλη ης   cloud, 105
νέφος ους   cloud, 105
νεω – new, 88
νεωτερικός ή όν   youthful, 89
νήπιος α ον   infant, 150

νηστ – hunger, 103
νηστεία ας   hunger, fasting, 103
νηστεύω   fast, 103
νῆστις ιδος   hungry, 103
νικ – victory, 97
νικάω   conquer, 97
νίκη ης   victory, 97
νῖκος ους   victory, 97
νιπτ – wash, 111
νιπτήρ ῆρος   washbasin, 111
νίπτω   wash, 111
νο – mind, 52
νοέω   understand, 52
νόημα τος   mind, thought, 52
νομ – law, 38
νομίζω   think, suppose, 38
νομικός ή όν   legal, 38
νομίμως   lawfully, 38
νόμισμα ματος   coin (> legal tender), 38
νομοδιδάσκαλος ου   teacher of law, 38
νομοθεσία ας   giving of the law, 38
νομοθετέομαι   be given the law, 38
νομοθέτης ου   lawgiver, 38
νόμος ου   law, 38
νόσος ου   disease, 150
νουθεσία   instruction, 52
νουθετέω   instruct (> place in mind), 52
νουνεχῶς   wisely, 52
νοῦς νοός   mind, 52
νυ – night, 77
νυκ – night, 77
νυμφ – bride, 103
νύμφη ης   bride, daughter-in-law, 103
νυμφίος ου   bridegroom, 103
νυμφών ῶνος   wedding hall, 103
νυν – now, 46
νῦν   now, 46
νυνί   now, 46
νύξ νυκτός   night, 77
νυσ – night, 77
νυστάζω   be asleep, drowsy, idle, 77
νυχ – night, 77
νυχθήμερον ου   a night and a day, 77

ξεν – strange, guest, 98
ξενία ας   place of lodging, room, 99
ξενίζω   entertain strangers, 99
ξενοδοχέω   be hospitable, 99
ξένος η ον   strange, foreign, 99
ξηρ – dry, 108
ξηραίνω   dry up, 108
ξηρός ά όν   dry, withered, 108
ξυλ – wood, 109
ξύλινος η ον   wooden, 110
ξύλον ου   wood, tree, club, 110

ὁ – the, 11
ὁ ἡ τό   the, 11
ὁδ – way, travel, 53
ὅδε ἥδε τόδε   this, 11

ὁδεύω   travel, 53
ὁδηγέω   lead, guide, 53
ὁδηγός οὖ   guide, leader, 53
ὁδοιπορέω   travel, 53
ὁδοιπορία ας   journey, 53
ὁδός οὖ   way, journey, 53
ὁδούς ὁδόντος   tooth (> dental, orthodontist),
    150
ὅθεν   where, from where, 150
οι – such, as, 84
οἰδ – know, 43
οἶδα   know, 33
οἰκ – house, 27
οἰκεῖος ου   family member, 27
οἰκετεία ας   household, 28
οἰκέτης ου   house servant, 28
οἰκέω   live, dwell, 28
οἴκημα ματος   prison cell, 28
οἰκητήριον ου   home, dwelling, 28
οἰκία ας   home, family, 28
οἰκιακός οὖ   member of household, 28
οἰκοδεσποτέω   run a household, 28
οἰκοδεσπότης ου   master, householder, 28
οἰκοδομέω   build, encourage, 28
οἰκοδομή ῆς   structure, 28
οἰκοδόμος ου   builder, 28
οἰκονομέω   be a manager, steward, 28
οἰκονομία ας   task, responsibility, 28
οἰκονόμος ου   manager, steward, 28
οἶκος ου   house, 28
οἰκουμένη ης   world, oikomenia, 28
οἰκουργός όν   domestic, 28
οἰν – wine, 93
οἰνοπότης ου   drinker, drunkard, 93
οἶνος ου   wine, 93
οἰνοφλυγία ας   drunkenness, 93
οἶος α ον   such, such as, 84
ὀκταήμερος ον   on the eighth day, 26
ὀλ – whole, all, 60
ὀλιγ – little, few, 91
ὀλιγοπιστία ας   little faith, 19
ὀλιγόπιστος ον   of little faith, 19
ὀλίγος η ον   little, few, 91
ὀλιγόψυχος ον   faint-hearted, 91
ὀλιγωρέω   think lightly of, 91
ὀλίγως   barely, just, 91
ὀλλ – destroy, 62
ὅλος η ον   whole, all, 60
ὁλοτελής ές   wholly, 60
ὅλως   at all, actually, 60
ὀμ – swear, 105
ὀμν – swear, 105
ὀμνύω   swear, vow, 105
ὁμο – same, like, 59
ὁμοθυμαδόν   with one mind, 60
ὁμοι – same, like, 59
ὁμοιάζω   resemble, 59
ὁμοιοπαθής ές   similar (> of same feelings), 59
ὅμοιος α ον   like, 59
ὁμοιότης ητος   likeness, 59

ὁμοιόω   make like, compare, 59
ὁμοίωμα ματος   likeness, 59
ὁμοίως   too, in the same way, 59
ὁμοίωσις εως   likeness, 59
ὁμολογέω   confess, declare, 18
ὁμολογία ας   confession, 18
ὁμολογουμένως   undeniably, 18
ὁμοῦ   together, 59
ὁμόφρων ον   of one mind, 61
ὅμως   even, 59
ὀνομ – name, 39
ὄνομα ματος   name, 39
ὀνομάζω   name, call, 39
ὀντ – be, exist, 12
ὄντως   really, 12
ὀπ – see, 58
ὀπισ – behind, after, 92
ὄπισθεν   behind, 92
ὀπίσω   behind, after, 92
ὁποῖος α ον   as, such as, 84
ὁπότε   when, 22
ὅπου   where, 43
ὀπτ – see, 58
ὀπτάνομαι   appear (> gain sight of), 59
ὀπτασία ας   vision, 59
ὅπως   that, in order that, 16
ὁρ – boundary, 66
ὀρ – hill, 78
ὁρα – see, 50
ὅραμα ματος   vision, sight, 50
ὅρασις εως   vision, appearance, 50
ὁρατός ή όν   visible, 50
ὁράω   see, perceive, 50
ὀργ – anger, 87
ὀργή ῆς   anger, punishment, 87
ὀργίζομαι   be angry, 87
ὀργίλος η ον   quick-tempered, 87
ὀρεινή ῆς   hill country, 78
ὀρθοποδέω   be consistent, 56
ὁρίζω   decide, determine, 66
ὅριον ου   territory, vicinity, 66
ὁρκ – oath, 111
ὁρκίζω   adjure, 112
ὅρκος ου   oath, 112
ὁρκωμοσία ας   oath, 112
ὁροθεσία ας   limit, boundary, 66
ὅρος ου   limit, boundary, 66
ὄρος ους   mountain, hill, 78
οσ – much, many, 50
ὅς ἥ ὅ   who, which, what, 11
ὅσος η ον   as much as, as great as, 50
ὅσπερ ἥπερ ὅπερ   who, which, 11
ὅστις ἥτις ὅ τι   whoever, whichever, 14
ὅταν   when, whenever, 22
ὅτε   when, while, 22
οτε – when, 22
ὅτι – that, because, 13
ὅτι   that, because, 13
οὐ – no, 12
οὐ   no, 12

οὐ not, 12
ου – where, 43
οὖ where, 43
οὐαι – woe, 89
οὐαί woe, 89
οὐδαμῶς by no means, 12
οὐδέ neither, nor, 12
οὐδέποτε never, 22
οὐδέπω not yet, 101
οὐκ – no, 12
οὐκέτι no longer, 47
οὐκοῦν so then, 24
οὖν – therefore, 24
οὖν therefore, 24
οὔπω not yet, 101
οὐραν – heaven, 34
οὐράνοις ον heavenly, 34
οὐρανόθεν from heaven, 34
οὐρανός οῦ heaven, 34
οὐργ – work, 30
οὐσ – be, exist, 12
οὐς – ear, 96
οὐς ὠτός ear, 96
οὐσία ας property, 12
οὐτ – this, 12
οὔτε not, nor, 12
οὗτος αὕτη τοῦτο this, this one, 12
οὕτως [οὕτω] thus (> in this way), 12
οὐχ – no, 12
οὐχί not, no (emphatic), 12
ὀφειλ – debt, 85
ὀφειλέτης ου debtor, offender, 85
ὀφειλή ῆς debt, 86
ὀφείλημα ματος debt, 86
ὀφείλω owe, ought, 86
ὀφελ – gain, 105
ὄφελος ους gain, benefit, 105
ὀφθαλμ – eye, 64
ὀφθαλμοδουλία ας eye-service, 64
ὀφθαλμός οῦ eye, 64
ὄφις εως snake (> Ophites), 150
οχ – have, 16
ὀχλ – crowd, mob, 45
ὀχλέομαι crowd, trouble, harass, 45
ὀχλοποιέω gather a crowd, 45
ὄχλος ου crowd, mob, 18
οψ – late, 108
ὀψέ late, after, 108
ὀψία ας evening, 108
ὄψιμος ου late rain, spring rain, 108
ὀψώνιον ου pay (> given late in day), 108

παθ – feel, desire, 93
πάθημα ματος suffering, passion, 93
παθητός ή όν subject to suffering, 93
πάθος ους lust, passion, 93
παι – child, education, 53
παιδ – child, education, 53
παιδαγωγός οῦ instructor (> pedagogue), 54
παιδάριον ου boy, 54

παιδεία ας discipline, instruction, 54
παιδευτής οῦ teacher, 54
παιδεύω instruct, correct, 54
παιδιόθεν from childhood, 54
παιδίον ου child, infant, 54
παιδίσκη ης maid, slave, 54
παίζω play, dance, 54
παῖς παιδός child, servant, 54
παλ – again, 53
παλαι – old, 98
πάλαι long ago, formerly, 98
παλαιός ά όν old, former, 98
παλαιότης ητος age, 98
παλαιόω make old, 98
παλιγγενεσία ας rebirth, new age, 15
πάλιν again, once, 53
παμπληθεί together, 39
παν – all, 13
πανδοχεῖον ου inn (> receive all), 49
πανδοχεύς έως inn-keeper, 49
πανοικεί with one's household, 28
πανουργία ας trickery, 30
πανοῦργος ον tricky, 30
παντ – all, 13
πανταχῇ everywhere, 13
πανταχοῦ everywhere, 14
παντελής ές complete, 45
πάντη in every way, 14
πάντοθεν from all directions, 14
παντοκράτωρ ορος the All-Powerful, 68
πάντοτε always, at all times, 22
πάντως by all means, 14
παρα – by, 43
παρά (*gen, dat, acc*) by, with, 43
παραβαίνω break disobey, 37
παραβάλλω arrive, 29
παράβασις εως disobedience, 37
παραβάτης ου one who disobeys, 37
παραβολεύομαι risk, 29
παραβολή ῆς parable, symbol, 29
παραγγελία ας order, instruction, 23
παραγγέλλω command, order, 23
παραγίνομαι come, appear, stand by, 15
παράγω pass by (away), 24
παραδειγματίζω expose to ridicule, 71
παραδέχομαι accept, receive, welcome, 49
παραδίδωμι hand over, deliver, 18
παράδοξος ον incredible (> paradox), 63
παράδοσις εως tradition, 19
παραζηλόω make jealous, 92
παραθαλάσσιος α ον by the sea or lake, 66
παραθεωρέω overlook, 68
παραθήκη ης something entrusted, 32
παραινέω advise, 100
παραιτέομαι ask for, excuse, 56
παρακαθέζομαι sit, 48
παρακαλέω beg, encourage, 23
παρακαλύπτομαι be hidden, 76
παράκειμαι be present, 68
παράκλησις εως encouragement, help, 23

παράκλητος ου　helper (the Paraclete), 23
παρακοή ῆς　disobedience, disloyalty, 23
παρακολουθέω　follow closely, 63
παρακούω　refuse to listen, disobey, 23
παραλαμβάνω　take (along), receive, 27
παράλιος ου　coastal district, 110
παραλλαγή ῆς　variation, change, 16
παραλογίζομαι　deceive, 18
παραλύομαι　be paralyzed, 46
παραλυτικός οῦ　paralytic, 46
παραμένω　remain, stay, 41
παραμυθέομαι　console, 60
παραμυθία ας　comfort, 60
παραμύθιον ου　comfort, 60
παρανομέω　act contrary to the law, 38
παρανομία ας　offense, 38
παραπίπτω　apostatize (> call away), 46
παραπλέω　sail past, 67
παραπορεύομαι　pass by, go, 38
παράπτωμα ματος　sin, 46
παράσημος ον　marked by a figurehead, 67
παρασκευάζω　prepare, make ready, 95
παρασκευή ῆς　day of preparation, 95
παρατείνω　prolong, 100
παρατηρέω　keep watch, observe, 70
παρατήρησις εως　observation, 70
παρατίθημι　place before, give, 32
παρατυγχάνω　happen to be present, 107
παραφέρω　remove, carry away, 40
παραφρονέω　be insane, 61
παραφρονία ας　insanity, 61
παραχρῆμα　immediately, 62
πάρειμι　be present, 12
παρεισάγω　bring in, 24
παρεισέρχομαι　come in, 13
παρεισφέρω　exert, 40
παρεκτός (gen)　except, 14
παρεμβάλλω　set up, 29
παρεμβολή ῆς　barracks, camp, 29
παρενοχλέω　add extra difficulties, 45
παρεπίδημος ου　refugee, 102
παρέρχομαι　pass (by, away), 13
παρέχω　cause, 17
παρθένος ου　virgin (> Parthenon), 150
παρίημι　neglect, 44
παρίστημι　present, 20
πάροδος ου　passage, 53
παροικέω　live in, live as a stranger, 28
παροικία ας　stay, visit, 28
πάροικος ου　alien, stranger, 28
πάροινος ου　drunkard, 93
παρομοιάζω　be like, 59
παρόμοιος ον　like, similar, 59
παροργίζω　make angry, 87
παροργισμός οῦ　anger, 87
παρουσία ας　coming, parousia, 12
παρρησία ας　openness (> all flowing), 60
παρρησιάζομαι　speak boldly, 60
πασ – all, 13
πᾶς πᾶσα πᾶν　each, all, 14

πασχ – suffer, 75
πάσχα　Passover, 75
πάσχω　suffer, 75
πατ – walk, 35
πατάσσω　strike, touch, 150
πατέω　walk, trample, 35
πατηρ – father, 25
πατήρ πατρός　father, 25
πατρ – father, 25
πατριά ᾶς　family, nation, 25
πατριάρχης ου　patriarch, 25
πατρικός ή όν　paternal, 25
πατρίς ίδος　homeland, 25
πατροπαράδοτος ον　handed from ancestors, 19
πατρῷος α ον　belonging to ancestors, 25
παυ – stop, 86
παύω　stop, 86
πεδ – foot, 56
πέδη ης　chain (for feet), 56
πεδινός ή όν　level (ground), 56
πεζ – foot, 56
πεζεύω　travel by land, 56
πεζῇ　on foot, by land, 56
πειθ – persuade, 69
πειθαρχέω　obey, 69
πειθός ή όν　persuasive, 69
πείθω　persuade, 69
πειθώ οῦς　persuasiveness, 69
πειν – hunger, 107
πεινάω　be hungry, 107
πειρ – test, 76
πεῖρα ας　attempt, 76
πειράζω　test, tempt, 76
πειράομαι　try, attempt, 76
πειρασμός οῦ　trial, period of testing, 76
πεισμονή ῆς　persuasion, 69
πεμπ – send, 63
πέμπω　send, 63
πενθέω　mourn (> penitence), 150
πεντ – five, 87
πεντάκις　five times, 87
πεντακισχίλιοι　five thousand, 87
πεντακόσιοι αι α　five hundred, 87
πέντε　five, 87
πεντεκαιδέκατος　fifteenth, 87
πεντήκοντα　fifty, 87
περα – far, end, 96
περαιτέρω　further, 96
πέραν　beyond, across, 96
πέρας ατος　end, boundary, 96
περι – around, 32
περί (gen, acc)　about, concerning, 32
περιάγω　go around, travel over, 24
περιαιρέω　take away, remove, 78
περιάπτω　kindle, 90
περιαστράπτω　flash around, 90
περιβάλλω　put on, clothe, 29
περιβλέπομαι　look around, 43
περιβόλαιον ου　cloak, covering, 29

περιδέω wrap, bind, 79
περιεργάζομαι be a busybody, 30
περίεργος ου busybody, 30
περιέρχομαι go around, 13
περιέχω seize, contain, 17
περιζώννυμι wrap around, 109
περίθεσις εως wearing (of jewelry), 32
περιΐστημι stand around, 20
περικάθαρμα ματος rubbish, 62
περικαλύπτω cover, conceal, 76
περίκειμαι be placed around, 68
περικεφαλαία ας helmet, 69
περικρατής ές in control of, 68
περικρύβω keep in seclusion, 86
περιλάμπω shine around, 101
περιλείπομαι remain, 57
περίλυπος ον very sad, 88
περιμένω wait for, 41
πέριξ around, 32
περιοικέω live in neighborhood, 28
περίοικος ου neighbor, 28
περιούσιος ον special, 20
περιπατέω walk, move about, live, 35
περιπείρω pierce through, 76
περιπίπτω encounter, 46
περιποιέομαι obtain, preserve, 19
περιποίησις εως obtaining, possession, 19
περισσ – abundance, 67
περισσεία ας abundance, 67
περίσσευμα ματος abundance, 67
περισσεύω be left over, abound, 67
περισσός ή όν more, 67
περισσότερος α ον greater, more, 67
περισσοτέρως all the more, 67
περισσῶς all the more, 67
περιτέμνω circumcise, 77
περιτίθημι put around, 32
περιτομή ῆς circumcision, 77
περιτρέπω drive insane, 80
περιτρέχω run about, 98
περιφέρω carry about, bring, 40
περιφρονέω esteem lightly, disregard, 61
περίχωρος ου neighborhood, 51
πετεινόν οῦ bird (> petrel), 150
πέτρα ας rock (> petrify), 150
πηγή ῆς spring, well, 150
πιάζω seize, 150
πίμπλημι fill, end, 39
πιν – drink, 71
πίνω drink, 71
πιπτ – fall, 45
πίπτω fall, 46
πιστ – belief, faith, 19
πιστεύω believe, 19
πιστικός ή όν genuine, 19
πίστις εως faith, trust, belief, 19
πιστόομαι firmly believe, entrust, 19
πιστός ή όν faithful, believing, 19
πλαν – error, wandering, 81
πλανάω lead astray, 81

πλάνη ης error, deceit, 81
πλανήτης ου wanderer, 81
πλάνος ον deceitful, 81
πλασσ – plague, strike, 105
πλε – sail, 66
πλει – more, 68
πλεῖστος η ον most, large, 68
πλείων ον more, 68
πλεον – more, 68
πλεονάζω increase, grow, 68
πλεονεκτέω take advantage of, 68
πλεονέκτης ου one who is greedy, 68
πλεονεξία ας greed (> have more), 69
πλέω sail, 90
πλη – full, 39
πληγ – plague, strike, 105
πληγή ῆς plague, blow, 105
πληθ – full, 39
πλῆθος ους crowd, 39
πληθύνω increase, 39
πλήκτης ου violent person, 105
πλήμμυρα ης flood, 39
πλην – but, 99
πλήν but, nevertheless, 99
πληρ – full, 39
πλήρης ες full, 39
πληροφορέω accomplish, 39
πληροφορία ας certainty, 39
πληρόω fulfill (> make happen), 39
πλήρωμα ματος fullness, 39
πλησίον (*gen*) near (noun: neighbor), 150
πλησσ – plague, strike, 105
πλήσσω strike, 105
πλο – sail, 66
πλοιάριον ου boat, 67
πλοῖον ου boat, 67
πλου – rich, 76
πλοῦς πλοός voyage, 67
πλούσιος α ον rich, 76
πλουσίως richly, 76
πλουτέω be rich, prosper, 76
πλουτίζω make rich, 76
πλοῦτος ου wealth, 76
πν – spirit, wind, breath, 26
πνευ – spirit, wind, breath, 26
πνεῦμα ματος spirit, self, wind, 26
πνευματικός ή όν spiritual, 26
πνευματικῶς spiritually, symbolically, 26
πνέω blow, 26
πνίγω choke, drown, 26
πνικτός ή όν strangled, 26
πνοή ῆς wind, breath, 26
πο[1] – foot, 56
πο[2] – drink, river (compare πιν), 77
ποδ – foot, 56
ποθ – feel, desire, 93
πόθεν from where, where, 43
ποι – make, do, 19
ποιέω make, do, 19

ποίημα ματος   something made, 19
ποίησις εως   undertaking, 19
ποιητής οῦ   one who does; doer, 19
ποικίλος η ον   varied, diverse, 150
ποιμ – sheep, 93
ποιμαίνω   tend, rule, 93
ποιμήν ένος   shepherd, 93
ποιμν – sheep, 93
ποίμνη ης   flock, 94
ποίμνιον ου   flock, 94
ποῖος α ον   what, what kind of, 84
πολεμ – war, 106
πολεμέω   fight, be at war, 106
πόλεμος ου   war, conflict, polemic, 106
πολι – city, 46
πόλις εως   city, town, 46
πολιτάρχης ου   city official, 46
πολιτεία ας   citizenship, state, 47
πολίτευμα ματος   place of citizenship, 47
πολιτεύομαι   live, be a citizen, 47
πολίτης ου   citizen, 47
πολλ – much, many, 30
πολλάκις   often, 31
πολλαπλασίων ον   more, 31
πολυ – much, many, 30
πολυλογία ας   many words, 31
πολυμερῶς   many times, bit by bit, 31
πολυποίκιλος ον   in varied forms, 31
πολύς πολλή πολύ   much, many, 31
πολύσπλαγχνος ον   very compassionate, 31
πολυτελής ές   expensive, 31
πολύτιμος ον   expensive, 31
πολυτρόπως   in many ways, variously, 31
πονηρ – evil, 47
πονηρία ας   wickedness, 47
πονηρός ά όν   evil, 47
πορ – journey, 38
πορεία ας   journey, 38
πορεύομαι   journey, go, live, 38
πορν – evil, 47
πορνεία ας   fornication, 47
πορνεύω   commit fornication, 47
πόρνη ης   prostitute, 47
πόρνος ου   immoral person, 47
πόρρω   far away, 38
πόρρωθεν   from a distance, 38
πορρώτερον   farther, 38
ποσάκις   how often? 51, 50
πόσις εως   drink, 77
πόσος η ον   how much, how many, 50
ποτ – drink, river (compare πιν), 77
ποταμ – drink, river (compare πιν), 77
ποταμός οῦ   river, 77
ποταμοφόρητος ον   swept away, 77
ποτέ   once, ever, 22
πότε   when? 21, 22
ποτήριον ου   cup (> place for water), 77
ποτίζω   give to drink, water, 77
πότος ου   drunken orgy, 77
πού   somewhere, 43

ποῦ   where? , 43
πούς ποδός   foot, 56
πραγ – matter, event, something done, 80
πρᾶγμα ματος   matter, event, 80
πραγματεῖαι ῶν (*pl*)   affairs, 80
πραγματεύομαι   trade, do business, 80
πρᾶξις εως   deed, practice, 80
πρασ – matter, event, something done, 80
πράσσω   do, 80
πραΰς, πραεῖα, πραΰ   humble, 150
πρεσβυ – old, elderly, 75
πρεσβυτέριον ου   body of elders, 75
πρεσβύτερος ου   elder, presbyter, 75
πρεσβύτης ου   old man, 75
πρεσβῦτις ιδος   old woman, 75
πρίν   before, 37
προ – before, first, 37
πρό (*gen*)   before, 37
προάγω   go before, 24
προαιρέομαι   decide, 78
προαιτιάομαι   accuse beforehand, 56
προακούω   hear before, 23
προαμαρτάνω   sin previously, 36
προαύλιον ου   gateway, forecourt, 109
προβαίνω   go on, 37
προβάλλω   put forward, 29
προβατ – sheep, 92
προβατικός ή όν   pertaining to sheep, 92
προβάτιον ου   lamb, sheep, 92
πρόβατον ου   sheep, 92
προβλέπομαι   provide, 43
προγίνομαι   happen previously, 15
προγινώσκω   know already, 25
πρόγνωσις εως   foreknowledge, purpose, 25
πρόγονος ου   parent (> progenitor), 15
προγράφω   write beforehand, 31
προδίδωμι   give first, 19
προδότης ου   traitor, 19
προελπίζω   be the first to hope, 70
προενάρχομαι   begin, begin before, 26
προεπαγγέλλομαι   promise before, 23
προέρχομαι   go ahead, 13
προετοιμάζω   prepare beforehand, 78
προευαγγελίζομαι   evangelize before, 23
προέχομαι   be better off, 17
προηγέομαι   outdo, lead the way, 24
πρόθεσις εως   purpose, plan, 32
προθυμία ας   willingness, zeal, 60
πρόθυμος ον   willing, 60
προθύμως   willingly, eagerly, 60
προΐστημι   be a leader, manage, 20
προκαλέομαι   irritate, 23
προκαταγγέλλω   announce before, 23
προκαταρτίζω   prepare in advance, 112
προκατέχω   have previously, 17
πρόκειμαι   be set before, be present, 68
προκηρύσσω   preach beforehand, 75
προκοπή ῆς   progress, 85
προκόπτω   advance, progress, 86
πρόκριμα ματος   prejudice (> pre-judging), 21

πόποτε   ever, at any time, 22
πῶλος ου   colt, 150
πῶς   how? in what way? 14, 16
πώς   somehow, in some way, 16

ῥαββί   rabbi, 150
ῥάβδος ου   stick (> rod), 150
ῥαδιούργημα ματος   wrondoing, 30
ῥαδιουργία ας   wrongdoing, 30
ῥη – word, 60
ῥῆμα ματος   word, thing, event, 60
ῥητ – word, 60
ῥήτωρ ορος   lawyer, spokesperson, 60
ῥητῶς   expressly, 60
ῥιζ – root, 110
ῥίζα ης   root, descendant, source, 110
ῥιζόομαι   be firmly rooted, 110
ῥύομαι   rescue, 150

σ – you, 14
σαλεύω   shake, 150
σαλπ – trumpet, 107
σάλπιγξ ιγγος   trumpet, 107
σαλπίζω   sound a trumpet, 107
σαλπιστής οῦ   trumpeter, 107
σαρκ – flesh, 48
σαρκικός ή όν   belonging to the world, 48
σάρκινος η ον   belonging to the world, 48
σαρξ – flesh, 48
σάρξ σαρκός   flesh, physical body, 48
σεαυτοῦ ῆς   yourself, 11
σεβ – worship, piety, religion, 82
σεβάζομαι   worship, reverence, 82
σέβασμα ματος   object / place of worship, 82
σεβαστός ή όν   imperial, 82
σέβομαι   worship, 82
σει – quake, 103
σεισμός οῦ   earthquake, storm, 104
σείω   shake, excite, 104
σημ – sign, indication, 67
σημαίνω   indicate, 67
σημεῖον ου   sign, miracle, 67
σημειόομαι   take / make note of, 67
σήμερον   today, 26
σθεν – strong, 70
σθενόω   strengthen, 70
σι – silence, 110
σιγ – silence, 110
σιγάω   keep silent, 110
σιγή ῆς   silence, 110
σιτ – food, fat, 108
σιτευτός ή όν   fattened, 108
σιτίον ου   grain, food (*pl*), 108
σιτιστός ή όν   fattened, 108
σιτομέτριον ου   ration (> measure of food), 108
σῖτος ου   grain, 108
σιωπάω   be silent, 110
σκ – dark, 75
σκανδαλ – scandal, 90

σκανδαλίζω   scandalize, 90
σκάνδαλον ου   scandal, 90
σκεπ – view, 99
σκευ – prepare, 94
σκευή ῆς   gear, 95
σκεῦος ους   thing, container, 95
σκην – tent, 94
σκηνή ῆς   tent, 94
σκηνοπηγία ας   Feast of Tabernacles, 94
σκηνοποιός οῦ   tent-maker, 94
σκῆνος ους   tent, 94
σκηνόω   live, dwell, 94
σκήνωμα ματος   body, dwelling place, 94
σκιά ᾶς   shadow, shade, 76
σκληροκαρδία ας   hardheartedness, 48
σκοπ – view, 99
σκοπέω   pay attention to, 100
σκοπός οῦ   goal, 100
σκοτ – dark, 75
σκοτεινός ή όν   dark, 76
σκοτία ας   darkness, 76
σκοτίζομαι   become dark, 76
σκοτόομαι   become dark, 76
σκότος ους   darkness, sin, 76
σκυθρωτός ή όν   sad, 59
σός σή σόν   your, yours, 14
σοφ – wisdom, 73
σοφία ας   wisdom, 73
σοφίζω   give wisdom, 73
σοφός ή όν   wise, experienced, 73
σπειρ – scatter, 60
σπείρω   sow, 61
σπερ – scatter, 60
σπέρμα ματος   seed, offspring, 61
σπερμολόγος ου   gossiper (> word scatterer), 61
σπευδ – speed, eagerness, 95
σπεύδω   hurry, 95
σπλαγχν – pity, 106
σπλαγχνίζομαι   have pity, 106
σπλάγχνον ου   affection, feeling, compassion, 106
σπορ – scatter, 60
σπορά ᾶς   seed, origin, 61
σπόριμα ων (*pl*)   grainfields, 61
σπόρος ου   seed, 61
σπουδ – speed, eagerness, 95
σπουδάζω   do one's best, work hard, 95
σπουδαῖος α ον   earnest, 95
σπουδαίως   eagerly, 95
σπουδή ῆς   earnestness, zeal, 95
στα – stand, 19
στασιαστής οῦ   rebel, 20
στάσις εως   dispute, revolt, 20
σταυρ – cross, 71
σταυρός οῦ   cross, 71
σταυρόω   crucify, 71
στελ – send, equip, 35
στέλλομαι   avoid, 36
στενοχωρέομαι   be held in check, 51

συναπόλλυμαι　perish with, 62
συναποστέλλω　send along with, 36
συναρπάζω　seize, drag, 101
συναυξάνομαι　grow together, 104
συνδέομαι　be in prison with, 79
σύνδεσμος ου　bond, chain, 83
συνδοξάζομαι　share in glory, 39
σύνδουλος ου　fellow-slave (servant), 44
συνεγείρω　raise together, 44
συνειδη – conscience, 101
συνείδησις εως　conscience, 101
σύνειμι　be with, be present, 12
συνεισέρχομαι　enter in, 13
συνέκδημος ου　travelling companion, 102
συνεπιμαρτυρέω　add further witness, 42
συνεπιτίθεμαι　join in the attack, 32
συνεργέω　work with, 30
συνεργός οῦ　fellow-worker, 30
συνέρχομαι　come togegther, 13
συνεσθίω　eat with, 73
συνευδοκέω　approve of, 63
συνεφίστημι　join in an attack, 20
συνέχω　surround, control, 17
συνηλικιώτης ου　contemporary, 92
συνθλίβω　crowd, press upon, 81
συνίστημι　recommend, show, 20
συνοδεύω　travel with, 54
συνοδία ας　group (> synod), 54
σύνοιδα　share knowledge with, 33
συνοικέω　live with, 28
συνοικοδομέω　build together, 102
συνοράω　realize, learn, 50
συντάσσω　direct, instruct, 57
συντέλεια ας　end, completion, 45
συντελέω　end, complete, 45
συντέμνω　cut short, 77
συντηρέω　protect, 70
συντίθεμαι　agree, arrange, 32
συντρέχω　run together, join with, 98
σύντροφος ου　close friend, 96
συντυγχάνω　teach, 107
συνυποκρίνομαι　act insincerely with, 21
συνυπουργέω　join in, help, 30
σύσσημον ου　signal, sign, 67
σύσσωμος ον　of same body, 51
συσταυρόομαι　be crucified together, 71
συστέλλω　carry out, 36
συστρατιώτης ου　fellow-soldier, 79
σφόδρα　very much, 150
σφραγι – seal, 99
σφραγίζω　seal, acknowledge, 99
σφραγίς ιδος　seal, evidence, 99
σχίζω　split (> schism), 150
σωζ – save, 59
σῴζω　save, rescue, preserve, 60
σωμα – body, physical, 51
σῶμα ματος　body, substance, 51
σωματικός ή όν　physical, 51
σωματικῶς　in bodily (human) form, 51
σωτηρ – salvation, 74

σωτήρ ηρος　savior, 74
σωτηρία ας　salvation, release, 74
σωτήριον ου　salvation, 74
σωτήριος ον　saving, 74
σωφρονέω　be sane, sensible, 61
σωφρονίζω　train, teach, 61
σωφρονισμός οῦ　sound judgment, 61
σωφρόνως　sensibly, 61
σωφροσύνη ης　good sense, 61
σώφρων ον　sensible, 61

ταγ – order, 57
τάγμα ματος　proper order, 57
τακ – order, 57
τακτός ή όν　appointed, fixed, 57
τάλαντον ου　talent (coin), 150
ταξ – order, 57
τάξις εως　order, division, 57
ταπειν – humble, 97
ταπεινός ή όν　humble, poor, 97
ταπεινοφροσύνη ης　(false) humility, 97
ταπεινόφρων ον　humble, 97
ταπεινόω　make humble, 97
ταπείνωσις εως　humble state, 97
ταρασσ – trouble, 110
ταράσσω　trouble, disturb, 110
ταραχ – trouble, 110
ταραχή ῆς　disturbance, trouble, 110
τάραχος ου　confusion, 110
τασσ – order, 57
τάσσω　appoint, 57
ταχ¹ – order, 57
ταχ² – quick, 95
ταχέως　quickly, 95
ταχινός ή όν　soon, swift, 95
τάχιον　quickly, 95
τάχιστα　as soon as possible, 95
τάχος ους　speed, 95
ταχύ　quickly, 95
ταχύς εῖα ύ　quick, 95
τειν – extend, stretch, 100
τεκν – child, 54
τεκνίον ου　little child, 54
τεκνογονέω　have children, 54
τεκνογονία ας　childbirth, 54
τέκνον ου　child, 54
τεκνοτροφέω　bring up children, 54
τελ – end, far, 45
τέλειος α ον　complete, 45
τελειότης ητος　completeness, 45
τελειόω　make perfect, 45
τελείως　fully, 45
τελείωσις εως　fulfillment, 45
τελειωτής οῦ　perfecter, 45
τελεσφορέω　produce mature fruit, 45
τελευτάω　die, 45
τελευτή ῆς　death, 45
τελέω　finish (make an end), 45
τέλος ους　end, 45
τελων – tax, 106

τελώνης ου tax-collector, 106
τελώνιον ου tax (office), 106
τεμν – cut, 76
τεν – extend, stretch, 100
τέρας ατος wonder, omen, 150
τεσσαρ – four, 63
τεσσαράκοντα forty, 63
τέσσαρες α four, 63
τεσσαρεσκαιδέκατος fourteenth, 63
τεσσαρακονταετής ές forty years, 82
τεταρ – four, 63
τεταρταῖος α ον on the fourth, day, 63
τέταρτος η ον fourth, 63
τετρα – four, 63
τετρααρχέω be tetrarch, be ruler, 63
τετραάρχης ου tetrarch (ruler), 63
τετράγωνος ον squared (> four-angled), 63
τετράδιον ου squad (of four men), 63
τετρακισχίλιοι αι α four thousand, 63
τετρακόσιοι αι α four hundred, 63
τετράμηνος ου period of four months, 64
τετραπλοῦς ῆ οῦν four times as much, 64
τετράπουν ποδος animal (> four-footed), 64
τηρ – keep, observe, 70
τηρέω keep, observe, 70
τήρησις εως custody, keeping, 70
τι – who, what, any, 14
τιθ – put, place, 31
τίθημι put, place, lay, 32
τικ – child, 54
τίκτω give birth to, yield, 54
τικ – child, 54
τίκτω give birth to, yield, 54
τιμ – honor, price, 48
τιμάω honor, 49
τιμή ῆς honor, price, 49
τίμιος α ον precious, respected, 49
τιμιότης ητος wealth, abundance, 49
Τιμόθεος ου Timothy, 49
τιν¹ – extend, stretch, 100
τιν² – who, what, any, 14
τις – who, what, any, 14
τὶς τὶ anyone, anything, 14
τίς τί who? what? (why? τι), 14
το – the, 11
τοιγαροῦν therefore, then, 24
τοίνυν therefore, then, 46
τοιοῦτος αὕτη οῦτον such, similar, 12
τοκ – child, 54
τόκος ου interest (> child of money), 54
τολμάω dare, 150
τομ – cut, 76
τομός ή όν sharp, cutting, 77
τον – extend, stretch, 100
τοπ – place, 64
τόπος ου place, 64
τοσοῦτος αὕτη οῦτον so much, so great, 50
τότε then, 22
τουαντίον on the contrary, 66
τουτ – this, 12

τράπεζα ης table, 56
τρεῖς τρία three, 49
τρεπ – turn, 79
τρεφ – feed, support, 96
τρέφω feed, support, 96
τρεχ – run, 98
τρέχω run, 98
τρι – three, 49
τριάκοντα thirty, 49
τριακόσιοι αι α three hundred, 49
τριετία ας period of three years, 49
τρίμηνον ου three months, 49
τρίς three times, a third time, 49
τρίστεγον ου third floor, 49
τρισχίλιοι αι α three thousand, 49
τρίτον the third time, 49
τρίτος η ον third, 49
τροπ – turn, 79
τροπή ῆς turning, change, 80
τρόπος ου way, manner, 80
τροποφορέω put up with, 80
τροφ – feed, support, 96
τροφή ῆς food keep, 96
τροφός οῦ nurse, 96
τροφοφορέω care for, 40, 96
τροχ – run, 98
τροχιά ᾶς path, 98
τροχός οῦ wheel, cycle, 98
τυγχ – obtain, 107
τυγχάνω obtain, 107
τυπ – type, example, 113
τυπικῶς by way of example, 113
τύπος ου example, pattern, 113
τύπτω beat, hit, 150
τυφλ – blind, 83
τυφλός ή όν blind, 83
τυφλόω make blind, 83
τυχ – obtain, 107

ὑγι – health, 108
ὑγιαίνω be healthy, be sound, 108
ὑγιής ές healthy, whole, 108
ὑδρ – water, 70
ὑδρία ας water jar, 70
ὑδροποτέω drink water, 70
ὑδρωπικός ή όν suffering from dropsy, 70
ὕδωρ ὕδατος water, 70
υἱ – son, 30
υἱοθεσία ας adoption, sonship, 30
υἱός οῦ son, descendant, 30
ὑμέτερος α ον your, 150
ὑπάγω go (away), 25
ὑπακοή ῆς obedience, 23
ὑπακούω obey, 23
ὕπανδρος ον married (> under + man), 40
ὑπαντάω meet, fight, oppose, 66
ὑπάντησις εως meeting, 66
ὕπαρξις εως possession, 26
ὑπάρχω be under one's rule, 26
ὑπεναντίος α ον against, 66

ὑπερ – over, 48
ὑπέρ (*gen, acc*)   over, 48
ὑπεραίρομαι   be puffed up with pride, 53
ὑπεράνω (*gen*)   far above, above, 48
ὑπεραυξάνω   grow abundantly, 104
ὑπερβαίνω   do wrong to, 37
ὑπερβαλλόντως   much more, 29
ὑπερβάλλω   surpass (>overthrow), 29
ὑπερβολή ῆς   the extreme (> hyperbole), 29
ὑπερέκεινα (*gen*)   beyond, 28
ὑπερεκπερισσοῦ   with all earnestness, 67
ὑπερεκτείνω   go beyond, 100
ὑπερεκχύννομαι   run over, 108
ὑπερεντυγχάνω   intercede, 107
ὑπερέχω   surpass, govern, 17
ὑπερηφανία ας   arrogance, 50
ὑπερήφανος ον   arrogant, 51
ὑπερνικάω   be completely victorious, 97
ὑπεροράω   overlook, 50
ὑπεροχή ῆς   position of authority, 17
ὑπερπερισσεύω   increase abundantly, 67
ὑπερπερισσῶς   completely, 67
ὑπερπλεονάζω   overflow, 69
ὑπερυψόω   raise to highest position, 83
ὑπερφρονέω   hold high opinion of, 61
ὑπερῷον ου   upstairs room, 48
ὑπέχω   undergo, suffer, 17
ὑπήκοος ον   obedient, 23
ὑπηρετ – serve, 108
ὑπηρετέω   serve, 108
ὑπηρέτης ου   attendant, helper, 108
ὑπο – under, by means of, 40
ὑπό (*gen, acc*)   under, by means of, 40
ὑποβάλλω   bribe, 29
ὑπογραμμός οῦ   example, 31
ὑπόδειγμα τος   example, copy, 71
ὑποδείκνυμι   show, warn, 71
ὑποδέομαι   put on shoes, 79
ὑποδέχομαι   receive as a guest, 50
ὑπόδημα ματος   sandal, 79
ὑπόδικος ον   answerable to, 34
ὑποζώννυμι   strengthen, brace, 109
ὑποκάτω (*gen*)   under, 22
ὑποκρίνομαι   pretend, be a hypocrite, 21
ὑπόκρισις εως   hypocrisy, 21
ὑποκριτής οῦ   hypocrite, 21
ὑπολαμβάνω   suppose, take away, 27
ὑπόλειμμα ματος   remnant, 57
ὑπολείπω   leave, 57
ὑπολιμπάνω   leave, 57
ὑπομένω   endure (> stay under), 41
ὑπομιμνήσκω   remind, 55
ὑπόμνησις εως   remembrance, 55
ὑπομονή ῆς   endurance (> stay under), 41
ὑπονοέω   suppose, suspect, 53
ὑπόνοια ας   suspicion, 53
ὑποπλέω   sail under the shelter, 67
ὑποπνέω   blow gently, 26
ὑποπόδιον ου   footstool, 56
ὑπόστασις εως   conviction, confidence, 20

ὑποστέλλω   draw back, hold back, 36
ὑποστολή ῆς   shrinking / turning back, 36
ὑποστρέφω   return, 52
ὑποταγή ῆς   obedience, submission, 57
ὑποτάσσω   subject, 57
ὑποτίθημι   risk (> place under), 32
ὑποτρέχω   run under the shelter, 98
ὑποτύπωσις εως   example, 113
ὑποφέρω   endure, bear up under, 40
ὑποχωρέω   withdraw, go away, 51
ὑπωπιάζω   control (> under the eye of), 59
ὑσ – last, lack, 92
ὑστερέω   lack, need, 92
ὑστέρημα ματος   what is lacking, 92
ὑτέρησις εως   lack, need, 92
ὕστερον   later, afterwards, then, 92
ὕστερος α ον   later, last, 92
ὑψ – high, 83
ὑψηλός ή όν   high, 83
ὑψηλοφρονέω   be proud, 83
ὕψιστος η ον   highest, 83
ὕψος ους   height, heaven, 83
ὑψόω   exalt (> make high), 83
ὕψωμα ματος   height, stronghold, 83

φα – say, report, 35
φαιν – display, appear, 50
φαίνω   shine, appear, 50
φαν – display, appear, 50
φανερ – display, appear, 50
φανερός ά όν   known, visible, plain, 50
φανερόω   make known, reveal, 50
φανερῶς   openly, clearly, 50
φανέρωσις εως   disclosure, 50
φανός οῦ   lantern, 51
φαντάζομαι   appear, 51
φαντασία   pomp, 51
φάντασμα ματος   phantom ghost, 51
φάξις εως   news, report, 35
φάσκω   claim, assert, 35
φείδομαι   spare, 150
φερ – bring, bear, carry, 39
φέρω   bring, carry, 40
φευγ – flee, 90
φεύγω   flee, 90
φη – say, report, 35
φημ – say, report, 35
φήμη ης   report, news, 35
φημί   say, 35
φθαρ – decay, 84
φθαρτός ή όν   perishable, mortal, 84
φθειρ – decay, 84
φθείρω   corrupt, ruin, 84
φθινοπωρινός ή όν   of late autumn, 84
φθορ – decay, 84
φιάλη ης   bowl (Grimm's Law), 150
φιλ – love, 75
φιλάγαθος ον   good-loving, 56
φιλαδελφία ας   brotherly love, 30
φιλάδελφος ον   brother-loving, 30

φίλανδρος ον   husband-loving, 40
φιλανθρωπία ας   kindness, 21
φιλανθρώπως   considerately, 21
φιλαργυρία ας   love of money, 97
φιλάργυρος ον   money-loving, 97
φίλαυτος ον   selfish, 11, 75
φιλέω   love, like, kiss, 75
φίλημα ματος   kiss, 75
φιλία ας   love, friendship, 75
φιλόθεος ον   God-loving, 13
φιλοξενία ας   hospitality, 99
φιλόξενος ον   hospitable, 99
φιλοπρωτεύω   desire to be first, 38
φίλος ου   friend, 75
φιλοσοφία ας   philosophy, 73
φιλόσοφος ου   philosopher, teacher, 73
φιλότεκνος ον   loving one's children, 54
φιλοτιμέομαι   aspire, 75
φιλοφρόνως   kindly, 61
φοβ – fear, 48
φοβέομαι   fear, be afraid, respect, 48
φοβερός ά όν   fearful, 48
φόβητρον ου   fearful thing, 48
φόβος ου   fear, 48
φον – murder, 95
φονεύς έως   murderer, 95
φονεύω   murder, put to death, 95
φόνος ου   murder, killing, 95
φορ – bring bear, carry, 39
φορέω   wear, 40
φόρος ου   tax (> burden), 40
φορτίζω   burden, load, 40
φορτίον ου   burden, cargo, 40
φρ – think, 61
φρήν φρενός   thought, understanding, 61
φρο – think, 61
φρον think, 61
φρονέω   think, 61
φρόνημα ματος   way of thinking, mind, 61
φρόνησις εως   insight, wisdom, 61
φρόνιμος ον   wise, 61
φρονίμως   wisely, 61
φροντίζω   concentrate upon, 61
φρουρέω   guard, 50
φυ – natural, growth, planted, 89
φυγ – flee, 90
φυγή ής   flight, 90
φυλ – tribe, 93
φυλακ – guard, 69
φυλακή ής   prison, 69
φυλακίζω   imprison, 69
φυλακτήριον ου   phylactery, 69
φύλαξ ακος   guard, 69
φυλασσ – guard, 69
φυλάσσω   guard, keep, obey, 69
φυλή ής   tribe, nation, 93
φύλλον ου   leaf, 93
φυσ – natural, growth, planted, 89
φυσικός ή όν   natural, 89
φυσικῶς   naturally, 89

φυσιόω   make conceited, 89
φύσις εως   nature, 89
φυφίωσις εως   conceit, 89
φυτ – natural, growth, planted, 89
φυτεία ας   plant, 89
φυτεύω   plant, 89
φύω   grow, 89
φων – voice, 41
φωνέω   call, 42
φωνή ής   voice, sound, 42
φωσ – light, 65
φῶς φωτός   light, fire, 65
φωστήρ ήρος   light, star, 65
φωσφόρος ου   morning star, 65
φωτ – light, 65
φωτεινός ή όν   full of light, 65
φωτίζω   give light, shine on, 65
φωτισμός οῦ   light, revelation, 65

χαιρ – rejoice, 52
χαίρω   rejoice, 52
χαρ – rejoice, 52
χαρά ᾶς   joy, 52
χαρι – gift, 36
χαρίζομαι   give, forgive, 37
χάριν   for sake of, because of, 37
χάρις ιτος   grace, favor, kindness, 37
χάρισμα ματος   gift, 37
χαριστ – gift, 36
χαριτόω   give freely (> make a gift), 37
χε – pour, 108
χειρ – hand, 43
χείρων ον   worse, 150
χείρ χειρός   hand, 43
χειραγωγέω   lead by the hand, 25
χειραγωγός οῦ   one who leads, 25
χειρόγραφον ου   record of debt, 31
χειροποίητος ον   hand / man-made, 19
χειροτονέω   appoint, choose, 100
χηρ – widow, 105
χήρα ας   widow, 105
χιλι – thousand, 97
χιλίαρχος ου   tribune, officer, 26
χιλιάς άδος   a thousand, 97
χίλιοι αι α   thousand, 97
χιτών ῶνος   tunic, 150
χοῖρος ου   pig, 150
χορτ – food, 100
χορτάζω   feed, satisfy, 100
χόρτασμα ματος   food, 100
χόρτος ου   grass, vegetation, 100
χρα – need, use, 62
χράομαι   use, 62
χρει – need, use, 62
χρεία ας   need, 62
χρεοφειλέτης ου   debtor, 86
χρη – need, use, 62
χρή   it ought, 62
χρήζω   need, 62
χρῆμα ματος   possessions, wealth, 62

χρήσιμον ου   good, value, 62
χρῆσις εως   sexual intercourse, 62
χρηστός ή όν   useful, 62
χρηστότης ητος   goodness, 62
χρι – anoint, 21
χρισ – anoint, 21
χρῖσμα ματος   anointing, 22
Χριστιανός οῦ   Christian, 22
Χριστός οῦ   Christ, 22
χρίω   anoint, 22
χρον – time, 80
χρονίζω   delay (> use time), 80
χρόνος ου   time, 80
χρονοτριβέω   spend time, 80
χρυσ – gold, 89
χρυσίον ου   gold, 89
χρυσοδακτύλιος ον   wearing a gold ring, 89
χρυσόλιθος ου   chrysolite, 89
χρυσόπρασος ου   chrysoprase (gem), 89
χρυσός οῦ   gold, 89
χρυσοῦς ή οῦν   golden, 89
χρυσόω   make golden, 89
χυ – pour, 108
χωλός ή όν   lame, 150
χωρ – place, 51
χώρα ας   country, land, 51
χωρέω   make room for, accept, 51
χωρίζω   separate, leave, 51
χωρίον ου   field, piece of land, 51
χωρίς   without, separately (*dat*), 51

ψευδ – false, 84
ψευδάδελφος ου   false brother, 30
ψευδαπόστολος ου   false apostle, 84
ψευδής ές   false, 84
ψευδοδιδάσκαλος ου   false teacher, 84
ψευδολόγος ου   liar, 84

ψεύδομαι   lie, 84
ψευδομαρτυρέω   give false witness, 84
ψευδομαρτυρία ας   false witness, 85
ψευδόμαρτυς υρος   false witness, 85
ψευδοπροφήτης ου   false prophet, 35
ψεῦδος ους   lie, imitation, 85
ψευδόχριστος ου   false Christ, 22
ψευδώνυμος ον   so-called, 39
ψεῦσμα ματος   lie, untruthfulness, 85
ψεύστης ου   liar, 85
ψυχ – self, soul / cold (unspiritual), 55
ψυχή ῆς   self, person, 55
ψυχικός ή όν   unspiritual, material, 55
ψύχομαι   grow cold, 55
ψῦχος ους   cold, 55
ψυχρός ά όν   cold, 55

ὧδε – here, 79
ὧδε   here, 79
ὦ   O! , 150
ωπ – see, 58
ὡρ – time, hour, 62
ὥρα ας   moment, time, 62
ὡραῖος α ον   timely, welcome, 62
ὡς – as, how (manner), 16
ὡς   as, like, 16
ὡσαύτως   likewise, 16
ὡσεί   like, as, 16
ὥσπερ   as, just as, 16
ὡσπερεί   as (though), 16
ὥστε   that, so that, thus, 16
ὠτ – ear, 96
ὠφελ – gain, 105
ὠφέλεια ας   advantage, benefit, 105
ὠφελέω   gain, help, 105
ὠφέλιμος ον   valuable, beneficial, 105